Comment on *Syria - A Decade of Lost Chances*

"Carsten Wieland plumbs the contradictions of contemporary Syrian life
and politics. He was among the first Westerners . . . in the early years of
Bashar's presidency . . . to interview Syrian opposition members as well as
government officials. He explored the reasons that many young Syrians
had such high expectations of their young president even as so many reviled the government and the Baath Party for its corruption and repression.
Their expectations, we now know, were dashed. Wieland is even-handed
and measured; he knows Arabic and has lived in Syria for years. Better yet,
he listens. *Syria - A Decade of Lost Chances* is timely and important. Everyone interested in Syria should read this book."

> —Joshua Landis
> Director, Center for Middle East Studies,
> University of Oklahoma and Founder of
> *SyriaComment* (www.SyriaComment.com)

". . . since Bashar Al-Assad became President in June 2000. The early hope
for change toward pluralism and democracy—a Damascene spring—was
not fulfilled. The tragic story of an unflinching opposition struggling for
democracy against a rigid authoritarian minority regime lead by the Assad
clan is told on the basis of many interviews with leading figures of the opposition while describing the savage repression of a regime which cannot
reform itself and is still not willing to give up its power and privileges.

". . . readers who want a better understanding of the root causes of Syria's
ongoing revolts, will be enthralled by this vivid account of Syria's recent
political history since Bashar Al Assad became President in July 2000."

> —Gunter Mulack,
> President of the German Orient Institute
> Past German ambassador to Syria

Cover Illustrations
Front cover: Homs
Back cover, background: Homs
Back cover, inset montage from left:
Regime supportsers; destruction in Homs; opposition funeral & headband;
flag of the opposition on the statue of Sultan al-Attrash, a leader of the
resistance against the French in the 1920s.
(All Photos: Picture Alliance)

Syria—A Decade of Lost Chances

Syria—A Decade of Lost Chances

Repression and Revolution from Damascus Spring to Arab Spring

By Carsten Wieland

《🕯》Cune

Syria—A Decade of Lost Chances
Repression and Revolution from Damascus Spring to Arab Spring
© 2012 By Carsten Wieland
Cune Press, Seattle 2012

Hardback ISBN 978-1-61457-001-1 $34.95
Paperback ISBN 978-1-61457-002-8 $19.95
eBook ISBN 978-1-61457-003-5 $4.95

Library of Congress Cataloging-in-Publication Data

Wieland, Carsten.
Syria--a decade of lost chances :
repression and revolution from
Damascus Spring to Arab Spring / by Carsten Wieland.
p. cm.
Includes bibliographical references and index.

ISBN 978-1-61457-001-1 (hardback : alk. paper)
ISBN 978-1-61457-002-8 (pbk. : alk. paper)
ISBN 978-1-61457-003-5 (ebook)

1. Syria--Politics and government--2000- 2. Syria-
-Social conditions--1971- 3. Political persecution--Syria-
-History--21st century. 4. Protest movements--Syria-
-History--21st century. 5. Assad, Bashar, 1965- I. Title.

DS98.6.W528 2012
956.9104'2--dc23

Photo Credits for Cover:
Picture-Alliance

Syria Cross Road

Select titles in the Syria Cross Road Series:

Steel & Silk: Men and Women Who Shaped Syria 1900 - 2000 - by Sami Moubayed

A Pen of Damascus Steel: The Political Cartoons of an Arab Master - by Ali Farzat

The Road from Damascus: A Journey Through Syria - by Scott C. Davis

Syria - Ballots or Bullets?
Democracy, Islamism, and Secularism in the Levant - by Carsten Wieland

www.cunepress.com | www.cunepress.net

For Yenith and Amélie

Contents

Foreword

WILL THE FUTURE FOR SYRIA HOLD BALLOTS OR BULLETS? This was the key question six years ago when we chose the title for my first book, an analysis of Bashar al-Asad's rule and developments in modern Syrian society. At that time nobody dared to anticipate how imminent this question would become in the near future. For years it remained an unresolved riddle whether Syria's young president would one day choose ballots or bullets to decide the fate of his country—and in the end, his own. Meanwhile, the sobering answer has been given within the context of the Arab Spring. After a decade of lost chances, the regime proved unable to reform itself. It was bullets and unfortunately much worse that filled the vacuum of ideas and that substituted an eroded ideology toward the foreseeable end of Asad's rule.

Pointing at various assets that Syria holds for the future, especially a peaceful living-together of religious groups, I wrote in the foreword of *Syria— Ballots or Bullets?* in 2006: "There is much to lose if Syria drowns in chaos." Unfortunately, losing some of Syria's most precious pieces of heritage may be just in progress while this new book is coming out. It is rather depressing to write or re-write a book on Syria at the moment when this country is passing through one of the darkest chapters in its history. The Syria that observers, analysts, and tourists have known for years or even decades has ceased to exist. Disbelief is the mildest expression to describe the feeling of those who have been following the events in the country since March 2011. Syrian society—situated in the heart of a battered region—has been known for its overall tolerance, civility, peaceful coexistence of religious minorities and mixed neighborhoods for centuries. After all, it was Syria that hundreds of thousands of Christian refugees from Iraq chose as their new home after they had felt insecure in their country of origin following the Anglo-American invasion and subsequent intra-state violence from 2003 onward.

For years, law and order and the practical absence of daily crime added to the characteristic of a laid-back, sleepy, and hospitable environment in Syria. Under the surface sectarian mistrust did always simmer but the widely accepted narrative was to focus on common experience, be it out of religiously inspired convictions of communal compatibility, out of fear, out of calculations directed at the delicate fabric of power, or out of personal or economic opportunism. At least, most of Syria's children grew up in a country in which it was forbidden to speak about religious antagonisms and in which it was a taboo to publicly drop the word *alawi*—the sect of the ruling dynasty since the 1970s. It sufficed to mention from which region or village people came, and the rest went without saying. Often, it did not really matter at all.

All of a sudden, Syrians lost the fear in the wake of the Arab Spring. After decades of stagnation and humiliation, Arabs discovered a common cause. They woke up from paralysis, dependence, and immaturity. And they lost patience. They ceased to accept the plethora of excuses: Why reforms were more sluggish than promised or why democracy was nothing really for the Arab people but a Western phenomenon. Modern technology, social networks, and amateur videos on the Internet helped to spread uncensored realities. They created a new esthetics of upheaval, often unusually cruel for laymen's eyes. After the Facebook-coordinated protests in Tunesia and Egypt, Syria experienced the first *youtube* revolution in history. Additionally, conventional Arab television channels had broadcast the demonstrations in Tunesia and Egypt into Syrian living rooms and tea houses. People took to the streets to reclaim their dignity, to protest against arbitrary treatment and suppression.

For Syrians more than for other Arabs, however, the Arab Spring meant also looking into the abyss of civil strife. They had to witness daily killings of unarmed civilians, mutilations and torture of the worst imaginable kind being inflicted on men, women, children and wounded people by security forces or pro-regime militias. What completed the horrifying picture were public rapes and arbitrary executions as an instrument of warfare and deterrence, sport stadiums turned into prison camps, the barring of wounded from treatment, the torture of wounded, assassinations along religious cleavages, the influx of weapons from porous borders, the rise of armed gangs, the lack of food and medicine as well as everyday crime. The Syrian regime brought in Shiite fighters from Lebanon, Iraq and Iran for support. Soldiers were forced to shoot on unarmed demonstrators; otherwise they risked being shot by their superiors or by secret service people. On the other side, armed resistance grew in self-defense, weapons were smuggled into the country, army defectors founded an insurgent's force, and criminal gangs used the power vacuum to intimidate citizens. The often subtle and implicit codes of conduct in the fragile societal mosaic under the umbrella of the powerful secret services (*mukhabarat*) gave way to open barbarism and poisonous propaganda.

The cruelty in the streets of Syrian towns and in the *mukhabarat's* dungeons that were documented in countless amateur videos despite all technical obstacles and personal risks exceeded what the world had witnessed in the Libyan civil war that led to the fall of Muammar al-Qaddafi in October 2011. The displayed degree of atrocities against a widely unarmed population was not at all necessary to suppress a rebellion. Technically speaking, it was counterproductive. The system had failed. Politically speaking, the regime chose to play the sectarian card and the tale of foreign conspiracies as a survival strategy.

In the light of events the question was not if but when to write a new work on Syria. Many books on the Middle East will have to be rewritten after the Arab Spring has swept the region that was mildewed for so many years of deceptive stability. The question was rather when to dare writing it despite the fact that the events have been following hot on the heels of one another. All in all, my editor Scott C. Davis and I came to the conclusion that the time had come to compile new facts and analyses one year after the Arab Spring changed the face of Syria for good. In an attempt to cover a decade of Bashar al-Asad's rule the book tries to balance previous insights and assessments with the stunning new unfolding. For it remains important to know at what point of development Syria found itself when the Arab Spring hit the country.

The book starts with the last day in which the old and the new Syria met, on 17 February 2011. Barely one month passed between an unexpected demonstration in the Old City of Damascus and the first casualties in Dara'a. These weeks altered the face of the country. The subsequent chapter guides the reader through the regime's reflexes and reactions to the unexpected wave of protests against the background of discourse and demands during Syria's most recent history. Parting from the immediate handling of the crisis, the next chapter widens the zoom toward a series of missed chances during Asad's decade of rule. It is puzzling how many possibilities of national reconciliation and political leadership the president had let slip through his hands, particularly when taking into account the advance praise that had accompanied his inauguration, his various waves of popularity throughout the years of external threat, and his personal nimbus. In the following chapters of the book, the circle of leadership and breaches therein are analyzed in more detail. Several of the personal fault lines broke open again during the revolt of 2011 and after, others closed in favor of the unifying goal of clan survival.

The middle sections of the book juxtapose strengths and weaknesses of the Baath regime before and during the rule of Bashar al-Asad. The "five pillars" of legitimacy help to explain why the regime was able to survive massive protests for such a long time. It was not hard power only that held the system together—even though state barbarism and system failure *were* escalating. On the other side, a rising negative balance over the years built to the point that the Syrian people took to the streets against their government despite a large ideological overlap between regime and opposition, particularly in questions of pan-Arabism and foreign policy. But the more Syrian civilians felt exposed to existential threat, the more their diffuse and general anti-Western sentiments gave way to pragmatism and even calls for protection by other Arab and even Western countries.

A large section of the book is dedicated to the country's long-standing opposition, the Civil Society Movement, and alternative currents. Attention is given to different forms and representatives of Islam and Islamism. Some of the currents had the potential to crystallize as political alternatives. In numerous interviews through the years I was able to trace developments and subtle changes. When I went through my hand-written notes for this new volume, I was particularly impressed by the mood that I had captured among key opposition figures as late as October and November 2010. Widespread resignation and a feeling of defeat prevailed—sometimes even melancholy. Paralyzed by prison sentences, travel bans, and intimidations, Syria's traditional opposition was preparing to hand over their political legacy to future generations in a distant future. None of them had anticipated that circumstances would change so unexpectedly. The Arab Spring created the foundation for a change that Syria's civil society activists had not been able to achieve with their means. But some of them quickly drew parallels between the Damascus Spring and the Arab Spring. They saw the failed first attempt to achieve freedom in Syria as a precursor to the Arab-wide wave of protests with regard to ideas and political discourse.

The state of Syria's traditional opposition at the end of 2010 was an indicator that Syria was not at all on the way toward relaxation and reform despite its foreign policy honeymoon between 2008 and the beginning of 2011. Instead, a third wave of suppression was in full swing when the Arab Spring hit the country. The hope that the regime would feel safe enough in the light of regional and international détente to grant more political freedom was not fulfilled. This appeared as a policy paradox compared to previous years when external pressure was linked to domestic developments and did not leave a lot of leeway for political experiments. On the other hand, this may have been not so much a paradox at all, if one implied that Asad had never really intended to walk the path of reform. In Syria, however, many people had still believed in reform and in the president himself. Obviously, the spectrum of Syria's opposition widened as events unfolded. So were their ideological backgrounds. New persons and groups entered the scene, including the Muslim Brotherhood and individuals in exile.

Farther along in the book, some more theoretical and historical chapters deal with the ideological background of Syria's political discourse. In particular, the meaning of secularism in the Syrian context is important also for future explanations as to why things develop as they do in new circumstances. It is furthermore important in order to understand what many Syrians fear to lose. To what extent has Baathism contributed to this secularism? is also dealt with in this part of the book. Baathism in tandem with socialism and pan-Arabism has been gradually eroding in ideological and practical terms. This became blatantly obvious with the Arab Spring that entirely changed discourse. In addition, the Asad regime had been undergoing a progress of sectarian contraction beyond ideology. This contributed to the loss of soft-power and the erosion of a sufficiently broad power base that was necessary especially in times of increasing challenges. In terms of foreign policy the Asad regime had allied itself with such contradictory partners such as Shiite Iran and Hezbollah, Sunni Hamas and atheist North Korea and Venezuela. A pro-European elite had been sidelined through the years. This composition raised questions of Syria's role as a so-called rogue state, including questions about Syria's nuclear program.

At the end of the book, general reflections on the Arab Spring embed Syrian developments in a broader context. The shifting of discourse and the realignment of power alliances deeply affect Syria which is situated in the middle of geographic, political, and ideological fault-lines. A remarkable collateral effect of the Arab Spring is the possibility of Arab and Western reconciliation with regard to the concept of democracy. Previous antagonisms that occurred after the terrorist attacks on 9/11, the war in Iraq, and missionary rhetoric on democracy were about to give way to a common understanding: Democracy and personal freedom were not a Western or even Western imposed concept but something that many thousands of Arabs took to the street for, and risked their lives for, without the involvement of any foreign power. The last chapter finally dares to draw different scenarios about Syria's future that still looked plausible at the time of writing. Dangers of civil war are weighed against more hopeful indications of Syria's societal and political history. Syria is not Iraq. But still the Iraqi scenario after the war in 2003 made many Syrians, especially minorities, shy away from changes to the status quo as flawed as it was.

Like *Syria—Ballots or Bullets?* (2006) and *Syrien nach dem Irak-Krieg* (2004) this volume is based to a high degree on first-hand sources based on a period of twelve years in which I have visited Syria at least once a year. Therefore, I was able to capture not just snapshots but changing moods through time. After I returned from my two-year residence in the Old City of Damascus in 2004, I kept visiting the country and previous conversation partners. If they were in prison, I spoke to those who had meanwhile been released. I interviewed analysts, journalists, parliamentarians, religious figures, and other people committed to Syria's development from within or sometimes close to the official polity. All of them have enriched my horizon with their frank and detailed accounts as well as their philosophies of life. Although recent events have caused a tremendous polarization even between friends and old acquaintances inside and outside the country, it is important to remember that the Syrian societal and political scene is highly complex. As one conversation partner put it, "Syria does not know black or white but many shades of gray." Several intellectuals, activists, diplomats, or politicians also passed through places abroad where we continued our discussions, especially in Berlin, Beirut, or Washington, DC. I deeply thank all of them for their hospitality, patience, time, personal dedication, and enriching discussions.

I feel also deeply indebted to Nikolaos van Dam, the former Dutch ambassador to several Islamic countries and Syria expert, for his guidance and reflections during the editing process. I am also indebted to Syrian philosopher Sadiq Jalal al-Azm for our frequent exchanges on Syria's past and present when we met in various parts of the world. Concerning conversation partners within Syria, it is difficult to mention names because the book would never have been the same if only one of them had been missing. Nevertheless, I would like to express my particularly deep respect and gratitude to Michel Kilo as well as to Riad Seif and Anwar al-Bunni—all of them part of the traditional intellectual opposition in Syria. They are men with very different personalities who have ideas of their own which we discussed in length, during the years of Asad's rule, whenever they were out of prison. From the cleric's side, Sheikh Mohammed Habash dedicated much of his time in sharing his Islamic philosophy and assessments of Syrian society and politics. I would also like to thank Radwan Ziadeh, director of the Syrian Center for Political and Strategic Studies and now also member of the Syrian National Council, for his endeavors to realize the publication of an Arabic version of *Syria— Ballots or Bullets?* in early 2011.

As the reader will notice, the named personalities and countless other conversation partners who remain anonymous hold diverging views and have very different personal backgrounds. They contribute to the rich Syrian mosaic that I have encountered throughout the years. My personal assessments remain independent, and I am solely responsible for any possible misjudgments or mistakes. At the same time I hope that also those who do not necessarily follow all my conclusions will gain new insights into the country. The book is an account of modern Syria, told for the benefit of a general readership, with the goal of providing a basic understanding of the country's social and political atmosphere. It has journalistic features but it is simultaneously meant as an academic contribution to Syria's most recent history.

This time, many of the interviewees have reflected hopes and disillusionment throughout breathless fluctuations. Coming to terms with the cruelties that were committed in 2011 and after will constitute an incredible challenge to Syria's society—if circumstances will one day allow for that account to be given at all. Like in other instances in history of unbelievable barbarism many people simply cannot or do not want to believe what is happening in their immediate vicinity. They close their eyes and hope that the storm will pass. In particular for those who had hoped and sincerely believed in Bashar al-Asad as a reformer, the awakening has caused shock. But after a decade of disillusionment more and more Syrians have come to agree with one Syrian analyst: "We are not going to lose Syria for the sake of two families," he said. Syria is much more, if it survives.

— Carsten Wieland
  Berlin, May 2012

1
Hariqa: The Fire Spreads

BLUE SKY ARCHED OVER THE OLD CITY OF DAMASCUS. Dusty yellow taxi horns blared unabatedly as usual while creeping along the chokepoint in front of Suq al-Hamidiya, the city's historic and more than 400 meter long covered street market. On this sunny and peaceful day nobody came anywhere close to anticipating that this was the last moment when the old and the new Syria would once again meet. It was on 17 February 2011, six days after the ouster of Egypt's President Husni Mubarak, when Syria's political culture started to change beyond recognition.

Suddenly, the traffic jam on *Shari' al-Thawra* (Street of the Revolution) became denser than normal. Cars clogged around the old Citadel and around the monument that displays Sultan Salaheddin on horseback, the mystified and tolerant Kurdish-Islamic leader who conquered Al-Quds or Jerusalem in 1187. A few steps away lies the Hariqa neighborhood that is sandwiched between the two historic commercial galleries of Suq al-Hamidiya and Medhat Pasha Street (or Straight Street).

Hariqa means "fire" or "conflagration." Although located in the heart of the Old City, this busy merchant area has wider streets arranged in rectangles that are delimited by low story stone buildings. By contrast, the rest of the old city is marked by crooked narrow lanes and century-old warped Ottoman adobe houses. The reason for this is that the neighborhood was set on fire on 9 May 1926 when the French colonial forces shelled the city. The Druze revolution had spread to Damascus from the Howran province, whose capital is Dara'a close to the Jordanian border.

Eighty-five years later it was the Hariqa quarter from which a fire was to spread, this time in the opposite direction toward Dara'a and soon throughout the entire country. In another parallel, Muntaha al-Atrash, the daughter of Sultan Pasha al-Atrash, the Druze leader of the Syrian Revolution against the French occupation, was soon to emerge as one of the supporters of the revolt of 2011. She was one of only a few members of the Druze minority who dared to engage publicly in favor of the revolution.

Somewhere in the streets of Hariqa among the textile shops the son of a shop owner was beaten up by policemen on this very Thursday in February 2011—nothing unusual in a police state, although not all too frequent in the public space in Syria. However, this time something extraordinary happened. People gathered in order to support the victim. The crowd grew larger and larger. People chanted: "The Syrian people will not be humiliated!" This was something completely unheard of—a whiff of the Arab Spring mixed with the odor of cardamom and apple tobacco in the old market of Damascus.

For the past thirty years, Syria was considered by many to be one of the safest countries in the world. Its citizens were rigorously controlled by numerous secret services. Syrians often stated with a mixture of pride and fear that their country was a place where "law and order" prevailed. The system of informers functioned smoothly. People mistrusted each other deeply. In this Arab country the word "prohibited" (*mamnu'a*) was a frequent companion. The time when policemen carried pistols in their belts was past. Syria was a safe and peaceful country. A truncheon was quite sufficient and even this was seldom put to use.

This time in Hariqa the ubiquitous fear of people had begun to dwindle away. More than 1,500 Damascus citizens gathered and brought the traffic to a standstill. The city had not seen such an uprising since the 1980s. Their chants became louder. Again and again: "The Syrian people will not be humiliated!" And: "There is no god but Allah!" The latter was an Islamic call for justice that sounded bizarre in a country that had branded itself with socialist and secularist Baathism for more than forty years.

Shortly afterward, something extraordinary happened—an event that, a month later after blood had been shed in Dara'a and other parts of the country, would seem surreal: In a manner typical of the old Syria, the Minister of Interior, Major General Said Sammur, drove into the middle of the crowd, got out of the car without any visible bodyguards around him, stood up on the door sill of his old white vehicle, and started to discuss with the protesters across the roof of the car. People cheered. Many of them were holding their mobile phones into the air and filmed the scene. For a few seconds some of the mostly young men even started to chant the familiar tune, "With our soul and our blood we'll fight for you, Bashar!" At this stage people still projected the evils of the country on the lower ranking officials, especially the police and the *mukhabarat*. President Bashar al-Asad was still viewed by ordinary Syrians as a problem solver. It was not yet the time to cross the notorious red line, namely criticizing the president himself.

Dressed in a dark suit and tie, Interior Minister Sammur looked calm and surprised at the same time. "This is a demonstration," he said as he stood on the door sill, slightly above the protesters. Somebody handed him a megaphone with which he addressed the crowd. The minister met the alleged victim of the attack and promised an investigation. He drove away together with the victim, and with him he took one of the last PR coups of the ancient regime.[1]

Had the authorities reacted in a similar fashion vis-à-vis subsequent protests, an escalation of violence may have been averted. But this was the last time when a high-ranking government official could dare to dive into a crowd. What Sammur did may appear strange to external observers. Yet, by the standards of old Syria this was a very typical approach, especially in a city like Damascus where people knew their neighbors in the traditional quarters and where conflicts were negotiated between citizens and also between them and policemen, for example. Apart from that, the demonstration in Hariqa was perceived as such a rare event that the minister had the time and the willingness to personally engage. Similar scenes had occurred in the past. For example, in 2005, the then interior minister personally appeared on the crime scene when a money-transfer agency was robbed in Damascus, simply because it was considered something so rare and outrageous. Large demonstrations were only known as pro-regime celebrations or in favor of causes that the regime supported, such as the large turnouts of people against the Iraq war in 2003 or ostentatious pro-Palestine gatherings.

It is true that singular and quite unusual events had occurred in Syria shortly before the Hariqa incident. On 26 January for example, Hassan Ali Akleh from the north-east Kurdish city of al-Hasaka poured gasoline on himself and set himself on fire. Thus he evoked the symbolic action of the young Tunisian vegetable seller Mohammed Bouazizi, who set himself ablaze on 17 December 2010 in Tunis and died of his wounds about two weeks later. His desperation had sparked off the protests in Tunisia and triggered the entire Arab Spring. In Syrian prisons, hunger strikes were reported, and on 2 February some fifteen people held a candlelight sit-in in the Christian neighborhood of Bab Touma in support of Egyptian demonstrators. They were beaten up and dispersed by the *mukhabarat*. In the two first weeks of February, Internet activists, possibly supported from Syrians abroad, started to become active and called for protests in Syria on *Facebook*. This call trailed off, however. The only other protests occurred later in al-Hasaka.

But the Hariqa demonstration represented a turning point. The sheer amount of people who dared to confront the authorities was novel. The method of conflict solution was old. But the paternalistic approach to placate the plebs proved no good in stopping the gradual erosion of fear. The slogans went far beyond the incident itself, although they stopped short of demanding regime change. The protesters called for dignity, a constant theme in the Arab Spring demonstrations. But this time it was not the Arabs that called for dignity and independence from colonial suppression. They demanded dignity from their own governments.

From Hariqa and al-Hasaka the revolutionary spirit reached the parliament in Damascus before it famously exploded in Dara'a. On 8 March—precisely the 48th birthday of the Baath Party's rise to power—during a routine session of the Syrian parliament, independent MP Abdul Karim al-Sayed proposed that emergency laws be reviewed. They had been in force in Syria since the first Baath coup in 1963 and legalized the easy detention of opposition figures. The abolition of emergency law was a year-old demand of the opposition. But it was unthinkable that a member of parliament would one day call to review its practice. Although his proposition was immediately quashed, Al-Sayed received some kind of support from another independent MP Sheikh Mohammed Habash said he "hopes and expects" that the state of emergency would be lifted this year, as part of "a formula that guarantees national security, and at the same time lets people feel relaxed and satisfied."[2] Habash is a remarkable religious and political figure who showed increasing signs of estrangement from the regime since at least 2010 (see Chapter VII "Opposition, Islam, and the Regime").

Since then the events escalated. On March 15 actions on a "Day of Rage" were announced on the new *Facebook* page "The Syrian Revolution 2011." Demonstrations took place in several cities across Syria. Thousands of protesters gathered in al-Hasaka, Dara'a, Deir al-Zour, and Hama. In Damascus an estimated 1,500 people came together again. The *Facebook* page showed pictures of supportive demonstrations in Cairo, Nicosia, Helsinki, Istanbul, and Berlin. The opposition figure Suhair Atasi gave interviews on Arab and international news channels in support of the uprising. She ran the banned Jamal Atasi Forum and is the daughter of Jamal Atasi, who was a prominent pan-Arab ideologue in the early Baath movement and who held government and party posts until he fell out with Syria's president Hafez al-Asad. The first major wave of arrests swept the country during and after these events.

Only one day later, the protest took a distinctive political direction. In Damascus' Martyr's Square (*Saha al-Merjeh*), a few steps from Hariqa among the few remnants of the city's colonial era, a crowd of some 200 demonstrators gathered in front of the Syrian Interior Ministry. Family members of political detainees demanded their liberation. They were joined by a mix of activists and jurists, writers, journalists and young academics. About two dozen people were arrested, among others Suhair Atasi and the well-known university professor and philosopher Tayyeb Tizini, who said that he was caught in the middle of the turmoil while he was trying to get to the Ministry to pick up his monthly pension check.[3] Both were soon released but Atasi fled to Jordan in November.

At this moment the fire spread as a conflagration and the upheaval entered into broader international perception. Violence started to take its course in Dara'a and soon beyond. From now on the Syrian revolt became a decentralized phenomenon in the provinces and in several towns. It left the capital of Damascus where the first demonstrations had taken place.

The developments in the March weeks can be viewed from two different or rather complementary angles. One approach concentrates on the deliberate decision-making in favor of a violent crackdown and the other one sheds a light on the structure of the regime apparatus:

While the first people in Damascus started to celebrate the fall of Mubarak or showed sympathy with the rebels in Libya, the Syrian regime became increasingly nervous. In February a special commission of the government analyzed the patterns of protest in Egypt and Tunisia and came to the conclusion that the regimes were toppled because they did not squash the protests in time. This shows that the Syrian regime had agreed on a security solution even before the protests really began.[4] On the other hand, what happened in Dara'a was also a regime failure. The protests triggered typical reflexes of a thoroughly authoritarian culture with a cruel history of civil wars and crackdowns. Survival was a zero-sum game where the winner takes it all. On closer inspection, it is no surprise that the Arab Spring protests hit the most oppressive states in the Arab world. Structurally, they had no room to maneuver, no means to absorb societal and political shocks.

The mindset of the authorities at all levels precluded de-escalating strategies. This manifested itself in an extreme way in the agricultural and mostly Sunni city of Dara'a—a place that had been affected by the repercussions of the drought in Syria's eastern regions. During the past six years thousands of displaced people settled in the town of some 300,000 inhabitants. State mismanagement of resources and corruption aggravated the crisis.

First, a telephone conversation between two women was tapped by the *mukhabarat* in Dara'a in which sympathy was expressed for the revolution in Egypt. Then a group of fifteen children painted anti-government graffiti on walls, inspired by the revolutions in Tunisia and Egypt. They painted "The people want the fall of the regime" (*as-sha'b yureed isqat an-nizam*) on the walls, something unheard of and unthinkable in old Syria. Instead of handling this incident with kid gloves in light of the revolutionary environment in the neighborhood, the secret police arrested the kids and threw them into prison.

What the authorities did to them proved maybe the worst "technical" mistake of the regime in retrospect (apart from an outrageous normative behavior). The children were tortured. Fingernails were ripped out. The parents who went to the authorities several times to ask for their liberation were rebuked by insulting statements: "Forget your children!" an officer said, according to reports. "Make new ones! And if you don't know how to do it, send over your women and we'll help you."[5] This was too much even for the rural Syrian people who had suffered plenty of arbitrariness in their lives.

The protests grew and more and more demands were added in frustration and anger. The violence began when a large group of people emerged from the Omari Mosque, marching and shouting slogans against corruption and calling for more political freedom. Security forces used live ammunition and cordoned off the main hospital to prevent families from visiting the wounded victims. The first three deaths of the Syrian Arab Spring occurred, others died later from their wounds. The funerals brought thousands into the street of the town and caused more retaliation. The funerals of the subsequent days attracted even more people. This is what created the dynamics that went out of control and that began to shatter Syria to its core. The deaths soon went into the dozens, hundreds then thousands. Cases of torture became the rule of the day. Ever more funerals caused ever more occasions for protests and new victims.

During the first days of 18 March and thereafter, people in Dara'a chanted, "God, Syria, Freedom" and slogans accusing the president's family of corruption. The list of demands were quite concrete: The dismantling of the secret police headquarters in Dara'a, the dismissal of the corrupt governor, a public trial for those responsible for the killings, and the scrapping of regulations requiring permission from the secret police to sell and buy property. The first wave of protesters in Dara'a did not topple Asad statues but burned down the office of the Baath Party, the court building, and the local outlet of Syriatel, the mobile phone company of Rami Makhlouf. Asad's cousin owned both of Syria's cell phone companies, all duty-free shops and almost everything else that promised quick profits. Like his counterparts in Tunisia and Egypt, Makhlouf was the incarnation of a classic predatory economy. The stories of forty-one-year-old Makhlouf's corruption incensed ordinary Syrians from the working poor to the endangered middle class.

The Dara'a uprising was done by rather rural or tribal people but their demands such as good governance and freedom were very modern, and their target of attack was a symbol of Syria's modern technological development under Bashar al-Asad. "We'll say it clearly," went a chant in Dara'a. "Rami Makhlouf is robbing us."[6]

The people's fury was also directed toward Bashar's brother Maher, who possesses a reputation for personal cruelty. As head of the Republican Guard—the elite force which protects the regime from domestic threats and is the only one permitted to enter Damascus—and commander of the fourth armored division, he was the backbone of the "security solution." Other names increasingly heard in the protesters' chants were Asef Shawkat, husband of Bashar's sister Bushra, who became deputy Minister of Defense in September 2011.

Ironically, it was Asad himself who made this form of upheaval possible. He became victim of his own modernization. He allowed satellite dishes and fostered modern communication infrastructure, albeit all in the hands of his clan. The result: He harvested a modern form of protest movement that exchanged videos via *youtube* and organized itself via *Facebook* and SMS. Syria experienced the first "*youtube* war" in history. Though several Internet sites were permanently blocked, Syrians had far more access to information and the outside world than before, through satellite TV and Internet media. Precisely these visible signs of modernization caused hope among many young Syrians for further changes and at the same time nurtured the yearning for more freedom when Asad took power.

Thus the people of Dara'a were searching for the culprits of social and economic frustration in Asad's surroundings as it had always been until then. It was still not the President himself who was attacked. The red line was kept even after the first deaths that Bashar al-Asad inflicted on innocent civilians during his rule. The victims that the upheavals in the Kurdish north-eastern regions had caused in 2004 were rather attributed to external factors, such as the turbulence in Iraq, than to Asad himself. But this time it was different. The forty-five-year-old president lost his innocence in Dara'a. He began to operate with blood on his hands, similar to his father after the Hama massacre in 1982.

There is a major difference, however, between Hama 1982 and Dara'a 2011. In the late 1970s and early 1980s, radical members of the Muslim Brotherhood, who were supported by Saudi Arabia, were fierce enemies of the Syrian regime. Alawite officers had become targets of sectarian killings. President Hafez al-Asad had narrowly escaped an assassination attempt himself. In this case it was them or him. In the end, he decided to put a bloody end to the tug-of-war with the notorious massacre at Hama that left thousands if not tens of thousands of people dead. The city was shelled and flattened without any mobile cameras filming the events like today. Hama became a mass grave secluded from the world's eyes. Even now nobody knows exactly how many people lost their lives. The number of twenty to thirty thousand people is most often cited.

Since the clampdown in Hama 1982, Islamic extremists had successfully been contained. They never again gained a foothold in Syrian politics as they did in other Arab countries. Nevertheless, they noticeably gained ground in recent years on the societal level. The "secular" regime presented itself as a bulwark against the spread of Islamic fundamentalism in the region. It derived its legitimacy partly from the struggle against those radical forces that had once hastened Syria into a bloody civil war. For most Syrians this argument still sounded convincing, and they mistrusted the unknown. Moderate Muslims and religious minorities especially pinned their hopes on Baath secularism, even though critics maintained that Islamic fundamentalism was only being used as a pretext for not carrying out political liberalization.

Whereas his father resonded to religious fanatics who had launched violent attacks leading to the brink of civil war, Bashar al-Asad instigated a civil war. While his father fought for his political survival, Bashar *chose* to kill, and thus put his political survival at risk. He and the system that he was responsible for adopted a "security solution" directed against unarmed civilians. Thus was the situation in Dara'a during the first days of the escalation of the Arab Spring in Syria. Soon, protests spread across the country to Jisr al-Shughour close to the Turkish border in the north, to Banias and Latakia at the Mediterranean coast, to Deir al-Zour in the eastern desert, to the major industrial cities of Homs, and—again—Hama in Syria's populated West.

When Asad realized how the fire was spreading, he attempted to tamp down unrest in Dara'a. The president sacked the hated Howran governor Faisal Kulthum and charged him with blatant mistakes in tackling the protests. Asad also ordered the release of the fifteen detained children who had painted the graffiti as well as those detained in the 18 March protests. He sent a high-ranking Baath delegation to offer his condolences. In another move Asad issued a decree that shortened mandatory army conscription from twenty-one to eighteen months. But these dodges proved insufficient and, above all, too late—like many subsequent political concessions (see Chapter II "Regime Reflexes and Reactions").

Referring to these actions Ayman Abdul Nour, a prominent Syrian dissident, who edits the online publication *All4SYRIA* (www.all4syria.info) from Dubai, told *TIME*: "It is the start of a Syrian revolution unless the regime acts wisely and does the needed reforms. It will continue in all cities, even small groups. But the brutality the regime will use—it will show its Qaddafi face, the one it has been trying to hide for the last thirty years after the Hama massacres," he said. (He referred to the Libyan leader, Muammar al-Qaddafi, who was killed at the end of October 2011 after a war against Libyan rebel forces and NATO.)[7]

However, at the same time when the regime made attempts to placate moods, it started to instigate its propaganda against the demonstrators. Syria's official news agency SANA blamed "acts of sabotage" for the events in Dara'a. "A number of instigators tried to create chaos and unrest damaging public and private properties and setting fire to cars and shops," it wrote, adding that the security forces stepped in "to protect citizens and their property." The regime started its eternal mantra of foreign conspiracies against Syria and the danger of Islamist attacks.[8] So Asad evoked the familiar and simplistic alternative of "us and stability or them and chaos and Islamism." This was a familiar tone to Egyptians, too, who faced chaos and bloodshed carried out not by the people but by the regime's police forces and armed thugs in the days before the decisive moment of the revolution in Tahrir Square.

The fact that most inhabitants of Dara'a are Sunnis does not mean that this was an Islamist uprising. Neither was the fact that the first bloody scenes took place in and around the Omari Mosque an indication of a religiously inspired action. For mosques remained the only legal places of assembly in a country whose regime did not leave any room for alternative spaces of civil society. Even Christians or atheists used to participate in Friday prayers throughout the years in order to discuss and exchange ideas.

Nevertheless, on the surface religion gained importance to furnish symbols and spaces for the upheaval. Twisting a common slogan often heard to praise the president, protesters across the country chanted "God, Syria, freedom and nothing else!" instead of the usual "God, Syria, Bashar and nothing else!" Others shouted "No to Iran! No to Hezbollah!" which delivered a foretaste to sentiments that opposed the rising Shiite influence in Syria. With the escalation of cruelty, demonstrators straightforwardly called for the execution of Bashar al-Asad.

The Dara'a events also produced the first fissures within the political fabric of the Baath regime. Youssef Abou Roumiya, a Member of Parliament from Dara'a, accused security officers of being responsible for the massacres and called on Asad to apologize to the people of Dara'a. Moreover, he demanded to open an inquiry into the matter, and to listen to the peoples' "legitimate demands." A video of his speech made the rounds on the Internet even though it was taped in the closed circuit TV of the parliament. Later on, more Baath officials resigned in areas of unrest in an unprecedented manner in Syria.

After Dara'a the Pandora's Box was opened. More and more demonstrators were shot in the streets after Friday prayers or funerals. And everywhere it appeared that the security forces committed the same mistakes. They applied the cruelest possible techniques in an attempt to deter others from protesting. One of the early victims of torture whose fate became widely spread in the conventional and social media was that of 13-year-old Hamza al-Khateeb. The boy was arrested during a demonstration on April 29 in Saida, ten kilometers east of Dara'a. After one month his body was returned to his family in a horrible state. There is nothing much to add to the media reports; one of them went as follows:

"Lacerations, bruises and burns to his feet, elbows, face and knees, consistent with the use of electric shock devices and of being whipped with cable, both techniques of torture documented by Human Rights Watch as being used in Syrian prisons during the bloody three-month crackdown on protestors. Hamza's eyes were swollen and black and there were identical bullet wounds where he had apparently been shot through both arms, the bullets tearing a hole in his sides and lodging in his belly. On Hamza's chest was a deep, dark burn mark. His neck was broken and his penis cut off."[9]

Anger and more funeral protests spread wherever victims had fallen in the hail of bullets or when their tortured bodies were dumped at their families' houses. The regime themselves created the heroes or martyrs of the Syrian uprising in the perception of the demonstrators. It happened in a similar way in Tunisia with Muhammed al-Bouazizi, who immolated himself after being humiliated by the police; in Egypt where the young Khalid Said was tortured to death by the *mukhabarat;* in Libya; and in Yemen. However, precisely in the "Cradle of Civilization" (as Syrian tourism authorities liked to refer to their country with regard to its centuries old civilization, traditions, and tolerance), the pictures that reached the world from Syria through *Facebook* and *youtube,* as well as eyewitnesses' accounts, outgunned the other Arab countries in cruelty and barbarism. The children from Dara'a who had their finger nails ripped out and Khaled al-Khateeb who died in unimaginable pain became the Syrian figures that raised shock and ire beyond fear. A government ban on iPhones and the targeted shooting of "civilian reporters," who filmed the activities of the security forces and uploaded them on *youtube,* did not stop the presence of amateur videos on the Internet.

Later on it was Hama and then Homs that emerged as the hotspots of the protests. For a few days demonstrators managed to occupy central places like the Clocktower Square in Homs or the al-Asi Square in Hama with up to 200,000 people. The Syrian army, which had withdrawn for tactical reasons alone, re-entered the scene with all the more determination. A Tahrir Square scenario represented a nightmare for the authorities. When soldiers and regime thugs entered the city of Hama on 4 July, they also killed protest singer Ibrahim Qashoush. He sang in the *'arada* style—a traditional genre, favored by the protestors, where the audience participates by repeating evocative refrains or by answering questions and declarations sung by the lead singer.[10] *'Arada* also used to be an element of demonstrations at national protests in the 1920s during the time of the Great Syrian Revolt. Qashoush fascinated thousands of protesters in Hama with his explicit criticism of Bashar al-Asad and his family clan. His body was found floating in the Asi River (also known as Orontes). When people took it ashore, they were shocked to see that his murderers had cut out his entire throat.[11]

In an interesting plot of cyber warfare, Qashoush was honored post mortem by Google Earth. The Internet map service unilaterally changed names of Syrian streets and places. The President's Bridge (*jisr ar-ra'is*) in Damascus, for example, appeared now to users as Ibrahim al-Qashoush Bridge. Was it possible that Egyptian activist Wael Ghoneim, Google's regional manager for the Middle East (who had played a major role in the Egyptian revolution), was responsible for the changes?

A few days after Qashoush's death, on 7 July, in an unprecedented diplomatic move, US Ambassador Robert Ford together with French ambassador Eric Chevalier visited the protests in Hama against the will of the Syrian government. This created a rise in diplomatic tensions. Both diplomats were greeted by the protesters with roses and olive branches. They visited hospitals and spoke to people in the street. Protected by activists of the Local Coordination Committee—a grass roots opposition movement—Ford even stayed overnight while the Syrian army encircled the city.

After the diplomats' departure tanks soon re-conquered Hama's central square where protesters had been celebrating and singing. Thus the Syrian revolution remained a decentralized movement, starting from the periphery and gradually moving to the urban centers, implying high logistical challenges for all sides. Coordination of the protesters remained difficult with an increasing number of dangerous checkpoints and with little public transport left. The sporadic availability of electricity and Internet connections made their coordination even more challenging. As to the government side, frequent troop movements had to be conducted over long distances. Buses normally for civilian use were taken to transport soldiers so that in some areas transportation came to a halt.

From the army that was estimated to consist of roughly 300.000 to 500.000

men,[12] the regime had only a limited number of soldiers on hand that could be trusted. The concentration on elite units, dominated by Alawites, limited the manpower and immediate availabilities. But those well-trained and well-paid elite soldiers were more effective and had more to lose. As clashes broke out simultaneously in the country's extremities the leadership's logistical capacities were challenged. Syria's basic army of conscript soldiers had always been badly equipped and oozed with corruption. Conscripts were in a state of frustration because of ill-treatment by their superiors. A frequent narrative was that they were frequently forced to build the houses of superiors instead of fulfilling their training schedule; otherwise they were denied holidays. Many young Syrians went abroad to work in the Gulf States in order to escape the abhorred military service. Apart from that, it was unlikely from the beginning that ordinary soldiers would shoot or torture unarmed civilians from their own villages or neighborhoods. Therefore, large troop movements were inevitable. When it came to military constellations, a Libyan scenario was more likely to happen in Syria than an Egyptian one. Throughout the months more and more soldiers defected and joined the newly founded rebel force coined the Free Syrian Army (FSA). According to the government, by the end of 2011 some 2,000 regular soldiers and other security personnel were killed by "terrorist groups."

Desertions were a logical development given the increasing death toll and the rising psychological pressure on ordinary soldiers to commit actions against their professional ethics. Some of the soldiers, including higher ranking officers, were shot because they refused to shoot civilians, according to various first-hand reports and human rights activists on the ground. Sometimes it remained unclear who was responsible for the soldiers' deaths.[13] On the other hand, the rise of the Free Syrian Army brought a new dimension to the conflict and led it toward civil war. This was true, even though they were far from a coherent and coordinated group with strategic aims but operated in rather isolated pockets, mostly in self-defense or protecting civilian demonstrators. The rebels whose "commando" operated from Turkish safe heavens in the border area defined their task to protect the demonstrators against the security forces. At times they succeeded in keeping the regular army at a distance like in Homs. As a result, the number of people in the streets grew larger.[14] Later the defected soldiers also embarked on attacks against military targets and personnel. Colonel Riad al-Asaad, who declared his defection in July 2011, led the Free Syrian Army from Turkey.

The chronology of events speaks a clear language. At the outset of events peaceful demonstrators protested against everyday grievances. The violent (over-)reaction of the armed forces and secret services in Dara'a and other places in March and April caused the escalation of violence. At the same time, anguish grew among many Syrians, especially minorities, who feared a scenario of civil strife. Indeed, armed groups popped up from different sides, some with criminal agendas and others with sectarian ones. The loss of the monopoly of power by the Syrian government and rising counter violence was a consequence of its harsh approach within a narrow "security solution" based exclusively on hard power. This scenario was no a priori characteristic of the Syrian street protests. Inter-religious mistrust and violence as well as a rising rampage of outlaws, external interference, influx of arms, and foreign fighters developed as a consequence or self-fulfilling prophecy. Without any doubt, this played into the hands of the regime's propaganda.[15]

With rising levels of violence and counter-violence unarmed protesters were caught in the middle. Thus the clientele in the streets began to change. Demonstrations could no longer be celebrated as popular fairs with dancing and chanting performances but resembled highly dangerous cat-and-mouse games with the security forces. The regime switched to survival modus willing to bear any cost while the demonstrations became more Sunni in nature. The minorities, apart from the Alawites especially Christians and—to a lesser extent—Druze, cuddled in their protected niches of the Baathist arrangement. They feared the unknown more than the known flaws of the secularist authoritarian regime. The group that would have been able to tip the scales, the moderate Sunni merchant class, joined the silence for a while hedging their bets. The deterring cruelty of the "security solution" and of the Alawite paramilitary militias (*shabbiha*), the well prepared *mukhabarat*, the restrictive access to communication, the expulsion of journalists, and the identification of many members of minority groups with the Baath regime contributed to the stamina of Asad's clan during the heated months.

In conclusion, one of Asad's strategies was to keep up the fragile alliance between religious minorities and the moderate Sunni merchant class. This worked as long as the state propaganda managed to uphold a completely different narrative of the crisis depicting it as being led by criminals and terrorists directed from abroad. It also worked as long as the clampdown did not pass a certain limit of atrocities and bloodshed. Beginning in February 2012, the military put Homs under a siege that included: indiscriminate bombardment of Sunni neighborhoods; the deployment of snipers on high buildings who shot at men, women, and children as in Sarajevo in the early 1990s; the slaughter of entire families including the youngest babies with knives or bullets. All this became unbearable for those who had access to *youtube* videos or who followed reports of foreign journalists who were smuggled into the site of the suffering. Thus it became more and more difficult for minority clerics, for example, to find supportive words in favor of the regime for normative reasons. The fear of post-revolutionary chaos and possible persecution of Christians or other minorities by radical Islamists as in neighboring Iraq floated in a delicate balance with the disgust with the regime's methods. It was up to Asad and his clan to define the tipping point.

2
Regime Reflexes & Reactions

B Y HOLDING OUT IN AN EXTENDED WAR OF ATTRITION against the uprising, the Syrian government regime proved much more able than those in Tunisia or Egypt to maintain coherent control over propaganda from state and the few censured private sources. This was possible because Syria had only selectively opened up to modern media and banned foreign journalists quite effectively since March 2011. The Asad regime also employed more shrewd and unscrupulous tactics against opposition figures and neighborhood demonstrations. Initially, it also dealt successfully with international pressure and pursued a time-winning strategy with the Arab League and the international community. Unlike Libya, Syria possessed powerful friends such as Iran, Russia and China who regarded Syria as an important strategic asset. Also Syria's neighborhood provided support for the regime or at least kept quiet. Syrian opposition refugees felt threatened in Lebanon and Iraq. These countries also refused to participate in anti-Syrian sanctions. Even Jordan tried to keep a low profile for fear of regional repercussions and concern about the stability of its authoritarian monarchy. Refugees to Jordan were barred from publicly pursuing opposition activities against the Asad regime and from talking to the media. The Kingdom also hesitated with implementing or calling for sanctions because of fear of the adverse effect on Jordan's economy since Syria is an important transit hub. King Abdullah also feared a boost for Jordan's Muslim Brotherhood who could feel even more encouraged to help the Syrian brothers.

Still in February and March 2011 experts and observers cited more or less plausible reasons why Syria was unlikely to be the next Arab Spring domino.[1] Indeed, Syria differed from other Arab countries in that she had been in the anti-Western camp, castigated by sanctions for most of Asad's rule, whereas Tunisia's President Zine al-Abidine Ben Ali and Egypt's Husni Mubarak were Western allies in the old constellation of Arab-world power; guarantors of the old notion of stability. Egypt had a peace treaty with Israel and kept the border to the Gaza strip sealed despite Palestinian suffering. Also Yemen's Abdullah Saleh, another victim of the Arab Spring, was a Western ally in the fight against al-Qaida. Only Asad saw himself in the pan-Arab tradition. He played the anti-Israel tune of resistance, together with Hezbollah and Hamas, and played upon Western double standards toward the Israeli-Palestinian conflict. Thus Asad had the Arab street support (see also Chapters III and V). Major elements of the domestic opposition shared these ideological assumptions. Baathist Syria, as the last pan-Arab mouthpiece and the frontline Arab state against Israel, seemed to have sufficient ideological resources and more political leverage than pro-Western Arab authoritarian regimes to weather domestic crises.

Because Syrian civil society was weak and Asad's grip on the Syrian people was seen as particularly effective, there seemed to be enough power to keep rulers and ruled on some sort of common ground. Apart from ideology the perceived stabilizing factors included the soft-spoken personality of the president himself, a notorious security apparatus, calm and stability inside the country, and peaceful coexistence of minorities.

These factors gave President Asad a sense of security that lasted far too long. He especially thought that this presumed common ideological ground granted him immunity against the novel demands and discourse of the Arab Spring. This was despite the fact that Syria's demography, socio-economic frustrations, corruption, poor governance, and high levels of repression were comparable to the Arab states where revolutions had toppled autocrats.

Asad's disconnect with reality had been pointed out by opposition figures going back five years or more. In his 31 January 2011 interview with the Wall Street Journal, Asad uttered words that must make him wince to recall. The president said that Arab rulers would need to move faster to accommodate the rising political and economic aspirations of Arab peoples:

> "If you did not see the need for reform before what happened in Egypt and in Tunisia, it is too late to do any reform," he chided his fellow leaders. Then Asad assured the interviewer (and perhaps himself): "We have more difficult circumstances than most of the Arab countries but in spite of that Syria is stable. Why? Because you have to be very closely linked to the beliefs of the people. This is the core issue. When there is divergence between your policy and the people's beliefs and interests, you will have this vacuum that creates disturbances. So people do not only live on interests; they also live on beliefs, especially in very ideological areas. Unless you understand the ideological aspect of the region, you cannot understand what is happening."

In this lengthy interview the president also opined that his people were not yet ready for reform:

> We still have a long way to go because it is a process. If I was brought up in different circumstances, I have to train myself and, to be realistic, we have to wait for the next generation to bring this reform. . . . If you want to be transparent with your people, do not do anything cosmetic, whether to deceive your people or to get some applaud from the West. They want to criticize you, let them criticize and do not worry. . . . I do not think it is about time [for faster political reform, representation of people, and improving human rights], it is about the hope, because if I say that in five years time or ten years time may be, if the situation is going to be better, people are patient in our region.[2]

Less than two months later, the people's patience ran out and confrontations between protesters and security forces across Syria shook the Baathist regime. In the final analysis, the nationalistic discourse, the antagonism toward Israel and the West in general, and the pro-Palestinian rhetoric did not outweigh the people's daily social and economic grievances, their wish for the end of tutelage, and the loss of fear after the successful popular uprisings in Tunisia and Egypt. The internal enemy overshadowed the external one to the surprise of many observers inside and outside Syria.

Despite its relaxed appearance, the regime in Damascus was well aware of their policies' wound spots. When the Arab Spring swept through Tunisia and Egypt, one of the first reflexes of the government in Damascus was to implement socio-economic measures. Social shocks had been caused by selective economic reforms by a corrupt and ineffective government apparatus, which added to the frustration of the many young and unemployed Syrians. At the beginning of the fateful year of 2011 the government swiftly increased state salaries (plus twenty percent), pensions (plus thirty percent), subsidies and social benefits. The income tax was lowered. While the regime did react relatively quickly, these measures did not have the desired effect: they did not suffocate the protests. In fact, they were detrimental to the government's long-term reform agenda. According to estimates, these steps cost the Syrian state one billion USD amounting to six percent of the state's budget.[3] At this point the regime's political survival became the top priority.

The key question was whether the Asad government would be able to meet people's economic expectations, especially those of the traditional Sunni merchant class that had been won over by Hafez al-Asad.[4] But reports suggested at an early stage that this pillar was crumbling, too. While publicly supporting Asad, parts of the Sunni merchant class in Damascus and Aleppo reportedly were hedging their bets by secretly financing the protesters. As soon as the protests started to ruin the economy, these technical win–win alliances broke apart and predominantly primordial ones remained. With its intransigent violent strategy and the deteriorating economic situation, the regime risked to lose the Sunni merchant class while the pillars of power were more and more reduced to Alawite clan coherence.

The second immediate reflex of the regime in the spring of 2011 was directed at religion. Although the demonstrators, especially in their early period, were Syrians of all backgrounds making purely technocratic and secular demands (i.e. an end of suppression and better living-conditions), the regime made concessions to Sunni Islamists at the very start. Although religion was not a driving force, local Sunni clerics or *ulama* were involved in the early provincial protests from Dara'a onward. Mosques served as the only available shelters.[5] But similar to Tunisia and Egypt neither religion nor the obsolete slogan "Islam is the solution" played a role in the streets. For the regime, however, the ghost of Hama and the fear of Islamists in a growing political and security vacuum became visible. Still during the year 2010 the Syrian government had felt secure enough to get tougher on Islamists again after having left them increasing leeway throughout the previous years (see Chapter VII "Opposition, Islam, and the Regime").

The first indication of an "Islamic reflex" occurred in early April 2011 when the government re-allowed female teachers to wear the *niqab*. The facial veil had been banned following a heated controversy in summer 2010. Some 1,200 instructors had been banned from teaching and moved to administrative positions instead. Simultaneously in April, the influential Sheikh Ramadan al-Bouti announced on Syrian TV that the government would give in to long-standing Sunni demands which included founding an institute for Religious Sciences, Islamic and Arabic studies, and establishing a religious TV satellite channel. A casino was closed and Islamist political prisoners released. These concessions had little impact on most opposition demonstrators who insisted on sweeping political reforms.

Bashar al-Asad kept a low profile during the first weeks of protest. This fueled gossip that he was feuding with his family over how best to respond to the uprising. Some observers speculated that the far-reaching reform package nervously announced by his adviser Buthayna Shaaban at a press conference on 24 March 2011 more closely represented Asad's real position than his surreal speech to Parliament, in his first public appearance since the beginning of wide-spread violence, one week later. Cameras showed a smiling and waving president surrounded by parliamentarian claqueurs. In his national address Asad asserted that Syria was "facing a great conspiracy" at the hands of "imperialist forces."

With his rare public appearances in the early weeks of protest, the president played the role of a quasi monarchical leader of what the Syrian opposition likes to call a *jumlaka,* characterizing the country's political system, as a melding of the Arabic words for republic *(jumhurriya)* and monarchy *(mamlaka)*. Staying aloof, assuming no responsibility for the crisis, Asad shunted the blame downward, offering to reshuffle the cabinet and sack the lieutenants responsible for the hot spots around the country. In trying to manage its public relations, the regime attempted to make do by sending advisers, deputies or ministers before the TV cameras to explain its position. The president was only trotted out in extremis. As the protests escalated, the regime first tried political accommodation— then appeasement. Military service was cut to eighteen months and the price for exemption reduced. In Tunisia and Egypt, concessions had no conciliatory effect on the crowds because they always came a few days or weeks too late. This proved true in Syria, too. The concessions appeared poorly chosen for the circumstances.

On 7 April 2011 Asad granted citizenship to some 150,000 of Syria's Kurds, who had been stateless, finally responding to a long-standing demand of Kurdish advocacy organizations (see also Chapter VII "Opposition, Islam, and the Regime"). The measure was so overdue that Asad got little credit for it. "Citizenship is the right of every Syrian. It is not a favor. It is not the right of anyone to grant," retorted Habib Ibrahim, leader of a major Kurdish party.[6] Nevertheless, the Kurds did not participate in the protest movement as vehemently as their deprived status might suggest.

In another move the government hastily announced the establishment of political pluralism under the pressure of the street. Suddenly, the ancient demands of the opposition were apparently picked up. In particular the law on new political parties was intended to break the Baath Party monopoly (Decree No. 100 of 3 August). The draft of this decree had been gathering dust in a presidential desk drawer for years (more on the stalled political reform process in Chapter VI "The Negative Balance"). Another law, Decree No. 101, promulgated a general law on elections. A new media law, also promised since at least 2005, was introduced on 2 September. On 16 October, the President established a national committee tasked with preparing a draft constitution, which would be subject to a referendum within four months.

In a reflective speech to the new government on 17 April Asad announced the reform package. He still sounded optimistic that the decreed changes would address the problems facing the country. Despite making the usual excuses as to why reform developments in Syria took so long, he used moderate words clearly intended at political accommodation. In his statement, Asad explained that "the lack of communication with the citizens creates a feeling of frustration and a feeling of anger, particularly when there are daily needs within the capacity of the state to provide and yet we do not provide them." The president recognized the failures of the state and dedicated a long passage to unemployment. "From my meetings with sections of the population last week, I found that there is a gap which started to appear between state institutions and the Syrian citizens. This gap must be closed; and we need to find channels between ourselves and the Syrian population."

Asad apparently sensed where the problem lay and even employed some revolutionary discourse from the Tunisian and Egyptian Arab Spring when he declared:

> The loss of dignity doesn't necessarily mean that an individual is directly humiliated or insulted by another individual in or outside the state. It rather means neglecting citizens. It means not dealing with a certain transaction that he has in a government department. It might mean asking for a bribe. All these are insults and forms of humiliation that we need to get rid of once and for all. All these elements are strongly connected: the economy is connected with services, services are connected to dignity, the economy is connected to dignity, and security is connected with all of the above. This means that all these elements are interrelated and need to be achieved in parallel and at the same time.

In a remarkable passage from this speech Asad tried to put himself at the forefront of Arab reform by borrowing from democratic rhetoric, thus proving his aloofness from reality: "If we succeed, this will be a historic response to the orientalists who in the past wrote many things about the Arab society. They said that as a result of the social structure of this region, it will not be able to proceed with democracy at all. This will be equally a Syrian response; and you will be able to provide a model in the Arab region or the Middle East in producing a civilized democracy which is in the best interest of all the population." Ironically, on other occasions Asad had been equally adept in explaining why the Western democracy model was inappropriate for countries and societies such as Syria (see Chapter VI "The Negative Balance").

With this speech to his new government, Asad made it clear that after this reform package was passed, there remained no legal justification for further protests: "With these laws, we draw a line between reform and sabotage; and there are clear differences between the demands for reform and the intentions of creating chaos and sabotage."[7] He made good on this threat without hesitation.

By Syrian standards, the political concessions were very far-reaching; resulting in what many years of civil activism had been unable to achieve. In the context of the times, however, the moves turned out to be inadequate. The same was true for the regime's other promises, like erecting a legal framework for NGO activities and promulgating a new media law. Even declaring an end to martial law proved to be inadequate; a step that, rhetorically, had always been tied to liberation of the Golan Heights from Israeli occupation and the end of hostilities with Israel. Domestic stresses clearly brought such measures to the forefront of regime calculations. The government was about to lose one trump card after another. Despite the lifting of emergency law on paper, the suppression of dissent and human-rights violations took place more intensely than ever before.

Asad was also unable to convince the various opposition groups to engage in a government-sponsored dialogue. On 2 June the president announced the establishment of a National Dialogue Commission as part of a "transitional process" toward a multiparty democracy. Leading opposition figures boycotted the initiative. The initiative failed for three reasons. The regime continued to use violence to suppress the protests: moderate opposition figures made the end of violence a precondition for their participation (see Chapter VII "The Opposition, Islam and the Regime"). A second reason for failure was the regime's attempt to drive a wedge between different opposition groups while winning time and continuing its military advances. The third reason for failure was an open question: With whom to lead such a dialogue? A Syrian researcher, based in France and linked to the foreign Syrian opposition, recalled that he received a phone call from Syria's Vice President Faruq al-Shara' who asked him if he would participate in the national dialogue. The researcher asked which protagonists would represent the government. Al-Shara' responded that it was himself and the President's adviser Bouthayna

Shaaban. The researcher replied that such a meeting would be futile because even these political veterans could no longer exert any influence on the Asad clan's decisions. According to the researcher, al-Shara' did not even try to contradict this statement.[8]

Meanwhile, the persistence and duration of the street protests turned into a war of attrition for both sides. While desperation and radicalization grew in the country, nervousness corroded the political leadership and the security personnel. At this point, Asad had already been under intense pressure in a far less dangerous, albeit highly sensitive, situation after the assassination of Lebanon's Prime Minister Rafiq Hariri and the subsequent withdrawal of Syrian troops from the neighboring country in 2005. Around that time a member of the opposition reported complaints about the president's "weak character." "He holds the opinion of the person he last spoke to," said a journalist who preferred to remain anonymous. Even his sister Bushra reportedly called him "stupid and nervous" when he was among a circle of relatives after the turbulent events in Lebanon, according to the same, well-informed source. Another credible source reported that Asad underwent psychological treatment after the events in 2005.[9]

Usually, presidents are described with a focus on their personality. In the Arab context personal leadership is considered important. Bashar al-Asad's cult and image also played a key role in shaping the president's perception (see also Chapters IV and V).[10] However, a personality-centered approach alone fails to explain the complexity of developments. The Baathist regime was a web of direct and subtle influences, priorities, jealousies and power struggles. There were indications that in some circumstances the president had not been able to enact his own decisions or fulfill promises made, because others were calling the shots. A leading opposition figure, Michel Kilo, stated in late 2010 that Asad was not the regime and that he had been left to act freely in only foreign policy; domestic policy making was in the hands of the secret services, the Baath Party, his clan, and representatives of big business. "The whole country is in the hands of the *mukhabarat*," he said. "Asad cannot even change his shirt without their permission."[11] As will be discussed later, opposition observers perceived a growing pluralization of power centers within the regime after the death of Hafez al-Asad.

This view was reiterated by the defector Mahmoud Suleiman Haj Hamad, Inspector General of the Central Financial Monitoring Commission at the Prime Minister's office and Defense Ministry's Chief Inspector. He told the media that "the responsibility for the violence against demonstrators lies with the military intelligence, with the directorate of the general intelligence service and with the air force intelligence." According to Haj Hamad, the government no longer exercised any real power. The members of the cabinet were "prisoners who cannot do a step anymore without being accompanied by the security forces."[12]

In earlier times, Asad reportedly confronted some of his cousins and friends who had formed wild street gangs and who caused trouble in particular in the northwestern port city of Latakia and the surrounding countryside. The *shabbiha* ("ghost") gangs emerged in the 1990s and were originally founded as the armed wing of the "welfare organization" al-Murtada led by Jamil al-Asad, Hafez's brother and Bashar's uncle. Since the uprising started they have lent welcome assistance to loyal army units in the fighting far beyond Latakia and were able to operate freely. The leaders of these *shabbiha* gangs were Asad's cousins Fawaz al-Asad und Munzhir al-Asad. They were among the first members of the regime apparatus to be put on the list of sanctions by the European Union in spring 2011. During the protests the *shabbiha* militia often acted in the bow wave of regular troops. When the army soldiers had subdued a neighborhood, the *shabbiha* spread out to loot and murder. According to eye witnesses, the *shabbiha* also executed those soldiers who refused to shoot on unarmed civilians. Apparently, these were not merely paramilitary groups but, according to high-ranking defectors, government-sponsored proxies. Haj Hamad pointed out that the regime had spent 2 billion Syrian Pounds (USD 34 million) on the *shabbiha* militias. He also confirmed that the regime had been getting financial aid from Iraq and Iran.[13]

In a stunning interview in the beginning of December 2011, a muddleheaded Asad said something that his father would have never uttered. When asked by ABC reporter Barbara Walters to explain who was responsible for killing the street protesters, the president of Syria said (following the literal transcription[14]): "They are not my forces, they are military forces belong to the government. . . . I don't own them. I am president. I don't own the country, so they are not my forces." Asad was tense but tried to remain calm and spoke in a throaty voice. It was Asad himself who had invited the US television crew to come to Damascus for the interview. He intended to present the regime's side of the story. Instead, he appeared weaker than anyone had ever seen him.

Al-Asad further stated in this interview that at least twice at the beginning of the conflict, he had given orders that the shooting should stop, but to no avail. He insisted:

> There was even written not to use guns, that's why I said it wasn't policy. Their job is to prevent people [from starting turmoil] like [in] any other country. . . . Whenever they used machine guns against civilians, this is breaching of the law. . . . Every "brute reaction" was by an individual, not by an institution, that's what you have to know. . . . No, there is a difference between having policy to crack down and between having some mistakes committed by some officials, there is a big difference. For example, when you talk about policy it's like what happened in Guantánamo when you have policy of torture for example we don't have such a policy to crack down or to torture people, you have mistakes committed by some people or we heard we have some allegations about mistakes, that is why we have a special committee to investigate what

happened and then we can tell according to the evidences we have mistakes or not. But as a policy, no.

This behavior of the Syrian president brings to mind the joke on the streets of Damascus in 2004: "Bashar is akin to the traffic signs in this country. It is in principle forbidden to use your horn and yet the noise is overwhelming," as a parliamentarian had remarked.[15]

However, the situation had become too serious to crack jokes about or to explain in such simplistic terms. Asad insisted at the beginning of December 2011 that no protesters were being tortured and that the United Nations had not handed him its report of human rights violations in Syria. He understated the UN's seriousness saying that while Syria did have an ambassador at the UN, "it's a game we play. It doesn't mean you believe in it." This position represented a serious departure from previous policies when Syria traditionally counted on the UN to counterbalance US policies supporting Israel. Syria had launched several initiatives in UN bodies to condemn the occupation of Palestinian territories and to establish a nuclear-free zone in the Middle East. In contrast, it had traditionally been Israel's public position to mistrust and even ridicule the UN. Now it was Asad who ridiculed his country's precious UN policies.

In this surreal interview Asad emphasized:

"We don't kill our people, nobody kill. No government in the world kill its people, unless it's led by crazy person. For me, as president, I became president because of the public support. It's impossible for anyone, in this state, to give order to kill people . . . No, no, no. We don't have—nobody—no one's command. There was no command, to kill or to be brutal. . . . most of the people that have been killed are supporters of the government not the vice versa." He continued by saying, "By doing the best I can . . . for this country. Whether you agree, or whether the people agree or don't agree, but at—at the end, I was not a puppet. . . . No, a regret—you regret when you do—when you do mistakes, when you commit a mistake. I always try to protect my people. How can I feel remorseful if I try to protect the Syrian people?"

The mere fact that he had to justify himself of not being a puppet was interesting since it reflected a discourse that had long been held inside the opposition. It also showed Asad's insecure self-perception. Of course, people, including a government spokesman in Washington, liked to pick up on the quote that only a crazy man would shoot on his people in this way. But there were more possible explanations for the president's behavior during the uprising. The first was that Asad was losing his grasp of reality, as observers had noted earlier. His performance before parliament in previous March, when he smiled and cracked jokes amidst the crisis, was one indicator. A second explanation could be that Asad was a great cynic who played a brutal role in a division of labor and power within his family clan but that he simply did not have the talent to be a great actor.

Ayman Abdul Nour, ex-member of the Baath Party and former college friend of Asad, said that the president "lives in a cocoon" opting not to see the reports of torture and killings. "He wants to deal with things with a cool mind," Nour said, who had broken with Asad in 2004 after a 20-year close acquaintance. In an interview after Asad's remarks on ABC Nour recalled an incident in 2000, shortly after Assad succeeded his father as president, involving a child who had been painfully injured. Nour told Asad that the sight of the child in pain had made him want to cry. According to Nour, Asad got angry and said: "You can't use such emotive words!' It was forbidden to talk about anything emotional while with him. He said he was the president and can't take decisions based on emotions and has to be cold, calculated and detached."[16]

Asad's "coolness" looked increasingly staged as the conflict in his country escalated. He had outsourced the "security issue" to his family members and drifted away from reality, if he had not been a cynic from the beginning. Certainly, Asad made a plethora of technical and strategic mistakes as president. Despite his initially soft image, Bashar gradually took on the cynicism, the loss of reality, and the apocalyptic will to cling to power at any cost that characterized other Arab dictators. In an interview at the end of November 2011, he said he would "definitely" be ready to die for his country, echoing the rhetoric of failed leaders such as Muammar al-Qaddafi. But he would not fight for his position as president, "for that would be fighting for myself and not for Syria," Asad said. "If I am to fight it will be for Syria and the people of Syria."[17] He still believed or wanted to believe that he was in tune with the majority of the Syrian people. In another interview cited below he contradicted himself and claimed that he would hand over his post to whomever would win the next presidential "elections" in 2014 or whenever he would lose "popular support."

Additional evidence supporting the Asad-as-cynic theory came from information provided to the author by a researcher close to the Syrian opposition who lives in Paris. He reported that, early in the uprising, Asad calmly explained during a private conversation that his strategy was not to let more than twenty-five to thirty people get killed per day, on Fridays maybe more, in order to avoid upsetting international public opinion.[18] This policy of murder was confirmed later in interviews collected by Human Rights Watch. Deserted soldiers and secret service officials reported that they had received clear orders to shoot unarmed protesters. One interviewee mentioned that he had been given a target quota: In a demonstration of about 5,000 people, some fifteen to twenty people could be killed. In December 2011 the human rights organization published seventy-four names of commanders who had issued orders to kill, to torture, or to carry out illegal detentions.[19]

To conclude this question of Asad's involvement, consider that reports differ over the degree of the president's personal responsibility for the government's response after protests broke out in 2011. To what extent were the cruelty and the numerous technical mistakes committed in suppressing the popular protests due to the multiplicty of power centers? Or, could they be directly attributed to Asad? In the end, however, it does not really matter if Bashar personally ordered each and every shot that was be fired, each child that was tortured and mutilated, every armed attack by the *shabbiha* Alawite gangs with the purpose of inciting sectarian hatred, for cattle and fields that were burnt to starve dissenting villagers. Neither does it matter morally, or politically, or in relation to international law. Asad was the president during this dark chapter of his country's history. He initiated the "security solution." Since 2000, he had inserted his loyalists into nearly all important positions in the *mukhabarat*, the military, and the government bureaucracy. He was in charge.

Since 2011, Bashar al-Asad has ordered the killing of many thousands of people. He had ten thousands arrested, tortured, and held under abysmal conditions in cramped dungeons or sport stadiums. He was well on his way to repeat the level of atrocity reached by his father in the 1982 Hama massacre. When the bloodshed is over, these cruelties are bound to be investigated, as they were in Eastern Europe. Then a fragmented Syrian society will suffer yet another trauma as it attempts to come to grips with its past. If for some reason blame is not assigned and justice is not meted out, then the barbarism of Syria's Arab Spring will join the cruel mysteries of Syria's history in the dungeon of the nation's collective memory.

During 2011, Syrian society began to segregate. On the popular level Alawites felt threatened, as a group that had most to lose and most to fear from a Sunni backlash in a worst case scenario. On the other hand, the violence did produce some instances of inter-religious solidarity. Some Alawites felt that they had been hijacked by the Asad family and made scapegoats for the massacres, especially since not all of them had necessarily profited from the regime in the past years. Courageously, some Alawite tribal leaders publicly distanced themselves from the Asad regime.

An example of Alawite discent came from the coastal region. The "Alawite League of Coordinating Committees and Figures on the Syrian Coast" was established at the end of 2011 and declared the Alawite community not responsible for the barbaric acts against demonstrators. The statement emphasized that *shabbiha* were "toys in the hands of the Asad family" and had no connection to the Alawite community. The authors equated Maher al-Asad's brutal elite forces to the militias led by Asad's uncle Rifaat in the 1970s who caused the Hama massacre. The text reads:

> Throughout the whole history of our homeland Syria Alawis as much as
> Druze, Sunnis, Shiites, Kurds and Christians and other components of Syrian

society have been part of the existence of this country, of its nascence and unity. Throughout the history of Syria no sect (ethnic group, religion) has excluded another one and treated them unjustly.

The text claimed that the Alawites had been active participants in Syria's revolutionary history, including resistance to the French colonial influence and continuing to the founding of nationalist, leftist and pan-Arab parties and movements. The authors explicitly mention the active role of Alawites in the Arab Socialist Movement of Akram al-Howrani, a pan-Arab minded Sunni and one of the founders of the Arab Socialist Baath Party. The declaration further stressed the nationalist credentials of contemporary Alawites, who "stood by their duties to liberate the Golan and carried the values of the entire democratic march of transformation."[20] The regime's brutal clampdown of the popular uprising led to a point that alienated vocal parts of its proper religious constituency.

During the escalation of events pressure on the regime was mounting from several sides including: the international sanctions; domestic armed resistance mounted by deserters from the regular military and a growing possibility of proxy battles fought in Syria by external powers. Accordingly, the regime increasingly fell back on threats in its statements. One of the early verbal attacks came from state entrepreneur Rami Makhlouf in May 2011—just at the same time when Asad tried to accommodate the protests with political concessions that were described above. Makhlouf burst out saying: "If there is no stability here, there's no way there will be stability in Israel. . . . No way, and nobody can guarantee what will happen after, God forbid, anything happens to this regime. . . . They should know when we suffer, we will not suffer alone."[21]

That a beneficiary of the regime could make such a public statement suggested a fracturing with the established elite. Makhlouf's threats prompted Syria's then ambassador in Washington, Imad Mustafa, to issue a statement in the New York Times one day later: "I wish to inform you that Rami Makhlouf, a businessman whom you interviewed at length, is a private citizen in Syria. He holds no official position in the Syrian government and does not speak on behalf of the Syrian authorities . . .."[22]

Soon after, Syrian state TV announced flimsily that Makhlouf had decided to give up his entrepreneurial activities in Syria, including Syriatel, and dedicate his profits to "charity organizations."[23]

A few months later, the also president himself began to use a more belligerent tone in his public statements. He warned Western countries to resist any thought of military intervention; as such action would result in an "earthquake" in the region. During the ABC interview, Asad interpreted the situation as follows:

Syria is the fault line in the Middle East. You know, the Middle East is generally it's very diverse in ethnicities, in sects, in religions, but Syria the most diverse

and this is the fault line where all these diversity meet so it's like the fault line
of the Earth . . . .. When you play with it, you will have earthquake that is going
to effect the whole region. So playing don't mean to overthrow me or to deal
with me it's not about me it's about the fabric of the society in this region that
is what I meant.[24]

In this respect, the Syrian president was correct. Any foreign intervention
in the Levantine powder keg would have dire consequences for many years
to come. This was exactly the fearful scenario on which Asad and his clan
built their confidence. The killing went on undisturbed for many months,
and as a strategy of self-defense the regime played with the angst of Syria's
population and of politicians in the region and beyond.

By using threat on one hand and offering symbolic and belated reforms on
the other in their political discourse, Asad and his government criminalized
and primordialized[25] the opposition's motives. Like always in such scenarios
violence and counter-violence became a self-fulfilling prophecy, whether
sectarian slogans played a role or simply criminal energy. The regime's regular
military forces acting hand in hand with the *shabbiha* staged incidents intended
to be seen as acts of sectarian violence in order to provoke an automatism of
sectarian violent responses, according to opposition reports from Homs and
other places. Such deceptions were also attempted by the former regimes in
Tunisia and Egypt but to no avail. The peaceful character of the Tunisian and
Egyptian demonstrators and their cross-sectarian solidarity prevailed.

In Syria, sectarian cleavages were more easily exploited because the Syrian
minority mix is more complex and a governing minority regime. Generally,
in better times, the Syrian polity has proven more inclusive than that of other
Arab states. In a bitter irony of events, the same regime that had officially
stood for anti-sectarianism and the protection of minorities had now chosen
sectarian strife as its emergency survival plan. Syria once stood as a regional
example for tolerance, but this model was seriously at stake (see Chapter V
"Pillars of the Ancient Regime's Legitimacy").

While targeted attempts to incite sectarian violence did occur and citizens
were killed at military checkpoints because of their religious affiliation, most
of these phenomena were restricted to Homs and its surrounding villages.
Despite the length of the crisis and the indescribable cruelties perpetrated
throughout the country by the regime, no country-wide sectarian rifts
crystallized. Inter-religious solidarity held especially during the early months
of the protests before the militarization of events. Several reports indicated that
Syrian Muslims and Christians followed the example of their counterparts in
Cairo's Tahrir Square. In Hama both groups exchanged gestures of solidarity
during the mass protests in June. In the Damascus Sunni neighborhood of
Midan Muslims and Christians marched together with Quran and Cross
protesting against the regime.[26] Despite differing attitudes toward the regime,
residents in the coastal town of Jebleh and inhabitants of Alawite and Sunni

neighborhoods in Homs established reliable channels of communication and thus counteracted violence meant to instigate sectarian unrest.

The opposition reported an incident in Darya near Damascus on 18 February 2012: A young Christian timidly carried a banner that referred to the constitutional debate, saying, "Why can a female Christian not become president?" A group of young Muslims approached her and politely asked her if they could carry the sign instead until the end of the manifestation.

Most of the slogans used by protesters emphasized the unity of the Syrian people and Syrian patriotic feelings. First in Hariqa in February 2011 and in demonstrations thereafter, the words Suriya (the Syrian nation), *as-sha'b as-suri* (the Syrian people), and as-Suriyyin (the Syrians) were used. Sometimes the protesters emphasized unity in diversity with the chants "Not Sunni and not Alawi: We want freedom" *(la Sunniyya wa la Alawiyya, bidna huriyya)* or "Syria in all its shades and sects" *(Suriyya bijami' atyafiha wa tawa'ifha).* From the very beginning, the movement has explicitly rejected sectarianism and so did the various programs of opposition bodies, including the SNC.[27]

The picture was complemented by the fact that the regime deliberately silenced moderate Islamic figures. The prominent Damascus preacher Mouaz al-Khatib was taken away by the *mukhabarat.* Khatib, head of the independent Islamic Civilization Society, was seen as an enlightened religious figure. He had moved to assure Syria's minorities that the diversity of the country would be respected if President Asad fell. "We call for freedom for every person. For every Sunni, Alawite, Ismaili and Christian, whether Arab or a member of the great Kurdish nation," Khatib had told protesters the month before his arrest. Opposition figures Aref Dalila, an Alawite, and Michel Kilo, a Christian, were by his side.[28]

As the violence escalated, secular Syrians and Alawites in particular worried about the rising influence of radical Sunni groups, of Saudi influence, and some outspoken Muslim preachers who used mosques as the only legal public platform to incite a religious antagonism during Friday prayers that has been absent from Syrian streets since the beginning of the rule of the Asads. Witnesses reported from the Homs governorate that Sunni groups allegedly entered Christian villages, threatening the populace to join the protests. The *takbir* (the words *"allahu akbar"*) called from balcony to balcony at night turned into a battle slogan for some protesters.

These actions frightened religious minorities and secular Sunnis who felt that religious radicalism represented a greater threat than a superficial secularist ideology and Baathist authoritarianism, regardless of the fact that they may have despised the regime's brutality as much as anyone else (if they had access to independent news at all). Several prominent Christian clerics declared their support for the regime, while many Christians joined the protests.[29] Christians were among the key opposition figures from the beginning. Conversely, amateur videos of battered minarets or aged imams that were beaten up inside their mosques contributed to the perceived religionization of the conflict. These images mirrored the worst fears of the Sunni population as much as the other incidents mentioned above scared the minorities. Alawites were reportedly preparing the Alawite mountains in northwestern Syria as a safe refuge with arms and money carried from Damascus. Some Alawites were selling their houses in the plains in Homs in order to withdraw into the mountains. Syrian society started to segregate. The longer the war of attrition between regime and opposition went on, the more Syria would change for the worse.

For several months the country suffered a ruinous stalemate between regime and demonstrators who were sometimes under rather symbolic protection by defected and lightly armed soldiers. The death toll rose to as many as one hundred persons daily. In Homs the world had to watch idly one of the most merciless military attacks against a civilian population in an urban setting since the war in Bosnia in the early 1990s. Despite suffering continuous attacks on civilian houses by mortar shells, despite the lack of heating, food and medicine, local activists managed to upload some of the cruelties on *youtube,* adding to dramatic reports from foreign journalists who were smuggled into the battle zone while risking their lives. According to the opposition, by the end of February 2012, more than 2,000 people lay injured in makeshift clinics in the Sunni neighborhoods of Homs, especially in Baba Amru. Hundreds had died in their houses or had been shot by snipers in the streets in Homs during this month alone. Homs suffered the scenario that Benghazi had been spared. In March 2011, French fighter planes had prevented a massacre by Qaddafi forces in Libya's eastern coastal city and thus heralded a UN-backed military intervention that arrived five minutes to twelve. In Homs, the people waited in vain.

Amid this situation of unstoppable military escalation in Syria that went along with tightening international sanctions and economic strangulation, the Asad regime made an attempt to prove not only its military effectiveness but also its capacity for political action. An appointed government commission that was composed of twenty-nine Alawite, Sunni, and Christian experts presented a draft for a new constitution. In this sense, Asad fulfilled an announcement that he had made eleven months before, following Russian pressure. Despite the raging war in parts of the country, the government managed to stage a referendum on the new constitution on 26 February. In the areas under government control and / or inhabited by Asad supporters, state TV cameras showed people casting their ballots while expressing their hope for stability and peace. The opposition called for a boycott and claimed that, in the days preceding the referendum, soldiers took away people's ID-cards at checkpoints with the hint that they would get them back in the voting station. It is hard to tell how many of the 14 million Syrians eligible to vote really made their cross on the ballot under these circumstances.

Internationally, the referendum was widely criticized as a farce of a drowning regime.

The constitution of 2012 replaced the one of 1973. The most revolutionary change at first glance was the abolition of the Baath Party as "leader of state and society" (Article 8). At closer inspection, this did not change much in practice since the Baath Party had already been a shell for years and an ideological decoration for the president's plenipotence. Real political pluralism was additionally impeded by article 60 of the constitution that stipulates that at least half of the members of parliament have to be "workers and peasants."

Despite this familiar vocabulary, any reference to socialism has been wiped out in the new document. The party's trinity of "unity, freedom and socialism," to which any president is sworn into office, became a thing of the past. Yet this second remarkable novelty was less spectacular in practical terms than in ideological or historical terms. Remnants of socialism have been replaced more and more by inhibited crony capitalism. Selective liberalization favored the new rich of the wider regime clan, as described in subsequent chapters.

In spite of the composition of the constitutional commission, no significant reference was made to Syria's religious and particularly ethnic minorities. Kurds are not mentioned at all in the document. The Arab character of the state has been carved in stone. The Arabic language is declared the only official state language (Article 4). However, religious minorities obtain the right to freely manage their legal relations with regard to family and religious matters. The Syrian state has thereby given up any secular pretensions, not only socialism.

Equally, the restriction of the president's rule to two 7-year-terms does not have much practical effect, because under this regulation Asad could remain in power until the year 2028. Before Hafez al-Asad's rule the term in Syria was a more realistic period of five years. The new constitution enables the president to continue to amass all important powers: He can issue decrees and remains the head of the executive branch, he nominates the prime minister and the ministers, he can dissolve the parliament, and he has the right to nominate the members of the constitutional court. All three state powers remain united in Asad's hands. In light of the bloody developments in Yemen, where beleaguered President Ali Abdullah Saleh granted himself "eternal immunity" before stepping down, article 117 of the Syrian constitution grants the president absolute immunity except in cases of treason. This passage is a back door in case Asad would opt for political asylum.

The fact that the Syrian president must remain a Muslim was kept from the 1973 constitution, although this was a controversial issue during the debates of the mixed commission. Apart from that, requirements for eligible presidents have been tightened to the extent that Asad himself would not have fulfilled them. The minimum age for candidates was lifted again to forty years and, more importantly, any candidate must be a Syrian by birth, married to a Syrian, and be a resident in Syria for at least ten years. Thus any opposition figures in exile would be excluded, such as SNC President Burhan Ghalioun.

Despite all caveats, given the domestic climate before the upheaval and even up to the spring months of 2011, the changes of the new constitution would have been a sensation in "old Syria." Now it came too late and offered too little, as it had happened with so many other political promises and gestures. The result of the referendum was a socialist-like approval rate of eighty-nine percent. The violent circumstances surrounding the election did even more to deprive it of credibility.

Six weeks after the referendum, parliamentary elections were planned. Even under normal circumstances the period would have been far too short for any opposition party to prepare for a campaign. According to the new constitution, any presidential candidate needs the approval of thirty-five of the 250 members of the People's Assembly that elects the president. This was hardly possible under the control of the Asad clan. In this regard, the Syrian constitution is inspired by the Egyptian one that was valid under toppled president Husni Mubarak. The power of Mubarak's party (NDP) enabled the regime to prevent the surge of unwanted opponents.[30]

The political theatre was to continue without any signs of rapprochement toward the opposition or an easing of the killing machinery in place. It is almost impossible to lead a serious discourse on the theoretical foundations of a state when state-sponsored barbarism undercuts any kind of positive domestic law, not to mention the essential humanitarian concepts that are the foundations of the Geneva Conventions. Meanwhile, opposition groups inside and outside Syria were failing to show more coherence and did not contribute to significant successes on the ground. At the same time, the societal and political structure in Syria was falling apart. It remained an open question: In the next presidential elections—planned for 2014 by the dictates of Syria's obsolete legal code—would the main candidate's name still be Bashar al-Asad at all.

3
A Decade of Lost Chances

THE AUTOCRATS IN TUNISIA, EGYPT, AND LIBYA—toppled during the Arab Spring—ruled for some 30 or 40 years before their power structure collapsed. Syria's President Bashar al-Asad only ruled for a decade before arriving at the end of his tether. His legacy was to leave his country in ruins, its morale and social fabric destroyed, perhaps beyond repair. He was the youngest of the Arab autocrats, born in 1965. No matter how the bloody revolt in his country will play out, his political capital will have been spent. How could this have happened after such a hopeful and auspicious start to his rule in June 2000? The story of his political career is a series of missed chances and practical failures.

Throughout his rule Asad emphasized his strong personal relationship to the "beloved people of Syria." Despite waves of significant popular support during the years of his rule, this rhetoric proved to be a self-delusion. In his first inauguration speech on 17 July 2000 Asad characterized himself as "the man who has become a president is the same man who was a doctor and an officer and first and foremost is a citizen."[1] Seven years later, during his second inauguration speech, he again touched on this theme: "I have worked during those years to enhance constructive values in my relationship with the people by rejecting the feeling of the man of authority in favor of the feeling of the man of responsibility, and by enhancing the image of the citizen before the image of the president in order to realize the concept of the responsible citizen and the official who feels and behaves as a citizen." He continued, "I have always respected the people by being clear and honest with them . . . . Our success in that regard depends on consistently providing the citizens with correct information so that they are aware of what is going on . . . ."[2] After 2011 the president was never again able to summon his previously cultivated image. He began a new chapter of his rule with blood on his hands.

Asad's choice of the "security solution" in 2011 was particularly disappointing, because the country had indeed made some progress during the ten years of his rule—at least in areas that did not touch on matters like democracy or human rights. The Syrian people enjoyed a greater access to a broader range of media and more plainspoken journalists than under Hafiz, but there existed unwritten "red lines" related to politics, religion and sex which could not be crossed. Arts and letters benefited from greater freedom of expression. Cell phones and other modern communications equipment became accessible to a wider range of people. Women's organizations gained strength and were granted some freedom of action even if they were not legally registered and not explicitly supportive of the government.

Clearly, the development of the country under Asad was asymmetric. While some reforms became evident especially in the macro-economic realm, political, administrative, and socio-economic progress came to a halt or was reversed. His first attempts of political pluralization soon appeared too risky. Therefore, the president reduced his aspirations to administrative reforms (eg. anti-corruption, efficiency). And when this was met with resistance, he concentrated on economic reforms that had been moving along a bumpy road since then but were indispensable for the regime's survival.

The following pages analytically condense and summarize some of the issues that are laid out in more detail later in this book.

Following the Baath Path

The chain of possible chances for a better development for him and his country started right at the beginning of Asad's rule. The first opportunity to change the course of suppression and to change his image into one of an accommodating leader occurred when the young heir to the republican throne was still highly dependent on the apparatus of his father. Bashar could not be sure how supportive the power circles would be if he deviated too quickly from the trodden path of Baathism. Asad was dependent on key players of the old power structure. He needed the loyalists of his father's era who had changed Syria's constitution to the effect that Asad was able to become president at 34 years of age (Syria's constitution had contained a minimum age of 40 years). Theoretically Asad could have put his legitimacy on a wider basis by instituting himself as a transitional president who would call for a popular vote. Since there was no other candidate around and much less any organized party, he would have won by a landslide.

But any direct election would have put into question the Baath system as a whole that had served his father as a stable basis for three decades and enabled the smooth succession. Moreover, competition from within the family ranks was still looming. His uncle Rifaat al-Asad, for example, never really thought that Bashar was the right man to do the job. He could have taken advantage of any mistake or volatility to snatch power himself. Similar ambitions could have emerged in the security apparatus or with other major political protagonists like long-serving Vice President Abdul Halim Khaddam (who defected in 2005) or Syria's experienced Foreign Minister Faruq al-Shara'.

Asad chose to stick to the Baath path. In reality, the Baath discourse camouflaged the ideological erosion of the system. There was not much left of socialism nor of pan-Arabism (see Chapter XI "The Bankruptcy of Baathism"). Asad weakened the influence of the Baath Party further during his rule but he never questioned the foundations of the system as such. Still, power relations were renegotiated, and Baathist functionaries were sidelined.

In times of crisis the circle of persons that the Asad clan could trust was contracting more and more up to the point that if the erosion escalated it might have become difficult to recruit enough staunch and qualified loyalists to effectively run a country.

Failure to Reach Out to the Opposition

A second opportunity for Asad to pursue sweeping changes was to come a few months after his taking over of power. In his inaugural speech on 18 July 2000 the president had called for Syrians to actively contribute to shape the country's future:

> . . . thus society will not develop, improve or prosper if it were to depend only on one sect or one party or one group; rather, it has to depend on the work of all citizens in the entire society. That is why I find it absolutely necessary to call upon every single citizen to participate in the process of development and modernization if we are truly honest and serious in attaining the desired results in the very near future.

Intellectuals were inspired and began to discuss freely in newly founded debating clubs in the halls of private houses. The most renowned one was the Jamal Atasi Forum of Suhair Atasi. The dynamics that emerged thereof in September 2000 became known as the Damascus Spring (more in Chapter VII "Opposition, Islam, and the Regime"). But the spring turned cold in only a few months as two key representatives of the Civil Society Movement, the economics professor Aref Dalila and the entrepreneur and ex-Member of Parliament Riad Seif, were arrested. The debating clubs in Damascus were forced to close down one after the other.

From the early years of his rule Asad plugged into the notorious discourse of other Arab autocrats in the region: Their people were not ready for democracy. Democracy was a "cultural phenomenon" of the West. In the Arab Spring of 2011 the people finally showed that, indeed, they were ready not only for practical changes but also for a new political discourse and even a new political culture. People demonstrated that it was their rulers who were responsible for keeping them in a state of poverty and intended political immaturity.

The clampdown of the Damascus Spring in 2001 represented the first wave of suppression against the moderate Syrian opposition. Asad decided to prioritize regime stability before democratic experiments. This was a conscious step to secure his power after he felt he would lose control. Then Vice-president Abdul Halim Khaddam was instrumental in putting the brakes on the development, and the Civil Society Movement went underground—in the Syrian context more appropriately put: into the tea houses. The Café Rawda was the most popular meeting point right around the corner from the parliament building. For the next couple of years the regime and the leftist intellectual opposition were to coexist side by side in a peculiar and very Syrian manner with protagonists of the Civil Society Movement taking turns in prison.

There was a time when even parts of the regime seemed to appreciate the constructive and prudent nature of Syria's opposition. Bahjat Suleiman, the feared and powerful former head of Syrian intelligence, wrote in the Lebanese newspaper *al-Safir* in 2003: "In Syria, the regime does not have enemies but 'opponents' whose demands do not go beyond certain political and economic reforms such as the end of the state of emergency and martial law; the adoption of a law on political parties; and the equitable redistribution of national wealth."[3] Forcible regime change, Suleiman knew, was only on the agenda of select exiles and US politicians.

But instead of reaching out to these opponents, who defined a gradual transition toward civil society and pluralism as a soft landing inherent to the system and who shared basic foreign-policy assumptions of the Baathists, the president treated these intellectuals like a gang of criminals in the subsequent years. Thus he disillusioned many Syrians who had hoped for a common ground toward incremental change. Looking back at Asad's first big opportunity, Sadiq Jalal al-Azm, philosopher and member of the Civil Society Movement, said: "Asad should have brought Riad Seif into a reshuffled government in 2001. His original sin was not to offer national reconciliation. Many even said that he would be ready to reconcile with Israel but not with his own people."[4]

Suleiman's distinction between opponents and enemies was to become highly topical again in the 2011 upheavals when the setting was much more polarized. It was part of the Syrian tragedy that even after the bloody escalation in 2011, some opposition figures tried to keep the doors open in the hope of dialogue for the sake of Syria's stability and in order to avoid a civil war, most notably the journalist and head of the Civil Society Movement, Michel Kilo. Ignoring the constructive opposition was one of Asad's gravest errors of his tenure. An elderly tribal leader in the northern province of Idlib was quoted as saying: "This revolution was led by the kids, the children. It's their revolution. This is the generation that didn't see the horrors of the 80s. If it was up to us we would have never started the revolution. We have been burned once. But they are brave. They led and we followed."[5]

External Shocks Add to Homegrown Mistakes

The clampdown on the Damascus Spring took place when the young Asad was still in a phase of political orientation. External forces would soon shock the Syrian regime. Looking at the chronology of events, it is important to keep in mind that the Damascus Spring was strangled *before* the attacks in Washington and New York on September 11, 2001—among other adverse events and circumstances.

Still, Syria's development took place in unusually harsh and unpredictable international conditions. The 9/11 attacks changed the whole board game in the Middle East and beyond, aggravated by the military approach of the US administration under President George W. Bush. The ensuing "war against terrorism" provided Arab autocrats with a pretext to get tough on opposition figures (many of whom were Islamists living outside Syria). It gave them a new context in which to frame their policies.

The 9/11 attacks can be viewed as a double-edged sword for Damascus. On the one hand, the Syrian *mukhabarat* now had the opportunity to use their year-long experience to fight Islamists of all kinds. Futher, the attacks strengthened Syria's ties with Western interests and was a welcome opportunity to underline the secular credentials of the Baath regime. Syria was to become a valuable partner for the West in the fight against Islamist terrorists. It was no coincidence that the United States and Israeli security establishments tended to take more conciliatory positions vis-à-vis Damascus than the respective political establishments. For example, George Tenet, who resigned from his position as head of the CIA, was, with his organization, one of the few moderating voices with regard to the Syrian regime within the US administration of George W. Bush.

On the other hand, despite Syria's willing cooperation in the fight against Islamist terrorism, it did not succeed in trading in this commitment for substantially better relations with the United States or Europe. Had this happened, the westward-looking and pragmatic technocratic and political elite in Damascus would have benefitted. Some of these figures lobbied for a rapprochement with Europe and favored signing the long-postponed EU Association Agreement. One of the key representatives was Sami Khiamy, Asad's economic adviser who later became the Syrian ambassador in London.

Syria's difficulty was that two different political pressures were simultaneously in play on the international stage. One was the discourse oscillating around the fight against Islamist terrorism, which included the debate over direct consequences from the 9/11 attacks. This discourse also posed fundamental questions about a readjustment and the value-orientation of Western foreign-policy vis-à-vis so-called pro-Western regimes that have nurtured Islamist terrorism for years, above all Saudi Arabia.[6] If this discourse had been put into political practice in a consequent manner, Syria could have gained a strategic advantage. It would have been a respected partner on the security level in view of its contribution against militant Islamism (much less, obviously, on the level of democratic governance).

The second discourse had less to do with protecting the United States from terrorist threats and more with catering for Israel's security concerns in the region. The pro-Israel discourse did not always overlap with the anti-Islamist-terrorism discourse. In this context Saddam Hussein's Iraq posed a threat to Israel and thus became a target of the Israel-friendly neo-conservative foreign-policy of the Bush administration. Other Western governments, especially France and Germany, were not convinced that Iraq had ties with al-Qaida (not to mention weapons of mass destruction) and consequently refused to support an attack against Iraq on the basis of these reasons.

What it meant for Syria was that the pro-Israel discourse proved stronger and in the end impaired efforts undertaken within the anti-Islamist-terrorism discourse. Because of Syria's political, ideological, and territorial issues with Israel, she would never be considered part of pro-Western coalition under the influence of the Bush administration and Israeli interests. Nevertheless, Syria continued to cooperate with Western secret services, even after the Anglo-American attack on Iraq up to the fall of 2003. When the regime in Damascus did not harvest any rewards from its engagement but threats of regime change instead, it was not interested in cooperation anymore.

This time it was the West that missed a great opportunity to focus on common secular values and the tolerance of religious minorities, on the fight against militant Islamism. This would have strengthened the pro-Western actors within the Syrian bureaucracy and political elite. It would have resonated among parts of the educated middle class as well. Around this time blue car stickers with yellow stars became popular in Damascus that served to imitate EU number plates. Instead, the Bush Administration placed Syria on the extended axis of evil pushing her closer to Iran, a country which many Syrians detested culturally, ideologically, and for religious reasons. Thus, secularist Syria began drifting more and more into the Iranian orbit and into alliances with Islamist groups.

The second and most serious external shock impacting the Asad government was the Iraq war of 2003. The Syrian regime was not ready to embark on democratic experiments at home while its eastern neighbor was in a state of war, and the Bush Administration was openly suggesting regime change in Damascus. In turn, the regional situation provided a comfortable excuse for the Asad regime to delay any political reforms and to further suppress its domestic opponents. It also presented a further opportunity for Asad to show the political shrewdness of his father.

Asad used the Iraq war to galvanize Syrian public support and to rally the entire "Arab street" behind him. The Syrian president became the hero, the only Arab leader between Baghdad and Casablanca who confronted a belligerent Bush administration. He even enjoyed the company of European countries like Germany and France in the anti-war camp. But it was Syria alone who again raised the anti-imperialist, pan-Arabism flag. The resistance discourse went down well and Asad enjoyed a period of almost unanimous domestic support. He was sure to have great parts of the Syrian opposition behind him, too. On another note Syria became the portal for Arab resistance fighters entering Iraq. The regime in Damascus was glad to get rid of Syrian Islamists who crossed over to Iraq where the Americans did the job of killing them. Furthermore, the Islamist foreign fighters helped keep the Americans from leaving Iraq and choosing Damascus as their next target for regime change. An American attack on Syria was a realistic scenario in the first months after the Iraq invasion.

Syria could have opposed the Anglo-American Iraq invasion. But the way in which Asad surfed on the wave of anti-Western, pan-Arab nationalism—that notably merged with staunchly Islamist discourse—did not leave much leeway for a future change of tactics. Moreover, this served as a catalytic to push Syria into the Iranian orbit (a process that had started with Israel's invasion of Lebanon in 1982). But in the big political scenario the Syrian regime had always been aware of the necessity of US support for any major achievement in the region, if only for the famous last mile in a possible peace agreement with Israel. Many of Asad's foreign policy endeavors after the Iraq war were indeed directed toward finding some kind of acceptance in Washington.

International pressure mounted on Syria in subsequent years, especially from Saudi Arabia, France and the United States to stop its meddling in Lebanon. As is further elaborated in Chapter XII, Asad lost his nerve and pursued an abrasive policy toward Lebanon. This culminated in the assassination of Lebanese Prime Minister Rafiq Hariri in February 2005, which increased Syria's isolation and entailed the forced withdrawal of Syrian troops from Lebanon.

Asad used to cite these external shocks and the problems in Lebanon to justify delaying domestic reforms. "We were affected by the situation in Iraq or in Lebanon. There are many things that we wanted to do in 2005 we are planning to do in the year 2012, seven years later! It is not realistic to have a time frame because you are not living in situation where you can control the events," he said in a *Wall Street Journal* interview at the end of January 2011.[7] Asad was definitely right about the fact that the foreign policy environment and the approach of some Western countries in the region were not at all conducive to the opening up of minds and policies in Syria. But despite pressures exerted from the outside, many mistakes were homemade.

Reference to the "old guard" of functionaries from Hafez al-Asad's times initially served as an argument not to embark on political change beyond administrative adjustments and insulated economic reforms. However, the picture was more complex. Old-aged functionaries were not necessarily part of the old guard, and young ones not necessarily reformers and westward looking. In any case by 2005, Asad had gradually placed his people in the key political and security positions. After 2011 Syria's foreign policy options narrowed down even further to only include alliances with, roughly speaking, Iran, Russia, China and Venezuela. Apparently, in times of crisis family members of higher regime loyalists did not see other options than fleeing to countries such as Malaysia, Iran, the United Arab Emirates, China, Ghana, and Nigeria.[8] Syria's foreign minister Walid Muallem announced, in anti-Western anger at the end of October 2011 in front of a group of Indian academics and journalists, that Syria would look more toward Asia now.[9] President Asad underlined this when talking to a Russian TV station. Interestingly, in this interview Asad antedated the decision to look to the far East to the year 2005. This was the precise moment when the economic reform program was announced in the Five Year Plan, and the European model of Social Market Economy was declared.[10]

Failure of Arab-Kurdish Reconciliation

Throughout his decade of rule, Asad had amassed numerous unresolved problems that combined to hit him in 2011. On the domestic chess board Asad missed another important chance to change the domestic discourse during and after the violent Kurdish protests in March 2004. Kurdish demonstrators rioted in several cities, including Aleppo and Damascus, setting fire to cars and fighting battles with the security police. Within a week Asad had the situation under control (more details in Chapter VI "The Negative Balance").

Two aspects are interesting here. First, the human rights lawyer Anwar al-Bunni, a member of the moderate opposition Civil Society Movement, tried to mediate and exert a moderating influence on Kurdish activists. The Syrian opposition considered it anti-patriotic to allow any form of Arab-Kurdish cleavage. Also Kurdish political leaders agreed to avoid a rift between them and the Arab opposition counterparts. They conceded that they had lost control over parts of their constituency. This would have been yet another opportunity for the regime to reach out to the opposition on behalf of the common national interest in times of external turbulences such as in Iraqi Kurdistan.

Secondly, after the riots Asad travelled to the neglected Kurdish region in northwestern Syria and promised to look into the Kurdish grievances. But the years passed without him doing anything to address these grievances. Restrictions against Kurds were even tightened. It was only under the existential threat of the protests in 2011 that the president agreed to grant citizenship to the Kurdish population. Thus he intended to prevent a strong Kurdish participation in the protest movements. The Kurdish issue was one of the easiest concessions to make. Asad lacked the political instinct to offer a solution to this problem at the apt moment.

The Lebanon Disaster

By 2005, Asad had gradually placed his people in the key political and security positions. Precisely at the hump day of his rule, when Asad felt relatively secure, he committed a grievous error and missed another formidable chance to establish himself as a moderate ruler who would set a course of his own. The error was to press for an unconstitutional extension of the mandate of Lebanon's pro-Syrian President Emile Lahoud at any cost. Asad's insistence in doing so bore heavy long-term costs for the Syrian regime. Among other repercussions Syria lost France as a European ally. France's President Jacques Chirac had been the only Western statesman to attend Hafez al-Asad's funeral in June 2000. In subsequent years French consultants had pilgrimaged to Damascus to help Syria to reform its administrative and judicial system. Now it was the personal friendship between Lebanon's Prime Minister Hariri and Chirac that proved stronger than the Syrian-French connection. Syria was isolated. Not a single Arab state moved a finger in her support. Syria became even more isolated after the assassination of Lebanon's Prime Minister Rafiq Hariri in February 2005. Asad was forced to withdraw all Syrian troops from Lebanon (for more details see Chapter IV "Bashar and Breaches in the Leadership"). Subsequently, the Special Tribunal for Lebanon, whose role was to investigate the Hariri assassination, became yet another political instrument for Syria's enemies to put pressure on Damascus.

During these months after February 2005 rumors spread of a coup d'état in the presidential palace in Damascus. Regime loyalists debated whether Asad was capable at all of defending Syria's national interests. Asad's power became challenged as never before. It was only in 2011 that a similar discussion was sparked again. This time the stakes were much higher. Asad piled up political debts from his family clan and the Alawite security establishment. The fact that he had missed earlier chances to strengthen his position began to take its toll. Without having risked a popular vote or at least reaching out for national reconciliation with the moderate opposition, Asad had nothing much but his clan and the security apparatus to fall back on. This made the president sink ever deeper into the self-interested power structure up to the point of no return. The political blunder of the Hariri assassination, whoever was behind it, marked the beginning of the decline of Asad. The trauma of complete isolation created certain paranoia that also had an influence in how he viewed opposition challenges at home.

Failed Reform Promises

Still, despite the foreign policy disaster at the beginning of the year 2005 resulting from events in Lebanon, the subsequent months yielded a valuable opportunity for Asad to reposition himself domestically. In June of that year Asad called the 10th Regional Baath Congress, the first one under his leadership. Expectations were high. But opposition forces and foreign observers were disappointed because they had expected more sweeping political reforms (more details in Chapter VI "The Negative Balance"). Instead, the results were merely announcements that never took effect until the regime struggled for survival in 2011.

Instead of working toward the fulfilment of the reform promises, a second clampdown on the Syrian Civil Society Movement was soon to follow. In face of the obvious turbulences of Asad's regime due to the Hariri assassination, the secular opposition caught momentum and was encouraged by Western diplomats and politicians. At that time a historic step toward a more unified opposition had been achieved through the Damascus Declaration of 16 October 2005 (see Chapter VII "Opposition, Islam, and the Regime").

The wave of suppression followed quickly in the first half of 2006 when those who had been spared in 2001 were arrested like Kilo and human rights lawyer Anwar al-Bunni. The hunt on signatories of the Damascus Declaration was based on the accusation against the opposition to pursue the agenda of Western interests. While The Syrian regime suffered from the "Lebanon trauma" of increased isolation and stigmatization, it became increasingly insecure. In this respect the suppression of civil society went hand in hand with external developments.

Not long after Kilo was arrested in May 2006 the summer war between Israel and Hezbollah broke out. Its result was a public diplomacy disaster for Israel, although the human and material damage on the Lebanese side was far higher. This war offered Asad yet another opportunity to turn popular enthusiasm into long-term political support. Instead, after Hezbollah declared "victory," Asad in a bigoted speech tried to cash in on the triumph as part as his own policies of resistance against Israel. Syrian public opinion stood behind him, while Hezbollah, and to some extent Asad, became the heroes of the Arab street far beyond the Levant.

Against this background, Asad was able to orchestrate the 2007 Syrian presidential and parliamentary elections with a comfortable cushion of popularity. Syrians were proud of their president for resisting international sanctions, the US intervention in Iraq, and international pressures connected with the Hariri Tribunal. And in their view Asad was the only Arab leader left who dared to speak out against Israel. With the main protagonists of the Civil Society Movement behind bars and the street behind him, this would have been another apt moment to convert his popular support into reformed political structures. Instead, Asad chose to be acclaimed again in a manipulated referendum for another seven-year-tenure.

On the public policy level, the selective economic reforms started to hurt the poor and the lower middle classes, while corruption and mismanagement thrived. Kilo criticized that transition in Syria toward a post-Baath era was achieved by an alliance of the *mukhabarat* with the new rich.[11]

Foreign Policy Honeymoon and Domestic Frustration

Some three years before the wave of Arab protests reached Syria in 2011, the regime in Damascus had started to regain the initiative in foreign policy matters. European governments and even the US administration had come to the conclusion that Syria was at least a stable, politically approachable, and important geo-strategic player in the Middle East, whose president was on the path of piecemeal reforms. Also US President Obama chose a strategy of engagement in his effort to reverse the Syrian drift toward Iran and sent an ambassador to Damascus in January 2011 after nearly six years of diplomatic vacuum. This represented the last foreign policy success for Asad before the popular protests began.

On the other hand, clinging to power by all possible means created common grounds with other autocratic Arab states. Syria was able to temporarily ease traditional tensions with Saudi Arabia and the other Gulf States. The Syrian regime declared its sympathy for the Saudi military invasion to crush the protests in Bahrain.[12] However, this overlap of authoritarian interests between Syria and the Arab peninsula's monarchies was fragile and short-lived.

Despite the international détente, the domestic secular opposition had not profited from the new dawn in Syria's foreign policy. Even benevolent dissenters and cautioning voices, not necessarily linked to the opposition, became increasingly frustrated. An experienced Syrian analyst, who worked in the government arena, conceded in an interview in October 2010: "I made the same mistake. I thought there was a correlation between foreign and domestic policy. . . . With or without external pressure we have no political change in Syria. Domestic pressure is a continuity, not a contradiction."[13]

A sheikh, who held political positions and was known to be pro-regime for years (but who also preferred to remain anonymous here), made a remarkable comment in visible frustration, also at the end of 2010: "Unfortunately, under the pressure of the US the situation here was better. Now they [the regime] think they have a strong message." He paused and added in a pensive tone: "We are going through a sensitive phase, through difficult times."[14]

These three quotes show that general frustration had been growing within the wider sphere of regime supporters before the upheavals broke out. Moreover, criticism that was directed against Iran was interpreted as a pro-American stance and sanctioned. The room for even cautious dissent had shrunk to a new low, not seen since Hafez al-Asad's times. Not even five months later, the exuberant self-confidence of the Asad regime, the arrogance of power, was seriously challenged.

Last Chances and the System's Failure

At precisely the moment when nobody in the international community, including Israel, had an interest in Asad's ouster, when many states tried to engage Syria as an actor in a regional peace scenario, the president committed his most grievous mistakes and missed the last chance of his political career.

The numerous lost chances due to technical and strategic mistakes during the revolt, especially after the incidents in Dara'a, have been described in detail in Chapter II. Authorities lacked the tools to cope with the situation.

The political class was petrified when the protests spread to other towns and regions. In August Asad "acknowledged that some mistakes had been made by the security forces in the initial stages of the unrest and that efforts were under way to prevent their recurrence."[15] By then the damage was irreparable.

For several weeks into the protests, it was not too late yet to preserve the most famous red line in Syria: criticizing the president. Initially, the demonstrators' wrath did not, by and large, target Asad himself. After so many years of stalled reforms and broken promises the president missed this last minute opportunity to convince his people that he was different from the other Arab dictators; that he had the corrupt and violent authorities under control. Several times Asad announced that the army would stop the killing of civilians, but nothing changed. The positive attributes of his character that had circulated among Syrians throughout the years, as well as his authority, faded away quickly. The former confidence that was once projected into the youngish leader would never be restored again. Asad lost the most important part of his political capital.

In addition, by playing the sectarian card as openly as never before during his rule, Asad destroyed his secular legacy that had been a Baathist trademark. He tainted the Syrian spirit of tolerance that has century-old roots in Syria's social history. The targeted violence, in order to instigate sectarianism, has become one of the greatest challenges of the Syrian people.

The most crucial chances that Asad missed during the upheaval were the political opportunities that presented themselves. He failed to deliver a political perspective as described in Chapter II. Instead, he promised overdue reforms too late and, in addition, never kept his word. Asad missed the chance to save his legacy by making a last-minute U-turn against internal resistance. After years of waiting, he could have finally portrayed himself as part of the solution instead of as a persisting part of a growing problem. Many Syrians would have preferred to embark on a transition in the framework of stability. To accomplish this purpose, Asad would have had to overcome his personality and to counter family resistance. Asad did not have the audacity and vision of his personal friend King Juan Carlos of Spain; he was no political hero who would become a champion of reform instead of resisting it within an obsolete and ideologically eroded system.

Even months into the brutal attempts at stamping out the opposition movement, the Syrian president could still count on a few illustrious opposition figures who were ready to risk their reputation in order to build Asad a bridge over the spreading fire. People like Michel Kilo in tandem with the secular editor Louay Hussein and a few others were yet one more window of opportunity for Asad. But the regime's continued and uncompromising "security solution" undermined all persisting efforts to search for a middle way.

Rebuff of International Initiatives

As long as the UN Security Council was at loggerheads with Russia and China holding on to Syria, the regime did not have to fear any foreign intervention, unlike in the Libyan case. Nevertheless, several external initiatives tried to build bridges for Asad to end the crisis. He rebuked all of them. The first important opportunity came from Turkey. In the years since 2004, the relations between Syria and Turkey had radically improved. Both governments held common cabinet meetings and talked of "family bonds" when they referred to bilateral relations. Not long before the crisis, Turkey's Prime Minister Recep Tayyip Erdoğan spent a few days of holidays with the Asad family. The countries abolished each others' visas and established free trade across their borders. The good relations with Turkey certainly represented the greatest success for Syria in the past years. Thus Damascus aptly managed to diversify its foreign policy.

The uprising in Syria put Turkey's pro-democracy stance to a serious test. After some hesitation, as in the Libyan case, the Turkish government finally opted for the side of human rights and democracy. Criticism from Ankara rose with the escalation of violence in Syria. Erdoğan followed through with his role as an advocate of change in the Arab world, voicing harsh criticism of Tunisia's and Egypt's autocrats.

Given the former harmony even on the emotional level and the practical improvements between both countries, the visit of Turkey's Foreign Minister Ahmed Davutoğlu on 9 August 2011 in Damascus represented a shocking change of paradigm. Davutoğlu came to Damascus to deliver an "earnest" message from Erdoğan that called for an end to the violence, and on the acceptance of a Turkish-sponsored peace plan. Asad reacted indignantly and said: "If you came for a compromise, then we reject it. If you want to have war, then you can have it—in the entire region."[16] This was an affront to Erdoğan, not only personally, but also vis-à-vis Erdoğan's envisaged role of Turkey as a regional player and mediator.

The giving away of friends and political trump cards in rage or short-sightedness deprived the Syrian regime of possible future options within the framework of steering out of the crisis. As mentioned above, the protests hit Syria at a time when Western governments had more or less accommodated themselves with the Syrian regime or at least with its strategic importance in the region despite Syria's tainted human rights record. European and US diplomats, high-ranking politicians, and academics went in and out of Damascus until the time when the revolt broke out.

As late as March 2011 US Secretary of State Hillary Clinton pointed out: "There's a different leader in Syria now. Many of the members of Congress from both parties who have gone to Syria in recent months have said they believe he's a reformer."[17] This tone was dramatically different—not only from the condemnations of the Libyan regime, but also from rhetoric once employed by President George W. Bush against Syria. This change of attitude in Washington had been the Syrian political goal for many years. And it was destroyed so quickly.

By July Clinton made clear that US Syrian policy has definitely changed, when she claimed that Asad had lost his credibility to rule. "President Assad is not indispensable, and we have absolutely nothing invested in him remaining in power," Clinton said.[18] In only three months Asad lost yet another important chance to become part of the solution instead remaining part of the problem.

Asad's tone vis-à-vis former friends and the international community became harsher the longer the conflict simmered. He burnt vital bridges and lost his soft-spoken and educated image that he had cultivated during various discussions with foreign heads of state and other politicians. In bilateral discussions as well as in interviews Asad used to impress his conversation partners with his friendly and reflective style. At the end of 2011 he had become nervous, confused, and sometimes aggressive.

Despite the rebuke of Turkey's peace offer, Erdoğan's hefty criticism of Asad's policies, and the hosting of Syrian opposition groups in Turkey, links between Ankara and Damascus were not cut. Economic cooperation continued for some time before being annulled. Davutoğlu returned to Damascus in October. But this meeting did not contribute to a settlement either. Damascus continued to issue threats. According to one Arab source, President Asad proclaimed, "If a crazy measure is taken against Damascus, I will need not more than six hours to transfer hundreds of rockets and missiles to the Golan Heights to fire them at Tel Aviv." The Arab source said that the Syrian president told the Turkish foreign minister that he would also call on Hezbollah to launch a rocket attack on the Jewish state.[19] Asad's warning came after Davutoğlu informed him that he would face a war similar to the one against the Libyan regime, with NATO support, if he continued to crack down on his people.

After alienating Turkey, it was up to the Arabs to offer Asad a way out. The Arab League headed by the former transitional foreign minister of Egypt, Nabil al-Arabi, presented two peace initiatives in September and November 2011. Reportedly, several Arab states and then Russia offered asylum to Asad to defuse the situation. The mediation attempts included a call to halt all violence against civilians and to withdraw Syrian troops from the cities. The League urged Syrians to avoid sectarianism and—entirely in line with the Syrian government—strongly recommended not to create a pretext for any kind of foreign intervention. It further called for compensation for the families of the victims and for a release of all political prisoners. The initiative moreover called on Asad to commit to the political reforms he had announced, including a multi-party system.

Asad chose not to benefit from either of the initiatives, although he formally accepted the second one. But no improvement occurred with regard to human rights, similar to the situation in April when he had declared reforms and an end of the shooting. Instead, the killing continued through November, escalating in the cities of Homs and Hama. In the end, the Syrian regime managed to play for time and to downscale the League's second peace plan. After weeks of negotiations—in which hundreds more people were killed—Syria agreed to allow an Arab observer mission into the country. When Arab observers were finally on the ground, the killing continued. First, individual members of the mission left the enterprise in disgust. Then, in the beginning of 2012, the Arab League called the observer mission a failure altogether. Having exhausted its means, the League turned to the UN Security Council in February in a dramatic appeal, brought forward by Qatar. But Russia and China blocked any condemnation of regime violence again and insisted on putting it on the same level as violence from the side of the opposition. The anti-Arab and anti-Western course of Russia and China was an important symbol for the Syrian regime that felt encouraged to continue with its "security solution." It also postponed a tipping-point at which those people within the regime, who were against the brutal strategy, would dare to defect.

A refreshed Arab League—composed of autocracies but also of post-revolutionary states in democratic transition—condemned the killing of civilians in unusually harsh terms. Anti-Syrian Qatar (yet another lost friend of Syria) was holding the presidency of the League, and Syria's adversary Saudi Arabia grew increasingly impatient, too. After it became clear that the killing in Syria was continuing unabatedly, in a surprising move the Arab League suspended Syria's membership at the end of 2011 and called Arab states to withdraw their ambassadors from Damascus. Only Lebanon with a pro-Hezbollah government and Yemen, which was equally disrupted by the Arab Spring, voted against this measure while Iraq abstained. The economic sanctions that followed cut off Syria from basically all trade from and with the Arab world on which it depended with fifty percent of its exports. Syria's membership in the Greater Arab Free Trade Zone (GAFTA) was suspended. A travel ban was imposed on members of the Asad regime, not only to Western countries but to the Arab world as well.

Even observers who supported the regime's policies, if not ideology, and believed in its ability to reform grew increasingly frustrated by the frittering away of political options. Finally, they distanced themselves from the regime and from their previous illusions. The historian Sami Moubayed, professor at Syria's prestigious private University of Kalamoon and editor-in-chief of *Forward Magazine*, reasoned after the failure of the first Arab League initiative: "It could have been a life jacket for the nation that would end the deadlock between the government and demonstrations which have continued non-stop, despite violence and the rising death toll, since mid-March. By snubbing it, the Syrians probably have lost a golden opportunity." Moubayed recommended: "What they should have done is take it as it stands, then rebrand it as a Syrian initiative—regardless of the Arab League and Qatar—because it is a win-win formula both for the Syrian government and the Syrian street. To quote the *Godfather*, it was an offer they shouldn't have, rather than 'couldn't have refused'."[20] It was the Syrian regime that closed the door to an inner-Arab solution and thus contributed to an internationalization of the conflict.

Since March 2012 Russia and China also started to become impatient with Asad. They urged the Syrian regime to cooperate with former UN General Secretary Kofi Annan, who was selected to act as a mediator. But Asad's forces chose to ignore Annan's peace plan, too, and continued shelling Syrian cities. Asad agreed on paper and failed in practice, as it happened with the Arab League's mission earlier. He tried to buy time since he knew that if his troops stayed out of the cities, the streets would quickly fill up once again with tens of thousands of demonstrators who would call for his ouster and demand revenge for the regime's atrocities. The regime had maneuvered itself into a dead end.

After the Annan plan, the conflict started to become more and more internationalized with the participation of observers and politicians other than Arabs, something that parts of the leftist domestic opposition had always feared. But it remained Arab countries like Saudi Arabia and Qatar that most openly supported the Syrian uprising militarily.

In the preceding years, Asad had managed to accommodate some of Syria's enemies, including Saudi Arabia, and he had made new friends in the region and on the international stage. Until the Intifada of 2011—as some Syrian opposition figures call it in Arabic—Asad's grip on power looked even stronger than that of his ally, Iranian President Ahmedinejad, in light of Iran's post-election Green Revolution in summer 2009. But every year, every month that went by, Asad gambled away remnant pieces of his credibility and political leeway. His painstakingly accumulated foreign policy successes lay in tatters. Moreover, Asad became isolated from his own people. After a decade of missed chances and numerous sacrifices Syrians finally longed for the fruits of the Arab Spring: better governance and the end of fear.

4
Bashar & Breaches in the Leadership

A SLIM YOUNG MAN IN SWIMMING TRUNKS is sitting on the Blue Beach of Latakia, Syria's Côte d'Azur. With its yachts, bungalows, and the luxurious Meridien Hotel, the seaside resort hardly differs from a coast in Greece or southern Spain. This is where the Syrian upper classes spend their vacations. Friends of the young man are sitting around him on towels and deck chairs. They are laughing because they are telling jokes about the Syrian government. Forbidden jokes. Even about the supreme father Hafez al-Asad, whose name is otherwise never spoken aloud without someone flinching or casting a frightened glance around. The young man is amused, pricks up his ears and cries, "More, more! Do you have another one?"

This was many years ago. The young man's name is Bashar al-Asad. At that time, he had not dreamt of one day acceding to his father's heritage. Friends from his youth describe him as frank, honest, and helpful. He never took advantage of his status as the president's son to show off his wealth or indulge in a wild life of pleasure. "After eating, he'd put his plate in the sink," recalls Asad's cousin, Rami Makhlouf. "At college, he parked his car outside campus like the other students. And he always scolds us for having chauffeurs."[1]

Bashar, the third child of the Asads and the second of four sons, is no fighter type and no braggart, as are so many sons of powerful fathers. He was perceived more of an easy-going and reserved buddy. Instead of exploiting his privileges as the president's son, Bashar had already taken measures to improve law and order in the 1990s by enforcing discipline on the teenage ruffians from powerful Alawite circles who spread terror in the streets of Latakia with their automatic weapons. In one case, he sent the bodyguard of one of his cousins to jail because he had screamed a litany of wild abuse in public. In 1996, Bashar fired thirteen of the nineteen Alawite professors at the Tishreen Medical School because they were involved in corruption. This was a sign that he rejected nepotism and would not spare members of his own religious group.[2]

A medical student, Bashar had prepared himself for a civilian's life. His father's political protégé was his elder son Basil, a passionate professional horseback rider who was very popular, especially among the ordinary soldiers. In previous times Syrians could admire him on numerous murals, mostly in uniform with a severe expression and black sunglasses. The elder Asad created the same kind of leader cult around his son as he did around himself.[3] Basil was systematically prepared to be his father's successor. It was therefore all the more painful for his father when the son on whom all hopes were pinned came to an early end. Basil died in a mysterious car accident in 1994. He was known for speeding. At any rate, this is the common story. Some people however speak in confidence of a rumor that he was murdered near the Beirut airport.

The story evokes memories of the Gandhi dynasty in India, though India enjoys a democratic system. Prime Minister Indira Gandhi, daughter of the father of Indian independence, Jawaharlal Nehru, prepared her son Sanjay to be her successor. He then was killed in a plane crash in 1980. Her (in this case older) son Rajiv had no political ambitions. His Italian wife Sonja had repeatedly begged him, "Please don't go into politics!"—but in vain. Rajiv became a weak prime minister, however, who began to open up the country economically. In the end, he paid for his efforts with his life. In 1991, Rajeev Gandhi was torn apart by a bomb in a Tamil attack in southern India.

Without dramatizing the parallels, like Rajiv Gandhi, Bashar al-Asad had never been interested in politics. He planned for a career in ophthalmology and went to England for training, where he kept his medical colleagues in the dark about his prominent background and drove a small car for the standards of presidents' sons, a BMW 3-Series. He got to know his future wife Asma during this time.

After eighteen months Bashar had to break off his training in order to submit himself to his father's strict schooling at home. Bashar was made the crown prince in the republic of Syria. Indeed, around the turn of this century, sons succeeded their fathers as heads of state in Morocco and Jordan. But these countries are ruled by royal and not by presidential families. Syria became the first case of a republican dynasty or dynastic republic in the Arab world. In Egypt and Libya the autocratic fathers hedged similar plans with their sons. But the Arab Spring spoiled these enterprises.

Bashar was the only person who would not upset the carefully balanced system of political power. Only thirty-four when his father died of leukemia, he was not strong enough to set his own mark immediately and defy adversaries. The fear of unrest between political, social, and religious groups was not unfounded at the time. Moreover, the somewhat sudden death of Hafez al-Asad left a tinge of uncertainty as to whether the way for Bashar had been paved sufficiently, although in the late 1990s the elder Asad had dismissed several leading figures in the army and the *mukhabarat* who could have become dangerous when the overarching authority passed away. Those in charge in June 2000 staged a surprisingly gentle transition. This does not mean that it took place without internal friction. Minister of Defense Mustafa Tlass, for example, used threats to force Vice President and acting President Abdul Halim Khaddam to sign the necessary documents. (This was the first visible sign of a power struggle between Bashar al-Asad and Khaddam as well as a prelude to Khaddam's spectacular defection to Paris at the end of 2005). In the parliamentary session that was broadcast live, a critical voice was raised asking why the constitution had to be adapted to Bashar's age.

But the parliament did change the constitution, lowering the minimum age required to hold the office of the president of Syria, and thus removed a formal hurdle. At the first Baath Congress held since 1985, the party elected Bashar secretary-general, while at the same time he became commander-in-chief of the armed forces, as his father had been.

At least formally, Bashar possessed the same amount of power his father had. However, the footprints which Hafez al-Asad had left behind were a few sizes too big, as would have been the case with any other successor. A friend from Bashar's youth said about Hafez al-Asad that "when you see a face on the front page of every newspaper and on every poster for thirty years, the person becomes like God for you. Bashar can't have this charisma now. But he'll have it in fifteen years if he's still in power then."[4]

Bashar, however, made it clear that he did not want to be on the front pages of the newspapers every day. Neither his photo nor an article about him was to appear on the front page unless it was necessary from a professional journalistic point of view. This is what he told overzealous writers in the state media. The same applied for state television. In the elder Asad tradition, the president's likeness would appear in a large format even when—as Syrians joke—His Excellency received a congratulatory telegram from the vice minister of infrastructure of Timbuktu. Bashar disliked his father's cult of personality. However, he changed his gusto throughout the years and acted more and more similarly to his father's habits. In the past years before the upheaval Bashar's portrait did hang in the streets almost as often as his father's counterfeit used to before, frequently with his father's head in the background. However, for some time Bashar reduced his presence in prominent squares like in the market in the Old City of Damascus. The traveler looked in vain for any statue of Bashar.

The vacuum left by the elder Asad's death was being filled slowly. In his fifth year in office, the young president was in the process of consolidating his power. Or putting it another way: in contrast to the monolithic rule of his charismatic father, Syria was in a process of power pluralization, the outcome of which remained in doubt. At any rate, courageous steps taken by Bashar or his government were improbable, for nobody wanted to take great risks or embark on political experiments.

The first years of Bashar's presidency were marked by cautious measures, which displeased even friends of the president. "People who know him very well from the time before he became president speak of him as a liberal, unideological person. He only became an opportunist after entering the machinery of power," said the journalist. Bashar was often said to be overtaxed.

Another person who is familiar with Bashar's surroundings complained after three years of Bashar's rule that "the president is increasingly suffering from a loss of reality," that he sees everything through rose-colored spectacles. Others accused him of having wasted the authority that was his father's heritage, making it impossible for him to instigate reforms. Clearly, the above statements expressed disappointment at the very high expectations that even Bashar's critics had held for his regime.

A friend of Bashar's countered that "it's easy for intellectuals to express opinions when they don't have to make decisions. Besides, every decision depends on the information and data you get. When the information changes, so does the decision. Everybody changes when they're suddenly in a position of responsibility." [5]

The lack of a strong and predictable leadership, which for decades was excessively provided to Syrians, created uncertainty. Bashar's network of supporters in the state machinery still had to prove stable. Back in early 2004, more and more ministers were said to be seeking backing from the conservative old guard instead of from the president. "Nobody would let himself down the well on the president's rope, for he would be afraid that it might be cut," an analyst explained.

On the other side of the spectrum, Michel Kilo, a leader of the opposition Civil Society Movement, observed that increasing opportunism among those holding high positions in politics and the media convey the message that they in effect share the critical analysis of the opposition. "They want to keep a back door open in case of a regime change." The forces at the margins of power are drifting away from the center. "People are leaving the sinking ship," Kilo pondered in the year of crisis in 2005.[6] Especially after the Lebanon disaster (in Syria's eyes), several retired, high-ranking officials, including former members of the secret services, were reported to have tried to sell their real estate and emigrate. Some bought land and houses in Jordan or took their money to Turkey. According to press reports, family members of ex-Prime Minister Mustafa Miro transferred millions of US dollars abroad, and even ex-*mukhabarat* chief Hassan Khalil attempted to leave Syria. The authorities managed to thwart these escape attempts to a large extent by issuing travel bans.[7]

These dramatic developments may also be positively interpreted. It could have meant that Bashar pushed the reform process so far that it had reached a point of no return. Those who had much to lose were trying to escape before it was too late. In retrospect, however, these hopes remained unfulfilled and the breaches were rather of personal nature than of ideological differences.

Syria expert Raymond Hinnebusch saw only one possibility for Asad's rule, namely that of a "consensual leader."[8] What was regarded as a weakness in the Arab political tradition could be seen in the Western view as conducive to the political culture of the country and the establishment of strong institutions—if this had taken place hand-in-hand with the strengthening of civil society and political reforms. But it is here where the sore point lies.

For several years a pluralization of authoritarian power took place, coupled with some economic reforms and a new and more open political atmosphere. "It isn't anymore the Syria of Hafez al-Asad," concluded Kilo. The deep-rooted fear people used to have during the elder Asad's time subsided for a while, or at least diminished, until it came back again with full vigor toward the end of the decade. Political discussions had become freer and criticism more open. In the years up to 2005 increasing numbers of people were professing to support the Civil Society Movement.

"The small Asad is a small step toward the great transition," was Kilo's hope in 2003. "During the times of Hafez al-Asad the dynamics of the regime came out of the fact that there was a clearly determined and well-defined power center. It was Asad and a small group around him. He exported the problems of power into a society that was apolitical. This made the impression that the power was stable and unified." Inside the circle of power, there did not seem to be any contradictions, any differing interests. "With this power center, Hafez could play the regional and international game and maintain stability in the regime. This is not the case anymore. The power is no longer being reproduced from its head, rather the head is being reproduced by different power centers," Kilo explained.[9]

Another influential person in the Civil Society Movement, who preferred to remain anonymous, went so far as to call Bashar a "junior partner" in the fabric of power. Strong personalities with their own power circles in the secret services, the military, and the intermarriages between the state economy and the machinery of government, had their own vested interests. The anonymous opposition figure compared Bashar's position in politics with that of Anwar al-Sadat in Egypt after Gamal Abdul Nasser's death in 1970. "He only became a proper president after he had been able to get his own camp behind him." Bashar was largely keeping himself out of some areas of domestic policy because he was powerless against the vested interests that controlled these areas. "Since Hafez's death the Baath Party, the different branches of the *mukhabarat*, and the army have become stronger," the opposition figure said. This turned out to be a crucial factor in the events of 2011.

Hakam al-Baba, ex-editor-in-chief of the banned weekly magazine *al-Domari*, made a similar observation. "Earlier it was one who ruled, now it is many who rule. This can be chaotic and dangerous," he said. People in the Damascus coffee houses remarked with a wink, "Nowadays the power lies in the hands of phantoms." Of course, impressions can be extremely relative following the experience of three decades of authoritarian rule. The human rights lawyer Anwar al-Bunni spoke of "a number of power centers" that were paralyzing each other. "No more is there a coherent political concept. This has become even more obvious after the war in Iraq."

In subsequent years the impression was fading that the power was in the hands of phantoms. The regime consolidated and contracted to predominantly Alawite circles. It crystallized in a narrowing circle of regime figures in the military, *mukhabarat,* and the president's family clan. Assessments differed on where the real responsibilities lay. Ex-Member of Parliament Riad Seif, for example, did not believe that Asad was controlled by his brother Maher, his brother-in-law Asef Shawkat, his cousin the tycoon Rami Makhlouf, or his other cousin Muhammad Makhlouf (Rami's brother) who heads one of the strongest *mukhabarat* branches. "Maher and Bashar are a team on equal footing," Seif commented in 2007.[10] This statement was to have clear implications for the interpretation of events in 2011. It underlines the thesis of Bashar al-Asad as a great cynic who appeared soft-spoken or clumsy at times but who followed a clear and unscrupulous strategy of power preservation.

Nevertheless, many decisions that had been taken throughout the years lacked cohesion. Critics pointed to a lack of vision except that of regime survival and reactive adjustments to external and internal challenges. One example is the turbulence that occurred among the top leadership on 22 May 2003 when the United Nations Security Council voted on Iraq Resolution 1483.

The resolution was meant to lift the sanctions imposed on the now-defunct Saddam regime and define the role of the UN in post-war Iraq. In addition, the United States and Great Britain were given authority as the victorious powers to rebuild the country and set up an interim government. Syria happened to have a seat on the Security Council as a non-permanent member and was especially displeased with the second point, since in the Syrian view it amounted to legitimizing the war.

The Syrian UN ambassador was mysteriously absent when the vote was taken and his vote was thus counted as an abstention. The resolution was passed with a majority of fourteen out of fifteen votes. The Syrian representative was not able to submit his vote in time because he failed to receive clear instructions from Damascus. At home, politicians were racking their brains and the decision process dragged on. The opinions of Foreign Minister Faruq al-Shara', backed by the Baath Party, and President Asad cancelled each other out—an indication that the time of clear command decisions was over. Reacting to events rather than defining long-term strategies in advance was the order of the day. Shortly after the vote, the Syrian ambassador to the UN was replaced.[11]

Incoherency affected even decisions about political prisoners. Some opposition figures were given indications of being released when other instances prevented it; or on the positive side judges sentenced political captives to fewer years than a branch of the secret service had wanted. Probably the most famous case was that of the arrest of Michel Kilo, which was publicly criticized as an error by people close to the regime and even by

Syria's ambassador to the United States, Imad Mustafa, in his personal blog in 2006. Kilo himself was told that even the president was against his arrest but did not prevail.[12]

International visitors were able to get a glimpse of illogical behavior of key authorities in Syria, too. The author David Lesch who had written a biography about Asad[13] was arrested in Damascus in 2007 when he was there to see the president. Lesch reportedly told the president that he would have to gain more control of the *mukhabarat;* otherwise it "would come back and haunt him."[14]

Up to the year 2010 many Syrian and foreign representatives that were interviewed coincided in the view that red lines were difficult to recognize or even to anticipate since those lines kept moving. Sometimes different ministries or different branches of the secret services drew different limits. Contradictions even occurred within one and the same institution or on different levels of hierarchy. For example, the private radio station Cham FM was forced to shut down a program that was explicit on sexual education and taboos. Shortly thereafter, the same Ministry of Information that caused the end of the program conferred a press award to the young female moderator who had run the show.

Local observers at the end of 2010 saw indications for power struggles in the fact that important Syrian embassies worked without an ambassador for a long time, for example in Moscow or Berlin. The haggling about filling the posts took longer than normal. Some chargés d'affaires were left with minor information. The delay of the 11th Regional Congress of the Baath Party to spring 2012 also pointed to a tug of war behind the scenes between reformers and conservatives.

At some occasions the Bush administration or Israel attempted to cause disturbances in Syria's power circle from outside, sometimes with military provocations. Such an attack took effect on 5 October 2003. On that day two Israeli F-16 jet fighters bombed an abandoned camp of the Popular Front for the Liberation of Palestine, only fifteen kilometers north of Damascus. "Threats mean a long-term erosion," commented analyst Samir Altaqi from the Center for Strategic Studies and Research (CSSR), a former think-tank at the University of Damascus. "The aim is to strangle political options and to provoke internal contradictions within the regime."[15]

If this was meant to further complicate business for Bashar al-Asad, it succeeded. But if the goal was to turn the majority of Syrians against their president and openly call for regime change, this was hardly achieved by external pressure. Syrians' patience was running out due to piecemeal reforms and a sluggish economy.

Critics complained sharply about the government, the bureaucracy, and the power structure. Yet, for many years Asad did not lose his image as a young and unblemished leader. He enjoyed sympathy, particularly among young people—more than half of Syrians are under the age of twenty—and among members of minorities, the traditional Baathist power base.

Since mid-2004, some observers concluded that Asad had finally been able to consolidate his position within the regime machinery. In July of 2004, he got rid of long-serving military Chief of Staff Hikmat Shihabi and replaced four-hundred-and-fifty army officers. "We get the impression that the president is beginning to overcome his indecisiveness," said an analyst in Damascus (only during the 2011 revolt Asad reactivated some of these figures since he was in desperate need of their military experience). Over the years, Asad managed to place a considerable number of technocrats and personal trustees around himself, some of whom he promoted to key positions at home and at embassies abroad, such as in Washington or London (see also Chapter VI "The Political Disillusionment").[16]

However, as mentioned in the previous chapter, just at the time that Asad began feeling more secure—maybe too secure—he committed his most grievous errors. Asad's decision to press the Lebanese Parliament to change the constitution in order to keep the pro-Syrian President Emile Lahoud in office was a very personal move against conservatives like former Vice President Abdul Halim Khaddam and the Baath Regional Command. Any other pro-Syrian figure could have done the job, as many critics pointed out, but Asad insisted on Lahoud.

With this move, Asad reaffirmed his strong grip on Beirut at a time of increasing international pressure to leave Lebanon. He also wanted to strike a blow against Prime Minister Rafiq Hariri. The multi-millionaire, pragmatic Sunni, and strongman of Lebanon had recently become more and more critical of Syrian influence, although he was known as a rather prudent and integrating figure compared to certain other Lebanese politicians. He was eager to point out, for instance, that an election victory by the opposition in May 2005 would not mean defeat for Syria.

It remains one of the riddles of political psychology why Bashar al-Asad and Rafiq Hariri clashed in such a personal way that no communication between them seemed possible thereafter. As reported by various observers, Asad met Hariri in Damascus on 24 August 2004. During their meeting in the presidential palace, Asad snubbed Hariri by not offering him a seat—a clear humiliation in the oriental context—and threatened him politically and, some claim, personally. The Lebanese strongman left the palace pale and shocked. Subsequently, Hariri resigned as prime minister in October and aligned himself more closely with anti-Syrian opposition forces in Lebanon. This was the point when disaster struck and, if this story is true, Asad had to take full responsibility. Nevertheless, Asad denied that he threatened Hariri's life.[17]

A few days after the extension of Lahoud's term on 2 September, the UN Security Council, led by the remarkable coalition of the United States and

France, passed Resolution 1559. Although it did not name Syria directly, the resolution was a clear challenge to Damascus, calling for the withdrawal of foreign troops from Lebanon, for the disarmament of militias (which meant, above all, Hezbollah), and for free and fair elections the following May 2005. There is hardly any doubt that Hariri's close relationship with French President Jacques Chirac helped bring about this scenario and caused the loss of France as one of Syria's more benevolent partners abroad. The resolution was in the pipeline even before the situation escalated with the extension of Lahoud's term.

In the following months, the resolution became the main tool for pressuring Syria to withdraw its troops from Lebanon and for considerably narrowing Syria's room for political maneuvering. Hariri joined forces with Druze leader Walid Jumblatt and with the Christian leadership to issue a call for the implementation of the resolution. Asad remained either steadfast or obstinate, according to one's interpretation. Two weeks prior to Hariri's assassination, Asad affirmed to his confidants that he had not the slightest intention of leaving Lebanon. This drastically changed after a three hundred kilogram bomb tore apart Hariri and members of his entourage in the convoy of armored cars on the Beirut corniche on 14 February 2005.

A wave of angry, anti-Syrian protests swept through the streets of Beirut. For the first time, posters of Asad and Syrian flags were torn from buildings and burned. Syrian workers in Lebanon were attacked and some killed. Via Saudi Arabia, the United States sent a stern message that included the threat of air strikes against Syria. Returning Asad's snub of Hariri, the Saudi Crown Prince Abdullah played tough with Asad when he saw him after the bombing. "Abdullah showed him a list of five hundred potential targets in Syria that the United States were ready to destroy," reported Michel Kilo. Abdullah was furious about Hariri's assassination because the tycoon held Saudi nationality and entertained profitable business connections with the country. "After this encounter, it became clear to Asad that he had committed the mistake of his life," Kilo concluded.[18]

In the initial days after the assassination, the Syrian leadership did not speak with one voice. Asad told then Arab League President Amr Moussa that a withdrawal from Lebanon was imminent, only to have the Syrian Ministry of Information later state that Moussa had got it wrong and Syria was only redeploying its troops to the Beqaa Valley. The tap dance continued a few days longer until Asad addressed the parliament in Damascus on 5 March, when he scuttled back to his pre-Moussa position. He did not speak of an immediate and complete withdrawal, but rather of a re-deployment step by step, first to the Beqaa Valley and then to the Lebanese-Syrian border. Soon after his convoluted speech in parliament, events overtook Asad once again and he ordered all Syrian troops home by 26 April, even before the US deadline.

Observers in Damascus considered Asad's speech a lost opportunity domestically and internationally. Although it should be recognized that he admitted that mistakes were made in Lebanon—probably alluding to the corruption and misbehavior of Syrian army and intelligence officers and maybe even to strategic errors—he did not offer an apology in order to win over the Lebanese people. He failed to deliver new insights, make bold announcements, and take the initiative. Ayman Abdul Nour said in frustration that "Bashar's speech was amateurish and full of mistakes. It was a golden opportunity to address the Lebanese people, especially the younger population. He should have played his age and said 'I'm young like you, I also want freedom, I can understand you; my country also needs freedom.' Instead, he threatened that problems will arise in Lebanon when Syria leaves."[19]

Apart from disappointing the reformers, the Lebanese disaster further damaged Asad's standing among the conservative hardliners, most outstandingly with Vice President Abdul Halim Khaddam. It was more grist for the mills of those who claimed that Asad was neither able to lead the country nor defend its interests against enemies during troubled times. For the first time, names of potential successors circulated among intellectuals and in the teahouses of Damascus in spring 2005, a development that would have been unimaginable during the reign of Hafez al-Asad. This scenario repeated itself in 2011.

All of this meant that a big struggle lay ahead for Asad to win back the confidence and advantage that he had gained by summer 2004. In one sense, leaving Lebanon helped him in the long run. He had already started a gradual redeployment in 2000, reducing troops from forty thousand to fourteen thousand, thus accepting additional pressure on the Syrian labor market in spite of the critical economic situation. Yet Syria had still failed to implement the Ta'if Accord that ended the Lebanese civil war in 1989, which called for a withdrawal of foreign troops when the security situation permitted. As years passed and Lebanese institutions began to function without external assistance, Syrian troops all over Lebanon became more and more unnecessary. Even if Asad had wanted them out, however, he would not have been able to push through a complete withdrawal against the will of nationalist hardliners. Only this unexpected turn of events made withdrawal possible and freed military and financial resources that were badly needed for the reform process at home.

Indications that Asad was able to again strengthen his hold on power arose again during the 10th Baath Congress on 6 to 9 June 2005, the second congress to take place after Asad's inauguration. On one hand, opposition forces and some foreign observers were disappointed because they had expected more sweeping political reforms, the end of martial law, immediate permission for the creation of independent parties, reform of the judiciary, and the abolishment of the Baath monopoly—as well as the release of the key opposition figures of the Damascus Spring, the democratic movement that took place in late 2000 and early 2001. In an open letter to the Baath delegates titled "Let the Damascus Spring Bloom," 226 intellectuals—among them Michel Kilo, philosopher Sadiq Jalal al-Azm, human rights advocate Anwar al-Bunni, and journalist Hakam al-Baba—summarized their demands.

On the other hand, unlike the Iraqi Baath Party, the Syrian organization proved its willingness and ability to embark at least on piecemeal reforms from within. Most importantly, Asad appeared able to strengthen his position of power. In this reading of events, the "Lebanese disaster" produced a shake-up that benefitted Asad in the long run despite the many temporary bruises. The most important outcomes of the 10th Baath Congress were a thorough reshuffling of top positions in the National Command and the Central Committee of the party, the government, and the military, as well as a recommendation—though not more—to allow independent political parties in the future, a separation of the party and government, further steps to combat corruption and open up the economy, and a relaxation of the emergency laws.

Although the influence of the Baath Party in government and society had been curbed, Syrian protagonists were not ready to bow to US demands and entirely dismiss the party's purpose and ideology. During the congress, Buthayna Shaaban, who had become a member of the Regional Command, made this clear. While accusing the United States of seeking to undermine Arab identity by fostering religious and ethnic divisions, she said, "If we are not Arabs what could we be? Do we want to be Sunnis and Shiites and Christians? Or do we want to be Arabs? I think I can speak in the name of millions of Arabs that we want to be Arabs. If the Baath Party were not here, I think we would have to invent it."[20] Sectarian politics in neighboring countries like Iraq and Lebanon gave weight to her arguments, although by referring to Arabs as an umbrella category, Shaaban once again ignored the Kurdish problem.

Contrary to these official statements Ayman Abdul Nour painted a different and bold scenario. In his eyes, the president had become tired of the old structures, despite the fact that he relied on them. "Bashar needs the Baathists for now. Otherwise, who will reelect him in 2007? But after that, he will try to get rid of the Party and found a party of his own. He is playing with time but feels the pressure because the US demands an immediate de-Baathification of Syria."[21] Thus the Bush administration was thinking in the same categories that it (falsely) applied in Iraq.

Whether Asad had this unfulfilled master plan in mind or not, during the congress the Baath Party experienced its greatest shake-up since 1970 when Hafez al-Asad took power. Out of the ninety-six members of the Central Committee—most of them nearly double Asad's age—seventy were replaced, among them former Prime Minister Mustafa Miro, former Defense

Minister Mustafa Tlass, and most importantly, Vice President Abdul Halim Khaddam, who announced his resignation from his powerful government post. Khaddam's action was received with respect even by his critics because voluntary resignations are uncommon in the Arab world.

Only a few months later, however, this respect was to turn into dismay and rage. At that moment, the breaches in the Syrian leadership became visible for everyone. For shortly after the Baath Congress, the staunch Baathist Khaddam, the only senior official who had remained in office since the Baath revolution in 1963, took residence in Paris. Finally, in December 2005 the seventy-three-year-old hardliner set out to take revenge on Asad and his family. In an interview, Khaddam accused Asad of threatening Lebanese Prime Minister Rafiq Hariri in August 2004, and said that Hariri's murder could not have happened without Asad's involvement. In addition, he listed many mistakes that the president made with regard to Lebanon. This was a decisive blow to Asad and represented the most eminent case of defection in Syrian politics since 1966. Moreover, the Sunni Khaddam announced his plan to organize a government-in-exile and invited defected military officers and other opposition groups abroad to join him, whereas the Syrian opposition at home swiftly rejected any form of cooperation because of Khaddam's anti-democratic and corrupt record. Consequently, the Baath Party stripped Khaddam of his membership and joined a unanimous vote in parliament calling on the government to try him for high treason.

Khaddam was a key player in Lebanese politics, helped to shape the Ta'if Peace Accord in 1989, was close to Rafiq Hariri, and backed his elections as Lebanese prime minister in 1992 and 2000. The former vice president, who used to be at the center of Syria's business mafia, shared economic interests with Hariri as his business partner in Syria, Lebanon, Saudi Arabia, and France. However, Khaddam and Hariri had an increasingly hard time fighting Asad's family cronies over investment in the Syrian market. From the beginning, the experienced Khaddam was reluctant to accept the young Bashar as the ruler of the country after Hafez al-Asad died, and he was at odds with the president over many issues ranging from domestic to foreign politics. The recent developments in Lebanon had caused the final rift between him and Asad.

The only old player left in the top ranks of the Syrian leadership was now Foreign Minister Faruq al-Shara', a long time rival of Khaddam and one of the few clean hands in the Syrian regime when it comes to corruption and nepotism. But it seemed that his days would also be numbered since speculation about his replacement had surfaced for years. But on the other hand, with so many experienced politicians fired or in exile, Asad soon started to count on Shara' more than ever, also as a reliable link to the Baath Party and its establishment. In early 2006 following another cabinet reshuffle, Asad made Shara' the new vice president of the country. This was the final victory of Khaddam's rival—a victory that was to taste bitter in 2011.

Another ideological hardliner was Muhammad Said Bukheitan who remained a member of the Baath Regional Command and head of the party's security committee. He and his supporters toppled several of the president's initiatives and continued slamming on the brakes, especially since Bukheitan was entrusted with the party office of economics and finance.

Another front for Asad was the *mukhabarat*. Above all, he had to regain control of the different branches that monitored the ministries and at times neutralized political decisions. Parts of the secret service had taken power into their own hands and operated against the president or became infiltrated by Islamists. This remained one of the greatest challenges for the president, and the restructuring of the security machinery was an initial step. Instead of being accountable to the Regional Command of the Baath Party as it had been since 1968, the political body of the *mukhabarat* was henceforth under direct control of the Ministry of Interior. The military part of the secret service remained accountable to the Syrian chief-of-staff and the secret service of the Air Force under control of the Air Force commanders.

The reform began in October 2004 after Ghazi Kanaan was appointed minister of the interior. On a formal level, Asad undertook several steps to curb the *mukhabarat's* influence, and the Baath Congress in June 2005 backed his efforts. The Regional Command decided that the secret service no longer had to be consulted in sixty-seven different circumstances that included the celebration of weddings and the opening of new enterprises, shops, social and educational organizations, and restaurants. Embassies can now inquire after missing persons and visit them in the central Adra prison without permission from the *mukhabarat*. Another far-reaching consequence of the congress was that security officers were no longer allowed to hold suspects in custody for longer than five days. After this period he or she had to be released or sent to court.

It remained questionable if the *mukhabarat* would toe the line. Asad could at least rely on the army, which remained largely under the command of Alawites, who had much to lose. This became all the more true when violence erupted in 2011.

Among the population there had always been widespread fear of an abrupt change or even a collapse of the political system. Asad exploited this fear to mobilize the population, particularly with international sanctions looming after Syria had been accused by the UN fact-finding team of involvement in Hariri's murder. During the last months of 2005, public rallies by different groups supporting the president became part of everyday life in Damascus. People, if members of the Baath Party or not, shouldered up with Asad's government, and even prisoners started a hunger strike for their president! A wave of patriotism swept the streets. Cities were plastered with huge posters and banners that concentrated on a message of support for Asad and a "unified Syria." It is noteworthy that Baath flags and symbols did not appear. In light of Iran's post-election Green Revolution in summer 2009 Asad's grip on power temporarily looked even stronger than that of his ally, Iranian President Ahmedinejad.

The analyst Samir Altaqi pointed out in 2004 that "any hope of a smooth landing of the reforms is through Asad. This is why, in the opposition, gambling is going on." Regime critics were torn between their opposition to the Baathist system and their loyalty toward their endangered home country. Threats from Washington boomeranged in many respects. Growing anti-Americanism, like in Iraq, had become the common denominator of rulers and ruled. Although disappointed and frustrated, the opposition made it clear that they would not challenge the Syrian regime "on the back of an American tank."[22] Michel Kilo emphasized at the end of 2010: "Give guarantees to the regime that the Americans won't attack it. Then you can do with Bashar what you want."[23] The antagonism with the US administration and the fear of a forced regime change initiated from abroad haunted the regime and parts of the nationalist opposition alike. The discourse represented a kind of umbrella under which other issues were subsumed.

When the Arab Spring hit Syria, however, the main debates were not about an American threat any longer. The resistance rhetoric had given way to other grievances, although the deeply ingrained fear of a US threat against Syria played a role again later with regard to cleavages among different opposition groups. In any case, Syria's circle of power was heavily tested by the challenge of the mass protests. Old breaches opened, new friction came to light, and many more remained in obscurity.

The system was exclusively based on hard power in its pure form, that is, on the eradication of dissenters and threats.[24] The circle of persons that the Asad clan could trust was contracting more and more to the point that it might have been difficult in the future to recruit enough staunch and qualified loyalists to effectively run the country without running the risks of defections. The circle of trust had been narrowing for a number of years. The regime had become more Alawite compared to Hafez's times, when Syria happened to be ruled by an Alawite but was not an "Alawite state."[25] However, with rising stakes in the conflict and increasing brutality it was above all Alawites (and to a lesser extent Christians, Druze and Ismailis) who were exposed to existential fear of retaliation, although some Alawite figures counted among important representatives of the opposition.

Interestingly, the second layer of regime functionaries after the Alawite elite comprised personalities from the Howran (especially from the south-Western town of Dara'a), including Vice President Faruq al-Shara'. Given the cruel events in Dara'a, this second layer of functionaries in the regime apparatus was regarded with more suspicion. The Sunni Shara' was still a man of the regime without any doubt but he was rumored to have had blatant differences of opinion with Bashar and especially with Maher al-Asad on the military crackdown in Dara'a. Moreover, the communiqué by the foreign Syrian opposition after their first conference in the Turkish city of Antalya in June 2011 called for power to be handed over to the Vice President. This did not necessarily serve him, although, as mentioned above, he was appointed by Asad to lead the "national dialogue of reconciliation" while the killing went on in Syria's streets. After having got rid of his rival Khaddam in 2005, it was now Shara' himself who found himself at the margin of trust and power. Conversation partners indicated that he lost access to the inner power circle although he had served in the Syrian cabinet since 1984. In times of existential threat Syrian politics was withdrawing into the caucus of the Asad extended family clan.

Shara' was known as an experienced and trusted politician. Many Syrians recall with glee one of Shara's political highlights during the Madrid peace conference in 1991. After Israeli Prime Minister Yitzhak Shamir held a flamboyant speech that branded Syria as a terrorist state, Shara' deviated from his moderate speech script and countered by showing a newspaper clipping depicting a photo of Shamir with the word "WANTED" as a bold headline. Shara' recalled in front of the world audience that Shamir had been wanted as a terrorist since, as a member of the militant Lehi group, he had been responsible for the murder of the UN envoy to Palestine, the Swedish diplomat Count Folk Bernadotte, in 1948. This scene in Madrid bolstered Shara's standing within Syria for years to come.

Another eminent Sunni of the Asad eras was Mustafa Tlass. He was a long-serving trustee of Hafez al-Asad and defense minister from 1972 to 2004. Tlass is originally from the town of Rastan, 20 kilometers north of Homs. This city experienced one of the worst clashes at the end of September 2011 because it harbored a considerable amount of defected soldiers of the Free Syrian Army. Rastan was attacked by hundreds of regular army tanks. Many houses were damaged, dozens of people killed, and numerous male inhabitants detained and tortured.

So due to their religious and regional background, Shara' and Tlass experienced the violence in Syria through accounts of personal contacts that obviously differed from the official state propaganda. In the past years, some of Tlass' family members had kept an intellectual distance to the Asad regime. Abdul Razzaq Tlass, the nephew of the ex-defense minister, even joined the Free Syrian Army and worked toward toppling the regime in which his uncle had served for so many decades. This was true for numerous less known officials, too. In other instances some active high-ranking *mukhabarat* officers from Homs and probably other places were sending hidden messages toward opposition members in Lebanon during the escalation of violence.[26]

In December the first ever defections of *mukhabarat* officers (in this case from the dreaded air force intelligence) became known in Idlib, a town close to the Turkish border and an early hot spot of the protest. The defectors escaped to Turkey under fire protection from members of the Free Syrian Army. Many more soldiers and *mukhabarat* officials would have been ready to defect throughout the months of the revolt if the Asad regime had not established such an effective system of deterrence, intimidation, and collective punishment. Even Syrian diplomats abroad conceded that their fears were of a very personal nature, since their families back in Syria would be put in danger. A long list of cases showed that family members of opposition figures and defectors were systematically tortured and murdered. Unlike Libya, Syria saw diplomats defect only one at a time. An example is Mohammed Bassam Imadi, former Syrian ambassador to Sweden, who joined the opposition Syrian National Council (SNC) and since then has lived under constant threat.

Despite the high personal risks involved, the cracks in the power apparatus became visible with defections on the political level, too. The first ones occurred in April 2011. In protest against the brutal violence in Dara'a, two members of the Syrian Parliament resigned. Khalil al-Rifaati and Nasser al-Hariri both came from Dara'a, and said that they were not able to protect the people who had elected them anymore. Hariri said that he "feels sorry for those who were killed in Howran by the bullets of security forces despite the fact that the president has promised no live ammunition by security forces at all."[27]

Through the months, political defections had gradually been gaining weight in the government's hierarchy. The crumbling of power started when not only the people but also politicians started to lose their fear. The first spectacular case occurred in January 2012 when Mahmoud Suleiman Haj Hamad, Inspector General of the Central Financial Monitoring Commission at the Prime Minister's office and the Defense Ministry's Chief Inspector, escaped with his family to Cairo and aired a series of discomforting truths. As mentioned in Chapter II, the most important information that he gave was the high financial support of the government for the Alawite paramilitary gangs *(shabbiha)* and his view that Syrian cabinet members were nothing more than prisoners of various branches of the *mukhabarat*. Also in January, the parliamentarian and financial expert Imad Ghalioun defected and said that numerous other Members of Parliament sympathized with the opposition but did not see any possibility to openly contradict the regime. "I had hoped that I could change the regime from within," Ghalioun pondered, "but I had to realize that I can't." The politician took the decision to flee with his wife and two small children after the president of the Baath Party in Homs, who had joined the opposition, had been killed. One day after Ghalioun's defection to Cairo, Asad issued a travel ban for all Members of Parliament and other public functionaries.[28]

The erosion of the government itself became visible on 8 March 2012 when Abdu Hussameddin, a high ranking functionary in the Oil Ministry, appeared on a *youtube* video in which he announced his defection. The engineer said he would join the opposition and added, "I recommend for all my friends who are still working for the regime to follow me and leave the broken ship of the regime." For more than thirty-three years he had been working for the government but now, "I do not want to end my working life serving the crimes of this regime." Hussameddin praised the Free Syrian Army and criticized the Russian and Chinese support of the Asad regime.[29] The politician said he took this step, although he was conscious of the fact that the regime would burn his house, chase his family, and try to kill him.

The "security solution" of 2011 shifted the power toward those organs who upheld the president's post. Neither diplomacy nor political aptness played a role in the suppression. Thus it was the military elite units and the *mukhabarat* that represented the sources of Asad's stamina—in particular the Fourth Brigade under Maher al-Asad and Asef Shawkat, who became deputy Minister of Defense in September 2011. As the threats to the regime grew, Shawkat, who had fallen out with Asad in 2008, saw his star rising again. He was a Sunni married to Asad's sister Bushra and had for a long time been regarded as the second most powerful man in the regime.

Several theories explained why Shawkat's star had waned. His downfall in 2008 came in the wake of a series of intelligence failures.[30] The first one was the embarrassment that Israel's planes were able to bomb a nuclear construction site in a desolate desert canyon east of the Euphrates River in September 2007. More importantly, the assassination of Hezbollah's military commander Imad Mughniyeh in Damascus in February 2008 marked a final breach of trust between Asad and Shawkat. The neighborhood in Damascus in which Mughnieh was killed by a car bomb fell under Shawkat's responsibility. It was unlikely that this could have happened without some complicity with Syrian intelligence. A more far-reaching theory went that Shawkat had planned a coup against Asad, and Mughniyeh tipped off the Syrian president to the plot. According to media reports, Mughniyeh was possibly killed by Shawkat associates a few days later.[31]

Mughniyeh's widow charged Syria with responsibility, although the official version was, of course, that Israel was behind the assassination. Moreover, defected ex-Vice President Khaddam, in his Paris exile, had stated that Shawkat would be the better president for Syria. Shawkat was soon put under house arrest and his wife Bushra, who had had frequent quarrels with her brother Bashar over the years, went to France and later to the United Arab Emirates. It was the name of Asef Shawkat that UN investigator Detlev Mehlis associated with the assassination of Lebanon's Prime Minister Rafiq Hariri. Precisely on the day of Hariri's death, on 14 February 2005, Asad had named Shawkat head of Syria's military intelligence. His family bonds to the

Asad clan saved Shawkat from worse. He was politically sidelined and named head of a toothless National Security Council for a while. Then in July 2009 Shawkat became deputy chief of staff of the Syrian army, a post that he held till his reemergence on the top political scene in September 2011.

A Syrian analyst in Damascus assumed in 2009 that "they are playing the theatre of confrontation to the outside but he and the president are hand in glove." This scenario served to show that Asad could play a hard hand against the background of the looming indictment of the Hariri Tribunal in Lebanon. "In the end it is the family that counts," the analyst mused. "A minority that is so much in danger cannot afford the luxury [of infighting]. If someone was to be eliminated, he would be so completely; he would not get a second chance."[32]

The more the ruling family came under external pressure the more old discords gave way to a common spirit of survival. But family survival did not necessarily mean the survival of Bashar al-Asad. During the revolt Bashar's uncle Rifaat al-Asad emerged on a side-stage from his exile residence in Spain. He had always felt that he would have been the better successor of his brother Hafez instead of the young and inexperienced eye-doctor Bashar. After his defeat Rifaat went into exile and was said to hold a group of sympathizers in the coastal town of Banyas where protests erupted in the first weeks of the revolt in March 2011. Rifaat had been instrumental in the massacre of Hama in 1982. Some opposition figures rumored that he travelled back to Syria when the country was on fire again. No proofs could be established but in November 2011 Rifaat emerged in international TV and radio stations with calls for a new president—one that should come, without much surprise, from the ranks of the Asad family.[33]

These and other episodes of family dissent showed that during the uprising Asad came under increasing attack from within his clan. If he was not directly attacked by family dissenters, he became deeply indebted to his entourage whom he had all reason to mistrust. After the Lebanon disaster in 2005 this was the second time that Asad's throne was seriously shaking. His most severe enemies then and now came from his immediate surroundings.

5
The Pillars
of the Ancient Regime

THE BAATH REGIME IN SYRIA MANAGED TO MOBILIZE LARGE numbers of people to publicly demonstrate on its behalf during the uprising, starting in 2011. This was a marked contrast to the lack of popular support for the regimes in Egypt, Tunisia and Yemen during the same period. Most of the street support for Asad happened in Damascus, while ongoing clashes with the opposition were occurring elsewhere in the country. On several occasions thousands of people demonstrated on Damascus' Mezzeh highway and in Umayad Square, coincidentally where the defense ministry and the Syrian state TV building are located. The demonstrators carried Asad banners, giant Syrian flags and delivered the traditional chant, "With our soul and blood we'll fight for you, Bashar!" These pro-Asad demonstrators filled the streets in Damascus when international sanctions against Syria were tightened or when the observer delegation of the Arab League was in town. This is reminiscent of the street solidarity for the Asad regime during 2003 when the Iraq war broke out and threats against the regime increased. Again, the narrative was framed as an external conspiracy against Damascus. Now it was the Arab League in its committed anti-Asad course that had fallen prey to US pressure, according the regime's propaganda. However, during the anti-war demonstrations in 2003 the protestors in the street were different.

The number of pro-Asad demonstrators in 2011 remained high for several reasons. Party members, teachers, trade unionists and other people from the inflated public sector were ordered to participate and sometimes paid to take part. Documented reports relate incidents of people, even school children, who were beaten and killed because they refused to participate in such demonstrations.[1] On Facebook some Asad supporters cited the large crowds on Damascus' urban highway as a proof for the regime's strong popularity (but failed to mention that pro-regime crowds diminished as opposition gunmen began shooting into the crowds). With escalating violence, pro-regime demonstrations became smaller, too. In an incident on 11 January 2012, a Syrian TV journalist was arrested because he privately shot and uploaded a pro-Asad demonstration with the participation of the President himself on the Umayyad Square in Damascus. But instead of a million-strong turnout claimed by the official state TV (showing close-ups in its broadcast) the journalist's video from the roof of the TV building showed that only a few thousands were present listening to Asad.

Having said this, support for Asad was not always artificial or staged. Syrian society was more polarized than in the other Arab Spring states. Many Alawites, with escalating violence, feared reprisals from Sunnis. Likewise, Christians, Druze, and other minorities found safe-haven niches in the minority-friendly Baath regime. Other groups supported Syria's pro-Palestinian stance and intransigent position against Israel despite the international headwind. International sanctions against Syria during most of Bashar al-Asad's rule also created a sense of unity-in-adversity among Syrians. And finally, the regime was able to rely on several sources of support that fostered its legitimacy in the eyes of many Syrians. Unfortunately, it frittered away these positive connotations through barbaric cruelty with which it hunted down civilians during the months of 2011 and after.

Despite all its short-comings, it makes sense to recall the stabilizing pillars of the ancient regime, which gave it long-lasting support from certain strata of society. Moreover, these achievements stand in stark contrast with a decayed reality that was to unfold. This discussion also ties to the material in Chapter III that examined the many missed opportunities of the Asad regime.

On the positive balance, Syria had remained stable despite contradictions within the regime since Hafez al-Asad's death—and despite long-lasting US political pressure under the Bush administration. The regime in Damascus could not be compared with Saddam Hussein's brutal dictatorship. The calm in Syria was by no means the result solely of an oppressive government machinery. Power in the country had several pillars of support that lent it legitimacy in the eyes of the public.

By contrast, the Iraqi leadership had made no compromises. Saddam Hussein did not pursue a strategy of balance among different interests as did his more flexible alter ego, Hafez al-Asad. Neither did Saddam need to do this, for he was able to buy loyalty very easily with his country's plentiful oil resources and supplement this strategy with brute force if necessary. Asad balanced conflicting interests with clever tactics and alternating concessions. A report by the International Crisis Group came to the conclusion that "ironically, the Syrian regime has become far more embedded in the nation's social fabric than was its Iraqi counterpart because of its comparative limitations and weaknesses."[2]

The sources from which the Baath regime derived its legitimacy were partly nourished by Hafez al-Asad's political legacy and partly by the new developments under Bashar. Among these were the consequences of the Iraq war. The sources of legitimacy can be summarized by the following points.

Pro-Palestinian Rhetoric

The two antagonized regimes in Syria and Iraq had distinguished themselves at home as advocates of the Palestinian cause and as hardliners against Israel. The Israeli occupation of Palestinian territory used to be the main topic covered by the Syrian state press each day. It was easy to gain the population's support for these matters, thus distracting them from economic and political problems at home. Syria never grew tired of proclaiming the Palestinian cause as its own, although its support was frequently no more than political rhetoric. Similar to other Arab states, many Syrians regard the some 500,000 Palestinians living in Syria only as tolerated guests, even if they enjoy equal rights with native Syrians.[3]

Rhetorical broadsides against Israel remained a welcome means of creating consensus. Asad sometimes tried to outdo the hardliners in this effort and clearly went over the top. In a speech at the Arab summit in Amman in March 2001, for example, he said that Israeli society was more racist than Nazism.[4] In his remarks welcoming Pope John Paul II to Syria two months later, he slipped into anti-Semitism when he referred to Jews as the killers of Jesus. "They try to kill all the principles of divine faiths with the same mentality of betraying Jesus Christ and torturing him, and in the same way that they tried to commit treachery against Prophet Muhammad (peace be upon him)."[5] Asad, however, dismissed his speechwriter after this faux pas.

Despite all the rhetoric, solidarity with the Palestinians gave way to pragmatism in dangerous situations. The younger Asad learned from his father, and his motto was "Give in as much as is necessary and persist as much as is possible." After the Iraq war, Asad's position on the Palestinian issue oscillated between readiness to compromise and an ideological hard line.

Asad gave in to American pressure and closed the contact offices of Palestinian organizations in Damascus. Washington, however, criticized this action as purely cosmetic as nobody really knew what "closure" meant. Most of the offices were only private flats, from which public relations work was done.

Demonstrations by Palestinians were banned or more strongly kept in check than before the Iraq war, but Asad made it clear that no Palestinian leaders would be expelled from Syria. He reaffirmed this position when on 12 May 2004 the United States stepped up its sanctions against Syria because of this stance among other things. The issue became more explosive after the Israeli government fired precision rockets at the Gaza Strip and liquidated the long-standing spiritual leader of Hamas, Sheikh Ahmed Yassin, at the end of March, and his successor Abdul Aziz Rantisi only two weeks later. This left Khalid Mashaal as the new leader of the Islamist organization. He had spent many years in Damascus and proclaimed from his new position that "it is undoubtedly safer in Syria than elsewhere."[6] At the same time, Mashaal publicly admitted to having close contacts with then PLO leader Yassir Arafat.

During the time of Syria's international honeymoon from 2008 to 2010 (see Chapter VIII "Syria's Policy Paradox") it became clear again that the Palestinian issue was a strategic trump card in Asad's hand. He ably played it to achieve foreign policy goals. The first signs that Damascus would expel

Hamas-leader Mashaal from Damascus emerged in the media in September 2008.[7] Although nothing came of this story, it was a clear indication that Asad was ready to make concessions on the way toward international recognition. Two years later, cables leaked by Wikileaks brought to light that for Asad support for Hamas was indeed negotiable. "Hamas is Muslim Brotherhood, but we have to deal with the reality of their presence," the Syrian president told a group of American lawmakers in March 2009, according to the leaked cable. In this conversation Asad called the Islamic movement an "uninvited guest."[8] This pragmatic attitude toward Hamas—one of the key Western preoccupations—was a great chance for both Syria and Western decision-makers, an opportunity that was never taken up. Perhaps, time was too short until the Arab Spring broke out. In December 2011 it was leaked that Hamas leader Mashaal had indeed left the country, and Hamas called his members to leave Syria altogether.[9]

Asad proved equally flexible on the Iraq issue. As Wikileaks cables suggested, the president was ready to tighten the Syrian border in order to prevent Islamists from pouring into Iraq in order to fight against the US troops there. But he said he would not do it "for free." Asad asked the US to lift sanctions that banned the sale of commercial airplanes and their parts to Syria. He added: "In the US, you like to shoot [terrorists]. Suffocating their networks is far more effective."[10]

The Iraq issue was indeed a source of popularity for Asad, and he used it in an environment of hostility against Syria. Encouraged by the severe problems the US troops were facing in Iraq, Asad sharpened his tone toward Israel and the United States in early 2004. Making up for his low-profile strategy during the first months of the war, he regained sympathy in the streets at home. Yet, as Samir Altaqi pointed out, "Syria is not able to make any further concessions [on the Palestinian issue]. This would harm the regime's identity."[11] Asad had already stuck his neck out in May 2003 when he promised to accept any decision by the Palestinian leadership in peace negotiations with Israel. Until then, Syria had always officially insisted on co-representing the Palestinians. In the peace negotiations with Israel in Shepherdstown, West Virginia, in January 2000, Hafez al-Asad had secretly signaled that he would accept a peace settlement even if the Israeli-Palestinian conflict had not been satisfactorily resolved. In this regard, Bashar's strategy of pragmatism concerning the Palestinian issue did not constitute a breach of domestic policy.

Immediately after the Iraq war, Asad signaled his readiness to hold talks with Israel and repeated his offer several times since, especially at the end of 2003, despite the continuation of the Intifada, and in 2007 in his second inauguration speech. He was said to have sent his brother Maher to Amman for secret negotiations with Israeli representatives.[12] As tensions and hopes ran high, every incident, no matter how minute, is subject to worldwide public scrutiny, as was the first handshake between a Syrian and an Israeli president, which took place at the funeral of Pope John Paul II on 9 April 2005, in Rome. When speculation arose, the Syrians hastened to clarify that this gesture between Bashar al-Asad and Iranian-born Moshe Katzav was nothing but "a formality."

In Israel voices increased that called for serious negotiation with Syria, with no preconditions. Syria always insisted on resuming negotiations at the point where the two sides had broken off in March 2000, shortly before Hafez al-Asad's death. Under these conditions, Syria would regain the entire Golan Heights in line with the borders of 1967. At the end of 2003, Asad surprisingly dropped this condition—which was based on a promise from the assassinated Israeli Prime Minister Yitzhak Rabin—thus placing Israel in a temporary predicament. He directed his strategy toward Washington in order to demonstrate his good will and avert its pressure on Syria. Asad declared his readiness to negotiate without preconditions several times, as he did in the speech to parliament on 5 March 2005, when he announced the withdrawal of Syrian troops from Lebanon.

Minister Buthayna Shaaban insisted, "Syria would be prepared to resume peace negotiations today if only the United States would induce Israel to negotiate."[13] But Washington was not interested at that time because it wanted to hold on to arguments for putting pressure on Syria in the "war on terrorism." Israel had no interest in peace negotiations because it would rather wait and see how much Syria was being softened up, which would strengthen the Israeli position in negotiations over the Golan Heights. And Syria could easily disseminate such expressions of will in the media because it could be sure that Israel at this point would not accept any offer to negotiate. This Middle Eastern vicious cycle left Damascus a free hand to go on playing the Palestinian card that it needed as a pillar of its legitimacy.

However, Syrian seriousness about peace talks with Israel became clear in 2008—the period of international détente for Syria—in exchange for a possible rapprochement with the United States. Syria and Israel conducted backdoor talks through the mediation of Turkey. One inch before the talks could have been elevated to direct bilateral negotiations, the Israeli side decided to break up the mediated efforts and started the war against Hamas in the Gaza Strip (at the end of 2008). On the one hand, this represented a considerable setback for peace efforts in the region. On the other hand, the brutality of the war in Gaza and the ire of the Turkish mediators added to Asad's boost in the Arab public opinion. He was once again able to use the Palestinian dossier and the rhetoric of resistance in the traditional pan-Arab framework.

Pan-Arab Rhetoric

As the Iraq war raged in Syria's neighboring country, as gigantic fireballs and bright flashes in Baghdad flickered on their TV screens, people in Damascus would meet each Thursday at the central Presidential Bridge. They marched through the streets with pictures and banners they had painted. Among them were many young people, mostly in jeans, some with baseball caps bearing the slogan, "We are all Iraqis." They gleefully carried placards mocking Jordan's King Abdullah II and Egypt's President Husni Mubarak in tight bras or black female clothing as George W. Bush's and the Zionists' whores. The American stars and stripes and the light blue Star of David against a white background regularly went up in flames. Yet beyond these common rituals, the strictly regulated marches (more reminiscent of theatrical performances with the *mukhabarat* officials as directors, very similar to the pro-regime marches in 2011 and 2012) were more of a social event, a chance to meet old friends and to get to know new people.

Surprisingly, of all countries Syria was an oasis of calm and stability during those tense weeks in 2003. Between the rulers and the ruled existed a complete agreement on the question of Iraq. It was quite different in neighboring Arab countries where mass demonstrations occurred against the ruling governments. Many Arabs looked with admiration at the regime in Damascus that demonstrated unqualified opposition to the war in spite of its vulnerability and intimidation from the United States. Faruq al-Shara', Syria's long-serving foreign minister, publicly called the Bush administration the "most violent and stupid" government the United States had ever had.[14]

A paradoxical situation arose after the collapse of the Baath regime in Iraq. The role of representing the sole pan-Arab, and thus anti-imperialist, mouthpiece fell to the Syrian Baathists who were happy to receive it. The Iraqi and Syrian branches of the Baath Party had been bitter enemies since 1966. The Syrian Baathists wanted social revolution in their home country first and concentrated on a strong Syria. The Iraqi Baathists criticized this national agenda and adhered to the pan-Arab goal of uniting all Arabs in a single state. With the fall of Baghdad, however, Syria obtained a monopoly on pan-Arab ideology, a source of legitimacy for the regime, with growth potential for the regime's popularity in the region that mirrored a rising anti-American sentiment. Syrian Baathists successfully played this tune, whereas Jordan, Egypt, and Saudi Arabia were seen as traitors to the Arab cause among the Arab population.

The opposition figure Michel Kilo warned, "There is a risk that Arab nationalism will turn into a dangerous demagogy and a means toward achieving internal unity in Syria."[15] As the anti-regime demonstrations in 2011 showed, pan-Arab rhetoric did no longer suffice to conceal Syria's real problems. Anti-American pan-Arabism was also a danger for the Syrian regime because the United States equated pan-Arab rhetoric with terrorism, which partly explained why the Syrian regime remained on the American and Israeli hit list for so long despite Syrian efforts of rapprochement in 2008.

In the aftermath of the Iraq war, some opposition members and also some within Asad's entourage complained about the hard line Bashar took in the Iraq war. He was blamed for having provoked an unnecessary confrontation with the United States that restrained political and diplomatic leeway for political horse-trading. His resolute anti-war stance was nonetheless very popular among the Syrian people, and the bloody scenes in post-war Iraq only served to reinforce this mood. These images remained well in the people's minds when the protests in 2011 lead the once stable country into an uncertain future.

Secularism

"We have a strong government that fights both radical Islamist and Christian fanatics alike and does not itself interfere with religion." This is how a young Christian from the Bab Touma quarter of the Old City in Damascus summed up Syrian secularism. It is not only the Christians who valued this principle of the regime.

Fear of political Islamization after a violent revolution, possibly supported by petro-dollars from Saudi extremists, was a trump card of the ruling Alawites and their secular supporters. Whether the danger was exaggerated is a matter of opinion, but it continued to serve as a strong source of legitimacy for the regime. In view of the fact that radical Muslims had previously been funded and supported in many places by the United States to serve its national interests, the Syrian status quo appeared quite acceptable. There was little confidence in any alternative that might have been put in place by the United States. Even a change that was not brought about by an external force from the West was viewed with suspicion, as became clear in 2011. "Just look at Iraq!" said Sadiq Jalal al-Azm. "If there is no higher civil national identity, people start to kill each other."[16] When he uttered these remarks in 2003 he could not have anticipated their sad truth only eight years later.

Syria's secular experience was a distinct facet of its society that had to be considered by any person in power. The regime did not show signs of making a Saddam-like u-turn from ideological secularism to populist Islamism in spite of the growing pressure by Islamists from within and without Syria. This was something that the West should have appreciated (more on this issue in Chapters IX "Che not Usama: Syrian Society and Western Ideals" and X "Excursus: Secularism in Syria.")

Religious Minorities

The thick walls of the Umayyad Mosque rise majestically in the heart of Damascus' Old City. For Sunnis, this is the fourth most sacred place in the world after the Kaaba in Mecca, the Prophet's Mosque in Medina, and the al-Aqsa Mosque in Jerusalem. It is also one of the most remarkable symbols of religious intertwinement in Syria's history. The main building behind the wide inner courtyard with its ornamented walls used to be a basilica, which can still be discerned today. Inside, Christians revere the alleged remains of John the Baptist and Muslims those of Prophet Yahia—both are one and the same person. When the Muslims took over Damascus in 636 AD, they allowed the Christians to continue praying in their church for seven more decades until it was converted into a mosque after the Christians had been paid compensation. Today there still remains a minaret dedicated to Jesus.

The Jewish community also has a place in Syrian society. Although their numbers have diminished to just a few hundred, they are not without influence, especially in economic life. For example, a Jewish meat entrepreneur supplies exclusive restaurants in the city from the Sheraton to the Cham Palace Hotel.[17] Hafez al-Asad lifted the travel ban for Jews in the early 1990s. To his disappointment a large number—far more than he had expected—emigrated to the United States or to Israel. Now Palestinian refugees live next door to the remaining Jews and some Christians in the Ottoman adobe houses near the East Gate of Damascus (Bab Sharqi), where the Jewish quarter once existed. An attentive visitor to the Old City can still see Stars of David on some walls. Nobody has chiseled them away in fury over their political archenemy Israel. The symbols have remained as a reminder of the long tradition of Jews, Christians, and Muslims living together. After all, modern anti-Semitism is no invention of Muslim Arabs, but was imported into the Middle East from Europe.

In my interviews, the large majority of Syrians repeatedly stressed that in their opinion there was a significant difference between the Jews who have always lived in Syria and speak Arabic as their mother tongue and the Zionists who have come to Palestine from all over the world and have often brought with them ethno-nationalism and the notion of territorial expansion. Syrians make an equally clear distinction between US citizens and the US foreign policy. One repeatedly hears in the streets that Americans as people are as welcome as anyone else.

Syrians mentioned with pride that people of nearly two dozen different religions and confessions have lived in their country for centuries. Of these, eleven alone are of Christian denomination, as there was not a central church that played a unifying force after Islamization. These include Roman Orthodox, Armenian Orthodox, Roman Catholics, Syrian Orthodox, Syrian Catholics, Armenian Catholics, Maronites, Protestants, Nestorians, Latiners, and Chaldeans.

The government deliberately did not keep official statistics on religious groups and so estimates differ. According to one older source, Sunnis accounted for sixty-nine percent of the population, while Christians of various confessions represented 14.5 percent, Alawites twelve percent,

Druze three percent, and Ismailites 1.5 percent.[18] Apart from this, there is also a small Shiite minority. Since Sunnis tend to have more children than Christians and Alawites, and because Christians tend to emigrate more often, the trend has been shifting in favor of the Sunnis. The figure of ten to eleven percent Christians and the same percentage of Alawites was often quoted. Many Christians have already emigrated but are still registered with the authorities as Syrian residents. More recently, however, the influx of Christian refugees from Iraq counteracted these numbers. Nevertheless, Christians raised concern of their marginalization not only in numbers but also through the more and more ostentatious presence of conservative Sunni elements. A senior Syrian analyst who feared to be quoted on the matter cited a figure that, according to him, stemmed from an unpublished Jesuit study of 2009. Thus the proportion of Christians in Syria had fallen to a mere 5.6 percent.[19]

Religious affiliation crosscuts with ethnic identity. Some ninety percent of Syrians are Arabs living alongside Kurds and Turks (mostly Sunnis), Christian Armenians, Circassians (whom the Ottomans removed from the Caucasus and resettled in Syria), and Assyrians of old Christian confessions who still speak Aramaic, the language of Jesus.

As a consequence of this mosaic, everyday life in Syria was regulated with ease and flexibility around religious traditions. Muslims closed their shops on Fridays, Christians on Sundays, and Jews on Saturdays. One religious group patronized the open bazaars of the others on their free days. Thus in Damascus, for example, an especially large number of Muslim women crowded into the modern clothing stores in Qasa' near the Christian quarter in Bab Touma on Friday evenings, some in tight jeans and with styled hair and others in long garments and headscarves. The accommodating system of holidays applied also to private schools. For example, the *muezzins* of mosques in any one quarter were prohibited by law from simultaneously broadcasting the call to prayer over loudspeakers. They had to take turns so as not to strain the tolerance of believers of other religions.

Minorities enjoyed equal rights under the law except for the clause in the constitution that stipulated that only a Muslim could become president. Christian churches developed freely in Syria and were often very well endowed financially. The government subsidized them by building asphalt roads to remote monasteries and other projects. Like mosques, churches were exempt from taxes on their purchases. Many Christians were traders, craftsmen, and merchants and had achieved a relative degree of prosperity. They were in a similar social and economic position as the class of Sunni traders.

That Syria was attractive for minorities in the region became more evident after the Iraq war. Christians living between the Euphrates and Tigris streamed West by the thousands to escape the daily violence in Iraq and settled in Damascus or on the coast of the Mediterranean. The migration swelled more and more after a series of attacks on churches in Iraq. The contrast between

Iraq and its calm and socially tolerant neighbor could not be more distinct. The former Mufti of Damascus, Ahmed Kuftaro, was quick to condemn the church attacks.

In the summer of 2004 alone, 250,000 Christians were reported to have fled to Syria from war-torn Iraq either for recreation or permanent residence. In the beginning of 2005 the number of refugees—whether Christians or other groups—rose to 700,000. UN officials say many were doctors, professors, business owners, and recent college graduates—the intellectual core that officials in Washington hoped would rebuild Iraq.[20] Syria was a generous host to Iraqi refugees in general. More than seventy percent of the Iraqi refugees registered in Syria in 2010 had lived there for over four years.[21]

As a result, rents rose considerably, particularly in the Damascus district of Jaramana, east of the Christian quarter Bab Touma. Because not all the refugees were poor, hotels were fully booked. Iraqi license plates on old and new American cars became part of the street scene in the Syrian capital. Damascus natives worried that the new arrivals would trigger a change in the city's relaxed and trusting atmosphere. An elderly Christian mosaic manufacturer in Bab Touma said that Iraqis had brought with them their "tough business methods" and "reckless attitudes" after decades of suppression under Saddam Hussein and the trauma of having to save one's skin after the Iraq war. Asked whether he was not happy that the refugees increased the number of Christians in Syria, he replied, "I don't care if they are Christians or not. Here, we Damascene people trust each other, Christian, Muslim, Jew, or whoever. We know each other and each other's families, we live together, and we do fair business with each other. The Iraqis are different. I don't trust them." In contrast, Anwar al-Bunni stressed, "Syrians have always proven hospitable to all kinds of refugees whether Palestinians, Lebanese, or Iraqis." However, he did not dismiss the current problems. "In Iraq, religious groups are used to living in separate areas and communities. Here, we are used to living as neighbors."[22]

In Syria, open conflict was rarely oriented along religious lines. On the whole, the different religious groups lived peacefully next to one another or even together, whereas in other countries in the region such as Jordan, Egypt, Iraq, and even in politically more open Lebanon religious communities have withdrawn into separate enclaves, cut themselves off, and become encrusted. They have entered into a competition of identity whose own dialectic momentum has created the compulsion for people to assign themselves more and more clearly along religious or ethnic cleavages. Also in Syria, the philosopher Sadiq Jalal al-Azm observed an increasing unrest among the minorities because of the rise of Islamic fundamentalism. "There is a kind of competition to demonstrate more clearly one's religious identity. The Muslims are building more mosques; the Christians organize more lavish processions and hang bigger crosses round their necks."[23]

Naturally, prejudices had also arisen among the religious groups in Syria before 2011 as has happened elsewhere. Every now and then people referred to the Christian pogroms in the Old City of Damascus in 1860. To this day, the exact reason and chain of events behind the murdering and looting suffered by the Catholic population in Bab Touma remains unclear, though academics are certain that it had political and perhaps socio-economic causes, but not religious ones.

The Catholics in the ailing Ottoman Empire had increasingly become protégés of French missionaries and French colonial policy that saw a bridgehead for French interests in the Lebanon Mountains. On the other hand, Russia made a show of being the protector of the Orthodox Christians, who in the Maydan quarter of Damascus mostly remained unscathed in the terrible summer of 1860. The English, in turn—for want of Protestants—concentrated on the Druze as protégés or accomplices for their interests.

Bloody battles between the religious groups in Mount Lebanon and on the coast reminded some Muslims and Druze of the Crusades. At last, the unrest spilled into Damascus on 9 July 1860. On that day, Muslims and Druze in Bab Touma slaughtered a great number of Christians and set fire to the quarter along the northern wall of the city. The reported number of victims varies between six hundred and ten thousand, depending on the source. People in Damascus generally speak of three thousand dead.[24]

Syrians today recall how many local Muslims ran the risk of hiding Christians in their houses, thus saving them from certain death. Sheikh Abdul Qadir al-Jaza'iri, the leader of the Algerian resistance movement living in exile in Damascus, also marched into the old quarter of Damascus with his men to help the Christians. The Ottoman administration had not been able to prevent the pogroms (most of their local police troops even took part in the persecution), but their headquarters in Istanbul organized a thorough investigation afterward and severely punished those who had perpetrated and planned the massacre. They were strongly supported by Damascus Muslims. At least one-hundred-and-seventy men were executed, including the governor of Damascus and the Ottoman ruler Ahmed Pasha. After this strict intervention by the Ottomans, the French no longer had a pretext for invading Damascus. Six thousand French troops had already landed in Lebanon and were waiting for their marching orders. The events of 1860 show that it was mainly Muslims who helped in time of need, who investigated the massacre, and who brought the culprits to justice. It always depends on which view of events prevails in a certain situation.

The Baath government made efforts to present itself as a mediator between the religions and guarantor of the religious tolerance that has evolved over the course of Syria's history. Asad liked to be filmed by Syrian television when he received Christian patriarchs. Pope John Paul II's visit to Syria with his much-publicized prayer in the Umayyad Mosque in May 2001 was a welcome highlight meant to underline the regime's political interest in propagating religious tolerance. During the Iraq war, Asad praised the pope for his anti-war stance. He said that the religions again had a common position after a disruption of Christian-Muslim relations following 9/11. To reinforce this welcoming attitude toward Christians in Syria, the government opened the world's first center for the Aramaic language in Ma'loula, north of Damascus, in July 2004. The remaining Christians who still have a command of Aramaic live in this monastery town.

As mentioned above, during the months of the protests in 2011 many Christians held on to their commitment to the Baath regime. Narratives of change appeared more threatening to them than the status quo, given the horrible pictures next door in Iraq where most Christians did not see any future. Christian religious leaders in Damascus publicly manifested their solidarity with Asad. The Catholic patriarch Gregorios Laham as well as the Syrian-Catholic archbishop of Damascus, Elias Tabe, and the Chaldean-Catholic bishop of Aleppo, Antoine Audo, expressed harsh criticism of international media reports of the protests and pointed to negative effects for Christians if the political setting should change. They emphasized their will to work toward a democratic solution that would prevent Syria from fundamentalism. "We don't want to turn into a second Iraq," they declared in mid-June as quoted by Syria's state media.[25]

In the provinces Christians were closer to the events on the ground but they still had their doubts. The Franciscan priest and head of the monastery in Knaye, a village not far from Jisr as-Shugour in the Turkish border area, recalled with relief the arrival of the Syrian army in a church report: "The army came to Knaye on 17 June [2011]. We received it festively."[26] Although the Franciscan monks had sheltered Sunni, Alawite, and Christian refugees alike during the clashes, the arrival of the army symbolized to the Christians the return of order.

Speaking from a similar vantage point, the Lebanese Maronite Patriarch Beshara Boutros Ra'i warned that a collapse of the Baath regime in Syria would endanger Christian minorities and called on the Western states to give Asad a chance for political reform.[27] The person who most strongly contradicted Ra'i was a Christian, too. Michel Kilo called the patriarch's statement "absurd" and "not acceptable."[28]

Only in December 2011, when the official number of civilian deaths had reached 5000, according to conservative UN estimates, the three Catholic patriarchs in Syria began to release more differentiated declarations. These included words on "deep pain about what had happened, grief about the victims and fear of an escalation of the economic situation." The clerics took a mediating position. They called on Syrians to reconcile and warned against foreign intervention. They also demanded an end to sanctions against the regime. In turn, they addressed the regime and asked to respect justice, freedom and human dignity. The declaration still contained enough sympathetic material to be useful to the regime. So the Syrian news agency SANA published a summary of the text that focused on the patriarchs' rejection of foreign intervention and of international sanctions.[29]

The Baathists had always been dependent on religious peace for they were, after all, also members of a minority. Opinions differ, though, as to whether the rule of the Asads had a positive influence on relations between the religions.

Nihad Nahas is a communist in the political opposition who spent fifteen years in prison. A Sunni by birth and married to a Christian, he said, "Syrian society used to be much more liberal and more secular. It was not until after the Alawites strong-armed Asad to power that tribes and religious groups gained importance. The ideological rift between them has deepened." His wife Leila Nahal, who was also in prison for being a communist, said in fluent French, "We never used to know what a person's religion was. Today young girls ask about a man's religion on their first date to know if there is any question of marriage." Mixed marriages are more difficult and less common than they used to be.[30] "In the 1950s," as Volker Perthes quoted an intellectual, "we were communists, Baathists, Nasserists, or Syrian nationalists. Today we are Sunnis, Alawites, Druze, or Christians again." Perthes attributed this development to the lack of an open political discourse.[31]

Salwa Ismail argued that the regime and to some extent the Syrian public had always anticipated a challenge to the predominantly Alawite government. At least this was among plausible scenarios. A social realignment along sectarian lines and retribution from Sunni circles against Alawites were obvious risks in such a context. "Within this perspective, the political sectarianism of the regime coexists with a dormant or hidden societal sectarianism," wrote Ismail. "Though references to an individual's affiliation to a particular sect were pushed out of public discourse, regime politics of 'divide and rule' is thought to have perpetuated social antagonisms and resentment along sectarian and ethnic lines."[32]

On the other side, the philosopher Sadiq Jalal al-Azm shared a different experience. He focused on the consequences of a modernizing economy. "If you compare modern Syria with the Syria of thirty years ago, society has become more coherent," he pointed out. The industrialization carried out under Hafez al-Asad made society more mobile. Towns grew and people began to travel and intermingle more. "When I was a small boy," the 1934-born intellectual reminisced, "you only heard about some minorities and religions from other people. The Druze all lived at the Druze Hill in Sweda and the Alawites in the mountains of Latakia. Society may not be so coherent as in developed countries but there are no longer any closed communities. Our feeling for Syrianness has grown."[33]

The Syrian Baathists counted on this form of Syrian nationalism. But the paradox remained. They ruled with a pan-Arab and nationalist ideology encompassing all religions. "Even the Christians hold up the flag of Arab nationalism and not the American one," said the historian Abdullah Hanna.[34] At the same time, the Baathists were dependent on clans and religious connections in order to support their rule, not exclusively but as an important pillar.

The relationship between religious groups still resembled a fragile mosaic, though overall the degree of social interaction and tolerance remained a model for the battered region. It at least gave the regime a significant plus in the minorities' view, with no sign either that the Sunni majority deemed the regime's minority policy a deficiency. Of course, this balance became tenuous in 2011. Did the Baath regime promote religious harmony or destroy it? The answer is not clear. The regime was conducive to religious harmony as long as it served the regime's interests of power, and it destroyed this harmony when it considered sectarianism a more promising agenda for the final struggle in power.

Domestic Security

Brandishing pistols with silencers and automatic machine guns, a four-member gang is storming a money-transfer agency in downtown Damascus on 7 February 2005. In broad daylight, the unmasked robbers force the customers to the walls. The bandits then fire two shots into the air and escape in a Mercedes with forty-three million lira (approximately $800,000).[35]

The ten-minute scene could have happened anywhere in the world, and is among the most familiar scenarios of Hollywood films set in modern urban landscapes. In Damascus, however, the crime was so unheard-of that Minister of Interior Ghazi Kanaan personally hurried to the site and, together with the chief of Damascus police, interrogated some of the customers and employees in an attempt to identify the robbers. The unusual personal involvement of a minister in this minor incident puts the robbery into perspective.

Syria was a police state *(daula al-'amniyya),* and according to one estimate there was one secret service member for every 153 Syrians over the age of fifteen.[36] Law and order in the country was proverbial for both the native population and its tourists. Of course, drug-trafficking and gang crime existed, especially in the commercial metropolis of Aleppo, but the overall crime rate remained extremely low, though it was difficult to obtain concrete figures. Crimes were not reported in the media and relevant statistics were kept secret. Not only was the strong state machinery the reason for this peace, but also the still largely intact traditions and a strict code of values (despite the growing challenge through social change).

It was safe for anyone, including women, to stroll through the streets at night. The narrow doors of the Ottoman houses in the old parts of cities used to stand open as a rule, allowing glimpses of shady inner courtyards and family life. Windows of parked cars were left ajar in the heat of summer without worry of car radios being stolen. "You don't need police on the streets when there is a hidden policeman in each of us," joked a Syrian, alluding to the ubiquitous *mukhabarat*.

However, worrying developments had taken place that undermined this pillar of regime legitimacy. Militia-like groups called *shabbiha* took to the streets from time to time in order to beat up opposition figures and human rights activists during demonstrations, sometimes more brutally than the police or the *mukhabarat* typically used. These gangs of thugs were sent in buses by family clans of the ruling elite surrounding the president who had much to lose if political change occurred. Such incidents increased in frequency and created fear among the population in the years before 2011. They threatened one of the essential elements of Hafez al-Asad's legacy.

Nevertheless, across the board, safety was a factor that all Syrians, including members of the opposition, spoke of positively when they described their country. The looting and excesses of violence in post-war Iraq made even more evident its contrast to the tranquility in Syria. The situation was likewise worse in Lebanon due to its greater social and sectarian divisions.

Because of this ambience, members of the government and even Syrians generally were initially surprised and shocked to see people gather to raise their voice in protest in February 2011. In a country where gatherings were strictly forbidden under emergency law, no tradition of collective civil dissent had been able to grow. Even more surprising were the peaceful and creative ways in which the initial demonstrations developed. Law and order was one of the biggest assets of the Baath regime. As the government proved incapable of calming and suppressing the Arab Spring protests and instead escalated the problem, it gradually lost the confidence of Syrians who had relied on this very order for their social and economic well-being.

Social Balance

Despite caveats, the gap between rich and poor remained tolerable in Syria, especially in comparison to Egypt where slums were part of daily life. The residual socialism in Syria did not fail to have a social impact.

Vital price tags remained fixed by the government and were marked on products, including restaurant menus, until some relaxation in 2005. The fact that Syria did not recognize international copyright laws enabled poor families to buy books, cassettes, music, and computer CDs produced cheaply in Syria or China. Numerous products were imitations of foreign brands, costing only a fraction of the originals. Affordable and acceptable medical care, cheap medicine, subsidized gasoline, free public schools, nursery schools, and universities, as well as free school uniforms and holiday youth camps, were made available by the government.

In order to secure the support of peasants, the government traditionally bought farmers' crops at twice the market price ("strategic crop"). In several stages the government increased the salaries and pensions of government employees. This was to counter inevitable price increases, especially for imports (due to a weak Lira) and for certain basic foodstuffs. It was, at the same time, an act of political defiance against the United States' economic sanctions. As mentioned above, an increase of social benefits also was among the first actions of the government in response to the looming Arab Spring.

Although the closed economic system became increasingly unstable and was unlikely to be maintained in the long-term, it served as an argument for maintaining the status quo, especially among the poorer classes. In Alan George's words, the situation can be caustically described as "a certain equality of misery."[37]

There are, however, two risks which will be described in more detail later (in Chapter VI "The Negative Balance"). First, the Syrian government had been finding it increasingly difficult to procure resources for redistribution, not least because of the international political constellation. Second, Syria's relative social balance had been tipping. The nouveaux riche started to flout their accumulated wealth more and more blithely, with expensive cars, high-tech TV sets, and exclusive restaurants. Access to modern equipment such as mobile phones, computers and satellite dishes created desires that could no longer be satisfied by an ordinary civil service salary.

Some progress was achieved during the second Five-Year Plan under Bashar al-Asad between 2006 and 2011. The investment environment was improved. Clearer rules were established and competition against monopolies was favoured, be they state owned or private. Import bans were lifted and the state gave up its monopoly on imports. Syria opened its market by signing the GAFTA (Greater Arab Free Trade Agreement) in 1997. This was followed by bilateral agreements with Iran, Iraq, and most significantly Turkey. The Central Bank was granted more autonomy in monetary policies, and a private banking sector was established. A stock exchange was founded and real estate laws relaxed. A sales tax was introduced and older taxes abolished. Foreign debts were comparatively low and foreign money reserves high. In good times foreign currency reserves amounted to more than sixty percent of the gross national product (a number that shrunk rapidly during the protests in 2011 because the government needed the money to finance the crackdown in an increasingly adverse environment of international sanctions).

As a result, economic performance improved and foreign investment had steadily grown. After Lebanon had become more volatile again in 2006 a surge of tourists and investors from the Gulf States came to Syria. Tourism boomed. All of these positive developments delivered a financial buffer for the government when the Arab Spring revolts paralyzed the Syrian economy.

Hopes for Modernization (Bread & Circuses)

During his years in office, Asad managed to introduce important changes in everyday life. For example, he cut required military service from thirty months to two years. And, during the protests in March 2011, cut once again to 18 months. Since the fall of 2003, children have been wearing new school uniforms. Instead of military green, the boys' uniforms were changed to dark blue/light blue and the girls' dark blue/pink. At the same time, corporal punishment in classrooms was abolished, and some military elements were deleted from the school curricula.

Despite a general frustration among opposition figures with regard to political reforms, it was nevertheless true that the areas of arts, media, and government-monitored NGOs were more colorful than under Hafez al-Asad's times. More art galleries existed, festivals were celebrated. Artists had more space for maneuver if they abstained from touching the issue of politics. Indirect forms of expression compensated for the lack of open discussion be it in the debates about corruption, homosexuality, or other subjects. Syrian TV series such as *Bab al-Hara, Boqa Dou* or *Maraya* have developed a tradition of social criticism and became popular in many other Arab countries as well.

Youth and education is traditionally a jealously guarded field of action in totalitarian systems. The Baath Party had monopolized education since taking power in the 1960s. One of the early measures of the young Asad was to break this privilege. Since 2001 local and foreign investors were allowed to engage in education. Private universities were granted licenses under strict surveillance of the state. The 10th Five Year Plan in 2005 brought further impulses of reforms with the purpose of tackling issues of overcrowding and improvement of quality of tertiary education.

By 2010 some twenty private institutions had been licensed, fifteen of which had begun operating. Most are located on large campuses outside the cities of Damascus, Aleppo, Latakia, and Homs. The best developed of these are: The private University of Kalamoon in Deir Atiyeh, ninety kilometers north of Damascus; the Arab-International University (former Arab European University), located forty-five kilometers south of Damascus on the way to Dara'a; and the International University of Science and Technology. Student numbers at private universities did not exceed 10,000 in 2010, but the sector was growing rapidly. The Ministry for Higher Education even invited the American University in Beirut to set up a campus in Syria. The private institutions complemented the five public universities in Syria: Damascus University, University of Aleppo, al-Baath University in Homs, Tishreen University in Latakia, and al-Furat University in Deir al-Zour.[38] In 2002, the Syrian Virtual University was founded, a distance-learning institution that utilizes online-delivery methods,

In comparison with students of private universities, students of public universities possessed stronger intellectual capacities because the entry criteria were not measured by purchasing power but by excellence tested in the entry exams. But students with sufficient financial resources increasingly chose to study natural sciences, medicine, and pharmacy at private universities due to their better laboratory infrastructure.

The relationship between the government and the private institutions was not without friction. In October 2010, the Ministry of Finance accused some private universities of withholding large amounts of taxes. At the same time the government prohibited the use of English in all institutions except in English language and literature courses. This went hand in hand with other attempts at Arabization such as a requirement to use Arabic script for public letter boards in front of shops. This aggravated the problem of Syrian youth who lacked the language proficiency to compete internationally.

Also, the media environment in Syria underwent a rapid change during Asad's tenure, although this change was more evolutionary than revolutionary. The development of Syria's media landscape had ups and downs as did most other reform activities. After an initial phase of where new media outlets were created, there followed a period of closures, restrictions, and contradictions.

Given its prosaic starting-point in the 1990s, the media developments were remarkable. Yet journalists nevertheless chaffed. Their expectations had been raised when Bashar became president in 2000. The results, however, were highly flawed and complex. Since the state of emergency that ushered in Baath rule was declared in 1963, the freedom of opinion and media that is mentioned in the country's Constitution (§32) and the Constitution of the Arab Socialist Baath Party was severely restricted.[39]

When Bashar took power, the country was one of the most isolated societies in the world: Almost no access to the Internet; satellite TV officially forbidden (although used at personal risk); and with a few state run media strictly controlling the flow of information. These were the three "revolutionary" newspapers *al-Thawra (Revolution), al-Baath (Rebirth),* and *Tishreen (October),* Syrian state TV and radio. Shortly before Hafez al-Asad's death, the first Internet cafés opened, and cell phones became available for the politically privileged for connection fees of about $1,000 per line.

After Internet cafés had mushroomed throughout Syria's urban areas, the authorities raced to safeguard control over information flow as the number of inormation sources rapidly increased. According to the Syrian Center for Media and Freedom of Expression, 241 websites were blocked by the Syrian authorities from mid-September 2009, of which 49 were Kurdish sites, thirty-five opposition sites, thirty-two social networking sites (including Facebook), thirty-one general media sites, and fifteen Islamic sites.[40] At the same time people were still able to access the blocked websites through proxies—and even the First Lady had a profile on Facebook. In the years leading to the grand upheaval in 2011 the secret services were clamping down more and more on bloggers. In addition, everybody who entered an Internet café was required to show a personal identification and obliged to sign a registration form. The best known case of punishment against a blogger was the arrest and draconian treatment of Tal al-Molouhi, a nineteen-year-old Sunni girl at the end of 2010.

The Publishing Law of 2001 was no impediment when the regime clamped down on the Damascus Spring, yet the law led cautiously toward greater diversity of published opinion. In 2001 private newspapers and magazines were allowed and approved by the Ministry of Information. In 2002, private radio stations followed, and in 2005 private TV.

Since 2001 the Ministry of Information has licensed 220 publications, mostly lifestyle magazines, 70 of which have been shut down again.[41] More than 50 newspapers and magazines were closed alone in 2009.[42] The government tolerated relatively free economic and cultural debates. It also promoted a diversification of published views beyond the traditional state newspapers. Still, for the most part, Syria's new media was "bread and circuses," since only two political publications were granted licenses: *Abyad wa Aswad*[43] *(Black & White)* and *al-Bilad (The Countries)*. The satirical paper *al-Domari (The Lamplighter)* was owned by the renowned cartoonist Ali Farzat and featured opposition figures such as Hakam al-Baba who wrote biting criticisms. It was forced to close in 2003. A traditional way for Syrian intellectuals to express dissent was to publish in Lebanese newspapers. The content, if not the papers themselves, were certain to be heard in Syria. The Syrian government tolerated this window as a pressure release valve for dissenters.

Several newspapers established their bases in the Adra Free Zone in Damascus where (in theory) publication laws did not apply. Examples include *Syria Today*, *al-Watan (The Nation or Motherland)* and *Baladna (Our Country)*. Despite being established as a privately owned paper in 2006, *al-Watan* soon developed as a mouthpiece of the Baath regime, indistinguishable from the state newspapers aside from its more modern style. Its editor in chief was linked to the presidential family, and the paper participated in the denunciation of intellectuals and opposition figures.[44] *Al-Watan's* role became particularly obvious in the 2011 protests when room for dissent shrunk to zero.

In contrast, the publication *Syria Today* at times crossed red lines. One example: when the journalists wrote about urban policies and how the Baath ideology contradicted the officially propagated Social Market Economy. In 2010, employees stressed that the publication had more freedom than it had six years earlier when the paper was founded. The publication was allowed to operate more freely simply because it was published in English, had a small circulation in 2010 of 7,000, and was scarcely read by Syrians aside from businessmen and decision-makers. Nevertheless, it addressed a wide range of critical issues such as corruption, judicial reform, social taboos such as homosexuality and drugs, and even interviewed the censorship office itself. This coverage touched upon the famous "forbidden trinity" of sex, religion, and politics. The magazine devoted a lot of space to women activists who criticized plans for a new but backward personal status law, and it dedicated an entire issue to civil society. "We can touch almost every topic as long as we have a government voice in the story," said Dalia Haidar, the chief editor who was in her twenties in 2010. She had plans to expand the publishing house to a training and media center that offered related media services.[45]

Private radio stations such as *al-Madina FM, Arabesque, Cham FM, Souria al-Ghad,* and *al-Arabiya* were all prohibited from carrying political news. But social problems found increasing space. Examples include sex education, child abuse, molestation, divorce, and marital problems.

The first private TV channel was *Cham TV* which was closed down in 2006 and moved to Cairo. In the same year, *al-Dunya TV* was established and was able to maintain its diverse program, including politics, without government harassment. Apparently, this was because of close ties with the government. *Al-Mashrek (Orient) TV* started broadcasting from Dubai in February 2009 and tried to make a difference in the style and content of its programming. In July of the same year its Damascus offices were closed by the *mukhabarat.*

Overall, the diversity and colorfulness of (non-political) information available to Syrians increased considerably. Even journalists in government media (who were at the same time government employees) developed a critical spirit and did not fall behind those colleagues who worked for private media.

On the negative side, journalists conceded that they worked under self-censorship. Moreover, most of the new media ventures were owned, financed, or influenced by people close to the government.[46] Yet there was hope that market liberalization would help to extinguish at least some sources of censorship. The state, for example, held a monopoly on distribution of newspapers and magazines and could use this to restrict the readership of publications that published inconvenient truths.

All these spaces of freedom collapsed with the rise of protests. The regime's propaganda worked effectively and ruthlessly up to the point that well-known Syrian journalists publicly announced their resignation despite the high risks involved for themselves and their families. One of the best known cases was the defection of Hani al-Malathi in August 2011. The state TV anchor of the evening news bulletin complained about "state-orchestrated misinformation." Malathi said, "Both state and private media were transmitting false information, and anything that didn't match up was portrayed as foreign meddling or a conspiracy." He also drew conclusions about the interaction between the media propaganda and the course of the conflict, thus adding to the thesis of a failure of the entire Asad system: "Our attempts to sell them a different story only added fuel to the fire. Instead of calming people down, we actually provoked the protesters to go further, fuelled their anger and reinforced a sense of shared hostility among the public."[47]

Bashar

My car mechanic in Damascus during the years 2003 and 2004 (who incidentally is also named Bashar) was hiding a banned opposition magazine with biting caricatures of those in power in the glove compartment of his Skoda pickup. At the same time he also had set a photo of the beaming president as the screensaver for his mobile phone. This was not a contradiction in Syria. Many taxi drivers displayed the president's portrait on the rear window of their cars—which was by no means prescribed!—often in the style of a pop star with abstract black and silver features and sunglasses, though sometimes in uniform, and occasionally in a family photo with his wife and two children. The leader cult that had originally been dictated from above became popularized.

After the thirty-year rule of the untouchable and inscrutable sphinx in the presidential palace, people liked to hear that Bashar occasionally went out alone to buy vegetables or dined with his family in a restaurant without visible bodyguards. Although his nimbus was fading as his promises of reform went unfulfilled, the young president still possessed an image that, from the point of view of most Syrians, was neither stained with blood nor corrupted by radicalism or incompetence. (Although some would have said more the latter than the former). He successfully distanced himself from his father's political Stone Age. Most Syrians tended to look for faults in Asad's surroundings rather than in Asad himself, which was a result of the leader cult and traditional taboo against directly criticizing the president.[48] Yet even with these restrictions, Asad was an incarnation of stability for many Syrians, as well as the hope for modernization.

Another factor in Asad's favor was his socially committed, politically active, and cosmopolitan-looking wife Asma Akhras. Born in 1976 into an affluent Sunni family with origins in Homs, she grew up in Great Britain, graduated with a degree in computer science, and enjoyed excellent training and professional experience in business, finance, and investment banking with Deutsche Bank and later with the renowned investment banking firm J.P. Morgan. In 2011, the opposition claimed that she was using her financial experience for large-scale money-laundering and arms deals. Yet prior to the opposition rallies she was noted for views that, by Syrian standards, were provokingly modern. And she had also made enemies within the power structure. Conservatives criticized her for exerting too much influence on the president and interfering in personnel matters.

Before becoming president, Bashar served as chairman of the Syrian Computer Society and received credit for the widespread introduction of the

Internet, mobile phones, and legal satellite TV. Thus, when he took office, Asad was regarded favorably by many Syrians. He was not only associated with the new technologies, but he knew how to use them effectively. A brilliant example was the then-largest ever pro-Asad demonstration in Damascus that followed increasing international pressure after the Hariri assassination in February 2005. Half a million people, many of them youngsters dressed in jeans and T-shirts or teenage girls waving pom poms, festively marched through the streets for their president after the mobile phone company Syriatel had sent an SMS calling for the event. This marked a new style of Syrian politics. A call from the Baath Party would never have gotten as many people into the streets as did a few text lines on a mobile phone.

Part of Asad's attraction was his youth which garnered support among the young. Yet he was also popular among many older and more traditional citzens who readily accepted his authority. Why? There were few alternative leaders within Syria to choose from. And Syrians lacked democratic experience and thus had few models to which they could compare Bashar. The greatest threat to Bashar politically—and personally—had always lurked in his immediate power circle and not among the Syrian people. He never realized this, and the scenario that evolved in 2011 confirmed this fatal misjudgment.

The following statements of Asad in his inauguration speech a decade earlier are surreal when compared to the unscrupulous "security solution" he loosed upon the mostly peaceful street protestors—his own people:

> I am not after any post nor do I avoid any responsibility. The post is not an end but a means to achieve an end. And now, and since my people have honored me with their choice of me as president of the Republic . . . I would like to say that I have assumed the post but I have not occupied the position . . . . I feel that the man you have known . . . will not change at all once he assumes his post. He came out of the people and lived with them and shall remain one of them. You may expect to see him everywhere whether in the work place or in the streets or at your picnics in order to learn from you . . . . The man who has become a president is the same man who was a doctor and an officer and first and foremost is a citizen.[49]

According to assertions of Sheikh Ahmed Badreddin Hassoun, the Syrian Grand Mufti, Asad had confided to him more than once that in his dreams he would like to return to his profession one day and run an eye clinic. Thus in November 2011 for the first time a confidant of the president spoke of the possibility of a voluntary and premature end of his rule—although the utterances had also tactical implications in the tense political situation.[50] One month later Asad himself offered a different version. In an interview with ABC television he said that he still had an emotional attachment to his profession as an ophthalmologist but that one cannot look back once one is in a more important position.

But he equally claimed in the same interview, that he would leave office if he lost in a future presidential "election" that was scheduled in 2014: "I'm here to serve the country, my country's not here to serve me."[51] Asad showed himself to be convinced that his reign was based on public support, although the presidential referendum amounted to nothing more than public acclamations similar to those of the former socialist countries in Eastern Europe. More than once Asad wanted to make believe that he would withdraw if the people did not like him anymore, while his troops continued to crack down on those who had already made it clear that they had withdrawn their support. Asad said (according to the ABC transcript):

> I don't have problem. For me Syria as a project, project of success, if you don't succeed you don't have to stay in that position and that success again depends on the public support without public support you cannot, whether you are elected or not. It's not about the election, now it's about public support. This is the most important thing. So when I feel that the public support declined, I won't be here even if they say, if they ask or not I shouldn't be here if there is no public support. . . . That's conclusive.[52]

Unlike his father, Asad had not been known for his brutality and self-assurance but for precisely the opposite: his restraint in private matters, awkwardness in public appearances, and even political ineptitude. As a result, during the gravest crisis of his political life foreign media described him as "the dictator who cannot dictate."[53] Asad displayed none of the arrogant, dissolute, and excessive life-styles of the sons of former Iraqi President Saddam Hussein or Libya's Revolutionary Leader Muammar al-Qaddafi. Asad was more interested in the Internet and computers than in conspiracies and arms. Nevertheless, he ended up displaying the same cynicism and the apocalyptic will to hold on to power as other Arab autocrats. This was reflected in his readiness to spill blood, to accept a high death toll, and to give a carte blanche to the security forces and Alawite militias.

Louay Hussein, the secular editor and a leading figure of Syria's domestic opposition, shed light on the differences between Bashar's and Hafez al-Asad's regimes in a conversation in October 2010. According to Hussein, the father could build his legitimacy on two pillars: social development and the liberation of occupied territories (or at least the attempt to do so). He had the power to control the Islamists and was ready to fight. "Bashar got the power on the silver plate," Hussein said. He has been lacking the two pillars of his father. The younger man and his circle had "no knowledge and vision of the state's identity. They are playing around. They don't know what losing means because they didn't fight for anything and didn't face any real challenges."[54] The moment to fight came unexpectedly, and it turned out that the system failed. In the end, it was based on nothing more than hard power.

Chaos in Iraq

For a long time the disaster in Iraq played into the hands of the Syrian regime. The failure of the US occupying forces to gain the Iraqi peoples' confidence, the moral catastrophe stemming from the pictures of torture that came out of the American-staffed Abu Ghraib prison and the uncertainty about the future of Iraq all had positive repercussions for Syria. True, the relatively easy victory of the Anglo-American troops was initially a slap in the face for Syrian strategists. But when it became clear that the reconstruction of Iraq would be an extremely arduous process, Syria was able to capitalize on the situation.

During the Iraq war Sadiq Jalal al-Azm said that "it would strengthen the position of the regime here [in Syria] if Iraq were to sink into chaos, resistance, and civil war. The argument would be that we don't want to end up like Algeria, Lebanon, or Iraq."[55] In this respect, the regime had the majority of Syrians on its side. In 2011 the memory of chaos in Iraq and the ghost of civil war knocking at Syria's door became major arguments for those who feared change in Syria. It did not matter that Syrian society and political structures differed from those of the neighboring country. In the long run, the Anglo-American adventure in Iraq turned out to become a stabilizing factor for the Syrian regime.

6
The Negative Balance

I N SPITE OF SEVERAL STRONG PILLARS OF TRADITIONAL SUPPORT, the Baath regime faced a growing crisis of legitimacy during the months leading up to the 2011 revolts. The reasons were structural in nature and concerned the economy and domestic politics. International pressure cannot explain all of the difficulties that Syria faced. This chapter pinpoints key factors that contributed to an erosion of the pillars of the regime's legitimacy and stability.

Political Disillusionment

In his inaugural speech in June 2000 Asad made his position clear:

> We cannot apply the democracy of others to ourselves. Western democracy, for example, is the outcome of a long history that resulted in customs and traditions, which distinguish the current culture of Western societies. . . . We have to have our democratic experience which is special to us, which stems from our history, culture, civilization, and which is a response to the needs of our society and the requirements of our reality.[1]

Simply, this meant that the Baath Party would retain political leadership. When asked about political reform, the president later answered with stilted formulations such as: "We need an intellectual basis. There should be a connection between the political proposal and the social structure in society."[2] By this he implied that Syrian society was not yet mature enough for the population to participate in politics as in a Western-style democracy. In this discourse Asad differed not at all from his elder Arab counterparts in Egypt, Tunisia and elsewhere.

However, it should be recalled that, for many Arabs, after the war in Iraq the term "democracy" had become nothing but a hollow shell put forward by the United States to pursue its interests in the region. At the same time, Syrian intellectuals were becoming frustrated by Westerners who now were ascribing culturally-relative meanings to "democracy" and "human rights" in the hope that this would lead to better relations with the Syrian regime.

Michel Kilo from the Civil Society Movement strongly criticized French President Nicolas Sarkozy. In Kilo's view, Sarkozy, after his visit to Damascus in September 2008, started to parrot back Asad's rhetoric that the West had created its own version of democracy according to its history and culture, while Syria, with its particular culture would create a democracy of its own style. Kilo said that he told the French ambassador in Damascus that it was the French who created the notion of universal human rights.

"May I remind you as a Syrian that the National Convent of the French Revolution decided to treat every person as a Frenchman whose human rights were violated in France or abroad?" And now, said Kilo, the French president came to Syria and conceded to Asad that Syrians had another set of human rights and democracy than the West. "They should be ashamed," the intellectual scoffed.[3]

Asad, in contrast, defended his different take on Western-style democracy with cultural, societal and developmental arguments. As the former president of the Syrian Computer Society he liked to explain hard realities with software analogies: Asad spoke to Western leaders as he addressed this issue in an interview with the American TV station PBS in March 2006.

> If they want to understand me as a president, they have to understand whom I represent, and this is related to the culture of my people. . . . So, this is the problem with the West: If I want to make an analogy to two computers with different systems—if we talk about Windows—we notice that they do the same job but they have different systems. So, you have sometimes some software to make the translation between the two systems. We do not have to talk about the events; we have to explain and analyze these events and translate them from our culture to another culture. That is what we want from the media in your country and from the politicians. That is how they can understand, and then they will understand that we need peace, we need prosperity and we need reform.[4]

Asad elaborated on democracy from his inauguration onward, suggesting that Syria would follow the Chinese example: economic liberalization without no more than minor political reform at home—or "bread before freedom," as expressed by the entrepreneur, ex-member of parliament and regime critic Riad Seif.[5] An increasing number of opposition figures wondered if Asad still wanted political reform at all or if he was aiming for bread instead of freedom.

However, there were indications that Asad did have some kind of political reform agenda in mind at the beginning of his rule. In August 2000, a go-between telephoned Kilo with a message from the president. The mediator assured Kilo that reform would begin in one year. Kilo replied that Asad had three years' time. The mediator answered: "No, [reform must happen] in at least one and a half years."[6] After three years had passed, the Damascus Spring had been suppressed, and political reform was not in sight. Frustration in the opposition grew higher and higher. Kilo complained in 2003, "Bashar has allied himself with the corrupt forces. Thus he has basically renounced reform. . . . Bashar is not only unable to act, he does not want to act either." The president, he lamented, wanted to circumvent the issue of democracy. "He only wants a reform of power, not of the system." The regime was not able to reform itself in Kilo's view. Another leading member of the Civil Society Movement, who preferred to remain anonymous, came to a similar conclusion. "Bashar is aware of his weaknesses." For this reason he largely kept out of domestic politics and abandoned his originally ambitious reform program. "He has capitulated to the hardliners and opted for stability instead of progress."

This was true for all authoritarian regimes in the Arab world, observed Kilo. "They are not in a situation of stability but in a stable crisis." The Syrian government lost the connection to its own ideology. "It does not have the same flexibility or the same unity anymore." The authorities knew they had to change but did not have the means to do it. "This is part of the drama of these regimes," said Kilo. "When the regime in the Soviet Union wanted to reform itself, the regime was gone. It will happen the same way with the regimes in the Arab world."[7] Seven years later Kilo added with regard to Syria's eroding regional power: "The situation of the country is as dangerous as never before."[8] Against the background of the Arab Spring, Kilo's analysis eerily anticipated the later struggle.

Asad had probably tried out several methods to enable him to implement reform without destroying the government. "If there were free elections controlled by the UN, the president would be sure to win," said former Baath member Ayman Abdul Nour in 2004 in a quite realistic assessment. "But if he did this, he would admit that the past thirty years were illegitimate." This was an ideological dead-end. Nour conceded that if there were free parliamentary elections with new parties, the percentage of Baath Party members in parliament would surely have slipped below fifty percent. He added cautiously, "I don't know how much below fifty percent." The engineer considered the hardliners within the Baath Party as the greatest obstacle to progress in Syria and remained impatient and critical also after the significant reshuffling of the Party Congress in June 2005.

Nour was playing out his personal confrontation with the hardliners on his Internet portal www.all4syria.com which quickly became the most popular forum for the exchange of political opinions both inside and outside of Syria. Nour also posted critical texts from the Civil Society Movement on the web and sent them as electronic circulars. "The country must become pluralistic," he insisted. His former closeness to the president suggested that it was at least thinkable that Asad sympathized with his demand, although the two men had drifted apart over the years. [9]

Observers who still believed in Asad's good intentions saw a desperate fight taking place. After becoming president, Asad first tried to ally himself with the people against the machinery of power. He thus conjured up a new Damascus Spring that soon got out of hand in the view of the regime and was put down. After that he made an attempt to reform the institutions and bring new people and concepts into the administration. As this proved much harder than he had expected, he then concentrated on reforming the party. "This is the last step he can take," one analyst held. "If this doesn't work, he will be overtaken by the crisis. He may remain in power but he will no longer be part of the solution."

Asad's former minister for expatriates did not mince words. "When the whole institution is rotten, you can't do anything about it. You have to rebuild the institution." Even though reform had proven harder to carry out than everyone had hoped, Buthayna Shaaban gave the reassurance. "The reforms are supported by the president and many others in the government," she said. "We need people who believe in reforms and carry them out. The president can't go into each institute and reform it. We must do this ourselves, and we have political backing and the political mandate."[10] This was in 2004. Seven years had passed and now it was Shaaban who was sent to the first press conference after the upheaval had begun in order to persuade the angry protesters to have patience and take seriously the government's offers of political reform. No one was willing to listen anymore.

A reform of the administration as Asad intended in the beginning did not suffice in the view of many Syrians. Above all, the opposition's frustration stemmed from the crushing of the Damascus Spring in 2001. It had been a kind of glasnost when, in his inaugural speech, the young Asad had spoken out in favor of "accepting others' opinions." The opposition took him at his word and political debating clubs mushroomed. Criticism of the state of affairs was voiced more and more loudly. Initially, the president went along and dismissed the heads of the state radio and television companies as well as of the three state daily newspapers, *al-Thawra, al-Baath,* and *Tishreen.* The new editor-in-chief of *al-Thawra* was not even a party member. The paper became a courageous forum against corruption and mismanagement.

In September 2000, Syrian opposition members wrote the "Manifesto of the 99" under Michel Kilo's lead, followed in December by the "Manifesto of the 1000." It was the heyday of the young Civil Society Movement, composed mainly of intellectuals and academics. Their aim was both bread and freedom. Riad Seif, an independent member of parliament and an entrepreneur, went the furthest. In his companies, he held up social standards and put forward social-democratic ideas. Politically, he called for a constitutional state, a fair market economy, an independent parliament, independent courts, and a free media. Seif, who had gained the highest number of votes—more than 180,000—among the independent candidates in the parliamentary elections in 1998, established the Independent Parliamentary Block and called for the break-up of economic and political monopolies. This was a direct broadside against one-party rule. He had crossed the red line. In addition, he had dared to air details of a shady mobile phone deal between Syria and Egypt in which Asad's cousin Rami Makhlouf was to get a fifty percent share without making any investment. At that time Seif appeared more dangerous than intellectuals such as Kilo and others from the Civil Society Movement. He became too powerful since he was well-known and had potential mass appeal.[11]

The conservative forces around Asad called a halt. The first warnings came in February 2001. Soon the sharpest critics of the regime were arrested one by one, among them Seif in September. Member of Parliament Maamoun al-Homsi was also jailed, as were other activists of the Civil Society Movement, such as the economics professor Aref Dalila and Riad Turk, leader of the banned former Syrian Communist Party Politburo.[12] As an Alawite Dalila received the longest prison term of all and was released on 7 August 2008 (Seif in January 2006).

The Publishing Law of September 2001 was also a giant step backward. True, it permitted the operation of private newspapers for the first time since 1963, and many specialist magazines appeared alongside the caustic weekly magazine *al-Domari* (that was banned once again in July 2003). However, the strict conditions limiting freedom of the press gave rise to angry criticism and disillusionment among the Syrian people.

The regime fought the Damascus Spring with arrests and bans. Although the president had for a long time defied the conservatives, backing the Civil Society Movement and even supporting some of their aims, he was finally trumped by the hardliners, led by Vice President Abdul Halim Khaddam.[13] This corroborates the theory that Syria was experiencing a pluralization of power centers, and explained as well why critics of the regime—such as Hakam al-Baba, the last editor-in-chief of *al-Domari*, and even leading human rights activists such as Haitham Maleh and others—continued to stand up for the president personally for a long time.

In the meantime, some members of the opposition started to reflect critically on the events of the Damascus Spring, conceding that supporters wanted too much too quickly. Tayyeb Tizini, a liberal philosophy professor at the University of Damascus who studied in East Germany, recalled the wild months of the Spring. "First, I was with the Civil Society Movement, but then I distanced myself from it. They wanted all or nothing, and they would have destroyed everything. They wanted to storm the Bastille."[14] Some of the movement's supporters stressed that a too abrupt swing to democracy could lead to chaos and to a reinforcement of sectarian and radical forces—a frequent argument heard in 2011 as well. This was similar to what the government was saying. In any case, opinions differed as to the timing and the manner in which the country should be democratized.

After the Iraq war there were initial signs that the government was taking a step toward the secular opposition. Opposition supporters pricked up their ears in surprise when in May 2003, just after the war's proclaimed end, a central regime figure voiced approval for the opposition's prudence and even for its goals. Of all people, Bahjat Suleiman, the powerful head of the Syrian intelligence service, wrote in the Lebanese newspaper *al-Safir* that "in Syria,

108 SYRIA—A DECADE OF LOST CHANCES

the regime does not have enemies but 'opponents' whose demands do not go beyond certain political and economic reforms such as the end of the state of emergency and of martial law, the adoption of a law on political parties, and the equitable redistribution of national wealth."[15]

At any rate, the first parliamentary elections under Asad two months earlier had not brought any progress as far as the opposition was concerned. Competition was limited to eighty-three independent candidates. The results for two-thirds of the seats were predetermined as in previous years. Opposition candidates had not put their names forward for election in the first place or had withdrawn their candidatures in protest. Only a small percentage of the population went to the polling booths.[16]

Furthermore, Syrians witnessed a bitter setback in June 2004, three months after the Kurdish riots, when the government instituted a ban on political parties outside the National Front. Those parties had not been official anyway, but they had at least been permitted to be active. The regime threatened the party leaders with serious consequences if they did not observe the ban. This affected Kurdish organizations in particular. It remained unclear if the ban also extended to Nasserist, nationalist and other left-wing parties united in the so-called National Democratic Block, which had so far enjoyed a relative degree of freedom under Asad. The contradictory and unclear instructions about the party ban again suggested that there was a power struggle going on behind the scenes. The challenge became more and more urgent with new (illegal) parties popping up such as the Movement of Free Patriots, founded in Aleppo in June 2005 by members of the mercantile, professional and landowning communities.

According to the opposition, a law permitting new parties had been laying in a drawer for years. However, a first step in this direction was made when the Tenth Baath Congress in June 2005 recommended allowing new parties to exist independent of the leftist National Front. The measures aimed at creating a safety valve for opposition groups, although an important restriction stated that no parties would be allowed that followed an ethnic or religious agenda. This left Islamists and Kurds out of the political system unless they allied with other political forces—a wise step with regard to the rise of sectarian politics in the region. There might be another reason as well, for behind the scenes in Alawite circles there was talk of possible Alawite opposition parties if new sectarian-oriented parties were allowed. This would have been a sensation in Syrian politics.

Despite the recommendations of the Baath Congress, Ayman Abdul Nour and others remained pessimistic in the short run. He estimated that a new party law would not take effect before 2007 when Asad's second term as president was to start. Nour's prediction remained overly optimistic. Asad's 2007 inauguration speech was peppered with excuses why the reform process did not advance as quickly as hoped, because of which obstacles this or that measure was not yet implemented. It took another four years before the party law was taken out of the drawer and became an issue again under the intense pressure of the street.

Other opposition figures were equally disappointed by the results of the 2005 Baath Congress. In his opening speech, Asad avoided any allusion to political reform. Instead, in a remarkable admission of government failure, he mentioned "numerous difficulties because of the weakness of the administrative structure, the lack of qualified people, and because of the chronic accumulation of these problems." Thus he continued to focus on administrative reform instead of political changes. Asad announced as well that the upcoming local elections were to be completely free. This reminded one of the early 1970s, when Hafez al-Asad held free elections and awakened democratic hopes that were later crushed in the civil war with the Muslim Brothers.

Despite some important changes, critics wondered how long Asad would be able to present himself as the "good guy among bad guys." The long-awaited formation of a new government in September 2003 was not very encouraging. First of all, Asad had promised to limit the power of the Baath Party in everyday politics and to confine it to its leading ideological role. He announced that technocrats would become more influential in politics. But in the end there were eighteen Baath members serving under new Prime Minister Muhammad Naji al-Utri rather than the previous fifteen. Nearly half of the new ministers had belonged to the previous government. The fifty-nine-year-old Utri was an easy-going but rather colorless Baath cadre from Aleppo and an uncle of Asad's wife Asma. He did not deliver a very convincing performance at that time. But he did become a stabilizing and reliable factor. He stayed in office for eight years up to 29 March 2011 when the entire cabinet resigned in response to the escalating protests. On 3 April Asad appointed Adel Safar, the previous agriculture minister, as successor in a country that had been suffering a drought exacerbated by the authorities' poor governance.

For the Utri government in 2005 the president had set the agenda to reform the economy, the tax system, and the administration in order to create a better investment climate. The cases of the key reform-oriented ministers of his first cabinet, Issam al-Zaim (Industry) and Muhammad al-Atrash (Finance) were a painful setback. Zaim, who had fought resolutely against corruption and the parasitical caste of entrepreneurs in Aleppo, paid the highest price. He was charged with corruption on specious grounds and imprisoned until a court rehabilitated him in August 2004. These incidents show, however, that in serious situations Asad was either unable or unwilling to support the people he himself selected. In a similar turn of events in January 2005, Hussein Amash, a staunch reformer and one-time presidential confidante, was abruptly fired from head of the Agency for Combating Unemployment (ACU) by the prime minister. This was Amash's punishment for an interview he had given to the state newspaper *Tishreen* in which he criticized the sluggish reform process. Shortly before, the prime minister had cut the ACU's budget and subsumed it under the Ministry of Labor. Founded in late 2001, the organization that was once a showpiece of reform had been reduced to a facade. Amash did not even get an appointment with Asad after the incident.

On the other hand, in the third cabinet reshuffle of his presidency in October 2004, Asad managed to increase the number of reformers, if only slightly. The most prominent figures were undoubtedly Minister of Information Mahdi Dakhlallah and Minister of Interior Ghazi Kanaan, who (reportedly) committed suicide on 12 October 2005 after the turbulent events in Lebanon.

The appointment of Dakhlallah came as a surprise to many. Prior to his appointment, he served as editor-in-chief of the *al-Baath* newspaper. After he stressed the importance of freedom of speech and publicly questioned the leading role of the Baath Party in politics and society, many thought that Dakhlallah had committed professional suicide. More importantly, he said that the Baath Party and the smaller parties in the National Front had to participate in civil society. But instead of falling into disgrace, he became a minister. In the same month, the independent political magazine *Aswad wa Abyad* criticized the suppression of freedom of the press in Syria in a similarly blunt manner. The author of the magazine article advocated a liberalization of the strict publishing laws. Shortly before that, the magazine had dared to call for martial law to be eased. Interestingly, the paper was published by the son of the new defense minister, Hassan Turkmani.[17]

Dakhlallah introduced what were revolutionary changes for Syria; state television started to broadcast the cabinet's weekly meetings, and journalists were allowed to interview all of the ministers, including the minister of defense. A television reporter, who was placed in the Supreme State Security Court, also filmed trials of Kurds and protests in front of the court building. The Syrian Arab News Agency (SANA) was given instructions to quote UN resolutions in full, even when they were directed against Syria. The minister replaced the old TV and radio presenters with younger ones. Observers expected Dakhlallah to reform the strict press laws and to permit private political media.[18] However, this hope was in vain and Prime Minister Utri continued to ban private magazines.

Michel Kilo remained pessimistic throughout the ups and downs. Dakhlallah was very bold, he conceded. But after encouraging the journalists to write freely, he soon called them traitors, criticizing their bluntness and saying that they should write in the Washington Post, but not at home.

"I don't believe that Dakhlallah's words mean real reforms. They [those in power] utter such diverging statements in order to confuse the opposition. I think Dakhlallah tries to wrap the existing reality in different catchphrases."[19] Moreover, his ministry was a hotspot where the *mukhabarat* chiefs reigned alongside the conservative Foreign Minister Faruq al-Shara' and, until his resignation, Vice President Abdul Halim Khaddam.

In the fouth cabinet reshuffle in February 2006, Asad launched two major coups. As mentioned earlier, he appointed Faruq al-Shara' as vice president. One month later came the real surprise: Najah al-Attar, a veteran woman of letters, became the second deputy of Asad's and the first female vice president of Syria and in the Arab world. She was the first non-Baathist in this job since the party came to power in 1963. More strikingly, her brother, Issam al-Attar, was the leader of the Damascus Faction of the Syrian Muslim Brotherhood and lived in exile in Germany since the 1970s. But Najah had never shared her brother's opinions. She had been with the government since the 1970s and, among other positions, worked as minister of culture and in 2002 became director of the Syrian Center for the Dialogue of Civilizations. Her appointment sent an important message with regard to the role of women in Syrian society. Attar was still serving when the Arab Spring broke out.

There was a continuous and considerable reshuffling of positions under Asad. After two years as president, he had managed to replace three quarters of the approximately sixty leading officials in politics, the military, and the administration.[20] Technocrats who had distinguished themselves by good performance rather than party connections were also appointed to a large number of positions in the middle levels of administration. The top officials and ministers had a relatively clean record and had so far not been known, at least not publicly, for being involved in corruption.

But new brains did not necessarily come with new ideas. A confidanteof the president conceded that Asad failed to create his own power base during his first months in office. "He ought to have placed advisors with their own staff in the government palace so that their offices could support him institutionally. But he failed to do so because he was afraid of conflict with the government. He lost a lot as a result." Hafez al-Asad, by contrast, had his advisors, at least at the beginning. However, he closed their offices when they took up other positions. "He thought he came from Allah, and who could be an advisor to Allah?" my source joked.

The mortal Bashar al-Asad realized too late that he was dependent on a new power base. It was not until 2003 that he appointed close, well-educated friends as economic advisors—Haitham Saytahi and Nabras al-Fadil—but neither of them with staff of their own. Fadil, who was in charge of administrative reform, left in frustration in early 2005. "This is bad news for Western actors," a European diplomat in Damascus said in regret. Alluding to the events in Lebanon, Michel Kilo quoted Fadil as having said that "Bashar is a man who does not need advisors, who takes the most dangerous decisions within five minutes, who leads a presidency in which nobody really knows what his responsibilities are."[21]

The president had to struggle with the reputation that his decrees tended to gather dust and did not get implemented. The fact that he was knocking his head against the wall of the government machinery dented his credibility. The effects of the Party Congress in June 2005 and the far-reaching reshuffle in the party, government, and military increased the pressure on Asad to deliver, as it made any pretext of being hampered by obstructing hardliners more flimsy.

Another problem neglected by the regime was the Kurdish issue. This became clear on 12 March 2004, when the government paid a price for having shelved urgent problems once again.

It started quite harmlessly with a soccer match. The local al-Jihad team in Qamishli, the center of the north-eastern province mostly inhabited by Kurds, was scheduled to play against the al-Futwa team from the east Syrian town of Deir al-Zour that is strongly marked by Arab tribal ties. The Arab fans suddenly started waving posters of Saddam Hussein instead of their team's banners, while the Kurds responded by waving US stars and stripes. Before the match could begin, the two sides went for each other with stones and knives. Shots were heard instead of the kicking of a football. The security forces fired into the crowd and the unrest soon spread throughout the town. Kurdish rioters attacked the station and set fire to other official buildings such as schools and a grain factory. Some twenty people were killed and dozens were injured.

In the days that followed, the risk seemed high that the entire country would erupt in violence. Troops of Kurdish demonstrators rioted in several cities, including Aleppo and Damascus, setting fire to cars and fighting battles with the security police. Syrians held their breath, for they had not seen anything like this since the civil war with the Muslim Brothers. How could it happen? Did Asad still have the situation under control? He did, for the whole scare was over in a week. More than a thousand Kurds were arrested, with estimates as high as six thousand. Hundreds were sent to prison for several months.[22] A total of thirty-one people were killed in the riots.

However, the danger continued to smolder. It was the first time that collapsing post-war Iraq had a direct impact on its neighbor Syria. The new federalism in the recently created Iraqi constitution that grants a large degree of autonomy to the three Kurdish provinces in the north brought the Syrian Kurds back to the forefront. The Iraqi Kurdish leader Masoud Barazani provoked even more discussion by using the expression "Syrian Kurdistan."[23] The Baath Party had always viewed northeast Syria as an intractable spot. Bedouin life, tribal loyalties, and conservative Islam, together with a neglected infrastructure, combined to make it difficult terrain to control from the center of Damascus. Prior to the advent of satellite TV, Syrian journalists interviewed some inhabitants in the far north-east and asked them who their president was. They had answered with all seriousness Saddam Hussein.

During the riots in March 2004, even Kurdish party leaders in Syria admitted that they had lost control over their own people. Young Kurds, mostly teenagers, had taken things into their own hands and carelessly defied the government. Moreover, the Kurdish Workers Party (PKK), that operated in southeastern Turkey and had been led by the imprisoned leader Ocalan, also became active in northern Syria. In addition, the Israeli intelligence service Mossad operated increasingly in the Iraqi, Iranian, and Syrian Kurdish areas and inflamed feelings against the central administrations in order to weaken the nation-states (which contributed, among many other things, to the dismantling of the once good relationship between Turkey and Israel). At the same time, suspicion circulated that Arab hooligans had received support from dissenting groups within the Syrian machinery of power. The Arabs were supposed to have provoked the Kurds in order to destabilize the regime.

It appeared that both sides, Kurds and Arabs, might have received backing from third parties. Without aid it would have been difficult to organize countrywide uprisings over such a long period of time.[24] If true, this meant that it was not an ethnic problem, but a political one through and through. But regardless of the events in Iraq, the Syrian Kurds had a score to settle with the Syrian regime. A Syrian population census in 1962 simply ignored about ninety thousand Kurds in order to stop the demographic balance in the north tilting to the Arabs' disadvantage. Incidentally, even the Syrian army's then-general chief of staff and his family were among the Kurds who were deprived of Syrian citizenship. As a countermeasure, the Baath regime tried to settle Arabs in a belt along the Turkish border.

An estimated two to three hundred thousand Kurds remained without citizenship, including their descendants, and subsequently arrived illegal Kurdish immigrants from Turkey and Iraq. Syria never registered them as refugees on an international level. They were not allowed to travel or to own land, among other things. Meanwhile a total of one-and-a-half to two million Kurds are estimated to live in Syria, some of whom have been there for centuries. During the time of the Ottoman Empire, Kurdish tribes started to migrate back and forth across the present border between Syria and Turkey. Even after the fall of the empire, the Kurds were still allowed to cross the border between the two new states from 1919 to 1958. Some of them fled from ethno-national Kemalism to the more tolerant Syria in the south, where they also found better economic conditions because of land reform and comparatively advanced agricultural techniques. Thus, until recently Syria was a refuge for Kurds from the north.

Many Kurds had become assimilated and considered themselves Syrians

114 SYRIA—A DECADE OF LOST CHANCES

more than Kurds. The Kurdish language was forbidden in schools and public life under the Baathists. By contrast, on the other side of the border, the first Kurds were just starting to get public secondary school education in their own language following Turkish reforms. Kurdish activists in Syria had long been calling for more cultural autonomy and an ethnically neutral state. According to them, the state's name should be changed from "Arab Republic of Syria" to simply "Republic of Syria."[25] This name issue became a bone of contention again between Kurdish and Arab opposition groups during their meetings in Turkey in 2011 (see Chapter VII "The Opposition, Islam and the Regime")

However, there was no political unity among the Kurds either. They continued to be so strongly entrenched in tribal structures that there were twelve major (illegal) Kurdish parties in Syria, each one associated with a different tribe. The majority of Syrian Kurds were neither ethno-nationalists as in Iraq nor did they show themselves particularly receptive to Islamic fundamentalism that could be propagated as a unifying bond between Arabs and Kurds. Many Kurds used to sympathize with communism, but this influence was in decline.

The majority of Syrian Kurds have not yet been radicalized in any direction. But time was running out for the regime in Damascus to address their concerns about citizenship. Unlike the issue of religious minorities, the pan-Arab Baath ideology could not provide a solution in this case but was rather part of the problem. The balancing act between ethno-national pan-Arabism and Syrian nationalism appeared increasingly paradoxical against the background of a growing ethnicization of the region following the Iraq war.

Ironically, the riots in Qamishli almost brought about historic cooperation between government and opposition. It was an extraordinary event when representatives of the Civil Society Movement and leading figures of the Syrian human rights movement met in the office of the head of the National Security Service. The opposition offered help in finding a peaceful solution to the Kurdish problem, for none of them were interested in a violent revolution. The opposition feared that such unrest would set the reform efforts back for years, giving the government a pretext for tightening the reins. An old supporter of the Civil Society Movement said in frustration after the Kurds' revolt that "during the last fifty years they have ruled us under the pretext of liberating Palestine, and during the next hundred years they will rule us on the grounds of preserving Syrian unity."

The meeting between the representatives of the government and the opposition turned out to be disappointing. "The government refused to talk about politics," reported Anwar al-Bunni, "although the problem is a political one and not one of law and order." Only a small Kurdish minority called for a Kurdish state. "Most of them would be satisfied if they were given normal citizens' rights. Otherwise they will only get more radical." Most of the leaders of the Kurdish groups exercised a moderating influence after the riots. The

Civil Society Movement, for their part, spontaneously set up committees. Their representatives traveled to Qamishli and Deir al-Zour to pacify those involved in the riots. It is quite rare that a country can enjoy an opposition with such a sense of responsibility.

Bunni spoke to the Kurds in the Damascus suburb of Dummar and tried to appease them. "Not all Arabs are in favor of the regime and want to oppress you. There are many who are on your side!" Although the government refused to cooperate in these efforts with the Civil Society Movement, the latter helped to restore peace. "We won't allow the regime to drive a wedge between segments of the population," Bunni explained. "We aren't helping the government, we are helping our country." [26]

The Kurdish problem was an example of the regime's obstinacy. It preferred to wait out problems, but what was supposed to be strength proved to be weakness in the end. In July 2002, Asad had visited the Kurdish region and promised to tackle the citizenship problem, though nothing happened thereafter. Insiders said that Asad long ago drew up a plan to grant some of the Kurds Syrian citizenship, but that hard-line pan-Arab chauvinists in the Baath Party blocked his initiative. The primary individuals obstructing the plan in the machinery of government were Vice President Khaddam and the Baath cadre Muhammad Bukheitan. It was five minutes to twelve when the government, in an act of desperation, finally granted citizenship to placate the Kurds in the spring of 2011.

Asad often worked around Baath obstacles and claimed small successes as in March 2005, at a time when external pressures on Syria were mounting. In a gentlemen's agreement with Kurdish leaders, and in the name of "national unity," he had a large Kurdish pro-government rally staged in Qamishli of all places. In return, he released 312 Kurdish prisoners and promised to found an association dedicated to the promotion of Kurdish culture and interests.[27]

Whether the riots in March 2004 sped up or slowed down a more profound solution to the problem was a matter of dispute among members of the opposition. Asad and some members of the government continue to pledge that they would tackle the matter "very soon." Insiders anticipated that fewer than one hundred thousand Kurds would be granted Syrian citizenship. The government would continue to regard the rest as illegal immigrants who had trickled in over the years.[28] At the beginning of 2006, after Khaddam's defection, word of solving the Kurdish problem "soon" spread once again throughout the teahouses of Damascus. But nothing happened.

It had always been the regime's tactic to play the role of rescuer and pull a solution out of its quiver at the last moment. "On his desk Bashar has several files of matters to be resubmitted for discussion," one of the president's confidants explained in 2004. "One is labeled 'Kurdish issue' and others 'Release of Riad Seif' and 'Release of Maamoun al-Homsi.' There was also a file labeled 'Pay Raise' for civil servants that Asad took out just when Washington imposed the sanctions. He always waits for a suitable opportunity." Interpreted in a less strategic manner, it could be said that the obstructionists kept their feet on the brakes until events made it unavoidable to react. To what extent Asad himself was able to get these files resubmitted was a secret that remained hidden behind the palace walls. In the end, he turned out to act as much as an obstructionist as many around him.

Actions lost their political value when they were accomplished at the last minute or under strong pressure. This is how many saw the sudden reopening of the files of ex-members of parliament Riad Seif and Maamoun al-Homsi. Surprisingly, both were released from prison in January 2006, along with three other opposition figures from the Damascus Spring: Walid Bunni, Habib Issa, and Fawaz Tello. Each had been sentenced to five years in prison for violating the constitution and inciting sectarian strife. They became free men seven months before their terms ended. This early release of some of the most charismatic figures of Syria's opposition gave hope to many of a revival of the Damascus Spring. This hope was dashed only a few months later when in the second wave of suppression Michel Kilo, Anwar al-Bunni and other leading figures of the Civil Society Movement were re-arrested.

However, liberated Homsi made his voice heard once more in 2007 when the president was "re-elected." From his exile in Lebanon Homsi dubbed the referendum illegal and cited a list of breaches and intimidations by the security services throughout the voting process. He even called on the international community not to recognize the result of the referendum and to consider Asad's new term illegal.[29] In the referendum Asad gained ninety-seven percent of the votes as the only candidate, according to Syrian government sources.

In his second inauguration speech Asad focused on foreign policy. He offered Israel peace talks in case Israel was ready to hand back the Golan and withdraw to the 1967 borders. But despite a new agility in international affairs, not much changed when it came to domestic reform. The third wave of suppression against Syria's opposition began at the end of 2009 (see Chapter VIII "Syria's Policy Paradox"). Senior human rights advocate Haitham Maleh, head of the Human Rights Association of Syria (HRAS), was imprisoned in October. Also the popular Kurdish human rights activist and moderate spokesman of the Kurdish Future Movement, Meshal Tammo, was arrested again in 2009 (Tammo was brutally murdered in his home in Qamishli on 7 October 2011, one day before he planned to flee across the Turkish border being a member of the General Secretariat of the newly founded Syrian National Council). Travel bans were issued and intimidations of intellectuals became more frequent again. This included many less renowned figures who were arrested in those months or years. In particular, secular-minded intellectuals were threatened with travel bans as a first warning, often preceding arrests.

Embassies, development and cultural organizations reported increasing difficulties in getting access to government officials. Diplomats complained that communication had become more difficult with Syrian authorities; travel restrictions were imposed more heavily; questions to the administration were ignored or answers dragged on for simple administrative matters as much as for highly sensitive issues such as human rights. According to multiple reports, it had become increasingly difficult to get access to captives of dual nationality, and in 2009 foreign observers were banned from attending military tribunals (where most political defendants were judged).

Cooperation with analytical voices that had previously been approved by the government became more difficult, too. The Orient Centre for International Studies (OCIS), a think tank established by the foreign ministry and headed by Sami Altaqi, was closed in 2010. Apparently, the Centre's analysts had become too frank in assessing such critical issues as economic development and foreign policy. Also their contacts with foreigners were misinterpreted as the regime pursuing two-track diplomacy. A disappointed member of the OCIS said that the government was not interested in professional analysis any longer but restricted itself to "intellectual masturbation" within a small circle of its own.[30]

The case of Anwar al-Bunni exemplified the deteriorating domestic situation at the end of the decade. Bunni was supposed to run an EU-supported academy of human rights in Damascus. Although he was arrested partly because of this endeavor, the mere fact of this project showed that the European Commission in Damascus had held plausible the establishment of such a human rights center in Damascus at that time. Such an endeavor would have been unthinkable under subsequent conditions. At the same time, several opposition figures expressed sadness that, in their estimation, imprisoned activists had been "abandoned" by the Europeans. "It will be hard to find anyone who is ready to engage with the Europeans to build up a human rights center again be it in Syria or in any other Arab country," a member of Bunni's family lamented.[31] Given this situation, the Syrian opposition was apprehensive. After years of "Syria bashing," would the West now deal with the regime in a business-as-usual manner, turning a blind eye to persistent human rights violations.

In 2009 Kilo described the situation in Syria as follows, alluding to the tense atmosphere of civil war and the subsequent massacre of Hama in 1982:

> The regime has the feeling that it is standing at the abyss and is facing nothing but enemies. The one who kills [Lebanon's Prime Minister Rafiq] Hariri, the one who kills [Samir] Qassir [an anti-Syrian journalist in Lebanon killed in summer 2005], the one who imprisons me who was committed to reconciliation, who was against the Iraq war and the United States, lives in the atmosphere of Hama.[32]

Corruption

Corruption pervaded all areas of public life. The Baathist system of patronage acted as a broad framework in which corruption flourished. The low pay of public service employees was another factor. Students were able to buy their degrees at universities, especially in the faculty of law. This frustrated a lot of young people and deprived bright students of possibilities for promotion. The recruitment of the elite was so distorted that many young Syrians only saw a future abroad.

Corruption in the administration, judiciary, police, and customs, and the awarding of public contracts was one of the main reasons for paralysis in the Syrian economy. The military was also affected. Officers and their soldiers had built up a parallel economy with little "military fiefdoms."[33]

Asad had had a Mr. Clean image when he took office and put the fight against corruption on his agenda. But the resistance inherent in the system proved stronger. After the Iraq war, a group of French experts was invited to Syria to inspect the system and make suggestions for improvements. There was little hope that this new attempt would bear fruit. According to Michel Kilo, the chairman of the new institute for administrative reform was himself "one of the most corrupt officials of the Syrian state," with a counterfeit degree and a record of embezzlement.[34]

The Economic Time Bomb

On the door of the Syrian Chamber of Commerce in Damascus is pinned a saying that merits thought: *Minuka al-'ata wa minna al-wala'*. You give us [prosperity], and we will give you loyalty.

This may sound like cynical opportunism in the environment of a Baath regime that demanded an ideological following, but the slogan is by no means new. The idea can be found in a similar form in Western state theories. Jürgen Habermas, for example, is convinced that in modern, democratic societies, commitment to the nation is linked to the efficiency of the welfare state.[35] But this saying was to be taken much more literally in Syria: if the regime distributed enough goodies to vital persons and posts, it could be sure that criticism of the leadership would remain low. If the economy was ailing and the predatory state was no longer able to hand out the same benefits, this lack would very soon have an impact on the stability of the regime.

Raymond Hinnebusch classified Syria as a model of a Middle East populist authoritarian regime that came into being after the colonial powers withdrew. The national elites of these regimes saw themselves exposed to external threat and internal instability. At first, they looked to the military and the administrative machinery for support. At the same time, these new leaders tried to extend their social base to the lower middle class and thus increase their legitimacy. Authoritarian regimes attempt to guard their independence with "defensive modernization." They enter the worldwide capitalist system, attempting to establish industries for imitating and producing cheap consumer goods in order to avoid becoming dependent on imports (import substitution). It is the state that takes charge in these matters while the industrial bourgeoisie remains weak.[36]

Dahi and Munif explained that through these kinds of policies the Syrian state was not able to accumulate capital of its own. The state maintained its role as a distributor being dependent on oil revenues, development aid and other payments. The government did not develop competitive sectors in manufacturing or industries of its own but remained dependent on revenues from the agrarian sector (precisely this criticism has been brought forward by the entrepreneur Riad Seif as depicted in Chapter VII). The regime used its oil revenues to finance social programs like free education, health care, and subsidized products. Despite their official cooptation, professional associations of peasants, workers or lawyers lost their autonomy and negotiating leverage. The main goal was securing the machinery of power.[37]

In Syria's state patronage system, big orders went to large families loyal to the regime or to members of the president's clan. Prominent examples were licenses for the mobile phone network and foreign car agencies. One of the richest beneficiaries of the corrupt patronage economy was the Makhlouf clan, from Asad's mother's family branch. A detailed, but anonymous, April 2011 study estimated the empire of Rami Makhlouf at 111 billion Syrian Pounds ($2 billion); others put it even as high as $3 billion.[38] Syrian analysts said he made a million dollars a day. Besides the two mobile phone companies, he also owned the port of Latakia, numerous key factories, hotels, duty-free shops, and private schools—or "half of the country," as Syrians lamented, shaking their heads in resignation. The fact that Asad allegedly kicked Makhlouf out of the country as part of an anti-corruption campaign in early 2005 diminished neither his wealth nor his political influence.[39] The same held true when Makhlouf surprisingly "resigned" from his economic activities in 2011 after he had uttered apocalyptic threats against the international community if the regime were to fall (see Chapter II "Regime Reflexes and Reactions").

The parasitical entrepreneurs depended entirely on the regime's protection. Political power and economic success converged in what leftist scholars call "authoritarian neo-liberalism."[40] The money flowed into their pockets and not into the domestic economy as new investments. This tendency was reinforced by the monopoly of licenses. Entrepreneurship thus remained politically conservative and sought the regime's cover, including protection from foreign competition. An economic divide-and-rule situation developed instead of an economically and socially vibrant entrepreneurship. A European diplomat in Damascus described it as a "segmentation of the bourgeoisie." The caste loyal to the regime, the oligarchic bourgeoisie, was especially strong in Damascus. In addition, there were those who worked as top bureaucrats in the state machinery and obtained juicy commissions. As a rule, they were also close to the president's family. Sometimes they were referred to as the "state bourgeoisie."[41]

Apart from this parasitic caste—or the Mafiosi, as Syrians called them—there were two other groups of businessmen. One group consisted of long-established merchants whose traditions go back hundreds of years as landowners and traders. Among them are merchants in the old suqs, whose shops may be less than three square meters in size, but who enjoy a surplus of profitable business connections. The other group was the new entrepreneurs, alternatively called the business society. Their members were often educated abroad and brought in foreign capital. These two groups were the "true entrepreneurs" who pressed especially strongly for the abolition of Mafiosi privileges and for liberalization of the economic system.[42]

Increasing friction developed between these groups. Their dispute reached violent proportions in the business metropolis of Aleppo, where rival gangs flourished. Segments of the *mukhabarat* were also said to be involved in the gang fighting. In this respect, the Syrian law and order state was losing its grip. This gave a boost to gangs and private security troops while frustrating the general population. One reason for the dispute was that the above-mentioned slogan at the Chamber of Commerce no longer applied across the board. The government was unable to hand out such large sums of money to the parasitic caste of entrepreneurs, who in addition were experiencing increasingly keen competition from the new business class. This confrontation extended into government circles, where those wishing to curb the reform process represented the interests of the parasitic bourgeoisie and opposed the liberals.

Michel Kilo accused the government of buying entrepreneurs and sectors of the middle class as an "alternative to reform." Without this strategy, Kilo said, there would be a risk that young members of the bourgeoisie in particular would dissociate themselves from the regime. "This is exactly the reason why the rulers need Iraq and Lebanon as sources of money," Kilo added.[43] What Kilo had in mind was, above all, the cooptation of the powerful Sunni merchant class particularly in Damascus and Aleppo who mostly stuck to the regime—or at least kept quiet—for a long time despite the escalation of protests in 2011. In an analysis of the historic alliance between the predominantly Alawite military officer corps and the Sunni merchant-business class from Hafez al-Asad times until 2009, Salwa Ismail came to the conclusion "that we are witnessing the reproduction of a religio-mercantile complex that may contribute to further disintegration of the regime."[44] By 2004, Samir Altaqi was painting a sober scenario. "This system is in the process of collapsing," he said dryly as he took a sip from his cup of strong Arabic coffee, sitting of all places in the Café Havana in the colonial center of Damascus.

Dahi and Munif pointed out that in more recent times the predatory oligarchy had stopped forming alliances. "The military junta became the new bourgeoisie itself." The political / military and economic spheres converged, while the cronies depended on a working measure of neo-liberal arrangements. This isolation from other societal actors narrowed their political options in times of crisis.[45]

Nevertheless, the alliance between the Alawite military officer corps and the Sunni merchant-class proved more resilient than many had thought during the protests in 2011. Part of the explanation was that prominent businessmen who had integrated into this stratum had high stakes in the regime. Among them were sons of high-ranking Baath politicians who profited from privileges and predatory arrangements of the status. Although some of them had pushed for reform, they were probably not interested in the collapse of the regime. An example was Firas Tlass, son of the long-term defense minister Mustafa Tlass, and Bilal al-Turkmani, son of Tlass' successor in the ministry, Hassan Turkmani. By contrast, traditional members of the "national bourgeoisie"[46] felt increasingly estranged by the abuse of influence and crooked business practices of regime cronies such as Makhlouf. Here was a possible breaking point the regime had to fear when tensions were rising. Some disillusioned members of this segment such as Ihsan Sanqer turned into major financiers of the rising opposition in exile in 2011 (see Chapter VII "Opposition, Islam and the Regime"). Against this background it was not surprising that ninety percent of financial support for the Syrian National Council came from such entrepreneurs, according to SNC President Burhan Ghalioun.[47]

In old times the elder Asad had run a clever foreign policy as far as securing sources of money, and his son attempted to follow in his footsteps. Analyst Samir Altaqi described the method as follows: Syria received money from Arab states in 1967 because it was engaged in a war with Israel, again in 1973, and once more in 1976 when Syrian troops intervened in the civil war in Lebanon. Then, in 1982, Syria was given support when Israel invaded Lebanon and occupied the southern part of the country. At the same time, Asad secured extensive debt relief from the Soviet Union in exchange for approving the Russian invasion of Afghanistan. In the Gulf War in 1991, Asad did a U-turn and accepted financial aid from the Gulf States, primarily Kuwait, as thanks for supporting the coalition troops against Iraq. Finally, in another U-turn, money flowed from Baghdad after an unexpected honeymoon with the Saddam regime after 1997, and especially after Hafez al-Asad's death. Altaqi concluded that "the best export product Syria has is its foreign policy."

"This explains why a Syrian employee only has to work thirty-seven minutes a day on average, and can still enjoy free health care and a free educational system," said the analyst with a grin. "The political welfare system is the main instrument of social appeasement. Redistribution, not production, is the priority of the Syrian government. The system of corruption is a political system of loyalty."The Syrian people were getting increasingly impatient for economic reform. Initially, hopes were high. Hafez Asad had placed foreign policy in the foreground, subordinating economic policy to "the requirements of the battle" and making reform dependent on peace with Israel. In contrast, Bashar, in his first years, turned the agenda upside-down and recognized that a modernization of the country was long overdue. Previously, reforms had only been doled out piecemeal to avert worse situations, without any logical overall concept. Asad wanted to change this. A number of draft laws had been gathering dust in drawers for years and were put on the agenda again after he took office. In spite of this, the few reforms that have materialized continued to resemble his father's patchwork approach.

It soon became clear that foreign policy and not economic development was and remained the first priority also under Bashar al-Asad. Otherwise, for example, Syria would not have suddenly opened its markets for Turkish products which flooded the Syrian suqs and aggravated the pressure on domestic manufacturing. And if economic development and well-being had been a state goal, the Syrian regime would have thought twice about rejecting the last efforts undertaken by Turkey and the Arab League to settle the conflict peacefully in 2011. Instead, the regime remained obstinate, put up with international sanctions and acquiesced to the erosion of its own economic foundations.

Later on when Syrian-Turkish relations had soured beyond repair and economic sanctions replaced free trade agreements, Asad suddenly admitted that the "agreement between Syria and Turkey wasn't fair." He acknowledged friction with the Syrian business sector about his open policies with Turkey. "It was against our interest. . . . most of the economic sector were against it, and they asked our government many times to stop working with this treaty."[48] From this new perspective Asad tried to justify sanctions against Turkey and played down the impact of international sanctions against Syria starting from the end of 2011.

While foreign policy goals dominated the agenda throughout the years, the regime had still implemented cautious economic reform. It granted relief for investments and foreign trade. Investors were allowed to buy land and had easier access to foreign currency. A stock exchange took up its work in 2009. Private banks started to operate in Syria in 2004, although with some bureaucratic restraints. For the average consumer, the most obvious signs of change were the automatic teller machines that mushroomed in the cities. Sometimes they were clad in white marble, as if to underline optically this precious achievement: the exit from the financial Stone Age. I can still remember, only a few years ago, when foreign students had to reserve a weekend to travel to Lebanon in order to withdraw US dollars to then exchange in Damascus.

Other reform measures included cutting lending interest rates, encouraging corporate ownership reform, and allowing the Central Bank to issue treasury bills and bonds for government debt. Despite undeniable progress, Syria could not compete with countries such as Jordan or Lebanon when it came to the investment climate, taking into account the regime, legal security, training and worker qualification. Syria's advantages were low production costs on the one hand and its geography on the other. Its proximity to the EU market has been an asset, as was its permeable border with Turkey until both countries turned against each other again in 2011. Syria could make more use of its central position as a trade hub. The rapprochement with Turkey and the booming consumer demand in Iraq were encouraging developments.

Asad has repeatedly admitted that economic reform was not proceeding as quickly as he would have liked. "It is true that there is tardiness," he conceded in an interview in May 2003. "We have somebody who is pushing the process in the right direction; there is somebody who is pushing it in the wrong direction, and somebody who is pulling it back." Thus he alluded to the so-called old guard who shied away from economic reform as much as from a political opening. "But this does not mean that I have changed," the president added, "and it does not mean that I'm not working to achieve what I have said."[49] This was a reference to his inaugural speech on 17 July 2000, when he underlined the need for change and gave the opposition reason for hope.

Syria, a country poor in raw materials, was still able to amass the third largest foreign currency reserves in the Arab world, at times between $12 and $17 billion. Compared to the size of the Syrian economy, these reserves equaled between six and eight months of imports at that time. The debt ratio in 2010 went up to an estimated twenty-eight percent of the nation's GDP from close to ten percent in 2004. If these figures can be believed (a caveat that has to be made for all the subsequent statistics, too), this remained a sound figure compared to other countries, including European ones. The current budget deficit of 2010 remained at a low 4.2 percent of GDP, according to international estimates. In late 2004 and early 2005, Syria achieved advantageous debt deals with a number of former Soviet Union countries, including Russia, Poland, Slovakia, and the Czech Republic. With Russia, for example, Damascus achieved a debt reduction of seventy-three percent from $14.5 billion.[50] The country was not able to uphold its trade surplus that it had held for years.

According to the World Bank, the average per capita income (GDP per capita) in Syria rose from $3,480 in 2003 to $5,120 in 2010. Despite the global economic crisis and decreasing oil exports Syrian economic growth remained in the four to five percent range between 2008 and 2010 with a peak of six percent in 2009. This coincided with the golden period of international and regional détente for Syria. The government strove to increase the growth rate to six to seven percent by 2010 with the help of advanced reforms. However, it growth came in at a disappointing 3.2 percent. The Syrian economy suffered far worse during the months of revolt and subsequent international sanctions. Economic growth slumped to minus two to minus ten percent, according to differing estimates.[51] These figures prove more painful when they are contrasted with Syria's demography. The country has one of the highest population growth rates worldwide, although it declined considerably in the recent years. In 2011, it was an estimated 2.4 percent; it reaches nearly three percent if one takes a longer time period into account.[52] During Asad's period of government alone the population increased by nearly eight million to twenty-two million.

Every year two to three hundred thousand young people crowded the labor market, and more and more of them were women. The public sector that employed about a quarter of the working population, did not create more than twenty thousand jobs annually since the mid-1990s.[53] Independent estimates put the Syrian unemployment rate as high as thirty percent, while official government figures put it at 8.2 percent in 2010.[54] It remained difficult to establish who could be counted as part of the labor force and who not in a setting where family businesses, irregular working conditions, and child labor played a role.

Although still better than neighboring countries, the gap between rich and poor had steadily grown in recent years. It was estimated around the middle of the decade that five percent of the population owned fifty percent of the nation's wealth, and it was probably higher at the end of the decade. Child labor, cuts in education funding, and growing poverty had a negative impact on the population's level of education.[55] Between eleven and thirty percent of Syrians are said to live below the poverty line, mostly in the less developed rural areas close to the Turkish and Iraqi borders, scenes of upheaval in 2011.[56] The system of traditional, extended families has still helped to prevent social need, but these issues were to become increasingly pressing in the future without a social security system. This was a crucial factor that threatened to undermine the legitimacy of the regime.

Asad himself posed the key question in an interview soon after the beginning of the Iraq war: "How do we achieve real economic reform without harming the social make-up of the country?" .[57] The call for a better and more coherent public policy was not restricted to opposition figures but could be heard from many Syrian observers and foreign experts as well. The major economic constraints included declining oil production, high unemployment, rising budget deficits, and increasing pressure on water supplies caused by heavy use in agriculture, rapid population growth, industrial expansion and water pollution.

A Syrian analyst said in 2009 with regard to the economy that Syria "is undergoing an existential crisis." An internal government study titled, "Syria 2025" supposedly projected various scenarios for economic reform was kept from the public because it described a "nightmare." Crop reserves had been exhausted and needed to be imported from the Gulf. Under Hafez al-Asad cereal had been a strategic asset of Syria. Desertification proceeded rapidly because of the illegal use of land and the destruction of plants. The poverty belts around cities grew and the middle class was weakened. The analyst said that Syria needed an investment of $50 billion to maintain and develop its infrastructure but investments from the Gulf sagged. Whenever Syria signed free trade agreements with Arab states or China it was the loser because Syrian domestic products could not compete.[58]

Reformers aimed to replace the costly and ineffective system of across-the-board subsidies with a social security system targeted at the needy. However, for this purpose they needed more statistics and data, and unfortunately few of the necessary preparations were taking place. Instead, the cutting of subsidies that amounted to some ten percent of GDP,[59] started without shock-absorbing measures in place, which ultimately hurt the poor much more than the rich. For example, in October 2004 the government increased the price of industrial diesel oil by a stunning 450 percent. Electricity and cement prices were next on the list.

These were hard but necessary steps toward a more liberal and dynamic economy. But changes remained selective in nature and were limited to measures that did not affect the vested interests of the president's immediate entourage or of the big businesses that had become the main pillars of regime support. In addition, external shocks such as the Iraq war, including US pressure, and the government's fear of social protests in the midst of other domestic challenges all led to a cautious approach. Inconsistencies were also due to a tug of war behind the scenes between those who promoted reform and those who feared the loss of privileges or even the collapse of the Baath polity. Therefore, public policy measures were often taken and afterward revised. During the controversial raise of diesel prices, eighteen different laws had been enacted. Trial and error instead of a long-term vision seemed to be the rule. Recommendations of various expert committees appointed by the president since 2001 were not implemented.[60]

In addition, Syrians experienced an inflation that was unprecedented for most of the young population. Semi-socialist coziness was giving way to harsher capitalist winds and created fear. By mid-2005, visitors could see that taxi drivers, shopkeepers, and traders were showing less of their characteristic *shami* (Syrian) relaxedness, instead becoming more insistent on making a living. Used to an inflation of less than one percent over the years, Syrians were confronted with price hikes such as 4.8 percent in 2003 that increased up to a stunning 15.4 percent in 2008[61] This was a consequence of rising consumer prices, the pay raise, the new Consumption Tax law (a temporary measure preparing the way for a more sophisticated value added tax or VAT), and of the strong euro. The latter put the Syrian lira under pressure, further raising the costs of imports. Moreover, real estate prices rose dramatically.

Among other causes was the influx of Iraqi refugees settling in Damascus. However, inflation soon settled down again to 2.6 percent in 2009 and 5.9 percent in 2010. But the positive signals were short-lived since in the year of the upheaval the Lira plummeted again. People also withdrew private assets from Syrian banks in great numbers and the government's foreign exchange cushion was used to finance the crackdown. During a tightening budget squeeze because of international sanctions, public salaries were not regularly paid anymore in 2011 and after, according to opposition reports.

The economic modernization in the growing private sector was in stark contrast to the encrusted state structures and the old-fashioned setup in the public sector. Up to 1991, Hafez al-Asad had inflated the public sector to 1.2 million employees. Under the first years of Bashar they grew to 1.6 million.[62] Thus, in spite of the generally low state salaries (plus benefits such as cheap housing and holiday chalets), a large number of families depended on the survival of the regime. And they were brought under direct control of the regime.[63]

The collapse of the Baath regime in Iraq dealt an additional temporary blow to the Syrian economy before it was able to profit from rising consumer exports to its eastern neighbor. Asad conceded that foreign investments declined, as not only foreigners but also Arab investors kept their distance.[64] Syria received a paltry $1.7 million in Arab direct investment in 2003, or 1.12 percent of all inter-Arab investments. This was less than a twentieth of what much smaller Lebanon received. In the same year, trade slumped by twenty-two percent from its previous level.[65] However, from 2005 to 2010 the Syrian economy picked up again and managed to attract considerable investment from the Gulf region. The growing antagonism between Syria and the most affluent Gulf countries starting with the protests in 2011 also dried up the flow of investments.

Nevertheless, Iraq's cheap oil was especially missed in Syria. Before the war, Syria imported oil at dumping prices behind the back of the UN-controlled Oil for Food Program, with the United States turning a blind eye. Syria was able to sell the surplus from its own production at a profit abroad in return for foreign exchange. Once the US troops gained control of oil production in Iraq, they turned off the tap for the pipeline to Syria. The loss of cheap oil from Iraq and falling oil prices was estimated at twenty percent of the official state budget.[66]

Decision-makers in Syria were aware of the fact that Syrian oil resources soon would be exhausted.[67] This produced an immense structural shock. The entire Syrian economic system was sitting on a time bomb. Hops turned to Syria's large natural gas resources. As this book was being written, the mid-term effects of international sanctions against Syria, including a ban of oil exports to Europe, could not yet be established. It can be assumed that the oil embargo which took effect on 15 November 2011 was a blow to the Syrian budget since an estimated ninety-five percent of Syria's crude exports were bought by European countries.[68] The scarcity of oil led to substantial power-cuts that caused production fallout in industrial areas around the country. A further reflection of economic decline was that the private weekly economic magazine al-Iqtissadiya halted its production at the end of December 2011. The reasons given were the economic situation and the lack of financial means.

Another significant income stream—tourism—collapsed entirely in 2011. After 9/11, because of stricter visa policies, many Arab travelers shifted from US and European destinations to closer resorts. In 2004, after the turbulence of the Iraq war had settled down, some two-and-a-half million tourists crossed the border to Syria, pouring $2 billion into the Syrian economy and creating approximately one hundred thousand new jobs. This number skyrocketed to more than 6 million tourists in 2009 with a growth rate of twelve percent compared to the previous year.[69] Nevertheless, the tourism sector did not live up to its full potential and was in urgent need of reform compared to the performance of neighbors such as Jordan or Lebanon.[70]

During most of Asad's rule, Syria lived under sanctions that progressed from bad to worse, a downward path punctuated with moments where relief seemed possible. Since 2004, the country was subject to a more stringent American embargo under the Syrian Accountability and Lebanese Sovereignty Restoration Act (SALSA). President George W. Bush hesitated for a long time before signing the sanctions into effect, finally yielding to great pressure from Congress. The consequences in Syria were economic but also political. They increased anti-American sentiment in Syria's streets.[71] The sanctions were controversial from an economic point of view. Even before their introduction, there had been no civilian airline flights to the United States, and the mutual trade in goods had been relatively small, accounting for only five percent of Syrian exports. Of course, there was one exception: American firms were still allowed to drill for oil in Syria and earn money in other sectors. Neither had there been any restriction in diplomatic relations.[72] Syrian Trade Minister Ghassan Rifai was one of the few to admit publicly that the sanctions were also harmful. They were deterring investors at a time when Syria needed them most. [73]

Syria's rapprochement with Turkey was not only a foreign policy coup but had also wide economic repercussions. In a quieter undertaking, Syria proved ready to restore relations with its southern neighbor Jordan. At the beginning of 2005, the two countries solved a border dispute that had been smoldering for decades, ever since the French and the British had drawn the line in 1931. Syria agreed to hand over one hundred twenty-five square kilometers of land to Jordan, while it recovered 2.5 square kilometers from its neighbor.

In its effort to find new partners, Syria put out feelers even further abroad. Asian countries strengthened their position as providers for the Syrian market with a considerable increase in import shares. Asad visited China in June 2004, the first time a Syrian president had been there since the beginning of diplomatic relations between the two countries in the late 1950s. In the beginning, however, China did not show overwhelming interest in an extensive and strategic political alliance. Instead, the Chinese pressed the Syrians to fight red tape and facilitate trade. Pragmatism prevailed even if the two socialist states had taken a similar path: a cautious economic opening without political reform. But Chinese support of Syria became a matter of principle and anti-Western ideology in the crucial months of 2011 when China blocked efforts to condemn the regime for its violence against the civil protests.

A new rapprochement with Moscow proved even more important because it had more strategic depth. Asad freshened up relations with Russia during his state visit there in January 2005, the first by a Syrian head of state since 1999. Besides boosting economic ties, he was interested in purchasing missiles and seemed to have found in Russia one of the few remaining states that would sell weapons to Syria. For the Russian government the military port in Tartous was of significant value: it represented Russia's only outpost on the Mediterranean. In 2006, both countries had agreed to develop the marine base that had previously existed in Soviet times and now hosted some 600 troops. In turn, Russia waived three quarters of Syria's old debts amounting to 13.4 billion USD. For this reason and for the big volumes of arms exports to Syria, the Russian government decided to support the regime in Damascus as long as bearable irrespective of breaches of humanitarian principles committed by the regime and despite Russia's deteriorating reputation among a growing share of Syria's population.

The rapprochement between Syria and Russia reflected a revival of Cold War alliances. After the fall of Libyan leader Muammar al-Qaddafi it was only Algeria and Syria that remained as Russian allies in the Arab world. The nascence of Cold War-style trench warfare has been boosted by efforts to contain US neoconservative aspirations in the region. Despite an intervention by then Israeli Prime Minister Ariel Sharon shortly before Asad's visit to Moscow in 2005 then Russian President Vladimir Putin stuck to his promise to sell the Syrians mobile short-range air defense systems. During his first visit to Israel in April of the same year, the Russian president justified his arms sale to Syria and stressed that it would not tip the balance of power in the Middle East. In a somewhat snide comment he added, "This will, of course, complicate low-flying flights over the residence of the Syrian president, but I'm not sure that such flights would be a good idea if we all, including in the interest of the Israeli people, want to create an atmosphere favorable to the pursuit of the peace process."[74] This must have filled Asad with glee, for he had been furious when Israeli warplanes buzzed his presidential palace in Damascus in August 2003.

With this stand, Putin suggested that he saw a new possibility of increasing Russia's curtailed influence in the Middle East through Syria, just like in old times. Both sides also agreed to intensify their commercial relations, which had fizzled out. In December 2005, Russian parliamentarians who visited Damascus underlined Russia's support for Syria in the aftermath of the Hariri killing. If Russia had to choose between defending US or Syrian interests in the region, it would definitely opt for Syria, they said.[75]

Another reason for Russia to support the Syrian regime has rarely been mentioned. It may originate from the ancient desire to act as a protecting power of the Orthodox Christian minority in the region. This reflects old alliances that are reminiscent of the Christian pogroms of 1860 when Russia appeared on the scene equally as a protector of the Orthodox population.

On another front, closer ties with the European Union did not materialize after a small window of opportunity had closed. Many Syrians saw Europe as a counterweight to the United States and as a moderate force that could have lent them support. As a result, Syria brought renewed energy to discussions of an Association Agreement with the European Union, after such talks had come to a standstill in 1998. Syria was one of the few missing links among the states bordering the Mediterranean in the brokering of the so-called Barcelona Process. The reformers also saw the agreement as an important step toward membership in the World Trade Organization (WTO).

Yet negotiations suddenly turned highly explosive when Great Britain and Germany wanted Syria to sign a more sharply worded memorandum against weapons of mass destruction. Damascus protested that the EU displayed a double standard in this matter, as it had long before signed an Association Agreement with the nuclear power Israel. The EU states were split down the middle: supporters of the agreement accused their opponents of pursuing an American policy and of attacking Syria too one-sidedly. The decision did not become easier with East European countries entering the EU. Syria has to take a share of the blame as well. When the Europeans were ready to sign the agreement, the conservatives within the regime had slammed on the brakes, warning that Syria was in danger of losing its independence. In reality, they feared that an open market would endanger their privileges. Apart from this, the majority of "ignorant apparatchiks" did not recognize the benefits of the agreement, as the former member of the Syrian negotiating team and today's ambassador to London, Sami Khiyami, conceded. "It was Bashar who spurred on the Syrian negotiating team to reach an agreement," Khiyami said.[76] But at the same time, it was Asad who, in the first months of 2004, rarely passed up an opportunity to make a provocative statement involving the issue of weapons of mass destruction. Such weapons were easy to get and could be justifiably stockpiled as long as Israel possessed them, he blustered. In addition, media reports speculated that Syria had tinkered with a nuclear program and also had chemical weapons.[77]

Have no doubt: the ball was in Syria's court. Those in charge had to consider whether it was worth sacrificing political rhetoric for the sake of economic opportunity, especially since they had already gone such a long and arduous way in their negotiations. During the negotiations, the Syrians were willing to make several concessions that they had previously refused to make. One point was the human rights clause, which was a normal part of the agreement, and the formulation concerning the fight against terrorism. It seems that American pressure had an indirect impact here.

Many of the benefits were more of a political value in the long run. The Syrian negotiators hoped that the agreement would bring Syria and the EU closer together (on the issue of the Israeli-Palestinian conflict as well), attract European investors, and above all trigger domestic economic reform. The cat-and-mouse game continued until October 2009. Then it was the Europeans who were ready to sign but Syria that decided otherwise. Europe had lost strategic importance to Syria after Syria felt increasingly comfortable in its new foreign policy setting, especially with Turkey as an ally. "The Europeans need Syria but Syria doesn't need the Europeans any longer," as a Syrian analyst summed up the attitude of the Syrian government. More and more voices also raised concern about negative effects of such an agreement on local manufacturers.[78]

Each side had its share of missing opportunities. Syria decided to look north and eastward instead of westward. In any event, when the violence in the country spread, cooperation between the EU and Syria was stopped. All bilateral cooperation programs were suspended as were all preparations for new bilateral treaties. The Association Agreement with Syria was definitely dead at that point. Moreover, in December 2011 Syria suspended its membership in the Mediterranean Union.

Instead of making compromises with the EU, Syria showed readiness to apply a different set of economic strategies to its economy by acceding to the Greater Arab Free Trade Agreement (GAFTA). Following this, Syria had reduced its tariffs to zero for its Arab neighbors by 2005. However, in the wake of a package of international sanctions GAFTA also suspended Syria's membership in 2011.

All in all, the greatest challenge was to cushion economic reform so that its social side effects would not endanger the complex web of alliances and thus the power base of the regime. This was a delicate tightrope walk for those in power. Social imbalance also brought also the risk of fostering the revival of Islamist forces that attracted supporters by offering social benefits in order to close the welfare gap, as in other Muslim states.

For this purpose the Syrian government introduced a new term in its 10th Five Year Plan during the Baath Congress of 2005. Taken from a particular German and European context of post-war development, "Social Market Economy" became the program, or at least the key term for economic reform in Syria. The promoter of this policy was the political reformer Abdullah al-Dardari, Deputy Prime Minister for Economic Affairs. Dardari gained credibility abroad and with foreign experts, mostly German and French, who were invited to support the government in this effort.

During its first few years in power, Asad's government helped the country to emerge from its socialist command economy. The transition was uneven and painful but it was real. Yet it soon became clear that the regime would miss the opportunity to create a sustainable socio-economic equilibrium. Instead of coherent attempts to implement the ambitious concept of a Social Market Economy, economic reform stopped short at the point where it would have curtailed the wider clan's privileges or interfered with their vested interests. The government even failed to issue a strategy paper that defined a Social Market Economy in the Syrian context.[79]

The term Social Market Economy was coined by the German economist Alfred Müller-Armack and politically implemented by West-Germany's first minister of economy, the liberal Ludwig Erhard, in the 1950s. The term has been widely used but not always understood in its complexity and necessary consequences. Basically, Social Market Economy attempts to establish a reliable general framework for competition in a free market to unfold its potential so that growing welfare for more and more people can be guaranteed through this system and through a minimum of social spending by the state itself.[80] It is a concept with clear economic, social and political implications. The traditional school of theorists implies that a functioning Social Market Economy is not thinkable without a functioning democracy. Deviations and selective implementations have been tried in state economies, most notably in China.

In Syria it seemed that the struggle between those who adhered to a more socialist-inspired model ("conservatives") and economic liberalizers ("reformers") led to various compromises. One such outcome was the use of the term Social Market Economy in the political discourse and even in the Five-Year-Plan. An economic analyst within a government institution said that the term was simply shaped out of a compromise between those who wanted to keep the system socialist and those who favored the market. Thus the term came to be, not because of any desire to implement the original complex concept. Moreover, the term fit the discourse of Western governments and donor agencies.

Asad expressed doubts about economic reform in his second inauguration speech on 18 July 2007:

> There has . . . been a lot of discussion or dialogue about the social market economy. . . . There are, of course, theories, ideas and academic research about that. But as far as we are concerned, as a state, our only concern is our people's interests. In other words, no term or method can be imposed on us. We decide what terms we want and what forms these terms should take. . . .

So, when somebody comes to us and says, "This is the dictionary, and the definition here is different from what you are doing," we say, "You have to excuse us, this is what we want, and these are our interests." So, any discussion about any term we use in any area should be based on our experience and our vision . . . .[81]

This false pride resulted in a lack of viable alternatives. Asad never presented any other coherent visions or concepts apart from giving excuses why this or that did not work in the Syrian context. His attitude suggested that broader political obstacles were in the way. A young economist and researcher in the First Lady's Syria Trust for Development admitted: "The President said that Syria has a version of Social Market Economy of its own. I don't know what the government means by it. You would have to ask Dardari."[82] Michel Kilo said he had done so. On this occasion, the Minister replied respectfully that he, Kilo, would know the definition much better himself. But after Kilo insisted on hearing a response from the Minister, Dardari smiled and dismissed it with a wave of the hand.[83]

The businessman Riad Seif was critical. In a real Social Market Economy, he argued, there were social partners and a system of collective bargaining. "You have at least workers rights like strikes, and here we have economic liberalization without any rights. It's worse than real capitalism combined with the socialist remnants of a dictatorial state."[84]

A foreign development expert who was based in Damascus said at the end of 2010: "I think two or three years ago one was more ambitious than today." Conservative forces realized that their vested political or business interests were in danger if the government got serious about reform and implemented a real Social Market Economy in Syria, and they started obstructing. In particular, the Minister of Finance and the Planning Commission were dragging their feet. They found allies among the economic conservatives within the Baath Party and the bureaucratic bourgeoisie in the inflated state sector: participants whose interests were threatened by sweeping change. Apart from this, the expert criticized a series of contradictory and technically flawed public policies.

Another foreign expert doubted if the term Social Market Economy would be mentioned again at all in the upcoming Five-Year-Plan. The term was used less and less by the government, he observed at the end of 2010. It looked as if the decision-makers wanted to keep more options open, in particular the Chinese model. This was underlined by an increased interest in China and visits to the communist power by the president. The foreign expert wondered why the Social Market Economy had only one visible face in Syria. He believed that Minister Dardari was serious about his reform efforts. Dardari also encouraged his subordinates to discuss with him openly and in a critical manner. "But maybe he is the only face of Social Market Economy in Syria because it is easier to pull the plug if necessary," the expert pondered.[85]

This is precisely what happened at the beginning of 2011 just before the protests started to gain momentum. Dardari was kicked out of the government. The chronology is important because this reform concept was meant to fail before widespread protests caused the need for pure crisis management. The term Social Market Economy did not find its way into the next Five-Year-Plan. With violence erupting and tightening sanctions doing more damage to the Syrian economy, whatever was left of economic reform lay in tatters. This caused a vicious circle for the regime because it endangered fragile socio-economic alliances. An Arab proverb says, "Those who eat from the sultan's table wield his sword (men ya'kul min sufra as-sultan, yadrub bisaifihi)." If there is no longer enough food for everyone at the table, those left out may well take up someone else's sword.

With escalating violence in Syria it was less and less likely that the regime would be able to provide enough economic benefits to maintain support that was essential to its survival. Economic experts in Syria made frightening forecasts for 2012. Tax revenues would dwindle to half. The government's access to international credit markets now came with increasing restrictions. Thus it fell upon private companies that had profited from the liberalization of recent years to lend money to the government.[86] In December 2011 Prime Minister Safar issued instructions to all State administrations requiring them to reduce all their overhead expenses by twenty-five percent, excluding salaries. The projected 5.8 percent fiscal deficit that was projected for the year 2011 will be topped significantly by additional expenditures anticipated during the year. The 2012 budget forecast a fifty-eight percent increase in expenses to SYP 1,326 billion. This large increase was mainly due to the fact that expenses previously not accounted for in the state's budget, namely energy subsidies, were now taken into account. [87] According to the Syrian Ministry of Labor, unemployment rose about one third during 2011. A Syrian businessman estimated that Syrian GDP plummeted by forty-five percent in this fateful year.[88] The fall of the Syrian Lira by fifteen to twenty percent soon consumed the rise in salaries that the government granted at the beginning of the year.[89]

However, up to the beginning of 2012 the Syrian authorities managed to keep a lid on inflation and to limit the decline of the Syrian Pound. Decreasing imports alleviated the pressure on price hikes, and a good rainy season brought higher crop harvests. The performance of the government was difficult to verify because transparent data was missing, as always. But reports indicated that financial support from Iran during the revolt also helped to alleviate the financial squeeze. However, these measures could not hide the fact that shortages of power, heating oil, and gas directly affected the population in urban centers such as Damascus that were less affected by the protests.

Looking back at the past decade, the visible aspects of modernization under Bashar al-Asad remained mostly restricted to urban areas. Investments in posh hotels for Gulf tourists, new cars, shopping malls, stylish restaurants, fancy cell phones, modern banking facilities, and a colorful variety of fashion and new technological products were achievements from which mostly upper social echelons profited. In contrast, modernization under Hafez al-Asad included the development of poor rural areas, infrastructure projects, schooling and sanitary facilities in remote villages. The ideological goal was to enhance the living conditions of workers and peasants and to weaken the hegemony of the Sunni landlords and commercial elite (before co-opting them in a power alliance). Those measures of modernization in the rural areas contributed to the country's coherence whereas modernization in the 2000s had centrifugal effects. Extended droughts, mismanagement, corruption, neglect and political indifference let the rural areas slip into dismal conditions. It is no coincidence that the most determined protests of 2011 started in Syria's periphery and found their way only gradually toward the urban centers of trade, consumption, and modern life.

Human Rights Violations

"It's a good thing that I became an attorney," joked Anwar al-Bunni with his distinctive mischievous humor. "I'm never without work." The human rights activist took a long draw on his cigarette stump. We were sitting in his modest apartment in the Damascus suburb of Masaken Berze, just next to the high walls of the military academy and, of all places, the *mukhabarat's* bugging service. Bunni calculated that members of his family had served sixty years in prison altogether. At that time things were already getting tight for him, too, as the *mukhabarat's* threatening warnings not to pass on any information about human rights violations to foreigners became sharper. He had loads of work, but most of it he did for free, serving as a messenger and mediator in conflicts between individuals and the government, lending a voice to people who needed help against the regime. Paying clients stayed away, and he was struggling for a living. When I visited him again in April 2005, he had sold his antique Opel Kadett and was just about to move to a smaller and cheaper office. In October, he spent ten days in hiding after he was framed for a fake crime meant to intimidate him into silence. After he came out of hiding, he was dragged from a car and beaten up in the street by unknown assailants.

His journalist brother Akram, who was released in 2001 after seventeen years in prison, remembers only too well the notorious—although meanwhile closed—jail in the Tadmur desert in the heart of Syria. Tourists are more familiar with the place under the name of Palmyra and associate it with one of the world's most impressive Roman archeological sites. While busloads of tourists were taking their vacation snapshots, the journalist was stewing in the ghastly prison nearby for five years. "There were no beds. We only had blankets on the concrete floor," remembered the forty-eight-year-old in a calm voice. "The prison is a round building with a space in the middle surrounded by cells. There are gaping holes in the ceilings of the cells so that the guards can look inside. In winter rain and bitter cold comes in, and in summer the sun beats down. We were tortured every day."

Arbitrary arrests, confiscations, torture, solitary confinement underground, ill-treatment, and dismal conditions in crowded prisons made up the dark side of everyday life in a Syria that otherwise appeared peaceful on the surface. Group arrests were notorious, as the *mukhabarat* would simply seize anyone who was sitting in a suspicious dwelling, even members of a family who had nothing to do with politics, and lock them up for years. Islamists and communists were most affected. The judiciary was corrupt, whereas it had still been considered exemplary in the democratic periods of Syria in the 1940s and 1950s.

In the spring of 2005 Bunni stated that the number of long-held political prisoners had gone down to about three hundred, according to information derived from reports by prison doctors. Taking new arrests into account— illegal fighters and Islamists who returned from Iraq, new radical Islamists in Syria—the number had risen again to some fifteen hundred. In addition, according to Bunni, there were more than a hundred Kurds still behind bars since the upheaval in March 2004, although the government claimed it released all of those involved one year later. During his first five years in office Asad released some twelve hundred political prisoners, Bunni said in an interview in April 2005.[90] For comparison: in the early 1990s there were still 7,500 dissenters behind bars, including many Muslim Brothers.[91] However, there remained seven thousand "missing persons" since the 1980s, according to the Bunnis. When I spoke to Bunni in 2005 only three large prisons remained in service in Sednaya near Damascus, Adra, and Aleppo. The others had been closed. Nevertheless, more cells could be found in the barracks of the police and secret service. Many of the notorious prisons, including Tadmur, were hastily reopened when the regime cracked down on the protest movement in 2011. In addition, sport stadiums were filled with prisoners whose numbers went up to tens of thousands. The middle of the decade looked peaceful in retrospect, although all along renowned and less renowned political prisoners (and with them their intellectual potential) rotted in the regime's cells .

In the years leading to the humanitarian catastrophe of 2011 opposition activists pursued advocacy work on the legal nitty-gritty of Syria's police state. The Islamic human rights activist Haitham Maleh, for example, took particular offense at Act Number 14 of 1969. Section 16 of this secret service law said that a supervisor could object to a criminal charge being raised against a member of his staff. "This makes employees even more dependent on their bosses, who can force them to commit an increasing number of crimes and exert pressure on them," said Maleh. "There has not been a single court case involving *mukhabarat* staff." Furthermore, any law could be suspended under the emergency law. Military tribunals instead of civil courts conducted the trials, if any. According to Maleh, the situation did not improve very much under Bashar al-Asad. "We don't notice any real change. The atmosphere is just a bit more relaxed," said the seventy-one-year-old lawyer in 2003, who also kept contact with the Muslim Brotherhood. "But young Bashar is a prisoner of his power clique."[92]

The changes in the atmosphere under Asad before 2011 manifested themselves, for example, in the fact that the secret service no longer necessarily entered homes and arrested people on the spot. Now persons were sent a written summons to present themselves to the *mukhabarat*. Some even reported lively discussions with *mukhabarat* staff about the country's problems. "They listen more now," members of the opposition agreed.

One sign of early change was the Human Rights Association of Syria that Maleh founded in July 2001. The government did not lodge an appeal against the establishment of the organization. Under Syrian law at that time, an association was automatically legal after a period of sixty days if there was no objection, says Maleh. The minister of home affairs had even replied to his letters, thus indirectly recognizing the organization. In February 2005, Justice Minister Muhammad al-Ghufri received Maleh for an unprecedented visit. This was interpreted as the final recognition of the Human Rights Association. Maleh, who was still barred from traveling abroad, handed over to Ghufari a forbidden copy of the organization's newspaper and letters that he had once sent to the president.

Diplomats reported that the government now at least gave reliable information on arrests and instituted court proceedings that were sometimes open to observers. The Bunni brothers saw progress as well. "Prison conditions have improved since Hafez al-Asad's death but they are not yet as they should be," said Akram. "There used to be perhaps fifty people penned up in one cell whereas today there are only ten." During the best of years, some prisoners were allowed books, televisions, radios, and telephones. Political prisoners were now also permitted to receive visitors.

During 2004 alone, hundreds of political prisoners were released, especially Islamists and members of their families. According to Muhammad al-Habash, a member of parliament, at this point three were no members of the former Muslim Brothers in Syrian prisons. Bunni, however, disputed this.[93] Members of the Iraqi Baath Party and communists were also released under the amnesties. In August 2004, fifty-one-year-old Imad Shiha, who held the unfortunate record for time in a Syrian prison—and even the world record at that time, according to Bunni—was set free after thirty years. He was jailed for belonging to the Arab Communist Organization. In comparison, Nelson Mandela spent twenty-seven years in prison in South Africa before being freed in 1990.

The Syrian Faris Murad also spent a longer time in prison than

Mandela—twenty-nine years, sixteen of them in solitary confinement in Tadmur. As a young man, he had demonstrated with friends against American policy in the Middle East and had detonated a homemade sound bomb at four o'clock in the morning. Nothing much happened and nobody was injured. At the beginning of 2004, the fifty-four-year-old communist resembled a living corpse. His hunchback forced him to look down at the ground. His face was pale. "Tadmur is a coffin," he said after his release. "We were buried alive without being alive. The food is awful, nobody cares about you, you are tortured day and night, you can't imagine how they beat you. It is like a miracle to leave Tadmur."[94] Some of those released with him had spent several years longer in prison than their actual sentences. Many of them were physically wrecked or terminally ill.

"Those [releases] are all measures with a placebo effect," said a Western diplomat in Damascus. "There is a temporizing policy in the human rights issue. The so-called concessions are only for things that were illegal and excessive anyway under international law."[95]

The regime seemed to have adopted a dual-track policy since the Iraq war. "The big names were spared because Syria now can't afford to have a bad image abroad," said the medical doctor Maya al-Rahabi from the Civil Society Movement. Those in power made compromises, especially when Syria was in the final stage of negotiations with the EU on the Association Agreement. "But work has become harder for most of us," complained Rahabi.[96] News of fresh arrests or attempts at intimidation were constantly circulating in opposition backrooms. According to Maleh, the regime arrested more political opponents on average after the Iraq war than it had before.

After the Kurdish unrest in March 2004 young people between the ages of fourteen and seventeen, among others, suffered torture in prisons for months. According to reports from human rights organizations, they were tortured with electric shocks and whipped with cables, their toe nails were torn out, their heads knocked together, and they were forced to strip naked. Some suffered constant nose bleeding, pierced eardrums, or infected wounds.[97] The fact that Syria signed the International Anti-Torture Convention in July 2004 sounded like mockery against this background and even more so with regard to the broad scale atrocities starting in 2011.

Not even the "big names" seemed to be altogether safe. Aktham Nu'ayssa, the fifty-four-year-old chairman of the Committee for the Defense of Democratic Liberties and Human Rights in Syria (CDDLHR), was arrested in April 2004. In spite of a heart disorder and other health problems, he was kept in solitary confinement in Sednaya with no contact with his family. The charge against him was worded in the old and familiar style: "activities against the socialist system of the state" and "rejection of revolutionary goals." Nu'ayssa had strongly advocated the abolition of martial law, for Kurdish rights, and for information about the fate of "missing persons." He was released on a symbolic bail in the late summer of 2004 and was even allowed to receive a human rights award in Brussels in October. Nu'ayssa had already spent the years between 1991 and 1998 in prison, where he was tortured.[98]

In May 2005, the regime decided to send a particularly strong signal. They arrested all eight board members of the Jamal Atasi Forum—the last political dissident forum remaining from Damascus Spring in 2001. Civil civil society activists were furious. The arrests occured just before the Tenth Baath Congress and sent a worrisome message that brought back memories of the clampdown on the Damascus Spring four years earlier. It turned out to be merely an act of intimidation because all eight men were set free after five days. Although the Jamal Atasi Forum was a secular debating club, the writer Ali Abdullah had read a message by the exiled head of the Muslim Brotherhood, Sheikh al-Bayanuni. And this action apparently provoked the arrests.

In a separate incident, also in May 2005, Muhammad Raadoun was put behind bars. The lawyer and chief of the Arab Organization of Human Rights in Syria (AOHRS) had warned Muslim Brothers in exile not to return to Syria, even though the government had promised them amnesty (often without keeping their word). Both Abdullah and Raadoun were set free six month's later in the November amnesty.

That May, prior to the Baath Congress, was a particularly dark month for all kinds of opposition figures, as a wave of arrests swept the country. The arrests hit many radical Islamists and also others, like the Kurdish sheikh Muhammad Mashouk al-Khaznawi. He disappeared and was later found murdered. His family blamed the secret service, but officials pointed to a criminal incident. The forty-seven-year-old was an advocate of Kurdish rights. Several other Kurdish activists were also arrested in May.

At that time the human rights policy in Syria was closely linked to the international setting. On one hand, the negotiations with the EU on the Association Agreement had a positive effect. On the other hand, the overall scenario of growing international pressure after the Iraq war, above all from the United States, as well as from Syria's self-inflicted humiliation in Lebanon, affected the opposition in a negative way. The rulers of Syria had become more nervous and reacted accordingly.

Asad and the regime felt threatened. This, more and more, determined political reflexes. The contraction of the regime gained momentum. The publication of the Damascus Declaration (see Chapter VII "The Opposition, Islam and the Regime") was a turning point in the relation between the opposition and the regime. It also caused confrontations within the circles of power. Finally, in May 2006 the Baath regime launched the biggest crackdown on the Syrian opposition since the Damascus Spring. Several key intellectuals and activists were arrested, among them Michel Kilo and Anwar al-Bunni.

Kilo did not return home after he had been summoned to a questioning by the *mukhabarat* on May 15. Two days later, Bunni was dragged away from his home under the eyes of his and his brother's family. While al-Buni, who is a lawyer was shouting and demanding to see an arrest warrant, he was forced into a car by two men and driven away. A few days before the incident, his license to practice law had been revoked for up to four years, probably because he had become the director of the EU sponsored human rights training center in Damascus that the regime had closed in March. Several other opposition figures were detained as well. At first glance, it was not clear whether the regime had just fired a warning shot or whether the crackdown represented a more profound turn of policy. Kilo, Bunni, and others were kept behind bars for many years. Kilo recalled that initially he thought it was a temporary measure but one that caused more stir than the regime anticipated.

The wives of Kilo and Bunni recalled in a conversation that their husbands, despite their prominence, suffered from dismal conditions. Bunni had to share a crowded cell with felons. On one occasion he was shaved, beaten and almost killed. However he was still bold enough to give interviews to foreign media from prison on cell phones. This act of defiance was just before the upcoming presidential "elections" in 2007. He bought cell phone minutes from mafia-type co-prisoners who, for some reason, were allowed to keep their phones while incarcerated. After this interview, he was relocated and his conditions worsened. Bunni suffered increasingly from rheumatism in his knees due to humidity and cold. Kilo at least was allowed to use the library and conducted philosophical discussions with whomever would listen. Still, Kilo was kept in a cell with sexual offenders.[99]

The Adra prison near Damascus had about 4000 prisoners when Kilo was arrested in 2006 and 9000 when he was released in 2009. Only thirteen inmates were political prisoners, according to a first-hand source close to the events. The compound had thirteen wings of one hundred twenty-five meters length each and halls of approximately seventy square meters on both sides. Each of those halls held thirty to one hundred inmates. They had at their disposal some thirty beds. At the end of 2007 a goup of criminal inmates hatched a plan to kill the political prisoners in the hope of receiving milder sentences. "Even criminals viewed us as their ideological enemies," Kilo recalled shortly after his release. "This was the most dangerous situation."[100]

Riad Seif also encountered hatred in prison. "We suffered from the police and the criminals. We were isolated. Others were punished when they talked to us," Seif recalled. "But I created trust without talking to them. I cleaned the toilet myself, repaired things in the room and paid for everything. I washed the stairs every day and told them that this was my sport. Thus I could gain respect from the people. Those dangerous criminals who were against me soon felt ashamed to attack me." In the two and a half years in prison he had no time alone with his wife and children. An officer stood always in the room. "Any criminal can get visitors freely without being monitored," Seif noted with scorn.[101]

Political prisoners in Syria lived in a state of uncertainty. Kilo received contradictory signals about his release. On 16 October 2006 the Office of the Public Prosecutor handed him a written statement ending his term. Shortly afterward it was repudiated. Kilo was convinced that parts of the *mukhabarat*, the party and the army were on his side, and that the president was against his release. In fact, Asad had originally opposed Kilo's arrest and was angry about the political fuss it created. As mentioned above, in his blog, the Syrian ambassador to the United States, Imad Mustafa, also called Kilo's arrest a mistake. Different authorities blew hot and cold. All this placed an additional psychological burden on the prisoner and his family. Twenty-seven months later another warrant for his liberation was issued, yet it was withdrawn once again.

This constantly changing treatment of Kilo provides an interesting view behind the scenes. The judge, who was supposed to sentence Kilo to 7.5 years of prison, insisted on a three-year sentence and prevailed. Kilo was released in June 2009 having served three years. Bunni was set free in May 2011 and found himself in a completely changed Syria. Kamal Labwani, another prominent figure of the Civil Society Movement, was freed in November 2011.

The human rights situation in Syria deteriorated markedly from 2006 and became increasingly decoupled from regional and international developments. What caused concern to the authorities was not only external threats—for the pressure on the country began to ease—but also increasing dissent in cyberspace. Asad had advocated Internet connectivity before he became president and, after coming to power, his pro-Internet policy had let the genie out of the bottle. Now the regime responded by tightening control on Internet cafés. Finally, at the end of the decade, the *mukhabarat* engaged in a type of cyber war. They were quick to track young bloggers which suggested that the regime had studied the Arab Spring protests in Tunisia and Egypt and was alert to the opposition use of Internet-enabled communications and social media. A widely-circulated incident concerned the fate of 19-year-old blogger Tal al-Molouhi. This young Sunni girl, pictured wearing a *hijab*, posted poems on Palestine and reform in Arab countries. She was arrested on 27 December 2009 and disappeared in the dungeons of the *mukhabarat* until a special military court on Valentine's Day, 14 February 2011 condemned her to five years in prison. This was three days after the fall of Egypt's President Mubarak and three days before the first demonstration in the Damascus neighborhood of Hariqa. Thy young blogger started the year 2012 with a hunger strike.

After March 2011, the degradation of human rights is hard to describe in its scope and barbarity. Some individual cases have been mentioned above (see Chapter I "Hariqa: The Fire Spreads") but innumerable cases could be added.

The unlucky ones died of torture and the more fortunate ones from bullets. At the end of November 2011, a special fact-finding mission appointed by the Office of the High Commissioner for Human Rights produced a report on the situation in Syria. At that time, a conservative estimate put the number of victims at more than 4,000 and the number of detainees at 14,000. Among those killed were 307 children. At least 12,400 Syrians had fled to neighboring countries, especially to Turkey. The commission had interviewed victims and witnesses of human rights violations, including civilians and defectors from the military and the security forces.

The report presented at the UN Human Rights Council found evidence of hundreds of summary executions; the use of live ammunition against demonstrators; the widespread deployment of snipers during protests; the detention and torture of people of all ages; the blockading of towns and cities by the security forces and the destruction of water supplies. Security forces were found guilty of systematic human rights violations. Soldiers were ordered to "shoot to kill" unarmed demonstrators. Patterns existed of arbitrary arrests and enforced disappearances. Torture was pervasive, which suggested that it was a state-sanctioned policy. Men and boys were sexually abused at military facilities.

The report cited the account of a defected soldier as follows:

> Our commanding officer told us that there were armed conspirators and terrorists attacking civilians and burning government buildings. We went into Telbisa on that day. We did not see any armed group. The protestors called for freedom. They carried olive branches and marched with their children. We were ordered to either disperse the crowd or eliminate everybody, including children. The orders were to fire in the air and immediately after to shoot at people. No time was allowed between one action and the other. We opened fire; I was there. We used machine guns and other weapons. There were many people on the ground, injured or killed.

In another incident on 29 April, "thousands of people walked from nearby villages to the town of Dara'a to bring food, water and medicine to the local population. When they reached the Sayda residence complex, they were ambushed by security forces. More than 40 people were reportedly killed, including women and children." Several defectors witnessed the killing of their comrades who refused to execute orders to fire at civilians.

At least two children were killed as a result of torture. The UN report cited the case of thirteen-year-old Hamza al-Khateeb that was mentioned in Chapter I. Another boy from the settlement of Sayda was taken to the notorious Air Force Intelligence Facility in Damascus. "The injuries described in the post-mortem report of Thamir al-Sharee are consistent with torture," the UN report concluded. "A witness, himself a victim of torture, claimed to have seen Thamir al-Sharee on 3 May. The witness stated that 'the boy was lying on the floor and was completely blue. He was bleeding profusely from his ear, eyes and nose. He was shouting and calling for his mother and father for help. He fainted after being hit with a rifle butt on the head'." X-rays presented by his father to a German TV crew showed that all teeth were missing in Thamir's skull.

An interviewed army defector stated:

> On Friday 12 August, we received orders to go to the Omar al Khattab Mosque, in Duma (Damascus governorate), where about 150 people had gathered. We opened fire. A number of people were killed. I tried to aim high. Later, I realized that security forces had been taking pictures of us. I was pictured firing in the air. I was interrogated. I was accused of being a secret agent. Members of the Republican Guard beat me every hour for two days, and they tortured me with electroshocks.

These horrific practices contributed to rising mistrust within army ranks and a growing number of defections. One military defector stated to the interviewers that he decided to defect "after witnessing the shooting of a two-year-old girl in Latakia on 13 August by an officer who affirmed that he did not want her to grow into a demonstrator."[102]

Opposition figures described a particular technique of revolving arrests. People were detained in masses, tortured for a few days and dumped at their homes in order to free space for new captives. This technique was imported from Iran where it was used during the upheaval in the summer of 2009. The idea was to intimidate demonstrators. Now, two years later in Syria, thousands were imprisoned. Exact figures were difficult to ascertain. The figures cited by some sources were as high as 20,000 or 50,000.

On 2 December the UN Human Rights Council strongly condemned Syria for the "continued widespread, systematic and gross violations of human rights and fundamental freedoms by the Syrian authorities, such as arbitrary executions, excessive use of force and the killing and persecution of protesters, human rights defenders and journalists, arbitrary detention, enforced disappearances, torture and ill-treatment, including against children." Taken together, these charges constituted crimes against humanity.[103] Thirty-seven countries voted in favor of the resolution, among them the Arab nations Jordan, Kuwait, Libya, Qatar, and Saudi Arabia. Only Russia, China, Cuba, and Ecuador voted against the resolution. Uganda, Philippines, India, Cameroon, Bangladesh, and Angola abstained.

Calls intensified, demanding that the UN Security Council refer the Syrian file to the International Criminal Court in The Hague. However, Russia criticized the actions of the Human Rights Council and continued to block further steps in the Security Council.

7
Opposition, Islam & the Regime

H E TOOK OFFICE AS A LIBERALIZER. PEOPLE were hopeful and many cheered in the streets. They were relieved to shake off his predecessor's authoritarian rule. The new statesman brought momentum to the economy by opening up the country. He restricted the power of the secret services, eased martial law, released political prisoners, held fair local elections, and promised further political liberalization in which political parties other than the Baath could participate. The new president promised an alliance with the people and the restoration of the citizens' "freedom and dignity."[1] The term "Damascus Spring" made the rounds.

The time was late 1970 and early 1971. The new figure on which all hopes were pinned was Hafez al-Asad. Although a general disillusionment soon set in, many Syrians believed the promises and kept the flame alive for years to come. When Bashar al-Asad became president in 2000, he, too, raised the hopes of Syrians. Five years later, some observers noted the public disenchantment with Bashar and wondered if history was repeating itself.

The elder Asad's relationship to the opposition became more aggressive in the 1990s. His Baathists systematically eliminated both moderate as well as conservative Islamic forces such as the People's Party and the National Party. The strong Sunni urban bourgeoisie became politically homeless. "For this reason, the social base of the Muslim Brothers broadened considerably," concluded Lobmeyer. Hafez al-Asad lashed out against all opponents. He fought not only the Muslim Brothers but the secular opposition, eliminating them in 1980. For a time, the only option for opposing the regime was to support the radical Islamists.[2]

Likewise, Bashar's relationship to the opposition left moderate forces such as the Civil Society Movement out in the cold. The regime treated Islamists and secular opposition figures more or less the same, apart from some cyclical fluctuations. Yet, as in earlier times, the regime put forward the fear of the Islamists as the reason for delaying the opening up of the country. The Damascus Spring of 2000-2001 was a unique opportunity to bring the regime and the secular forces in the country into closer alignment. The highbrow Civil Society Movement could have been strengthened and used as a counterforce to the more populist Islamists. This could have served the interests of both Bashar and the reformers. Sad to say, both sides missed this chance.

The Secularists

In the old days the opposition in Syria could be roughly divided into two camps: left-wing secular forces and Islamists of different stripes. The secular Civil Society Movement has been mentioned in this book, since it was the most talked about movement in the semi-public debate and its members published quite a lot. The movement was an amorphous network of intellectuals, journalists, actors, doctors, attorneys, and professors with a colorful range of opinions. No one knew how many Syrians supported it. The movement used mobile phones in place of conferences, personal contacts instead of legal statutes, formed working groups instead of boards of directors, and managed websites instead of using paper files and index cards.

Especially after the arrest of several activists during the Damascus Spring, Michel Kilo filled the role of the Civil Society Movement's spokesman. A Christian, Kilo studied several years in the northern German town of Münster and speaks fluent German. His philosophy of a grassroots democracy stems from that time, and he preferred a small and amorphous group to a large party. The smaller and more ambiguous group could issue many small initiatives. Kilo felt that this approach made persecution by the state machinery more difficult. The former communist described himself as a humanist. "The regime has to accept that freedom is the greatest principle in life," he said. "In a modern society you can no longer separate state and society because the free human being is the central principle." Kilo was convinced that every ideological party in power would enter a period of crisis because real life was much more complicated than any *Weltanschauung.*

Many of the old secularists have, for their part, shed ideological ballast after the collapse of communism and with the growing distance from colonial times. With new flexibility, these secularists now concentrate on humanistic ideas and democratic goals. A symbolic incident was the renaming of Riad Turk's "Communist Party–Politburo" as the "Syrian Democratic Party." This happened at the first party conference held in twenty-five years in May 2005, when Turk finally gave up his post as general secretary. On this occasion, the members called for the abolishment of the death penalty for Muslim Brothers. (In November 2002, Bashar had released the seventy-one-year-old Riad al-Turk after his arrest during the Damascus Spring because of poor health and his record of having spent almost twenty years in prison.)

Michel Kilo, in a contemplative moment during a lengthy conversation, referred to his father when he described his political motivations. Hanna Kilo served as a policeman in the Christian mountain village of Kassab on the Turkish border when, in 1946, Syrian Prime Minister Shukri al-Quwatli came to town. Quwatli asked the policemen if they needed anything. Hanna Kilo answered, "No, we don't have any problems but the people are poor." Qawatli replied angrily: "I didn't ask you about the people. This is my problem. I asked you, policemen." Kilo countered, "And I told you that the people are poor." For his boldness Kilo was sent to prison for forty-five days. "He always fought for the poor, never accepted grapes or bananas from the people and stayed humble himself," remembered his son, sitting in an old pillowy sofa in front of a ceiling-high book shelf in his modest apartment in the Damascus neighborhood of Qasa'. His father was one of fifteen people in Syria who had a higher college degree, according to Kilo. He fought against the French and had illusions about Stalin. He encouraged the poor to cultivate waste land and helped them to claim ownership after ten years according to Ottoman land law.

Michel Kilo continued the struggle of his father with similar personal enthusiasm and sacrifices. While he assumed the role of a front-line activist in tirelessly writing petitions and articles, Sadiq Jalal al-Azm was more the philosophical mastermind behind the movement. He has been living in Beirut in the past years because of increased troubles with the *mukhabarat*. A Sunni by birth, Azm has a Marxist background and is known as the "Heretic of Damascus." He was professor of philosophy at the University of Damascus and the American University of Beirut (AUB) and had completed his doctorate at Yale University, where he also taught. Azm has stood for a strict separation of religion and state throughout his life. His father, who belonged to the high aristocracy of the Ottoman Empire, was an ardent supporter of Ataturk. Azm wrote about Immanuel Kant's Theory of Time and called on Arab Muslims to take the European Enlightenment as a model for their reforms. In 2005 / 2006 he returned to the United States as a visiting professor at Princeton University.

Azm made most of his enemies after the Six Day War with *Self-Criticism After the Defeat,* published in 1968. In the book, Azm held Arabs responsible for their disastrous defeat by Israel, blaming outmoded traditions, insufficient modernization, and a lack of societal progress. He also criticized the strong influence of conservative Islam that obstructed scientific learning. Finally, he accused the Arab states and societies of avoiding self-criticism. Only one year later his collection of essays titled *Critique of Religious Thought (naqd al-fikr ed-dini)* created one of the biggest literary scandals in modern Arab history. Azm lost his teaching position at AUB and went to prison, but was freed after only a few days. The Azm Affair made him into one of the most controversial symbolic figures in the contemporary Arab world.[3]

Another ideologue of the Civil Society Movement was Ahmed Barkawi, professor of philosophy at the University of Damascus. He is the author of leading discussion papers about the path to freedom and democracy in Syria, the role of civil society, nationalism and democracy, women and democracy, and many other fundamental issues. The Civil Society Movement was supported by many nationalists, communists, and other left-wing groups— often splinter groups formed out of the bigger block parties that are coupled with the Baath Party in the National Front.[4] Other names associated with the founding of the movement are Riad Seif, Aref Dalila, Anwar al-Bunni, Walid al-Bunni, Abdul Razzaq Eid, Fayez Sarah, and Najati Tayara. During the Damascus Spring in September 2000, they and others composed the "Manifesto of the 99" followed in December by the "Manifesto of the 1000."

Hardly had Baghdad fallen in the US invasion of 2003 when the members of the Civil Society Movement saw their opportunity to turn up the heat in Damascus. Their first action was a petition, designed by Kilo, and presented to the president in May 2003. The text emphasized the new strategic "challenges and perils" for Syria following the occupation of Iraq. As a common denominator with the regime in Damascus, the opposition figures mentioned the "aggressive, racist, egotistical, and evil policies and ideology" of the Bush administration and Israel. "Honorable President," the petition continued, "our country faces this looming danger without being prepared for it. [Syria] must strengthen itself against [this danger] and enhance its ability to confront it, after having been weakened by cumulative mistakes that distanced the nation from public issues, exhausted the country and society, and exposed them [to dangers] like never before."[5]

The signatories called for "sweeping reforms," including the lifting of the state of emergency that had existed since 1963, curbing the power of the security machinery, permitting freedom of the press, freedom of speech, and freedom of assembly, as well as the freedom to be politically active, move around the country freely, and travel abroad. There was no official reply from Asad.

The opposition continued to strive for a revival of Damascus Spring, and international pressure was providing them with arguments. In their petition, they called on the president to act before the United States did, arguing that only a free state was able to withstand such pressure from outside. Seven years later in 2011, some of these Civil Society figures used the same arguments in the context of the new street protests. There were indications that in this difficult situation and facing US pressure, the regime was seeking discussions with the Civil Society Movement, though on an unofficial level. Some members of the opposition reported that attempts had been made to win them over as collaborators against the new opposition or to convince them of the wisdom of the government's policy. It is hard to judge if this was an attempt to co-opt parts of the opposition or a step toward greater intimidation. This pattern was repeated several times in 2011 as we will see later in this chapter.

Azm once received a personal summons from the head of the *mukhabarat*, Bahjat Suleiman. Azm's supporters reported the gist of the meeting. "Syria is currently in greater danger than you think. You must rein in your criticism!" This message was a serious warning meant to reach the Civil Society Movement as a whole. The fate of Seif and other prisoners of the opposition was ever-present. The regime tried to exploit the common denominator shared by government and opposition: the danger lurking from outside, the threat to the home country, a conspiracy from the United States and Israel.

The regime blew hot and cold. At the moment when everybody was holding their breath, the opposition was suddenly given encouragement by the government. Michel Kilo experienced this several times. In February 2004, a member of the regime close to the president called on Kilo to publish his critical articles not only in Lebanese newspapers but also in Syrian ones. "He promised me that not a single word would be left out," rejoiced Kilo. In March 2004, he was allowed to appear on a talk show on Syrian television for the first time. He was filmed live as he criticized the delay in reforms in the presence of a government representative, saying that "Syria needs a different beginning than that of March 8," referring to the day in 1963 when the Baathists staged the coup and took power.

After the broadcast, Kilo was given a tumultuous welcome in the popular Café Rawda opposite the parliament building in the modern business quarter of Damascus. During countless evenings, the journalist used to meet there with acquaintances and while away the hours. They sat at small tables with the apple-tobacco scent of the water pipes and the clicking of chess and backgammon pieces on wooden mosaic game boards. The noise level was so high in the large, covered inner courtyard that a spy could scarcely eavesdrop. "People hugged me, clapped me on the shoulder, and kissed me when I came into the café," Kilo remembered. "They told me: 'You said exactly what we think. We would never have thought that one day we would see this on Syrian television.'" The program was not broadcast live, but nothing was cut. Then-Minister of Information Ahmed Hassan had taken full responsibility for the experiment. Kilo was pleased that afterward the state newspapers also jumped on the bandwagon and praised the critical discussion that had taken place on the talk show.[6]

Fear of government reprisals for speaking your mind was fading and cautious concessions by the government were the rule of the day. This had led to the formation of new alliances. The secular opposition was marshalling its forces. At the beginning of 2005, twelve non-licensed parties and groups united to form a committee for the "national coordination of the defense of basic and human rights." Among them were members of the Civil Society Movement, human rights activists, communists, and Kurdish activists.[7] Without a doubt, the political debates in Syrian life became more colorful and lively. Yet the opposition regarded such surprising leeway with skepticism and saw it as a maneuver to distract attention from undiminished authoritarian practices.

Other Syrian opposition figures were operating from abroad and for the most part endorsed regime change. Among them was Farid al-Ghadry, who played more or less the same role as the dubious businessman Ahmad Chalabi had done in the US invasion of Iraq before he ultimately fell into disgrace with the Americans. Ghadry, who was in his 30s at that time, had been built up by the neoconservative US government as "the opposition leader" and the American media promoted him. In Syria, on the other hand, this head of the Syrian Reform Party was barely known. He had no backing among the Syrian population or other opposition groups. Some observers claimed that Ghadry's father, Nihad, who published a newspaper and lived in Lebanon, collaborated with the CIA. However, Nihad had fallen out with Farid over politics and said that his son was being used by the United States. Ghadry senior added that Farid was so distant from Syrian affairs "that he thinks Aleppo is located in Sudan."[8]

Kilo got angry when he spoke of the US-based Syrian opposition. "They want the same as we do, only under American patronage," he said tersely. Kilo would have preferred it if the Europeans had adopted the role of nurturing the Syrian opposition.

Following the Iraq war, the opposition in exile had been gathering force. In June 2004, the European Union organized a meeting of various individuals and groups in Brussels, where Farid al-Ghadry acted as spokesman. This, in turn, affected the activists in Syria itself. "Because of it [the joining of forces abroad] our voice has become much louder and bolder," admitted Kilo. "The regime will have to give us more leeway since they're afraid we'll join up with supporters abroad. We have threatened to do so. We have to become even more aggressive!" Kilo was convinced that the regime could take no action against the present leaders of the Civil Society Movement. "It would also strengthen the Syrian-American opposition. This is a battle that Bashar can't win."[9] On the other hand, by inviting Ghadry to a hearing in Brussels in mid-March 2005, the Europeans annoyed many Syrian opposition members and the Syrian ambassador to the EU, who had wanted to participate in the meeting, cancelled his visit in protest. "This was a big mistake," a European diplomat in Damascus later concluded.[10]

Despite such fickle relations among opposition figures in Syria and in exile (a cleavage that was to become paramount again in 2011) domestic activists continued to count on the indirect effect that the US-supported opposition abroad had on the regime in Damascus. They hoped to profit from the fear of those in power that "it could be worse," and thus extract concessions. However, opposition leaders had divergent agendas and conflicting personalities. It was unlikely that they could join forces to topple the regime at home. The mistrust of the domestic opposition also arose from the fact that those in exile would likely take the leading positions in government if the Iraqi model of toppling the regime through US military intervention were followed.

By contrast, at home a historical step toward a more unified opposition was achieved through the Damascus Declaration of 16 October 2005. For the first time, all major opposition groups—reaching from the secular Civil Society Movement to Kurdish activists, moderate Muslims, and even the outlawed

Muslim Brotherhood in London—issued a broad call for democratic change in Syria. The lengthy document called for an end to emergency laws and other forms of political repression, for a national conference on democratic change, as well as for a constituent assembly that was to shape a new constitution "that foils adventurers and extremists."

The signatories bluntly condemned the policies of the regime "that have brought the country to a situation that calls for concern for its national safety and the fate of its people." They also criticized "the stifling isolation which the regime has brought upon the country as a result of its destructive, adventurous, and short-sighted policies on the Arab and regional levels, and especially in Lebanon." Directed at Baathists as well as radical Islamists, the document called for "shunning totalitarian thought and severing all plans for exclusion" and underlined that "no party or trend has the right to claim an exceptional role. No one has the right to shun the other, persecute him, and usurp his right to existence, free expression, and participation in the homeland." The aim was the "adoption of democracy as a modern system that has universal values and bases, based on the principles of liberty, sovereignty of the people, a state of institutions, and the transfer of power through free and periodic elections that enable the people to hold those in power accountable and change them." The signatories did not intend to spur on a revolution but reached out to progressive forces of the present regime and invited them to take part in the proposed national conference for democratic change.

The Damascus Declaration called for a "new social contract" which leads to a "modern democratic constitution that makes citizenship the criterion of affiliation, and adopts pluralism, the peaceful transfer of power, and the rule of law in a state all of whose citizens enjoy the same rights and have the same duties, regardless of race, religion, ethnicity, sect, or clan, and prevents the return of tyranny in new forms." The principles of that society ought to be "moderation, tolerance, and mutual interaction, free of fanaticism, violence, and exclusion, while having great concern for the respect of the beliefs, culture, and special characteristics of others, whatever their religious, confessional, and intellectual affiliations, and openness to new and contemporary cultures." Acknowleging the Muslim Brotherhood's contribution, the document read: "Islam—which is the religion and ideology of the majority, with its lofty intentions, higher values, and tolerant canon law—is the more prominent cultural component in the life of the nation and the people."[11]

Regarding the broad alliance of highly heterogeneous signatories, the Damascus Declaration's far-reaching political demands, its conciliatory tone, its denouncement of any form of violence as well as social and political totalitarianism, particularly its vision and readiness to incorporate all kinds of "contemporary cultures" and beliefs, makes this document among the most remarkable papers of contemporary Arab political culture. Intellectually speaking, it also led the way toward the Arab Spring.

The idea for this Declaration arose during an international conference in Marrakesh. Kilo composed it in night-long discussions with representatives of the Muslim Brotherhood. In retrospect, Kilo was not so content about the text since it was subsequently watered down in a tiring discussion process about the role of Kurds, Arabs, history, etc. that dragged on for months with many parties involved. "A complicated and contradictory text emerged finally. But we said, OK, the text as such is not so important, let's sign it!"[12]

Al-Azm said that Kilo's approach was definitely very far-sighted, although he was accused by some of being too soft on the Muslim Brothers. "He thought that they were inspired by Turkey," said Azm skeptically, "but they were not so inspired yet when Kilo tried to win them over."[13]

Beyond its humanistic and ideological value, however, it remained an open question whether the Declaration would have a political impact in Syria. Observers doubted that it strengthened the opposition or that it represented a bulwark that could hold together the different opposition streams of thought if dramatic political change should occur.

Only a few months later, the surprising alliance between defected Vice President Abdul Halim Khaddam and Sheikh Bayanuni, head of the Muslim Brotherhood in London, gained visibility when both participated in the newly founded National Salvation Front, an organization that became a rallying point for opposition figures in exile. The Front was composed of members in the triangle that stretched from Paris (Khaddam), London (Bayanuni), and Washington, DC. Its adherents included activists such as Najib Ghadbian, Ammar Abdulhamid, and others. The National Salvation Front drove a wedge between these expats and groups within Syria, who despised Khaddam and the exiled Brotherhood. The difficult rapprochement in the name of "national unity" between secular and moderate Muslim groups within the country and the Brotherhood in exile was about to be disrupted altogether. A unification of secularists, moderate Muslims, and the purged wing of the Muslim Brotherhood, which could have had a moderating effect and been a model for other Arab countries, looked unlikely in the light of the National Salvation Front. The opposition has remained fractured ever since. Opposition figures abroad who rallied behind the Khaddam-Bayanuni tandem lost credibility at home. An Islamic figure in alliance with a long-time Baathist hardliner who suppressed the Damascus Spring was hard to bear for many in the opposition inside Syria. They called it an irony that both figures had all of a sudden become the champions of democracy, civil society, and political and economic reform in Syria. The Syrian domestic opposition showed reactions ranging from hostile rejection to benevolent indifference. As the pragmatic Riad Seif put it: "We let them do their thing. But we have more credibility with the Syrian people because we stayed and confronted the regime at home."[14]

The National Salvation Front broke apart in 2009. Among other things,

Khaddam did not live up to the exiled opposition's expectations. The anticipated insights into the eye of the power in Damascus that Khaddam promised lacked value that could have endangered the regime. Financially, Khaddam did not contribute as much as hoped. Khaddam suggested that his grand family that he had brought into exile might contribute. But his sons went into business and lacked an interest and appreciation of their father's political legacy. Later on, during the challenge of 2011, some figures from the former National Salvation Front and from inside Syria, also Seif, reconciled in order to join efforts against the regime. The credibility of opposition activists in exile was rising again.

Back in 2006 the opposition inside Syria felt a temporary boost with the release of Riad Seif and Maamoun al-Homsi in January 2006 (Homsi fled the country in 2007). Some even hoped for a possible revival of the Damascus Spring. For, hardly out of prison, Seif boldly announced the formation of a new political force under the name of National Liberal Party. The founding of an independent party (in parliament, at that time) was exactly the point where he had crossed the red line in 2001, and the reason why he was incarcerated. Déja-vu five years later: Seif was once again challenging Asad. The president, who felt strong enough or pressed enough to release a key and charismatic opponent, had to find a strategy to show that times had changed. He knew that a second arrest of Seif would not be possible without high political costs.

While defying Bashar and the Baath monopoly, Seif carefully followed the moderate line of the rest of the heterogeneous Civil Society Movement. In his first interview after his release he emphasized:

> We honestly seek to change the regime in a very peaceful way...not by overthrowing the current regime. There are many clear indicators to the incapacity of the Syrian regime to go on or achieve reform. . . . If President Bashar al-Asad decides to accept the change and real democracy, ... then the transition toward democracy would be easy, at a very low cost, and achievable by the end of his term in 2007. President Bashar al-Asad would go into history as the man who took a nationalistic [i.e. patriotic] position and spared his people from a lot of anguish.[15]

Even though the secular opposition reinforced its ranks with Seif and Homsi, it still lacked organization, coherence, and a broad popular following. Also, Seif who had preferred to go into business instead of finishing his degree of economics at Damascus University and was not an undisputed figure among mostly highbrow intellectual Civil Society activists. Despite his political prominence, Seif remained an outsider. This gave him more grounding, however, with regard to political and economic practice. A consensus on a roadmap for an efficient and prudent political transition was far from established. It depended on both sides of the table. Could a transition really be achieved at "low cost" as Seif hoped?

The hope for peaceful change that had gained ground again in the tea houses of Damascus in 2006 was short-lived. The Syrian regime further estranged moderate secular forces that were Syrian patriots. Kilo, for example, tried to push for a technocratic solution that would lead into a more pluralist political system. He, like many others, repeatedly distanced himself from US attempts to establish democracy in the Middle East by forced regime change and refused any form of cooperation with US-supported opposition figures. Kilo was at least as pan-Arab as the Baathists.

At the same time, the power circle was narrowing considerably, and Asad's regime underwent a period of contraction. Except for political veteran and Vice President Faruq al-Shara' all key figures in politics, the intelligence, and the military were replaced by Alawites. The circle of trust had narrowed. In reality, the outlook for the Civil Society Movement became bleaker: The intellectual and moderate opposition forces inside Syria were intimidated or imprisoned, and those outside Syria temporarily compromised themselves by allying with the Khaddam-Bayanuni tandem.

The tipping point toward more trouble was the disaster in Lebanon. If Bashar was involved in the killing of Hariri or not, he had by far underestimated the international reaction and the determination of Western countries, especially the United States, to pursue an uncompromising stance toward Syria. A sense of panic and helplessness was in the air in Damascus. This explained many short-sighted decisions taken by the regime in the months that followed. Asad not only gambled away the goodwill of many opposition figures but he also lost leeway in pursuing foreign policy strategies. Moreover, the weakness of the regime contributed to the fact that it could less afford to confront struggles at home and thus provided less resistance to Islamists in everyday life. When a leader and a regime become insecure, they commit mistakes. Measures become defensive and short-sighted. Arrests become unsystematic. Asad's actions had finally given way to the priority of securing power.

The Lebanon disaster escalated into another major crackdown on the Syrian opposition. Kilo, Bunni, and other intellectuals from Syria together with Lebanese intellectuals drafted and signed the Damascus-Beirut Declaration that was published on 12 May 2006. It called for mutual respect of interests and sovereignty of the two countries. It also urged the Syrian government not to interfere in Lebanese affairs. This was the red line. The fact that the petition appeared on the eve of a UN Resolution draft put forward by the US, France, and Britain in the Security Council aggravated the situation. Resolution 1680 stipulated the necessity to take measures to prevent the entry of Syrian arms into Lebanon, the demarcation of the border between Lebanon and Syria, and the exchange of ambassadors. Such a resolution represented an attempt to clip Syria's wings. The regime might have inferred—or looked for a pretext to infer—that the signatories of the Damascus-Beirut Declaration lined up with the foreign powers in this matter. But those who know Kilo and most of the other intellectuals agreed that this was pure fabrication. Kilo, Bunni,

Labwani, and other activists were arrested.

Lebanon became a dangerous emotional issue for the weakened Baath regime. The Damascus-Beirut Declaration was the first common petition of Syrian and Lebanese opposition figures, and it added insult to injury. The Syrian government sent a clear signal that its patience had run out. It was still time for Asad to use his pillars of legitimacy within the population and the resources passed down to him from his father to re-embark on a program of reconciliation and reform. Even now, the numerous moderate opposition figures would not have slammed the door at an honest invitation to common endeavor. The chances for Syria to return to a more hopeful and prosperous path without political upheaval or an Islamist intermezzo still existed. The obstacles and stakes, however, became higher every year.

Despite the depressing situation, parts of the opposition gathered their forces and tried to revive the spirit of the Damascus Declaration. On 1 January 2007 in the apartment of Riad Seif in Khaliye Qudsiye in the bare mountains half an hour drive from Damascus 167 personalities came together at 7 AM in the morning and left at 2 AM the following day. Alawites, Christians, and Sunnis attended. The group included people from different mostly academic professions. Despite being watched by the *mukhabarat* on guard they founded the National Council for Democratic Change *(al-majlis al-watani li i'lan Dimashq li at-taghyir al-democrati)* or simply the organized form of the Damascus Declaration. This time, however, without Kilo. He was not able to resolve differences of opinion with the new leadership. Thus Seif, the outsider from the business sector, once again became the center of Syria's organized secular opposition. Kilo, in the meantime, remained a highly respected and oft-published voice for change in the media and opposition discourse. The female doctor Fida' al-Howrani, who owned a hospital in Hama, was elected president of the Damascus Declaration. She is the daughter of Akram al-Howrani, who had been one of the founders of the Arab Socialist Baath Party and minister in several cabinets until he went into exile in 1963. Seif became head of the board.

This new network stuck to the traditional principles of the Civil Society Movement and worked toward a transition in Syria with a soft landing and sought to avoid violent revolt. The circle attempted to incorporate moderate Islamists on the basis of the Damascus Declaration. Seif spoke of creating a model similar to the Turkish AKP. In addition, he remained always much more open versus Western policies than other members of the more pan-Arab wing of the Civil Society Movement such as Kilo, for example. Seif was a pragmatic businessman rather than an ideologue. He saw a reflection of his own thinking in the mosaic of ideologies within the opposition. No other entrepreneurs exposed themselves by supporting the Civil Society Movement for fear of reprisals and a painful push into bankruptcy, as Seif himself had the misfortune to experience.[16]

154 SYRIA—A DECADE OF LOST CHANCES

In contrast to the discourse of the Damascus Spring, Seif now avoided approaching the regime head on. "We don't use the word democracy so often anymore because it has been discredited through the wrong approach of the United States in Iraq and through violence in Lebanon," Seif explained. "We prefer to speak about human rights and economic liberalization." The war in Iraq had damaged opposition efforts in Syria, Seif was convinced. Now people preferred stability to insecurity. "But one day the tipping point will be reached when only a small spark suffices to trigger resistance in a broad front. The rising consumer prices could become one cause among various others."[17] With this interpretation—that in many ears did not sound more than wishful thinking at that time—Seif clearly anticipated the dynamics of the Arab Spring in 2011.

It did not take long, however, for the regime to strike back at this new network of the Damascus Declaration. Twelve of the leading figures were arrested one by one, including Fida' al-Howrani. Riad Seif followed last, about one month after the foundation of the Council. He had been barely out of prison two years (and was set free again two and a half years later on 29 July 2010 as were the others).

In the following years the thinkers and leaders of the Civil Society Movement were silent. Single issue groups with new faces and new forms of organization with a higher degree of cyber literacy temporarily replaced the old opposition as the main actor of change from below. The secular and intellectual civil society activists had pursued a holistic approach of society and politics including conceptions of an ideological überbau, did not shy away from delicate issues such as political pluralism and democracy, and posed demands of domestic and foreign-policy relevance. The new single issue movements did not deal with these dangerous and sometimes unwieldy aspects but focused on immediate priorities such as women's rights, on the fight against so-called honor killings or on opposing the planned reform of the Personal Status Law. As long as they did not mention democracy and criticize the President, these local NGOs enjoyed a greater amount of tolerance for the time being. Whereas the Civil Society Movement with its discourse posed a threat to the regime as the real secular alternative, the Islamists and the "sub-political" single issue groups could be played out against each other beyond ideological questions of principle.

The Kidnapping of Civil Society

By 2010 the Civil Society Movement was functionally defeated and the notion of civil society itself had become a taboo. Instead, the regime was making efforts to appropriate the term. Civil society in Syria—as it was frequently used by the government, international donors, and agencies—was not civil society as understood in the historical context of Europe as an enlightened, self-determined, critical, and politically active bourgeoisie or *societé des citoyens*. This is what the Civil Society Movement had in mind when they founded the debating clubs during the Damascus Spring. Accordingly, Kilo defined civil society as "a society of free citizens, exclusively defined by their freedom, independently of any objective ascriptions such as religion or ethnicity. If you define a human being as a believer, you lose the intrinsic essence of the human being."[18]

Sadiq Jalal al-Azm called this notion of citizenship the essence of civil society as the Civil Society Movement understood it. It was not necessarily the rule of law since this could be defined as Islamic Law (*sharia*). The problem that the regime saw in the "remnants of civil society" in Syria is that it could offer alternatives to the simplistic dualism of either the present regime or the Islamists. Almost prophetically, Azm said at the end of 2010, "The civil idea of citizenship of the Civil Society Movement could become interesting again when a crisis arises and the danger of civil strife looms. But there is no guarantee that it will succeed."[19]

Until the fundaments of the regime were shaken in 2011, those in power made an increasing effort to redefine "civil society" and make the public forget any more profound notions of the term. Syria's First Lady Asma al-Asad put herself to the forefront of civil society development in the government's formal sense of "non-government" organizations that did work on the grass root level but with clear restrictions. Freedom was not part of this definition of citizenship. When asked about the definition of "citizen" and "civil society," representatives of the Office of the First Lady did not give clear answers. Statements remained fuzzy and, at best, were given in the context of the president's definition of the term as an active citizen who cares about his country, society, and surroundings.[20]

In 2007 the First Lady formed an umbrella for the NGOs in Syria called the Syria Trust for Development. These civil society activities were given access to shared resources, research and administrative services, and at the same time were restricted by the red lines of the regime because there was no legal activity outside this realm. The most visible programs that Asma al-Asad initiated or brought under the Trust umbrella were FIRDOS (development of rural areas), MASSAR (social uplifting of youth) and SHABAB (qualifying youth for the economy).

The Trust was part of a strategy to enhance the Syrian image abroad by plugging into widely accepted international discourse. It also served the purpose of repairing distortions of unequal economic development and employing NGOs in a buffer function against socio-economic shocks. Syria Trust was certainly also a tool in the power struggle between conservative ideologues and reformists, an attempt to gain the upper hand and to create incremental action and change. Finally, it was an attempt to fill the vacuum against potential Islamic charities.

In a bitter irony, considering the clampdown on the Damascus Spring, the

Syrian Government's Five-Year-Plan (2006-2010) addressed the limited role of civil society in Syria's development. Recognizing that "the role of the civil associations and institutions in the socio-economic development wasn't as good as desired," the plan envisaged "radical changes in order to activate and enhance the capabilities of the civil society role in the coming stage." The First Lady conceded in an international Civil Society conference in Damascus in January 2010, "The government alone cannot move this country forward."[21]

Despite public skepticism, these NGOs represented an important step forward and a radical change from decades of socialist etatism under Hafez al-Asad—where Syrians had nothing but the state as their reference point in life, from charity to education to rural development. Nevertheless, NGO activists hoped in vain for a more liberal NGO law. Since 2005 a new NGO law was "in planning" but never materialized. The same was true of the long-awaited law to liberalize the party system, announced at the 10th Baath Congress in January 2010.

At the Civil Society conference, the Ministry of Information and state press outlets continued to use the term "paternal society" instead of "civil society" in their Arabic-language coverage. This, observers claimed, signaled that the will to loosen government control over the sector remained limited.[22]

Syria's NGO law stemmed from 1958. It granted a Baathist monopoly on such activities. Like other things in Syria, this law had been consciously eroded in favor of a more open development, but it could be strictly enforced again if needed. Meanwhile, in line with above mentioned restrictions, the rules of association were tightened by the government. Earlier, NGOs could start working if their applications of registration had not been answered by the Ministry of Labour and Social Affairs in three months. Now the NGOs had to wait until they received official approval.

The magazine *Syria Today* quoted a Syrian consultant: "Civil society in Syria needs to become more active in the places where market forces leave the country with unwanted results."[23] In other words: The government needed new—but restricted—social forces to buffer the effects of economic transition from a command economy to a market economy.

Two problems arose. One was articulated by a researcher of the First Lady's NGO Research Centre: "Ideally, civil society can play a buffer role. But for that you need strong advocacy, and this we don't have." Nevertheless, he saw progress on the advocacy front in the ban of smoking in public places and improved environmental practices. He saw the biggest deficiencies in Corporate Social Responsibility (CSR) and corruption.[24]

Resignation

In November 2010, when the protests that began a few months later still seemed a remote possibility, I visited Michel Kilo in his small apartment in Qasa' and asked him to reflect on the failures of the Civil Society

Movement. After three waves of suppression, nothing much was left of the hopes and aspirations of the Damascus Spring. "The political opposition today has hit rock bottom," Kilo pondered, sipping black tea in his living room and holding in his hand a sesame-pistachio cookie from one of the Bab Touma bakeries. The journalist had a text of Max Weber ("The Protestant Ethic and the Spirit of Capitalism") in front of him on the lounge table that he had just agreed to translate from German into Arabic. Kilo had gained a weight since we had last seen each other in the summer 2009, a few days after he had left prison.

In 2009 in the lane outside his old apartment building, young *mukhabarat* watchers had taken positions or drove by on their motorbikes. Kilo was under strict surveillance, and a travel ban was imposed on him. Still, he used to converse with the *mukhabarat* guards. They respected him, called him *ustath* (master, teacher) in the old Syrian tradition of respect for the wisdom of the elderly. Some guards even gave him hints when they planned to take their lunch breaks, so that his visitors could slip in unseen. Kilo sadly admitted, "The political opposition are at loggerheads with one another. They jointly signed the Damascus Declaration, and now one suspects the other of being an American agent."

Despite all disappointment, Kilo was proud of the Civil Society Movement's achievements. "We were the driving force, not the political parties," said Kilo, referring to the legal parties within the Baath-dominated National Front and other parties that were illegal yet tolerated to some degree. "The intellectuals delivered the proof that the Syrian street was not dead, and that the middle class was vibrant and full of ideas. But the intellectuals who moved things became the main target of the regime." He paused for a while, slowly stirring his spoon in the tea glass, and continued, "We were persecuted at a very early stage. We had less than a year," he said referring to the Damascus Spring. The Movement had a plan of several stages. Reiterating European patterns of revolutions and theories of early nationalism, Kilo continued, "We wanted first to recruit the middle class that is always sensible for freedoms. We wanted to win over the nervous center of the middle class, the students, etc. But we did not have a mass basis. We got stuck in the first phase."

The political parties in Syria did not take the lead to renew society. "We have always said we don't want to become a political party," said Kilo. "Only when the society becomes independent of the existing parties, can we think of founding parties of our own." Drawing a parallel to Poland before the fall of communism, he referred to the Polish trade union Solidarność that embodied the popular movement and later turned into a political party. "Our parties did not have the [same] intellectual, political, and organizational capacities," he stated.

Another reason that the Civil Society Movement did not bear fruit was the fact that, as Kilo said, it presented "so many new ideas that were politically unfamiliar to our society. Our notion of civil society did not take root." The gap between highbrow discussion in the tea houses and reality in the street was a shortcoming of the Movement that became an issue again during the protests that began in 2011. The new demonstrations proved Kilo wrong in one regard: the early protests, at least, did come close to grass-roots civil society action as Kilo experienced when he was in Paris in 1979.

Another problem that the Civil Society Movement confronted was finances. No material sponsors existed for this independent group. "We had collected 2,500 Lira [$50]," Kilo explained. "Every paper that we printed, we paid from our own pockets." At the end of 2010, Kilo nourished the hope that by publishing the history of the Movement it could find a way to revitalize its ideas, especially among the youth. He pointed to several youth organizations in Syria that were interested in the Movement's ideas but for fear of reprisals did not call themselves Civil Society Movement. "The discourse is dispersed but not lost," he said. "Once the spark ignites the younger generation, we can withdraw," Kilo concluded prophetically. "At least we have paved the way."[25]

On another occasion, Kilo framed his hope in the following terms: "We were not created by God to be suppressed. Days will certainly come in which we will play a great role in this country. As rebels and freedom fighters we already play a great role for the young people of today. They know that we fought for them without demanding anything in return."[26]

In a similar conversation about possible failures of the Civil Society Movement Sadiq Jalal al-Azm reflected in Berlin that he could see no other reason why the Civil Society Movement had failed except suppression and military rule. "It was really very moderate and shunned any kind of radicalism. Those who paid personal prices for it have my highest respect. Actually, the regime is radical, not the Movement." Azm did not accept the criticism that the Movement might have been too detached from the people or that it had oscillated mainly Western ideas of secularism and civil society that were not in tune with Syrian culture. "These criticisms are really old stuff," Azm said defensively. "These states are all Western, they are Western founded, they share a Western notion of sovereignty. The word Western becomes bad only when it is about rights, democracy and so on." Azm was convinced that although the Civil Society Movement had failed in terms of achieving tangible goals, it had done a good job in leaving a mark and raising consciousness for times to come.[27]

The challenge to walk the walk in practice approached much faster than any of the protagonists could have expected. At the end of 2010, a mildew atmosphere lay over Damascus. The intellectual opposition was in a state of internal emigration while people in every-day life enjoyed the distractions of consumerism and an increasingly modern lifestyle or they struggled to purchase the basics for survival.

In this climate of intimidation and desperation I met Riad Seif again.

He sat in the living room in his modern white-clad apartment building in Khaliye Qudsiye, a neighborhood that was experiencing a construction boom for upper middle class apartment buildings in proximity to Damascus but with the advantage of a fresher climate and cleaner air. The ex-member of parliament and textile entrepreneur was in a highly contemplative mood. His prostate cancer was progressing and was far from eradicated by the operation he received in prison. Several attempts to leave the country for better medical treatment had failed. Seif was still one on the top of the regime's list. But he had changed.

"I have the feeling they want to silence me forever," said Seif in a low and soft voice. "They will put me into prison or kill me. In order to save myself and the Council of the Damascus Declaration I resigned from my position. I will not act as an opposition figure anymore if things don't change. I don't think that I can add anything because I'm not allowed and under too heavy surveillance." Seif, the relentless fighter for political pluralism and a social market economy, appeared broken. "We have at least to live and don't feel afraid to lift the white flag. Enough!" he said, glancing at his wife seated next to him. (She is younger than Seif and works at the Goethe Institute, the German cultural center in Damascus.) "You can say the regime won the war."

On the other hand, Seif did knew that the Civil Society Movement still had supporters from all sections of society.[28] "If people were not afraid of punishment, the support would be unlimited." Especially younger people shied away from exposing and black-listing themselves. A public film screening was enough to put some of the younger members into prison. "We are liberals, nationalists, Islamists, Kurds, Arabs, communists, etc. We are a team that represents Syria as it is. Our commonness was democracy," Seif said. In an arrangement with the authorities Seif withdrew from any opposition activities but could maintain his personal contacts abroad.

Seif showed bitter disappointment with the Europeans. Like Kilo he had hoped that European countries would do more on their behalf. "The Europeans should feel ashamed at least for Anwar al-Bunni," he said, referring to Bunni's arrest after he had taken over the position of director of the newly founded—and immediately closed—Institute for Human Rights in Damascus 2006. "He was their partner. The Institute was a European-financed NGO." Seif felt that the interest in human rights in Syria had faded due to the focus on regional issues like negotiations with Israel or the situation in Lebanon or Iraq. Pressure on the regime was fading. "That's why I thought they would keep me forever [in prison]."

In his "new life" Seif committed himself to charity projects in the manufacturing sector. He was very concerned about the rising gap between rich and poor. In the current drought, hundreds of thousands of people from the arid areas in the eastern part of Syria had fled into Damascus, he said. "This is a very dangerous bomb that will explode one day. We have to create jobs in the rural areas." Seif called for the urgent necessity to support Syria's industry and make it more competitive as well as offering better working conditions for employees. As an MP he had presented a project to develop the garment industry in the villages. The government rejected his project. Under the reign of Hafez al-Asad in the years between 1990 and 1998 Seif's company exported textiles for Adidas International worth $16 million per year and employed 1,200 workers, of whom were 500 young women. "They offered to sell their gold to keep the factory running in bad times," remembered Seif. "In one bad year we voluntarily reduced the wages by fifteen percent for six months and the people felt as a team. This is no fairy tale, all this happened in Damascus," he said with nostalgia.

In the coming years, Seif planned to establish a kind of hobby consultancy that helped create industries in rural areas. He said he still had many plans. "I want to do something good for the country. People trust me. I'm not selfish. I'm ready to teach. To give is the best joy." In Germany he once saw an old man who worked as a school crossing guard. "He was so proud to guide the pupils across the street. He was so happy." Seif smiled softly.

Despite his illness he was not suffering, he insisted. Seif's thoughts carried a peculiar melancholy on that day. "I have had one of the most wonderful lives that you can dream of. God always supported me. If I live one, five, or ten years more, it's all an extra gift," said the ailing entrepreneur who had lost his 21-year-old son in 1996 under "mysterious circumstances" as he called it. Almost spiteful he continued: "I feel proud. I deserve to be happy. I have a wonderful wife, family, children, and grandchildren. If there is a paradise I'll be in the first class there because I did a lot for society and the human being."[29]

These words almost sounded like a farewell. But only a few months later when a new opposition was forming in the streets, Seif abandoned his agreement to stay out of politics. He became the most outstanding member of Syria's traditional Civil Society Movement who went out to protest in the street hand-in-hand with the youngsters. Thus he built a bridge between the generations. He also linked domestic and foreign-based opposition groups. Fida' Howrani should be added here, too. She operated on injured demonstrators round the clock in Hama, free of charge, and under the mortal risk. Seif was temporarily arrested in May 2011 and again released. He was beaten up and suffered a broken arm in October during street protests in the Damascus neighborhood of Midan. Yet, still he continued. Seif also became the highest ranking representative of the old opposition in the new Syrian National Council that was founded in October 2011.

The Islamists

The best known Islamist group in Syria has been the Muslim Brotherhood, the organization that had nearly driven the "Alawite heretic" Hafez al-Asad out of office in 1982. Since 1980, membership in the banned organization was punishable by death. The leaders lived in exile in London, but numerous sympathizers sneaked into the Syrian, among them intellectuals, members of the military, and even members of the Baath Party.[30]

As the Damascus Declaration demonstrated, some representatives of the Civil Society Movement and of the exiled Islamists were by no means irreconcilably opposed to each other. There were regular personal contacts between them, as a member of the Civil Society Movement in Damascus told me. Islamists also signed some of the secularists' petitions. They were both pursuing the same end: democracy. Or so they said.

This surprising compatibility did not stem merely from opportunism. There was also a more profound intellectual dynamic behind it. By contrast, the Kifaya Movement in Egypt since the end of 2004 saw hardcore Muslim Brothers and staunch secularists march side-by-side against Husni Mubarak's reign. Yet they had no common goals beyond *kifaya!* (enough!). Another difference between Egypt and Syria was that Kifaya attacked the president directly, whereas in Syria this still was not the main focus of the opposition.

One reason why Civil Society activists and Islamists in Syria got along was that the Syrians had developed a movement of political Islam that was more moderate than in neighboring countries. Many people recalled with horror the Muslim Brothers of some thirty years before and the situation in Syria that had resembled a civil war. Radical Islamism would probably have had no broad following in Syria, not even among Sunnis, at least under peaceful circumstances. Another restraint on radical Islamism lay in the many decades of secular experience under the Baath and its predecessor regimes.

Yet something extraordinary and contradictory took place around 2004. For the first time since the 1982 bloodbath in Hama, the Syrian regime began to cautiously seek talks with the Muslim Brotherhood. True, Bashar stressed to American journalists in May 2004 that no apologies would be made for the action in Hama. Yet a month before, he had met with leading Islamists from neighboring countries who had connections with the Syrian Muslim Brothers. The late Mufti of Damascus, Ahmed Kuftaro, and a member of parliament, Muhammad al-Habash, acted as mediators. Later, the government established direct contact with Syrian leaders of the Brotherhood. However, details were difficult to uncover because of the delicacy of such developments, and the information was partly contradictory as well.[31] At any rate, Habash was a leading advocate of abolishing the death penalty for members of the Muslim Brotherhood in the name of national unity. He reiterated this stance during the upheaval in 2011 for the same reason of national reconciliation.

Whatever the exact circumstances, there were increasing indications that something remarkable was happening. The political scientist Salam Kawakibi sharply criticized this move. "The regime is now doing all it can to survive. This includes approaching the Muslim Brothers. It is trying to curry favor with everyone except the secular Civil Society Movement. From the beginning the other secular forces have been the Baath Party's greatest enemies."[32] Fear was growing that the regime was slowly but surely abandoning the foundation of secularism in Syria. Observers saw the temporary arrest of the intellectual Nabil Fayyad as one indication of the growing influence of Islamist forces. Fayyad had written about the spread of radical Islam in Syria.

Asad was playing with fire. Anti-Americanism and the isolation of the regime were bringing pan-Arabists and Islamists closer together. When it came to foreign policy, the once-hated Alawites in the Damascus regime became the Sunni extremists' best option. The Syrian ambassador to the United States, Imad Mustafa, who was known for unconventional statements, went even further than Asad when he said what was previously inconceivable: Hama had been a "tragic event." It was not so long before that the Syrian government had enveloped Hama in a mantle of silence. Mustafa's statement tested out a new tone in the movement for national reconciliation. After examining their individual cases, the government allowed many former members of the Muslim Brothers to return to Syria. However, one of the conditions for their return was that they had to apologize for Hama.

London based Sheikh Ali Sadr ad-Din al-Bayanuni was the moderate head of the Syrian Muslim Brotherhood, who oscillated between striving for reconciliation with the regime and forging unconventional alliances against it such with as the National Salvation Front during his tenure from 1996 to 2010.

Encouraged by the Damascus Spring, the Muslim Brotherhood published a statement in May 2001 that on its face announce a significant change of direction. In it, the movement committed itself to democracy, free elections, and the primacy of law—without reference to the Sharia, separation of powers, or a pluralistic modern state. "The time is gone when one party claims it is the homeland," the statement said, and went on to assert that each party was entitled to present itself only in accordance with the power it had derived from free elections. The conflict between secular Arab nationalism and Islamism was "a stage in history that is now past."[33]

In an official statement, the Syrian government declared that the Muslim Brothers wanted to distract from their internal crisis, to create for themselves a new identity, and to regain influence in Syrian politics. The Islamists remained a "terrorist organization" who believed that there was now a political vacuum in the country that they hoped to fill.[34] The renewed activity of the Muslim Brothers after years of silence worried Asad. He feared that, with the Muslim Brothers in the mix, the impetus for civil reform could get out of hand. This was an essential reason why the Damascus Spring was ultimately crushed.

In August 2002, the Muslim Brothers met again in London to convert their 2001 statement into a national charter. Opposition figures from the left-wing and nationalist camps were present this time. However, the new document contained slight differences from the previous statement: the role of Islam with its "noble objectives, sublime values, and perfect legislation" was emphasized more strongly. The passage stating that Islam may also be understood merely as a "cultural affiliation" was deleted.[35] Such a statement would have meant that the Islamists were suddenly on the same wavelength as Baath founder Michel Aflaq.

In November 2005, al-Bayanuni reiterated his pragmatic stand and emphasized that the Muslim Brothers were not interested in a coup in Syria, nor in a revenge campaign against secularists and Alawites. "We want a civil and not a religious state," al-Bayanuni vowed.[36]

Pragmatism was no novelty for the Muslim Brothers. In the struggle against Hafez al-Asad, the Islamists had displayed contradictions and breaches in their ideology, although Asad himself was no more consistent. In the 1940s and 1950s, the Muslim Brotherhood sympathized with socialist ideas, even with secular elements of socialism, and later with a capitalist economic system coupled with the call for political liberties and human rights. It had the quite worldly objective of getting rid of a dictatorship in the interest of the bourgeoisie. Their arguments were influenced by the overall political mood of the time and by strategic considerations.[37] During the first decade of this century the Muslim Brothers, not only in Syria but in almost all authoritarian Arab states, discovered popular issues, most of which were commonly associated with Western-style democracy. They converged with the secularist opposition movements on four key issues: the call for human rights, emphasis on encompassing humanist elements in Islam, respect for an ideological and political pluralism, and the guarantee of freedom of speech.

This pragmatism made the new Islamists acceptable to the rest of the opposition. The Christian Kilo even compared some of them to European Christian Democrats, or the ruling moderate Islamist party in Turkey, AKP (Party for Justice and Development), under Prime Minister Erdoğan. "I believe they are a moderate force with a strong democratic tendency," Kilo said in 2003. "Therefore we won't give the regime the chance to play us off against each other." The readiness for dialogue "is a basis for the time being to challenge the power of these people [the rulers]." Political change was the first priority. "If my opinion is the expression of a civil and secular democracy and theirs is an Islamic one, this is all right as long as we have democracy as a common denominator. We will accept the Muslims coming to power through elections, provided that they accept the democratic system."[38] Similarly, Riad Seif put it after his release from prison: "We have no problems with Islamic groups and organizations. I mean when the Islamists become democrats, they won't frighten us anymore."[39]

Islamic currents in Syria traditionally rejected the radicals in Saudi Arabia and elsewhere. Especially after the terrorist attacks on 11 September 2001, Kilo was convinced that "Saudi Arabia has no more credibility in the Islamic world." Neither did Iran serve as a model even for faithful Muslims. Sadiq Jalal al-Azm agreed: "Radical Islam has been in decline worldwide since September 11." This held true for Syria as well. "If there were a regime change, a moderate Islam of the merchant middle class would prevail," Azm said. But only a strong civil society could act as a "shock-absorber" against conservative Islam and dampen the apprehensions of religious minorities who feared oppression by the Islamic majority.

The pragmatist lawyer Anwar al-Bunni shared this view. "Of course, there is a danger when Islamists are allowed to return to the country. But the Syrians will not put up with a second dictatorship, with a transition from a nationalist to an Islamist one. Syrians don't want to become a second Afghanistan. I'm not afraid of the Muslim Brothers. Syrians have always had a loyal relationship among each other. Even if the Muslim Brothers came to power, they would not be as radical as in Egypt."[40]

Of course, Sadiq Jalal al-Azm admitted that doubt existed. "But I think the risk is worth taking." The regime only used the fear of radical Islam as an excuse for not changing anything in the encrusted system, he pointed out.[41] The philosopher Tayyeb Tizini went a step further. "The regime has sometimes actively supported the Islamists because they wanted to keep them as a visible danger to the secular opposition: 'Just look, this is the danger. Either you have us or you get them.'"[42]

Azm's relaxed attitude toward political Islam was all the more remarkable since the philosopher had often disparagingly called Islam a "backward folklore" and repeatedly warned that "the Islamists are always in favor of democracy when they know they have the political majority behind them and against democracy when they are afraid of losing the elections." In Syria not only the Islamists but also the left-wingers had come a long way.

The moderate line taken by the Muslim Brothers' political leadership in London also led to rifts in the movement itself with the political wing opposing the so-called Jihadis. The moderates were even willing to close ranks with the United States in order to put pressure on the regime in Damascus. Yet the Jihadis, some of whom lived in exile in Saudi Arabia, demanded that anti-Americanism be more emphatically stressed than anti-secularism. One of the radical Jihadi figures was Sheikh Mohsen al-Qaqa who held his hate sermons in an Aleppo suburb. He called for an Islamic state in Syria and openly supported the Iraqi resistance to the United States. His CDs laced with anti-American slogans found an enthusiastic market in Baghdad and other Sunni cities in Iraq.[43]

The fundamental policy disputes among the Islamists could not be resolved. The moderates got increasing support from Sunni entrepreneurs.

Observers saw this group distancing itself from the government because the latter was no longer able to ensure a profitable environment. The moderates were also turning away from Islamic rhetoric, realizing that it was not credible to pursue a policy of liberalization with Islamic populism that demonized the West in general and the United States in particular. The more radical Muslim Brothers, for their part, no longer had their social base in the Sunni business class and were looking for support in the lower urban classes and the urbanized country population—exactly where the Baath Party had traditionally anchored their social base.

Here is where the conservative current of the Qubaisis is located, too. They operated a powerful network among the wives, daughters and mothers of affluent businessmen in Damascus. They also came up with a more conservative version of the *hijab*. According to their design it came with dark stockings and a long coat in dark blue, navy blue, or black. In contrast, the traditional Syrian headscarf reminded one more of an Audrey Hepburn-like scarf, as Sami Moubayed wrote. It adorned more for modesty, rather than religiousness. The Qubaisis controlled schools, mosques, and entire neighborhoods, where alcohol, for example, was not served at restaurants, and where *hijab*-wearing young women drove around in brand new BMWs and Audis, as Moubayed critically observed. "They are rich, socially prominent, and influenced by Islam." "The Great Sheikha" Munira al-Qubaisi, born in 1933, founded the movement in Damascus and has managed to gather an international following. Different currents from Sufis to Salafis have been attracted to the circle. Qubaisi was also closely linked with the ideas of the late Grand Mufti Ahmad Kuftaro.[44]

On the societal level, conservative Islam and the worldly achievements of modern Syria did not stand in contradiction. On the political level, the discussion was in full sway about how compatible this kind of Islam was with modern values and politics. There was disagreement within the Civil Society Movement about how to assess the different streams of the Muslim Brotherhood. Not everybody followed Kilo's strategy of chumming up with them. The economic historian Ali Saleh, for example, warned that "the risk of political Islamization will exist as long as the country doesn't have a secular constitution that is accepted also by the Islamic forces. As it was in Algeria, as soon as the Islamists come to power, they will want to have an Islamic state and an Islamic society because it's Allah that is the supreme master for them."

In the 1980s, Muslim Brother ideologists had admitted that democracy was only a means to their ends. One of their leaders asserted that "the Islamists are fighting democracy in the world . . . [but] democracy is a suitable means to prepare the way for an Islamist victory."[45]

Therefore, Saleh stressed that AKP politicians in Turkey were forced to keep the secular constitution, although they themselves were, for the most part, strict Muslims. Unlike in Turkey, however, the Islamists in Syria had a leg up on the left-wing intellectuals. The Islamists had an existing infrastructure consisting of numerous Quranic schools and mosques. Meetings of more than five people in public places were forbidden by martial law. "This applies to us in the Civil Society Movement," said Saleh, a Sunni by birth. "But nobody forbids people to go to the mosques in crowds and assemble for talks."[46] Opposition members reported that "large numbers" of Christian and communist reformers entered mosques during Muslim Friday prayers just to meet without government surveilance.

Salam Kawakibi, who himself comes from a famous family of Islamic scholars, offered criticism. "Nowadays there are hundreds of mosques in Damascus but not a single meeting hall for secular people. This says everything. The truth about the Islamists will come out once they're in power." According to Kawakibi, they pretended to be moderate on the outside but they preached intolerance and missionary zeal inside the mosques. The problem was, he said, that the Islamic forces consisted of two pillars: narrow-minded theologians and ignorant masses.[47] The secular historian Abdullah Hanna also warned that "the religious opposition is stronger than the secular one. At present, the Islamists are operating under the cover of a ritual exercise of religion. But the ground has been prepared for an explosion once the lid is lifted."[48] Tizini added that "this state is a band of robbers. Of course, the Islamists would win [in the case of democratization] because they do everything for their masses. The state doesn't do anything." [49]

Indeed, the question had to be asked: in the case of an abrupt regime change, who would be able to fill the power vacuum more quickly—a group of mainly elder intellectuals who represented Western secular philosophy and a modern civil society, or an Islamist movement, possibly supported by Saudi petro-dollars or by the more radical Muslim Brothers in Jordan and Egypt? If a violent upheaval took place, those who seized the reins of power would write the constitution. In this case, it would not have a corrective function. This was an argument in favor of a cautious transition, which is what most Civil Society activists (and also moderate Muslims) were striving to achieve.

In August 2010 Bayanuni was replaced as the head of the Muslim Brotherhood by Muhammad Riad Shakfa. The engineer is counted among the more hard-line veterans from Hama with less interest in reconciling with the regime. In order to dispel concerns about an Islamization of Syria after the revolts that started in 2011, Shafka emphasized that Turkey continued to represent the model for the Muslim Brothers after the Asad regime had toppled. He rejected any notion of pursuing the Iranian model of a theocratic state. The Brotherhood had no intention to impose anything on the population, he promised.[50] Especially his antecessor Bayanuni and his people became heavily involved in the process of forming the opposition Syrian National Council in 2011.

The New Islamic Alternative

Apart from the purged Muslim Brotherhood, another Islamic force surfaced in Syria that presented itself in an even more moderate manner. The focal point of this current has been Sheikh Muhammad al-Habash, former director of the Islamic Studies Center and grandson-in-law of the long-serving Mufti of Damascus, Ahmed Kuftaro.

In March 2003, Habash was elected to parliament with the largest number of votes among the independent candidates from Damascus, according to the official count. An Islamic scholar, Habash saw the late Kuftaro and himself as "chosen by God" to counteract religious fanaticism and intolerance, which he tried to convey to Muslims in his writings, with the help of appropriate *suras* (chapters) from the Quran. In Habash's view, state and society were in a "harmonious relationship" in "secular" Syria. Nevertheless, he complained that more radical forces were also gaining ground. They reviled him as a heretic, sometimes as a Christian, and sometimes as a "secular Imam." Habash did not even find the last two titles offensive.

Habash has drawn his ideas about the renewal of Islam exclusively from the Islamic sphere itself. Born in 1962 in Damascus the scholar was educated in Quranic schools, where he concentrated on recitation of the Quran. At the age of twenty, he started publishing writings on Islamic law, which distinguished him from those past and present reformers who tried to renew Islam using religious and non-religious elements.

In 2003 when I firrst met him, the Islamic Studies Center was not yet closed by the regime. The telephone was ringing constantly in Habash's office pavilion, located in the garden of the institute in the Rukned-din quarter of Damascus. The institute was humming with conferences, interviews, and publishing ventures. Habash was a man in great demand. Dressed in a dark suit, he sat in front of a wall of bookshelves filled with Islamic volumes with golden calligraphy on their spines. After the interruption of every telephone call, Habash picked up the thread of thought again exactly where he had left off.

"We regard Islam as one among many religions," he said, knowing that this provoked the ire of the largest number of Muslims. "We reject the idea that Islam has superseded all religions that existed before. We are against a monopoly of the doctrine of salvation. You are a good person when you do good, no matter in what religion." Even for moderate Muslims it was hard to swallow the idea that redemption should be possible without believing in the Prophet Muhammad, which is what Habash was implying.[51]

Habash just as boldly criticized the schizophrenic Muslim view of women either as "saints or whores." According to him, this had a destructive impact on Muslim community life. Habash wrote that women were endowed by God with intellectual and spiritual abilities that they should use freely, and that they should be able to decide their own fates and what happens to their bodies. Nevertheless, Habash supported Islamic restrictions such as no sex before marriage, no free social intercourse between the sexes, and "moderate clothing" for women.

Habash is convinced that Muslims can only correct their relationship with God if they change their relationships with other people. This contrasts with the belief of the extremists who try to fix their relationship with God by breaking off their connections with others who do not agree with such a monopolization of Islam, be they Muslims or non-Muslims. In Habash's view, only dialogue can rescue Islam from its internal crisis. Islamic critics accused him of wanting to merge all types of faith into a new religion.[52]

Habash believes in an inclusive cosmos where everything is interrelated. This brings him close to Sufi-inspired teachings such as those of the great Islamic mystic and philosopher Ibn Arabi, who was born in Andalusia in Spain in 1165 and died in Damascus in 1240. Habash's beliefs also evoke parallels to the Indian Mogul ruler Akbar (1556-1605), who strove for a lively spiritual exchange between the different religions in his kingdom and even envisaged a common religion, the "divine faith" *(ad-din al-ilahi)*. Akbar, too, ceased to be regarded as a Muslim by many.[53]

Looking around the world, there were several Islamic scholars who advocated dialogue between the religions and cultures as well as the importance of a secular state. Among these scholars were Abdul Rahman Wahid, the former president of Indonesia (1999-2001) and chairman of the Islamic organization Nahdatul Ulama (Renaissance of the Religious Scholars) who died in 2009.[54] Habash personally knew Wahid and other like-minded Islamic figures such as Iran's Shiite philosopher Abdolkarim Soroush or Turkish Prime Minister Erdoğan. "We consider ourselves of the same stream of renewal," Habash said. "We have individual connections but we don't form a big common movement. Our main focus in Syria is domestic politics."

Habash himself likened his ideas to those of the European Enlightenment. Whereas early Islamic pantheism defined human beings as Allah's passive creatures, Habash is among the ranks of rational Islamic thinkers, such as the Mutazilites, who ascribe to human beings a large amount of freedom to determine their individual fates.[55] Democracy was Habash's political objective, he said. But in his view caution should be exercised on the way toward it: "Our priority is to bring about an Islamic renewal before we move toward democracy. We have to first correct our ideas of Islam."

The Islamic faith was a "collection of ideas over the course of history," said Habash. "We can choose from a large number of ideas." According to him, conservative Muslims interpret the Quran selectively for their purposes. Habash has particular aversions to Saudi Arabia, which in his opinion sends a radical message of Islam out to the world. In a letter to Crown Prince Abdullah in April 2005, Habash expressed his frustration over a new translation of the

Quran published in the birthplace of the Prophet that used the most radical way "out of more than one million traditions" of interpreting the *suras* and *hadiths*. "Why do we translate the Quran in such a way and then send it to England or the United States? If Westerners read this, of course they will want to fight us," he said scornfully. "The misunderstanding of Islam is not only the fault of the Western people, but also Muslims' responsibility when we convey a misguided understanding of Islam."[56]

His pragmatic interpretation of Islam had also alienated Habash from Kuftaro, who died on 1 September 2004, at the age of eighty-nine. Kuftaro had issued a written statement saying that Habash no longer spoke for him. Habash attributed this to the "conservative people" around the Mufti in his old age. Other voices had also expressed the criticism that Kuftaro was spreading an increasingly conservative brand of Sunni Islam. He had also called on Muslims worldwide "to use all means and martyrdom operations to defeat the American, British, and Zionist aggression on Iraq."[57] Thus, Kuftaro had once more shown himself true to the political line of the Syrian regime.

Habash, on the other hand, was even "more secular" than the Syrian constitution, for he rejected the *sharia* as a law for everyday life. The Syrians had always been a people with a will of their own, he said, as shown by the difficulty the French had in establishing colonial rule. "Now we have the risk of another kind of colonization: Islamist movements from outside."

Two things were especially important for Habash. First, the state should remain neutral and not dictate to its citizens any public dress code, including the veil. Second, radicals have misinterpreted the Islamic jihad, which in fact merely means defending oneself, one's family, and one's homeland, not fighting other religions and forcing their members to convert to Islam.

On the one hand, Habash thought in the cultural and dogmatic paradigms of Islam. In one of his books, he condemned the West's "spiritual emptiness" and idealized Islamic societies as "clean areas" with peace, no crime, alcohol, or rape. On the other hand, he also expressed sharp criticism about Muslims in the West who saw their host countries as "a pasture for their lusts and desires and a market for their profits, without feeling loyalty toward the land that protects or welcomes them."[58] Again on the one hand, Habash hoped for a growing Islamic influence in Europe. On the other hand, he preached tolerance and rejected religious zeal. Habash regularly held religious services in the Al-Zahara Mosque in Mezzeh and was pleased about the good attendance. "More than five thousand people come every Friday."

One of his mentors was Jawdat Said, a liberal sheikh from the Quneitra region on the Golan Heights. This popular old man, whose trademark was a pointed fur hat, championed vehemently for democracy, even if the Syrian majority would decide against an Islamic form of society. He liked to use the European Union as a model for the open dialogue among peoples and a balance of interests among countries. According to him, the Arab world should take the EU as an example of how to live in peaceful coexistence with ones neighbors instead of fighting with each other. "We need education, not nuclear bombs," Said insisted. "We must use our brains and the Internet, not weapons." The old sheikh ran his own website. He was a humanist through and through who liked to refer to Plato's cave parable in conversation, especially the passages where the human being frees himself from darkness and sees the light of truth at the end of a difficult path. Said opposed the dogmas of monotheistic religions. At the same time, he openly saw how disappointed he was with the US and also with the Europeans who had once been "the nation of discoverers and thinkers." With regard to the Middle East policy of Western countries in Iraq and Israel, the old man lamented that "today there are no more values. Only muscles and violence count." This applied to both sides, he said self-critically. The phenomenon of Islamic violence was the result of an unresolved intellectual crisis in the Islamic world, Said held.[59]

In the moderate Islamic camp, there were also businessmen pressing for an economic opening up of the country. One of their spokesmen was Ihsan Sanqer. "In Syria conservative Islam is only a reaction to socialism, a reaction to the regime," he said in 2004. "It doesn't belong to our culture." The stocky, energetic, almost bald fifty-one-year-old ran a financial empire with his family in Damascus. He was an agent for Daimler Chrysler, Porsche, Siemens Nixdorf, and other international firms in Syria, and owned a food-processing company. When the corrupt regime protégé Rami Makhlouf schemed to take over the Mercedes agency, the Stuttgart company backed Sanqer. Daimler Chrysler accepted the consequences and was barred from importing new cars to Syria for a period of three years. Officially, the ban was lifted in January 2005, and the Sanqer family was supposed to be able to deal once again with the limousines with the Mercedes star. It seemed that the businessman had won a long legal dispute. But "administrative burdens" and sudden "new taxes" imposed on Sanqer prolonged this war of nerves. It was indeed difficult to advance in Syria once one was a public enemy of the Makhloufs.

Certificates, pictures of Syria's sights, and a photo showing Sanqer with Hafez al-Asad hang next to the heavy bookcase in Sanqer's former office in the central Damascus quarter of Baramke. The businessman occupied an independent seat in parliament from 1990 to 1998. He was a committed supporter of a social market economy. "When I read German post-war history and Ludwig Erhard's concepts, it reminds me of our history," he said, alluding to the German minister of economy and later chancellor, who became a symbol of the model of the social market economy and the economic boom in Germany in the 1960s. "This is in line with our culture."

The word "culture"—above all with an Islamic connotation—frequently occurred in his lively flow of speech. Sanqer held that something of this culture should resurface in politics. "Turkey is a very good example for the whole of the Middle East," Sanqer was convinced, looking toward the AKP government. "For this model doesn't leave religious people abandoned but gives them a political umbrella. Like the Christian Democrats in Europe, these forces can absorb the conservatives. This has nothing to do with Islamic fundamentalism. On the contrary, they can draw the Muslim population into the moderate center." Syria, too, needed such a party to compete with the Baath Party, said Sanqer. Islam might be an integrating factor: the mostly Sunni Kurds, who felt excluded by the pan-Arab ideology, could find their political home in such a party. Sanqer hastened to say that the party should be so moderate that it could also attract Christians. "My feeling is that the president wants to allow such a party but he isn't able to because the pressure from outside is so great at the moment." No doubt about who would found and lead such a party—Sanqer himself. "I'm just waiting for the chance, for I don't want to burn myself too early," he said impishly and quoted an Arab proverb. "Put the honey in the store so that it increases in value." One like Riad Seif was enough to overstretch the bow during the Damascus Spring.

Sanqer stressed that he certainly favors reforms. "But here we have the problem that people still act too much with emotions. This is dangerous." In such a society, democracy had to come slowly and from above to guarantee a "soft landing." The businessman showed a great grasp of reality when he insisted that "we have to carry out reforms before there is peace between Israel and the Palestinians so that we are prepared. For it will only be after peace that the economic problems will begin."[60]

Shortly thereafter, Sanqer emigrated out of frustration with the regime's practices toward his business. Finally, in 2011 he saw his time coming and turned into the one the major financiers of the new opposition movements that gradually merged into the Syrian National Council. Among other things Sanqer financed flight tickets and the venues of the countless gatherings in which the opposition figures from inside and outside Syria negotiated their alliances and programs in Turkey and elsewhere.

Habash, Said, and Sanqer used to be friends and in old times supported each other politically. They also had contact with Civil Society activists on the other side of the political spectrum. Both sides invited each other to meetings and gave each other space in their publications. Habash's position in relation to the government was typically ambivalent. On the one hand, his institute worked illegally because the Baath ideology allowed no room for such Civil Society institutions outside the official associations. On the other hand, he had "good relations" with the government, at least at that time. Habash saw himself as following the same line as the president with respect to democracy as his long-term goal (this is where he differed from the Civil Society Movement who wanted it faster) and in the fight against radicals.

Sheikh Habash was definitely a person with a sense of power. Sharp tongues had even called him Machiavellian. In order to gain influence, he did not shy away from making pacts with those in power. In the parliamentary election in 2003, Habash snubbed supporters by forming an alliance with a list of candidates with well-known associations among the parasitic business class. Muhammed Hamsho, a former teacher who became rich with a range of firms that supply state institutions, was also on the list. Hamsho represented the mobile phone manufacturers Sony and Ericsson in Syria, among other companies. During the elections, Hamsho promised a free mobile phone to anyone who delivered a certain number of voters for him.

Skeptics always saw both the respective Great Muftis and Habash as the regime's accomplices. With the Kurdish Ahmed Kuftaro, who was the state-recognized authority of the Syrian Sunnis from 1965 until his death in 2004, and with his successor, Sheikh Ahmad Badreddin Hassoun, the ruling Alawites tried to clear themselves of the charge of neglecting Islam, to shake off their heretical image among Sunnis, and to broaden their constituency. The Asads could always count on Kuftaro. In 1991, the sheikh declared the reelection of the president to be a "national obligation and religious duty."[61] Equally reliable proved his successor Hassoun who was internationally known for his tolerant dogmatic sermons—and once was invited to speak in front of the European Parliament—but who was a staunch defender of the regime domestically. Contrary to the contents of his preaching during inter-religious dialogue forums in which he defended the strict separation of religion and politics, he boosted his rhetoric especially after the revolt broke out in the country. Hassoun was also known for participating in security sessions of the government. In a heated speech on 10 October 2011 he threatened that suicide bombers could become active in Europe and the United States if Syria were attacked from abroad.[62] A few days earlier Hassoun had lost his son Saria who was murdered in a series of possible revenge killings of professors, nuclear scientists, and other scientists in Homs and Aleppo.

When Hassoun took office in July 2005 he looked more progressive than the old Kuftaro. For example, he criticized the kidnappings and suicide attacks in Iraq. Within the Syrian *ulama* he was not alone in this opinion. In January 2004, the dean of the Faculty of Theology of the University of Damascus, Said Ramadan al-Bouti—otherwise a staunch religious conservative—made a controversial statement, describing the killing of American civilians as "un-Islamic" and the calling for the death of Americans as "ignorant." Bouti, who became head of the Umayyad Mosque in Old Damascus in 2008, was said to have intentions of founding an Islamic political party, too, but the regime refused to allow him to do so.[63] An analyst in Damascus called Habash an opportunist and Hassoun a dangerous demagogue. Secular opposition figures had mixed feelings about Hassoun in particular. The Syrian historian Sami Moubayed pondered in 2011 that the regime-friendly sheikhs were very likely to engage in an Islamist party if the system broke apart. Bouti and Hassoun had a hidden agenda, wrote Moubayed: "All talk about them being 'secular clerics' is pure nonsense, marketed by them during the heyday of the secular era, in order to cuddle up to officials."[64]

Habash for his part was welcome to the Baathists in the sense that he emphasized the national Arab character of Islam, unlike Sanqer, for example. Thus, Habash strengthened the historically weak link between religion and pan-Arab nationalism.[65] Similarly, Hassoun signaled a willingness to bridge the gap between Arab nationalism and Islam.

However, despite all criticism, it can be considered progress that the Baathists—for whatever reasons—had created an environment where such a liberal Islam not only established strong institutions but has also found committed followers. This was a valuable social and political asset, especially since 9/11. Yet another protagonist, the Syrian author and engineer Muhammad Shahrur, used very moderate arguments. He called for the Quran to be interpreted in a new and pragmatic way for each epoch instead of centuries-old interpretations being constantly held up as eternal truths.

Habash estimated that half of the Syrian population was secular and the other half religious. By his reckoning, eighty percent of the religious Muslims were conservative, twenty percent identified with the "enlightened trend," and two percent were radicals of whom less than one percent were ready to use violence. In his very active political life Habash started efforts to create inroads into the large conservative crowd. In April 2005, he stood for election as the president of the conservative Syrian League of Islamic Scholars *(rabitat al-ulama')*. To his own surprise and the surprise of others, he was elected. Habash's explanation was interesting. "The conservative direction in Syria has no political agenda at all. They prepare for life after death and observe strict traditions and values. That's all. It's very easy to influence the conservative direction in favor of Islamic renewal. But they can as easily turn to Islamic radicals for the same reason."[66]

For some time it looked like that a moderate Islamic party in Syria would have had the potential and also the ability to catch traditional Muslims before they turned to more radical pied pipers. A respective party would have had appeal for those who are looking for some connection to Islam in politics without wanting to islamicize politics. This was the constituency to which the "infidel," secular Civil Society activists could hardly appeal.

The political landscape in the moderate Islamic camp changed considerably throughout the years. As mentioned above, Sanqer emigrated and became part of the foreign-based opposition. The Mufti of Damascus went hand in hand with the regime through the bloody months of the upheaval, and Habash stayed somewhere in between.

Indications proliferated that more and more people who operated in the wider circle of the regime had become frustrated by the end of the decade.

Support was fizzling out at the margins. In other words, the contractions of the regime entailed the estrangement of supporters in the wider orbit of regime loyalty. This also applied to Habash.

By the end of 2010 Habash's Islamic Studies Center had been closed[67] (as well as the moderate Islamic Abu Nour Foundation). The sheikh was banned from holding sermons in his Al-Zahara Mosque in Mezzeh, and trouble with the Ministry of Religious Endowments *(wazarat al-auqaf)* was rising. Habash was highly frustrated at the end of 2010 and saw himself being pushed into an opposition corner where he actually did not intend to belong. In an attempt to control Islamic preachers the government now obliged the imams during their sermons to stick only to religion, Quran recitation and family matters. This was strictly applied to Habash, too, who was of a more political nature and used to talk about his controversial convictions. "In my Islamic speech I have a different agenda. It's a huge mistake to believe that God is ours," insisted Habash in October 2010, sitting between a home gym machine and high shelves of books with Islamic calligraphy in his roof top apartment in the modern Damascus suburb of Telat al-Rabia. His voice was as soft as always, his English had improved considerably but the tone of his voice was filled with frustration. "The Ministry is very intolerant. They want to convert everyone to conservative Islam and we as imams should be instruments for this." Despite his marginalization, however, Habash was allowed to continue his speeches on three private radio programs at that time.

Habash's wife, Asma Kuftaro, who headed the Association of Syrian Women *(muntada as-suriyyat al-islami)* had been banned from travelling abroad. Habash was torn between his loyalty to the Syrian system and adverse developments within it. "I believe the system in Syria is secular. I prefer that to a religious regime. My enlightened Islamic path would be impossible in Saudi Arabia, Yemen or elsewhere," he said. "The government should not fight the path of renewal but the conservatives."[68] He also thought that the president himself headed in the right direction and allowed important freedoms but that there was obvious resistance within old Baathists and Islamists alike. Without any doubt, Habash needed the remnants of Syrian secularism to survive politically and religiously. On the other hand, he thought that with diminishing pressure against the regime from abroad, the authorities should feel more relaxed allow more freedom inside the country. Apparently, his voice was no longer welcome. His words about granting more freedom almost turned to sound like those of representatives of the Civil Society Movement. Indeed, an opposition figure had indicated in another conversation that Habash had expressed remorse of having attacked members of the civil society so harshly during his years in parliament. Now it was him who used the word dictatorship in reference to the regime.

When violence broke out in Syria Habash remained in his uneasy position. In June 2011 he tried to establish a kind of forum on his own where a dialogue between the domestic opposition, moderate Islamic representatives and regime people were supposed to exchange ideas. In the light of the escalating violence and upcoming other forums his attempts remained not very successful. The conference that he had organized took place in the same Hotel Semiramis where the domestic opposition had met in their historic meeting a few days earlier. This time, however, a hotel technician unplugged the electricity.

Within his parliamentary activity Habash raised his voice in favor of reform in order to save as much as could be still saved. From the beginning of the protests in March he said he "hopes and expects" that the state of emergency would be lifted as part of "a formula that guarantees national security, and at the same time lets people feel relaxed and satisfied." For a long time Habash was one of the champions within the regime's orbit who called for abolishing emergency laws and for legalizing the Muslim Brotherhood in Syria as a matter of reconciliation. "During the 10th Baath Party congress in June 2005, one recommendation was to reduce the instances in which the emergency law was applied," Habash said. "Now we think it is a suitable time to ask what has happened to that recommendation."[69]

However, the sheikh remained in his difficult middle position and later called some slogans of the opposition "unrealistic and unreasonable" at that moment, and that they were combined with insults to the president. "The ballot box should be the judge between us," he added solemnly in a TV interview in October 2011. A military intervention was a "criminal act" that would cause even more bloodshed, Habash said, in line with his traditionally hard-line foreign policy views that had never deviated from the regime's position.[70] But as it became clear by 2010, his increasing frustration led him to more daring criticism even in connection with the regime's ideology of resistance. In the magazine *Syria Today* Habash was quoted in June 2011: "People's political rights had been suspended under the pretext of the state of war with Israel. The development [of political rights] should continue."

With his Third Way initiative Habash positioned himself notably between the regime and the opposition in statements such as: "We believe that the best way to protect civilians is diplomatic pressure and pushing the regime to sit and talk with the opposition and pushing the opposition to sit with the regime."[71] In November 2011 he supported the offer of the Arab League as "logical" and hoped that the government would agree to it.[72] He suggested inviting military pensioners from Egypt, Algeria, and Sudan to replace Syrian troops in the cities. Syrian state media started to refer to him as an opposition figure, which was obviously rejected by the opposition. Habash's influence during a process of political polarization, however, remained limited since he had temporarily lost basis and backing from either side.

Playing with the Islamic Fire

In the long run, the status quo in Syria benefited conservatives and radical Islamists. Moderate Islam and civil-secular representatives were suppressed and not allowed to emerge as alternatives to authoritarian Baathism. The question posed by many Syrians was how long would the regime be able to play with Islam without losing control? Exclusively ethnic or religious parties did not make sense and would quickly tear Syrian society apart. Yet new ways were needed to give a fresh social and political value to moderate Islam in Syria in order to provide a counterweight to conservatives and radicals.

Of all actors, the secularist Baath regime had silenced the moderate and secular voices calling for a pluralization of Syrian society and piecemeal reforms. Indeed, the fact that Islamist currents were gaining ground in the past years was partly due to the general trend of Islamization in the Arab Middle East from which Syria could not wall itself off. But apart from that, there were more reasons behind this development: a) A strategy of the ruling elite in Damascus was to let the Islamist danger simmer and present it as a deterrent in the sense of "either you get them or you have us." In this sense it was possible that the Baathists were more afraid of Islamic moderates becoming a stronger force than of the extremists. b) During the confrontation with the United States, violent Islamists served as a convenient instrument to weaken the occupying power in Iraq. c) Despite its secular orientation, the Syrian regime in its foreign policy allied with Islamist partners like Iran, Hezbollah and Hamas (albeit not necessarily with enthusiasm). d) In a delicate international environment the Syrian regime was not able to afford a war on two fronts, externally and domestically.

"The resistance discourse has taken a religious connotation from *muqawama* to *jihad*," said Louay Hussein, juxtaposing the words (national) uprising and the Islamic term for struggle. In his tiny office in a small side street close to the Café Rawda in downtown Damascus the secular publisher (Petra Publishing House), who gained prominence as a voice for dialogue in the 2011 upheavals, continued: "The regime of Bashar has no understanding of what the identity of the state is. They don't recognize the true meaning of secularism. This is why the Islamic discourse can spread in Syria."[73] Michel Kilo summarized the division of power between the Islamists and the regime with the pointed words: "Ours is the power, and you get the society."[74]

At times, this had led to bizarre concessions up to the legislative level. In May 2009 a highly controversial draft for a new Personal Status Law *(qanun al-ahwal ash-shakhsiyya)* was leaked from the cabinet to the public, apparently by the communist minister of irrigation who passed it on to the communist Syrian Women's League (SWL).[75] Finally, the paper was published on the websites of al-Thara (a group of secular young opposition figures) and the Syrian Women' Observatory (SWO), one of the independent single-issue groups that had managed to carve out some political leeway for its advocacy.[76]

A committee assigned by the Minister of Justice, Mohammad al-Ghufri, had drafted the paper behind closed doors. According to multiple sources, the circle consisted of highly conservative Sunnis: one ex-minister of justice, four sheikhs and one or two professors of Islamic Law *(sharia)*. Only one of them, Hassan Awad, professor at the *sharia* law school in Damascus, came forward publicly. The conservative mufti of the Umayad Mosque in Damascus, Said Ramadan al-Bouti, was said to be at least indirectly involved as well.

The conservative orientation of the reform of the civil code from 1953 (amended in 1975) caused a scandal with civil society actors, with religious minorities, and with moderate Islamic scholars. The sheikhs Hassoun and Habash were two of ten major Islamic leaders who opposed this law as backwards and inacceptable. Habash spoke of "Afghan conditions" and a "Talibanization of Syria"[77]—precisely the country that used to be a bastion against the Muslim Brotherhood in the time of Hafez al-Asad. Habash's wife Asma Kuftaro criticised in a paper that "the committee has chosen the strictest interpretations in Islamic jurisprudence." She objected to the absence of heads of minority religious groups in the secret committee, the sustaining of marriage to minors, the strengthening of Muslim men's prerogatives at the expense of women with regard to polygyny, and the choice of orthodox jurisprudence in determining apostasy and separation of couples in cases of interfaith marriage.[78]

Kuftaro was one of the signatories of four open letters that were signed by ten prominent civil society groups. They directed their protest to President Bashar al-Asad, First Lady Asma al-Asad, the Women's Union and the Syrian Commission for Family Affairs (SCFA) with direct organizational links to the Council of Ministers headed by the Prime Minister.[79] The signatories demanded the abolishment of the draft law and the inclusion of broader segment of the population.

The draft displayed Sunni Islamic doctrinal terminology based on orthodox interpretations of *sharia* principles and jurisprudence *(fiqh)*. Terms were applied such as *dhimmi* (ward, a non-Muslim under the protection of Muslims), *kitabiya* and *kitabi* (female and male member of the People of the Book, i.e. a Christian or a Jew), *murtadd* and *murtadda* (female and male apostate). The text also legitimized polygamy in contrast to the existing Personal Status Law of 1953 that forbade it. Male rights in the fields of divorce and heritage were strengthened as well as male custody and guardianship over females and children. The marriage between minors—thirteen years for girls and fifteen years for boys—was sustained.

With regard to religious minorities, the draft introduced major disadvantages and a higher dependence on the state's control over marriage and divorce. Thus it restricted the authority of the Christian clergy (no restrictions for the Druze community was envisaged). This counteracted the recent freedom that had earlier been granted to other religious denominations. The Catholic Church of Syria under Bishop Antun Mosleh of Damascus had elaborated a more liberal and women-friendly personal status law that had passed the Syrian parliament in June 2006.

The controversial draft also included a provision that made possible enforced separation of a married couple by a third party when it claimed that the couple had difference in faith or that one or both members of the couple were guilty of apostasy. If the draft had become enacted as a law, people in Syria could have suffered the fate of the Egyptian Nasr Hamid Abu Zaid in 1995. An Egyptian family court under Islamic influence forcibly divorced the liberal thinker and academic of literary studies from his wife. Because of his hermeneutics of the Quran in a modern historical context, Zaid was declared an apostate. Thus the divorce became legal according to *sharia* law. His case had caused an outcry in the academic world.

Bassam al-Kadi from the SWO was sure that the Syrian authorities were out of step with the general public on women's issues: "I am certain that the Syrian street is more liberal and open on women's rights than the government is," he said. "Women's rights are a bargaining chip. Religious conservatives support changes to the economic system in exchange for moving women's rights backwards."[80] Kadi's NGO also fronted the first nationally publicized civil campaign against honor crimes in Syria. In this context Syria under Bashar al-Asad achieved some progress. For example, a nation-wide public campaign regarding violence against women was carried out in 2005, yielding the publication of a study on violence against women and the establishment of public shelter homes for women who experienced violence in each governorate in 2009.[81] In the summer of the same year Asad issued a decree that increased punishment for honor killings from a few months to two years, possibly in an attempt to dampen the outcry against the proposed new Personal Status Law. Women rights groups were striving for the abolition of this crime and for making it equal to the charge of murder. Yet this was a first step. A new law against human trafficking in 2010 constituted another success that was welcomed by activists such as Kadi.

The heavy protests against the planned Personal Status Law unleashed new forms of organization in Syria like Internet signatory campaigns, advocacy work on the Internet and lobbying. This also triggered unusually lively debates within the government. Following the pressure a revised draft was created in July 2009, and after continued protests, the matter was shelved as had happened so often with other controversial laws. But this time it constituted a remarkable success. New forms of political action began to alter the political culture among regime opponents. Sub-political single issue groups, whose weapons consisted of hardly more than computers and websites, resisted a measure planned by the government in alliance with moderate sheikhs. The Syrian parliament, otherwise a rather toothless body, rejected the draft as well, including Habash. The Minister of Justice was replaced.

In these debates the protagonists of the Civil Society Movement hardly played a role. In conversation, Kadi did not conceal his disrespect of the old opposition. After all, it did not come out to defend the specific issue of women's rights but insisted on promoting the larger issue of human rights and political change. "Where is our Civil Society Movement?" Kadi asked. "They have no organization," he said and attacked them directly: "You have nothing to tell me. I'm more active. All what you wrote fits into a small book. In contrast, we have more than 100,000 users per month on our website and a network of journalists." Kadi dismissed the National Council of the Damascus Declaration as an organization that dealt with political problems but that had nothing to do with civil society. He also criticized its accommodation with the Muslim Brotherhood.

"Here is no democracy, freedom, and so on," Kadi admitted in his humble and somewhat chaotic apartment in the old Damascus neighborhood of Suq Sarouja. His power consisted of not more than a tiny desk, a personal computer, and a handful of volunteers who worked on the website and translated texts into English. Heaps of cigarette butts filled the ashtray. For his living, he gave private Arabic classes to foreigners. He was tired, he admitted, working day and night. "But you can change things slowly," he rejoiced. "The red line is much higher than you think. We have to further push it." He characterized the Syrian regime as a "special dictatorship" not like the "personal dictatorship" of Saddam Hussein in Iraq. "Our dictatorship is a regime as a whole. So, civil society organizations can help the government to go the right paths." Kadi spoke positively of the First Lady and the NGOs under the umbrella of Syria Trust. In an aside, he complaint about the opposition abroad and well-equipped international NGOs: "We have to stay here to change things. This is more effective than going to x [number of] conferences abroad."[82] Kadi himself was not keen on collaborating with other women's rights groups. In turn, those other groups charged him with obstruction. Thus they perpetuated the traditional fragmentation of actors in the Syrian opposition spectrum.

Despite the remarkable success in averting the backward Personal Status Law, the fear of rising Islamist influence persisted. Analysts pointed out that the prime targets of Islamists in Syria were the elementary schools and to a lesser extent the secondary schools. Even some public schools were exposed to strong influence where women teachers as well as girls wore the *hijab* (veil covering the hair). Some ministers' wives wore the *hijab*, including the one of Prime Minister Utri who had endorsed the controversial draft on the Personal Status Law.

This controversy that started in 2009 and the cancellation of an international secularism conference organized by Louay Hussein at the University of Damascus in January 2010 were indications that conservative Islam was gaining more influence. Surprisingly, however, a counter-movement set in during the following months. Since the beginning of 2010, measures were taken against Islamist tendencies in general and against Islamic institutions and clerics in particular.

Prayer rooms in popular middle class restaurants were closed as well as public prayer rooms during Ramadan. Girls and teachers dressed with a *niqab* (full scale veil) were banned in schools. "This is a historic step," commented Kadi. "Something like this has never happened since the 1980s."[83] In addition, imams were more restricted in their sermons as mentioned above, and laws to regulate the noise of loudspeakers on mosques were enacted and more strictly pursued. Also in 2010 school curricula were reformed to the effect that they had become more secular and less ideologically Baathist. The regime had the stamina to kick out influential radical Islamists from Islamic organizations, too.

In the last months before the grand upheaval, the regime had become more astute in their restriction of Islamic social and political influence. Observers speculated on the reasons. After many years of negligence, would such an approach be effective? Some argued that these steps could be the first fruit of international stability. Since the regime felt safer now, it had the strength to clamp down on the Islamists, although some Islamic groups had already become dangerous. These repercussions of Syrian strength in foreign policy might have affected some Islamists in the short run but had not helped the secular opposition. The secular opposition constituted the real competition and alternative in the regime's ideological proximity.

Other factors might have contributed to the the regime's new stance toward Islamists. One was that the concessions in the Personal Status Law had gone too far and that "we have reached a critical point" as one conversation partner put it. Another reason was the growing uneasiness of Syrian Sunnis, minorities, and secular-minded people with the increasing Iranian-Shiite influence as witnessed by the influx of pilgrims, refugees, and others immigrants.

Syrian Sunnis tended to look at the deepened Iranian-Syrian relations with great suspicion in general. Sunnis in particular hardly concealed their disrespect vis-à-vis the Persians who, in their view, had been traitors from Mohammed's time onward. "The rejecters are worse than the Israelis," a conservative Sunni put it in an interview at the end of 2010, referring to the Shiites.[84] Despite their religious conservativism, such Sunnis described themselves as westward-looking instead of Iran-oriented. Not surprisingly, early in the protests of 2011 some street slogans were directed against Hezbollah and Iran.

The Cage Breaks Open

The Arab Spring and the mass protests in Syria have changed the entire setup of the Syrian opposition. In the old days, resistance to the regime consisted of drafting manifestos and engaging in discussion in the back rooms of teahouses suffused with the aromatic smoke of water pipes. Now the opposition rallied in the streets and the smoke that rose carried the smell of gun powder.

The Syrian scenario provided ample ammunition for propaganda. There was some truth in the fact that Syria's protests were probably more influenced from abroad than those in Tunisia, Egypt, Libya, or Yemen. This was true because, in Syria, there were more international interests at stake. Apart from regional powers, such as the antagonists Iran and Saudi Arabia, Syrian players were meddling from a distance. Many opposition figures had been forced into exile over the years and were now turning up the heat. The external opposition had traditionally been more emphatic in its demands for regime change. The protagonists were diverse. They included intellectuals and scholars in exile in Washington, London, Paris, and elsewhere. They included as well figures with highly controversial records, such as former vice-president Abdul Halim Khaddam. Another person who had a score to settle with Bashar al-Asad was his uncle Rifaat who was said to have supporters in the coastal town of Banias, one of the hotbeds of the early protests.

The street revolts caught the traditional opposition in Syria by surprise. As we have seen in previous chapters, the intellectuals had carefully analysed the situation over the years and expected a break-up due to the grave social and economic challenges, political stagnation, the nervousness of the regime, breaches in its leadership, and the dispersion of authority within the regime. Other factors included a contraction of power that narrowed the country's power elite down to Alawite circles. But the experts did not anticipate anything such as the protests of 2011. Syria's traditional opposition were caught in an atmosphere of resignation, defeat, and melancholy. Thus, when the cage suddenly broke open, it took some time for them to gather their thoughts, define their positions, and negotiate common platforms inside and outside the country. The escalation of atrocities and the unwillingness of the regime to implement a "security solution" increased the sense of urgency among the established opposition and contributed to polarization. It also led to a shifting of alliances and positions.

Syria's domestic opposition was far from homogeneous and was scarcely linked to the opposition abroad. The first legal conference ever of Syria's domestic opposition took place in the mist of bloodshed on 26 June 2011 in the Semiramis Hotel in downtown Damascus. It was a reunion of many familiar faces from the debating clubs of the Damascus Spring. Louay Hussein and Michel Kilo played key roles in this event. The participants who gathered in the hotel's conference room provided yet one more window of opportunity for Asad since they stopped short of calling for immediate regime change. It was also an opportunity for figures of the wide and complex network of the Civil Society Movement to redefine themselves in heated debates, while an escalation of the conflict was looming at the horizon. Critics said that the regime allowed the meeting with the intention of driving a wedge between the opposition groups inside and outside Syria.

Hussein, in turn, attacked opposition figures in exile and the Arab TV programs on which they enjoyed considerable air time, for intending to undermine the Semiramis conference. Hussein criticized them for spreading the view that there was no real opposition in Syria unless allowed or formed by the regime itself. "These charges—and not the pressure of the regime— were responsible for the fact that we were not able to organize subsequent meetings," Hussein scoffed, "and the youth movement—which had been part of the people's movement from the beginning—was discouraged from joining new political groups or parties." Echoing the traditional Syrian anti-imperialist line, Hussein charged the foreign opposition with wanting to put the solution of the conflict into the hands of the UN Security Council and "foreign big powers."[85] (Hussein had been in prison for seven years (1984-1991) for being a member of the forbidden Communist Workers' Party. In October 2011 he founded an independent group called Constructing the Syrian State that concentrated on a domestic solution to the conflict.)

By the time of the Semiramis conference, opposition groups in exile had already held three major meetings: in Istanbul (26 April), in Antalya (2 June), and in Brussels (8 June). While those abroad had always rejected anything less than regime change, the declaration of the Semiramis Conference called for a peaceful transition to democracy. But in their final declarations, the conference of the domestic opposition formulated goals very similar to those of the opposition abroad. The call for free elections under these circumstances, however, was likely to have the same effect to set an end to the Asad family's 40-year-old monopoly on power. Asad was not seen by anyone anymore as part of the solution but as part as the problem of the country. At best he could serve as a transitional figure to avert worse.

Both external and domestic opposition circles increased efforts to coordinate themselves and connect their meetings via teleconferences, although subsequent Damascus meetings were disrupted by the secret services. What divided the currents were the means how to get to the goal of change (apart from personal jealousies). The Semiramis Conference also called for an immediate end to the security crackdown and the army's withdrawal from towns and villages. This demand remained pending throughout the bloody months without having ever been fulfilled.

In the private Syrian press Kilo was quoted as saying: "We are in front of two solutions: either security or political. There is no way the authorities could combine both of them. Dialogue will never lead to a political way out as long as the security [solution] continues." Also Hussein pledged to "transfer the battle from the streets to the political struggle." Kilo made it clear that the regime was facing more than one group now that it needed to talk to. Thus he reacted to the offer of a "national dialogue" that implied a pre-selection of who could take part in it. Kilo saw that the opposition leadership in Syria "cannot and does not want to" speak for the protestors. "Representatives of the street should contribute to this dialogue themselves," was his conviction. "This is especially important since [the protestors] have chosen dialogue instead of trying to topple the regime as the solution to the current crisis."[86] At least this was still the case by then.

A tweet that was sent out from the Semiramis gathering attributed the following quote to Michel Kilo: "Eighty percent of the Syrian population are under thirty-five. Where are they in this conference?" Indeed, the young people seemed uninterested in declarations and debates. Most of them had never been involved in the discourse of the traditional Civil Society Movement either. These young people were now in the streets. The links between the traditional thinkers of Syria's opposition and the new opposition were slight, if they existed at all. Nevertheless, the people in the street risked their lives for the same principles and rights that the intellectuals had demanded for years and for which they went to prison.

The Semiramis Conference was yet another last-minute opportunity for the regime to engage with the opposition before Syria headed one step further toward civil war. Yet it did not seem to have been a serious attempt at dialogue. The minimum condition required was never met. Specifically, the violence never ceased. Instead, the regime tried several times to launch a national dialogue on its own. It announced its own conditions. But it failed to convince most opposition figures inside and outside Syria to participate.

Despite his years-long struggle against the regime, in this situation Kilo was among those opposition figures who had been invited to meet with high-ranking government officials in May, including Buthayna Shaaban. Other opposition figures who attended the meeting were Aref Dalila, Louay Hussein, and Salim Kheirbek—some of the original signatories of the Damascus Declaration in 2005. The government aimed to drive a wedge between young and old opposition groups. All of a sudden, Kilo and even more Hussein, who had just left prison in summer 2009, found themselves on the regime's list as being part of the "good" or the "nationalist opposition" *(al-mu'arada al-wataniyye)* in contrast to the foreign elements of conspiracy against Syria in exile *(al-mu'arada al-charijiyye)* in the regime's new terminology.

Kilo tried to justify his willingness to build bridges despite his reservations in articles he wrote for the Syrian and Lebanese press. The writer feared the collapse of Syria's social fabric and civil war. "[If this situation continues] Syria's future will be black," Kilo said in *Syria Today*. "That is, if there is a Syria left."[87]

In the leftist independent Lebanese newspaper *al-Safir*, Kilo underlined his moderate position in April 2011:

> This civil / consensual Syrian possibility implies two things. The regime's abstinence from relying on the security related solution in confronting the

current situation; and the abstinence of the current movement from calling for ousting the regime. There must be a solution entirely based on a global national dialogue that would push away these two situations in order to prevent the country from turning into a fighting arena . . . . No matter who will be the victorious side, the cost of the confrontation will be deadly for the regime . . . . In addition, [there will also be a hefty price to pay] for the other side, which must realize that erroneous calculations will not lead to the desired freedom but rather to the collapse of the Syrian society's unity in addition to the destruction and dismantlement of the state. The only side that could benefit from a security solution . . . will be Israel.[88]

This discourse once again demonstrated that imporant figures in the traditional Syrian opposition were embedded in the Pan-Arab nationalist discourse.

Kilo's stance against the polarizing currents in Syria brought him considerable criticism from opposition figures who were being hunted down, who feared for their lives, who spent every night in a different bed, or who had friends tortured. Others applauded Kilo's far-sightedness in such a crucial moment of Syria's history. Kilo's travel ban was lifted. He went to Europe and Cairo to defend his mission. The prominent writer possessed a wide intellectual horizon and knew that he was walking on a fine line, especially in a situation in which it was not clear where the regime defined its limits of violence. While his method might have been controversial, Kilo's goals remained clear. He intended to work toward change "from the status quo to the revolution; from tyranny to freedom; from change driven by the authorities to societal change; and from the familial society to the civil society."[89]

Meanwhile, Syria's opposition abroad held a significant conference in the Turkish Mediterranean city of Antalya on 2 June. Three hundred people attended from Europe, the US, Australia, and Syria. They were predominately Sunni Muslims, as the opposition movement as such enjoyed little representation of religious minorities like Alawites, Christians, and Druze. Beforehand, the attendees had rejected the participation of three tainted protagonists—ex-Vice President Khaddam, Asad's uncle Rifaat al-Asad, and Farid al-Ghadry, the self-proclaimed opposition leader who previously was supported by US neoconservatives. Thus, the opposition abroad avoided the mistakes of 2006 when they allowed Khaddam to participate in opposition activities and, as a result, put at risk their credibility inside Syria.

The Antalya conference was financed to a great extent by the Sanqer family. Ihsan Sanqer, the old Damascus Sunni merchant and Member of Parliament in the 1990s lived now in Turkey and in the Gulf. His fight with the presidential family, especially with regime entrepreneur Rami Makhlouf, prompted him to turn his back on the Asads. In 2004 when I had visited him in his office in Damascus, he still had a photo on the wall that depicted him with Hafez al-Asad. At that time, Sanqer said that he was waiting for his chance to engage politically. Now his time had come. According to its leadership, the Syrian National Council received ninety percent of its funding from (probably mostly Sunni) Syrian businessmen.[90]

Another indication of the maturity and self-restraint of the opposition conference in Antalya was the fact that participants with different ideologies found a common voice. This was reminiscent of 2005 when secular and leftist forces temporarily collaborated with the exiled Muslim Brotherhood in London and drafted the Damascus Declaration. In Antalya, the Muslim Brothers once again accepted the notion of a secular state.

In a statement blended with wishful thinking, Sadiq Jalal al-Azm pointed to the fact that during the Arab Spring in Egypt and Tunisia the "people in the street" had learned to avoid the "Arab reflex" of infighting and rivalries. Therefore, he called on the Syrian opposition to unite: "The blood of Syrians is boiling. We should not exclude one another. Who can claim to have a superior understanding of how history will go?"[91] But the heterogeneous composition of Syria's opposition—ideologically, intellectually, individually, and geographically—made it difficult to find a common platform. In Libya, the opposition participated by tribe which tended to inflame rivalries. Yet the Libyan National Transition Council had a territory—eastern Libya—as its base, whereas in Syria the protests were spread throughout the country and failed to take hold of a piece of ground not to mention a region. With regard to international law, this also made it more complicated to recognize the Syrian National Council as some form of transitional government. Most of its active members were not even inside Syria.

Fragmentation & Congregation during the Arab Spring

Roughly speaking, the cleavages in Syria's newly emerging opposition were as follows: a) domestic versus foreign-based opposition (Syria-specific); b) secular versus religious (also a problem in the other Arab countries); c) pan-Arab versus civil-democratic (which raised the question of ethnic minorities such as the Kurds); d) violent versus non-violent (a rising issue with the escalating militarization of the conflict and need for human protection); and e) cyber-literate versus cyber-illiterate. The latter implied the question of ownership of the Syrian "revolution." Who laid the ground for the protests? Was it the grey-haired civil society people, the youngsters in the street who, too often, failed to communicate, or was it Syrian exiles who fostered the upheaval with their reporting of events and political advocacy?

Although the protagonists of the Civil Society Movement held multiple views and ideological bents and were separated from the discourse of the younger people, the far-sightedness and intellectual maturity of the Syrian opposition became clear ten years after the suffocation of the Damascus Spring. Al-Azm drew a parallel between the Arab Spring of 2011 and the Damascus Spring of 2001: "The Charter 99 contained all the slogans, demands and aspirations wherever there is an *intifada* now. The Damascus Spring created the first documents that emphasized freedom, democracy, human rights, civil society, and so on and avoided the typical attacks on Israel. The Damascus Spring was a dress rehearsal of the Arab Spring."[92]

The philosopher, who now has his main residence in Beirut for his personal security, observed a maturation of Arab society during the upheavals. Azm pointed to the

> . . . incessant efforts of the tyrannical and coercive regimes that had worked so hard to present themselves as the loci of the most rational, enlightened, inclusive, patriotic, and civilized tendencies in Arab societies plagued by sectarian, ethnic, tribal, and regional divisions, divisions that had always reinforced their backwardness and anachronism. The usual assumptions about enlightenment and backwardness were suddenly upended by the popular uprisings from Tunisia to Yemen, Egypt, Syria, Bahrain, Libya, and so on. Now we saw those very "enlightened" Arab regimes, at the moment of truth, clinging mechanically, repetitively, and neurotically to the lie of a 'conspiracy', and persisting against all odds with the Kafkaesque absurdities of their delirious logic . . . .[93]

Bashar al-Asad's words during his second inauguration speech in July 2007 underlined the phenomenon of lacking trust in one's own people:

> We also had to think carefully of the prevalent cultural structure, the mentality which controls the behavior of some of us and the negative traditions which do not encourage creativity and taking the initiative and do not promote respecting the values of collective work and the team spirit. This leads to an absence of the culture of work for many people, which obstructed professional and mental involvement in the modernizing project we are implementing.[94]

Asad devoted no words to the possibility that it was the structure of the regime itself that fostered this kind of behavior.

Indeed, the opposition movements during the Arab Spring swung between a civil and enlightened discourse—one that many Westerners until recently would have never attributed to the Arab world—and a relapse into primordial thinking and infighting. In Egypt after the first democratic elections in November 2011, Islamist tendencies overshadowed the civil-democratic discourse and actions during the revolution. Similarly, in the Syrian case highly progressive thoughts and intentions mixed with quarrels that relitigated issues from the past. Besides religion, it was the pan-Arab tradition in particular that proved pertinacious and caused friction. During the second opposition conference in Istanbul in mid-August, for example, a confrontation occurred between those opposition figures who insisted on keeping the name "Syrian Arab Republic," while Kurdish participants adhered to their proposal of changing it to simply "Syrian Republic." In the end, after their proposal was denied, the Kurds quit the meeting in anger.[95] Despite a long history of conflict with the Baath regime and significant ideological differences, Kurds did not participate in the protests as they could have. They had at least two reasons: First, they did not know whether they would profit from the revolution's outcome; second, if the upheaval failed, they would be punished even more harshly than others.

The bickering among opposition members caused disillusionment among intellectuals like Azm who preferred to stay above the everyday turmoil. Current circumstances reminded him of the situation in 1967 when he worked with the Palestinians. "If I had believed what the Palestinians said about each other, I would have probably thought that each Palestinian was a traitor," he said referring to similar developments within the Syrian opposition. "It is always about persons not about programmatic issues, the direct problems or ideas. Carrying out conflicts on a personal level is an old Arab malaise." At the same time, Azm was disappointed in the attitudes of other Arab Spring countries toward Syria. Especially the Egyptians were "emotionless" toward the Syrian uprising and had not developed a "revolutionary feeling of togetherness," Azm complained.[96] The only ones who started to support the Syrian revolution at an early stage and who even sent former rebels to assist were the Libyans. However, the Syrian opposition did receive informal help. Sections of the Arab committee to support the Syrian revolution were formed in Jordan, Kuwait, and Libya. This committee aimed to provide political and humanitarian support to the demonstrators.

Despite the personal and ideological ruptures that prevailed in the heterogeneous Syrian opposition inside and outside the country, the movements organized themselves in small steps. Innumerable committees and councils were formed; a dozen conferences took place, the early and most important ones in Turkey. When a Syrian National Council was announced for the first time at the end of August 2011 in Istanbul, most of its members were surprised when to find that their names were not on the list. Apparently the public announcement of the council was made without prior agreement from the leaderships of the still divided movement. Another source of division: the internal and external leaderships were ill at ease with one another. The domestic opposition feared a takeover by the diaspora groups and demanded higher representation. Another fear was the strong representation of Islamists.

In a counter initiative, less than a week after the second Istanbul meeting, a new National Transitional Council was presented in Ankara headed by Burhan Ghalioun, a political scientist and professor of political sociology at the Sorbonne University in Paris. Three deputies were listed, including Riad Seif. This was the second national council founded in less than a week. Rifts grew between the ideas of protesters in the street—represented by the various Local Coordination Committees—and the political platforms. The regime attempted to split the opposition within Syria, and bickering among the different opposition groups created a blurred image on the international stage where support was urgently needed.

From the old guard of the Damascus Spring it was Riad Seif who most visibly took part in the 2011 anti-government demonstrations in the streets of Damascus. The ailing entrepreneur and former Member of Parliament had spent most of the previous ten years in prison. As the events unfolded, he could not sit quiet. If Seif had been included in Asad's new government in the spring of 2011, this would have silenced half the opposition, opined Azm.[97] Yet once again, Asad had missed a chance at rapprochement.

Coordination among different groups was difficult partly due to the technical problems of secure communication within Syria. Nevertheless, a common denominator among the different opposition groups was gradually emerging. Three Nos materialized: No to Bashar al-Asad; no to sectarianism; no to foreign intervention (except for the protection of civilians). The latter point, however, became an bone of contention as the military crackdown intensified.

Amr al-Azm, a professor of anthropology based in Ohio (USA) and son of Sadiq Jalal al-Azm, said that he regretted that the opposition devoted considerable resources trying to find a common political platform for its international message rather than assisting people on the ground within Syria. However, international leaders insisted on dealing with a unified forum, a la Libya, as a precondition for official support. Amr al-Azm, decided to enter politics in 2011 in the light of the humanitarian catastrophe in Syria. In a conversation held in Vienna, he reflected:

> One positive outcome of these conferences is that they have offered the opposition the opportunity to meet, discuss, agree and disagree in a public competitive arena, something that they have been denied under the Asad regime. Further, it has been clearly demonstrated that the opposition is at least united in its goals of bringing down the Asad regime and establishing a democratically-based, inclusive society.[98]

Despite the obstacles, the pressure to find a common denominator among opposition groups gradually began to bear fruit. At the beginning of October 2011, at another conference in Istanbul, the opposition forces succeeded in uniting a majority of the different opposition fronts and branches. The head of the newly founded Syrian National Council (SNC), Burhan Ghalioun, announced that the following key opposition groups had approved a common platform: The National Council for Democratic Change (Damascus Declaration) that was founded in Riad Seif's house at the beginning of 2007; the Syrian Muslim Brotherhood; several Kurdish and Assyrian groups; the Syrian Revolution General Commission; several Local Coordination Committees; the Supreme Council of the Syrian Revolution; and other grass root groups. Some people were renowned scholars such Radwan Ziadeh, visiting scholar at Harvard University and founder of the Syrian Center for Political & Strategic Studies (SCPSS). He became the Council's foreign affairs coordinator. Subsequently, more and more individuals and groups joined or recognized the SNC. Soon the European Union and a number of individual countries had accepted the SNC as the official body that could serve as the kernel of a future Syrian government.

When the SNC was founded, it announced its composition as follows: From the one hundred forty members, fifty-two percent belonged to the new grassroots movements that sprouted from the 2011 revolution; sixty percent of the SNC members were inside Syria and forty percent abroad. The names of seventy-one members were announced. Others were not disclosed for security reasons. [99] The SNC issued a National Consensus Charter emphasizing that the Syrian Revolution was about dignity and freedom: The revolution should remain peaceful, inclusive, and opposed to foreign military intervention. Under a future civil state, all minorities would have their rights guaranteed without discrimination, including recognition of the Kurdish identity and rights within the concept of national unity. It also rejected foreign intervention. The SNC defined its mission as the effort as to "deliver the voice of the Syrian revolution and its demands to the international community," to secure political support for the "peaceful revolution," to promote national unity during the transition phase, to ensure there is no political vacuum, and to develop a roadmap for democratic change in Syria.[100] Nevertheless, in the eyes of its critics, the SNC did not undertake sufficient efforts to include Syria's religious and ethnic minorities and to reconcile them with the concept of post-Asad Syria.

Internally, the main points of criticism were the lack of a transparent democratic procedure within the Council as well as the strong influence of the Muslim Brotherhood. Externally, the SNC leadership tried to split the difference between its two remaining competitors, the so-called Antalya Group and the Coordination Committee for Democratic Change (CCDC). The Antalya Group was composed of those opposition figures (most but not all of whom had met in Antalya for the first time) who advocated international intervention to protect Syrian civilians on the ground. The Antalya Group considered called for protection zones: A buffer zone installed by Turkey in the north; a no-fly-zone; or other measures such as a UN blue helmet mission to protect civilians. In the face of atrocities committed in Homs, Haitham Maleh's Syrian Progressive Front split from the SNC in February 2012to pursue similar demands.

For its part, the CCDC was a domestic group that for a long time remained highly skeptical of any form of international intervention. They feared that Syria would become a playing field of proxy interests like Iraq or Lebanon. Michel Kilo, Haytham Manna, and for a time Louay Hussein were part of this group. Kilo, however, admitted that it was the Syrian regime with its violent clampdown that was the most likely to provoke an international military intervention that would destroy Syria.[101] Even the Iranian government reached out to the group at a point that the regime in Teheran was hedging its bets.

In November 2011 several members of the CCDC left the organization because they suspected cooperation between the regime's secret services and the Committee. This remained unconfirmed but it was clear that Syria had become polarized in complex ways—not only between pro and anti-Asad camps. The deep rifts among the opposition became tangible when, on 10 November 2011 in Cairo's Tahrir Square, four representatives of the CCDC—Hassan Abdul-Azim, Michel Kilo, Louay Hussein, and Monzer Haloum—were physically attacked on their way to a meeting with the Arab League. The Syrian assaulters blamed them for cooperating with the regime in Damascus and called for international protection of civilians in Syria.[102]

The regime's continued and uncompromising application of the "security solution" impelled the militarization and radicalization of the crisis. It also undermined all efforts to find a middle way. In this polarized environment, moderate opposition figures who had advocated a "soft transition" to democracy for over a decade found their authority being eroded.

At the end of 2011, the SNC and the CCDC were close to agreeing on a political platform. At the last minute, however, a document that was supposed to seal the agreement was withdrawn. The two sides were unable to establish a consensus on three main points: The SNC rejected any dialogue with Asad who, in its view, had lost all legitimacy; the SNC did not exclude foreign intervention, whereas the CCDC insisted on a Syrian solution; the CCDC continued to reject the Free Syrian Army as a participant in opposition leadership while the SNC attempted to coordinate its efforts with this group of defectors.

Starving and wounded citizens on the ground in Syria desperately called for help during continuous bombardments and sniper attacks, especially in the Baba Amru district of Homs. Yet the SNC was paralyzed by its lack of agreement on the question of violence vs non-violence. At the beginning of March 2012, the SNC issued a statement that, in light of the escalation of violence, "a new-found reality has been formed in which citizens are forced to bear arms in self-defense. Moreover, the regime's use of the military forces to terrorize and kill innocent civilians has led to the defection of soldiers and officers who refuse to fire at civilians." Therefore, the SNC announced the formation of a "military bureau" to strengthen the Free Syrian Army (FSA) and to coordinate command structures and strategies. What the statement did not mention was that only a few weeks earlier the FSA commander in Turkish exile, Riad al-Asaad, had fallen out with the SNC and called its members "traitors." Others said that the military bureau had, in fact, never been officially decided upon. The infighting among opposition players did not find an end. Syrian and international observers remained at a loss. The SNC's coherence and strategy remained a muddle.

For months, the foreign-based SNC had faced a increasing criticism for doing too little for the protesters and civilian population on the ground. It was an unmanageable tightrope walk. Should the SNC safeguard the revolution's moral supremacy by endorsing only peaceful protest? Or should it defend the lives of innocent civilians facing violence on the street? In the end, the balance shifted toward military means as a legitimate method of self defense. The SNC underlined the new policy in its March statement: "The Syrian Revolution began as a non-violent movement and has maintained its peaceful nature for months. The situation has changed and the SNC will shoulder its responsibilities in light of this new found reality."[103] Almost inevitably, Civil war had come one step closer.

In April, the SNC failed to gain international recognition as the sole legitimate representative of Syria—or as the Syrian government in exile. The recognition they sought was similar to that granted by the international community to the Libyan National Transition Council in Benghazi. Still, the SNC did make progress toward such recognition. The newly founded international contact group "Friends of Syria" (with members from 83 countries and organizations) did recognize the SNC as the umbrella organization of the Syrian opposition.

The question of hard power was not the only problem on the SNC's agenda. It tried to reach out to the frightened minorities in the country but was far too late. In an interview in December 2011—five months after the SNC's foundation—Ghalioun said:

> We strive now . . . to open up the council to new political forces and personalities to improve the participation of minorities and of females. We are aware of the importance of minorities, even beyond proportionately, to ease their fears. . . . Syrians have a national identity beyond the sectarian divide. Syria's national identity would be weaker and poorer if it didn't have this beautiful pluralism between Arabs, Kurds, and sects.

At the same time, Ghalioun tried to dispel fears of the growing influence of Islamists:

> Being someone who prays or fasts doesn't mean you want an Islamic state. Islam in the form of the Iranian state has been defeated in the Arab world. All Islamist movements now want to copy the Turkish model. The model we really need to look at is Tunisia. The [moderately Islamist] Nahda party won the majority—but they went for a coalition government.

Within the SNC, the Syrian Muslim Brotherhood was strong, yet it tried to keep a low profile. Moreover, the most active participants came from the moderate camp of Ali Sadreddine Bayanuni, who had led the Brotherhood until 2010 when he was replaced by a more conservative successor, was now attempting to regain influence.

Bayanuni is known for his orientation toward Turkey. In an interview published in mid-2011 he stressed that the Brotherhood had experience in parliamentary democracy since the group participated in Syria's 1961 elections. Today, Turkey's AKP has provided it with a blueprint for reform. "The AKP is neutral in the area of religion—neither does it impose religion on Turkish citizens nor does it seek to fight religion," the sheikh noted, "and for this reason we find [it] to be an excellent model." Moreover Bayanuni underlined two prime principles of his ideology of state and society: "Firstly, we believe that the state in Islam is a civil state, not a state ruled by any religious leaders or clerics. Secondly, we cannot impose any particular way of dressing on citizens. We do call for and encourage [women] to wear the *hijab* and to follow Islamic behavior and action, but individuals must be free to choose what they want."[104] Despite the strong influence of the Muslim Brotherhood in the SNC, the organization has tried to avoid being characterized as an Islamic group.

In the same December interview mentioned above, Ghalioun also articulated his political strategy. According to this professor of political science, the SNC tried to avoid mistakes that the Americans made in Iraq. The US-led administration in Baghdad had sacked all Baath members from the army and public positions which resulted in these people joining the anti-American resistance. In the interview Ghalioun underlined "that the regime and the state are separate. We don't want the state to collapse. We want to make use of the different agencies of the state and make them function. A national reconciliation committee will be formed during this period." Equally, he remained skeptical about an externally induced regime change: "We say it is imperative to use forceful measures to force the regime to respect human rights.

"But this doesn't mean military intervention to topple the regime. This is different than the organized military intervention that happened in Iraq for regime change. We count on Syrians to bring down the Syrian regime." Ghalioun added that the future of Syria would be clearly within the Arab context, avoiding yet another mistake made in Iraq.[105] Beginning in November 2011, members of the SNC began to coordinate their positions and strategies with the Free Syrian Army in the Turkish border zone. From this point on, Syria's opposition gained a new quality. Now it was composed of a political and a military wing. Both sides agreed that regular army soldiers and military facilities in Syria should not be targeted. It was more important in their view to uphold the possibility of reconciliation between regular and rebel units in the event of regime change and to avoid free-floating insurgent groups later on.

Syria's moderate opposition was still traveling a rocky road. It was tough to set aside old rivalries—especially between exiled and domestic groups— and to develop a counterweight to radical and sectarian tendencies. Part of the fragile compromise between the groups that now formed the SNC was a rotating presidency. The international community had to get used to a changing "face of the opposition." Ghalioun was a respected academic in the Western world who had, however, little standing within Syria. Yet the SNC was uncertain what would happen if a representative of the Muslim Brotherhood assumed the SNC presidency. Would he do an equally good job of homogenizing Syria's opposition? At the end of 2011, the SNC decided, for the time being, not to change horses in mid stream.

Despite friction among and within opposition groups, the SNC carried home its biggest political success to that point on 27 February 2012 when it was recognized by the European Union as a legitimate representative of the Syrian people. Most Arab states signaled their intention to follow.

Still, no charismatic figure had emerged to lead a transitional government. The need was for a person with sufficient determination, credibility, and legitimacy. Nor was there an established institution that could have taken on the task, as the military in Egypt or Tunisia. Yet the painfully long period of Syrian upheaval, in comparison to the other Arab Spring states, had at least one advantage: It gave the Syrian opposition more time to organize themselves and, more importantly, to thoroughly prepare the political, technical, and legal ground for a transition into post-Asad Syria.

Can the opposition steer Syria along a stable and peaceful path? The answer depends to a large degree on the physical and psychological damage inflicted by the regime's violence. Ghalioun was still optimistic at the end of 2011, when he stated:

> There's a deep change in the Arab psyche. No one can tolerate any longer the rule of regimes that have lost their legitimacy in the eyes of people. In the past ten years people's aspirations changed. The idea of an Islamic state or nation reached a deadline. The general trend in the population in the last ten years was towards democracy. All these attempts to democratize or reform brought no fruit.

According to Ghalioun, it now was impossible to turn back, no matter what the sacrifices:

> People in Syria were terrified of the security services. Tunisia and Egypt brought new horizons, new light to Syrians. When the volcano erupted it was clear there was an accumulation of disappointment that couldn't be quelled. This explains the courageous determination of protesters today. Freedom for Syrians today comes before bread, before life.[106]

8
Syria's Policy Paradox

NOT LONG BEFORE THE WAVE OF ARAB protests reached Syria, the regime in Damascus had started to regain the initiative in foreign policy. The years between 2008 and 2010 can be regarded as the golden period for Syria's foreign policy under Bashar al-Asad. Much of the pressure and insecurity of the preceding years was easing. European governments and even the US administration seemed to have come to the conclusion that Syria, at a minimum, was a stable, politically approachable, and important geo-strategic player in the Middle East whose president was on the path of piecemeal reform. It was hard work for Asad to get to this point after years of isolation and stigmatization following the Iraq war. What many Western governments did not see—or did not want to see—was that in the shadow of a more pro-active approach and considerable successes in amplifying spaces of maneuver abroad, the regime in Damascus had launched a new wave of suppression at home against human rights activists and mostly secular opposition forces well before the unprecedented street protests started in March 2011.

Against this background, criticism had risen of the cautious, but strategically reasonable, involvement of Syria by Western governments. The question was if Syria was too easily getting out of its pariah role. Others emphasized that Syria had been stigmatized for years without due reason and that things were getting back to a normal balance. One of the irritating factors for Damascus, shortly before the upheavals broke out, was obviously the rising insecurity in Lebanon and political repercussions after the indictment of the Special Tribunal on the Hariri assassination. Only a few months later, the dimensions of Syria's domestic protests dwarfed any other political problem in the region and Asad's foreign policy successes lay in tatters.

Syria was about to take its head out of the noose of isolation that had been tightened after the Iraq war by the United States and subsequently by European countries. The cause of Syria's success lay in a series of decisions that, on the one hand, reflected a break with past shades, even changes of paradigm, and, on the other hand, displayed a growing maturity of President Asad in foreign policy matters. There was a new Syrian pragmatism after a phase of ideological encrustation during the Iraq war. This falling back into old pan-Arab and intransigently anti-US positions with a dosage of clash-of-civilization-rhetoric (especially by Asad's adviser Buthayna Shaaban) had not left many doors open for backstage diplomacy (as Bashar's father Hafez would have done). On the other hand, the defensive stance of the regime during and after the Iraq war can be explained by both raison d'état and emotional desperation in an environment that had put the existence of the Syrian regime in danger.

Interestingly, the new agility in Damascus was not linked with Barack Obama being president of the United States. The most important decisions for this new course were taken in 2008, before it was clear who would become the new strongman in the White House. From a Syrian perspective, any change in Washington was a glimpse of hope. This was after the simplistic good-bad rhetoric and exclusively military approach of neo-conservative President George W. Bush, who placed Syria within the extended Axis of Evil. This happened despite Syria's intelligence cooperation against militant Islamists after the 9/11 attacks which lasted until well into 2003. Many chances had been missed to keep constructive relations with Syria and to lend support to West-centric elements within Syria's power circles.[1]

Until the beginning of 2011, Syria had rebounded from its worst shocks. The most significant developments in Syria's foreign policy in the period starting in 2008 can be summed up as follows:

- Syria's historical separation from Lebanon both on the level of ideology and in constitutional terms. This, of course, does not exclude the continued exertion of strategic-political influence.
- The start of talks and personal encounters with representatives of anti-Syrian camps in Lebanon.
- Indirect negotiations with Israel about the Golan Heights via Turkey, although they were interrupted shortly before they could turn into direct talks due to the war in Gaza in 2008 / 2009.
- The rapid deepening of relations with Turkey.
- The start of diplomatic relations with Iraq and bilateral cooperation in the fields of economy and security, although not without friction.
- Détente with Saudi Arabia and thus with the Hariri camp in Lebanon.
- Silent resumption of intelligence cooperation with the US and the UK which was interrupted in 2003.
- Becoming presentable again in most European capitals, especially in Paris, and being invited to the Mediterranean Conference there in July 2008.

Lebanon

Few were willing to bet on Bashar al-Asad's political future after the assassination of Lebanon's President Rafiq Hariri in February 2005. Hariri had criticized Syria harshly in his last months. Syrian troops had been present in Lebanon since 1976. But International pressure on Syria grew to the point that it caused a hasty military withdrawal from this country.

In 2009 and 2010 Asad had gained confidence and even felt secure enough to openly concede Syrian mistakes in Lebanon and to receive then

Prime Minister Saad Hariri, son of the late Rafiq, in Damascus with a state reception that included a visit to the well-secured presidential palace. Even Druze leader Walid Jumblatt, who in the past years had been one of the hardest and most eloquent critics of Syria in Lebanon, travelled to Syria and met Asad for an ice-breaking encounter.

For the first time in post-colonial history, Syria and Lebanon became two sovereign countries who exchanged ambassadors and agreed on its bilateral border drawing. This had been one of the main demands of Western actors toward Damascus. Step by step, the countries established a relationship that would have been unthinkable only a few years ago. After a long period of political bickering, Syria finally played a constructive role in the difficult formation of a Lebanese government. The deeply divided Lebanese parties managed to negotiate a breakthrough in the Doha agreement in May 2008. Thus, they cleared the way for the presidential election, and in November 2009, after another tough tug-of-war, the government of National Unity under Saad Hariri could take up its work.

From their perspective, Syrians complained about a lack of recognition from Western states, given the significant change of direction in their policies. The government in Damascus had given up Greater Syria as an ideological premise of Syrian nationalism. Still today, many Syrians see Lebanon as a French colonial construct rather than a full-fledged state due to tight family bonds, cultural relations, and the lively economic exchange between the two countries.

At the same time, Syria did not stop exerting political influence in Lebanon. The game was simply played with different means. As long as the conflict with Israel is not solved, the tiny neighboring state will continue to represent an indispensable strategic space. The Syrian regime knew that it would not have any chance in a direct military confrontation with Israel because of Syria's hopelessly corrupt, technically obsolete, and underpaid troops. Syrian soldiers were conscripts whom the regime did not trust in the clampdown on the protest movements in 2011. The country needed Hezbollah's asymmetric guerrilla capabilities. This alliance was without alternatives for Syria. Therefore, a continued influence of the Shiite organization in Lebanon's domestic politics remained important. All in all, Hezbollah obtained more political influence over Lebanon's state institutions than in the period before the summer war of 2006. This crisis was a disaster for Israel from a public diplomacy perspective but also a backlash with respect to Lebanon's domestic fabric since political and thus sectarian polarization had grown. After the ousting of Prime Minister Saad Hariri and the change of government with pro-Hezbollah businessman Najib Mikati in charge since January 2011, Hezbollah—and Syria—managed to tighten its grip on Lebanon. From a Syrian perspective this power constellation came about just in time. It was crucial to keep the Lebanese flank quiet during the escalating popular revolts in Syria, and it kept Lebanon supportive of Syria in the Arab League as well as during the critical debates in the United Nations.

But the fact that even Western ally Saad Hariri in April 2010 said that Syria did not channel Scud missiles into Lebanon and that he uttered increasingly cautious statements concerning the International Tribunal was an indication to what extent Hariri was already moving within the Syrian orbit.[2] In March 2010, the Lebanese newspaper al-Akhbar quoted Hariri as warning representatives of his media outlets: "I have made the decision of building a special relationship with Syria. And in the same way that it is forbidden to [negatively] allude to Saudi Arabia in our media institutions, you must know that from now on, [negative] allusions to Syria will be unacceptable under any form. Anyone who violated this rule should be leaving."[3] In September 2010, Saad Hariri told the paper al-Sharq al-Awsat, "We assessed the mistakes that we made with Syria that harmed the Syrian people and relations between the two countries. At a certain stage we made mistakes and accused Syria of assassinating the martyred premier. This was a political accusation, and this political accusation has finished." Though he added, "The Tribunal is not linked to the political accusations, which were hasty . . . The Tribunal will only look at evidence."[4]

For the sake of domestic peace, both Hariri and Jumblatt apologized for having blamed Syria for Rafiq Hariri's assassination. Hariri feared civil strife and the consequences of this for his position. He might have learned from Jumblatt's biography that in this delicate region one can seek the truth but not justice. It is unlikely that justice will be done after this assassination, even if the Tribunal named the real culprits. So hedging against further negative repercussions became the order of the day. The Hariri Tribunal turned into a thorn in the side of each camp for different reasons. This was due to the delicate situation in Lebanon and the region and was accentuated by the blunders of the Tribunal itself, especially in its early years, which called its credibility into question. What started out as an example of international law and justice that gave hope for the future turned into an impending disaster for political stability in the region.

None of Lebanon's problems have been definitively solved. The UNIFIL troops took their observation positions in southern Lebanon after 2006, but no one dared to mention Hezbollah's disarmament. The warnings were all too clear in May 2008 when Hezbollah's fighters for the first time turned their weapons inward and occupied several Beirut neighborhoods, stopping just short of a coup d'état. Many non-Shiites and Hezbollah critics still see the militia of the Party of God as a guarantee of Lebanese sovereignty in the face of Israeli military might. They understand that Lebanon's state organs remain fragile, and Lebanon's military is unable to defend the country.

In a more long-term perspective, Syrian influence in Lebanon threatened to diminish. The question was how much leverage would Damascus still have on Hezbollah in the future and to what extent Hezbollah had gained power to such a degree that it was able to dictate terms of its own. Moreover, Iran's direct influence in Lebanon was rising and a Syrian nightmare was that one day Syria would be reduced to a logistical interface between Iran and Hezbollah. The overwhelming welcome of Iran's President Ahmedinejad in Lebanon in mid-October 2010 is the more visible aspect of this development. During Ahmedinejad's visit, the British Daily Telegraph was prophetically titled: "A landlord visiting his domain."[5]

Israel

In contrast to the changes in its neighborhood, Israel remained caught in political stagnation. After the war in the Gaza Strip and the start of the new legislative period in early 2009, Israel did not make any discernible gestures toward its neighboring Arab countries or toward the Palestinians. Turkey's confidence in Israel was deeply shattered after the Gaza war, and the problems in the Gaza Strip and the West Bank were far from resolved.

There was no visible strategy except a continued push to extend Jewish settlements in the West Bank and Jewish presence in East Jerusalem. As Israel continued to feel little pressure, time was running in favor of political hardliners. The security situation was relatively stable in comparison to previous years when Palestinian suicide bombers took their toll on Israeli civilians almost monthly. The launching of rockets from Hamas positions in the Gaza Strip diminished too, at least temporarily.

Satisfaction with the status quo was coupled with a lack of initiatives from Washington and deep divisions within the Israeli government itself. This became particularly obvious with regard to Syria. Benjamin Netanyahu and his foreign minister Avigdor Liebermann aired contrasting positions at the beginning of February 2010. Liebermann warned Syria that if a war broke out, Israel's goal would be nothing short of the collapse of the Asad dynasty. Moreover, he admonished, Syria should stop dreaming of recovering the Golan Heights. Netanyahu, however, declared that Israel was still interested in negotiating peace with Syria—without preconditions—and was open to the mediation of a "fair third party." Without preconditions meant: Netanyahu distanced himself from promises made to Syria by previous Israeli governments to hand back the (whole of the) Golan. Apart from that, the Prime Minister banned his cabinet members from speaking about Syria.

In his statement, Liebermann had reacted to an attack by Syrian foreign minister Walid al-Mu'allem, who said that a future war would not stop short of Israeli cities. Before that, Asad had expressed the apprehension that Israel did not want peace, but instead would try to push the region into war.[6] Elsewhere, Asad added that only peace could protect Israel in the long run.[7]

Several times earlier in his political career Netanyahu had hinted that he was open to a deal with Syria. This would give him a free hand to tackle the Palestinian issue. But after the Iraq war Israel's enemies linked up more tightly. This raised the question for Israel's strategists: Was a peace with Syria still equivalent to the pacification of the region as it had been considered in the past? Or, had the interests of Hezbollah—increasingly in alliance with Hamas—and of Iran with its nuclear program become self-sufficient enough that Syria would fail to moderate them? This is another aspect of the argument, made above, that Iran's direct influence in Lebanon was rising while Hezbollah was becoming more astute in lessening its dependence on Syria by deepening of direct links to Iran. This would become even more significant in case of a Hezbollah-hostile and more Sunni-oriented new political scenario in Syria. In anticipation of possible antagonisms, Hezbollah tried to keep a rather low profile during the upheavals in Syria and sent support without causing a stir.

In the rhetorical exchange of blows between Syrian and Israeli representatives during 2010, Syria did seek to deter Israel when "sources close to the power center" in Damascus leaked their vision of a war "imposed on us" by Israel. The decisive phrase was: "This command is now convinced that there will not be any future war in the region with Syria not being part of it."[8] Therefore, Israel should know, it was implied, that should it initiate a regional conflict it would not be able to unilaterally control its scope.

Israel and Syria basically have a territorial conflict "only"—and to a lesser extent an ideological one similar to that between Iran and Israel. A peace treaty would be a strategic gain for Israel. But even if Netanyahu wanted a treaty, it is far from clear if he—or any other Israeli head of government in the extremely fragile party landscape—would politically survive the handing over of the Golan Heights in whole or even in part.

Precisely in order to avoid such a risky decision, Netanyahu's Likud party pushed for a change of procedure for handing over annexed land. This made it even more unlikely that either the Golan Heights or East Jerusalem would ever be returned to Syria and the Palestinians respectively. According to this new law, approved by the Knesset at the end of November 2010, the Israeli parliament needs a two-third-majority for such a decision or a national referendum to grant approval.

Both Syria and Israel (at least in words by senior figures in their governments) declared at various times that they would be interested in negotiations. The question is if they had the process of negotiations in mind as a political asset, as such, or if they aimed at tangible results. The Syrian side claimed that there was no serious negotiating partner on the Israeli side. At the same time, the Syrians tried to send positive signals toward Washington to demonstrate their readiness to negotiate, in the hope of ending the sanctions imposed during the Bush era.

Two theses existed with regard to Syria that seemed to contradict each other at first glance: (1) Bashar al-Asad needed the tug of war about the Golan for his ideological legitimacy as the Arab voice against Israel and to divert domestic problems; and / or (2) the liberation of the Golan would boost his legitimacy to a greater extent than the present situation. In fact, Asad had to swallow several foreign policy defeats that raised doubts about his capability to represent adequately the interests of his country. A perceived just settlement over the Golan could have improved his domestic and international standing if things had not changed so unexpectedly in 2011.

Even in the unlikely event of a peace agreement Israel and Syria would easily find sufficient arguments to keep the image of the external enemy alive in order to divert attention from domestic problems. From the Syrian point of view, Israel would remain an occupying power, either because of the remaining occupation of the Shebaa farms at the border to Lebanon or because of the unresolved conflict with the Palestinians. Asad hinted in this direction in a conversation with US journalist Seymour M. Hersh at the end of December 2009: "If they [the Israelis] say you can have the entire Golan back, we will have a peace treaty. But they cannot expect me to give them the peace they expect as long as other problems remained unsolved."[9]

For Israel, on the other hand, Syria would remain an anti-Zionist and pan-Arab mouthpiece. As long as no reform of the election law stabilizes the party spectrum in Israel, strong unpopular decisions will remain difficult, and an external enemy will remain beneficial to advance domestic agenda. An agreement between both sides could indeed aim to establish a peaceful neighbourhood policy (as was discussed in the 1990s). Experience in the Middle East has shown that both sides unleash propaganda according to their domestic political needs.

Hezbollah, too, sufficiently diversified its basis of legitimacy so that it could continue to play a role even after the (although incomplete) withdrawal of Israeli troops from south Lebanon in May 2000. The Shebaa farms were only a small piece of the whole picture. Strictly speaking, Hezbollah did not need the argument of the occupied Shebaa farms any longer to justify its military role. Its mission had increasingly drifted away from its self-defined original task of Lebanon's self-defence toward its involvement in the Israeli-Palestinian conflict. This was done by supporting Sunni Hamas and by fostering direct Iranian involvement. Still, the interest for Israel to exert a moderating influence on Hezbollah by signing a peace agreement with Syria remained (since Hezbollah could hardly be destroyed militarily), as it might have represented the beginning of a long path toward regional pacification.

There were three main points of criticism that the West raised against the Syrian regime: a) relations with Iran, b) support of Hezbollah, and c) asylum for Palestinian organizations, also of Islamist color, like Hamas. Of these three the bond with Hezbollah appeared to be the strongest one, while the alliance with Iran was the weakest component for some time—until Syria needed urgent support from Iran in 2011. In the end it was the Hamas bond that broke first, when the organization withdrew its headquarters from Damascus during the revolt in 2011.

Syria offered several indications—publicly and between the lines—that even sensitive issues were negotiable. An analyst in Damascus said in a discussion about the European role in the Middle East: "This region is like a bazaar. If you pay your price, you get everything. Our regime is very pragmatic. So far, the Europeans have not paid enough."[10] The same held true with regard to the United States.

In the constellation before 2011, Syria became increasingly important for Israel and the United States should a confrontation with Iran escalate. The difficult diplomatic task, in the case of an attack against Iran, was to keep Syria quiet. A simultaneous war with Iran, Syria, and Hezbollah in Lebanon would have been a disaster in the region and beyond. However, the possibility of just such a war grew suddenly tangible as an outcome to foreign military intervention in Syria triggered by the escalating protests.

Turkey

Relations between Turkey and Syria had changed radically. It was only in 1998 that the two countries were on the brink of war. Ankara accused Damascus of supporting Kurdish rebels in Turkey, and Syria reproached its neighbor for withholding precious water from the Euphrates River. Syria gave in at the last minute and expelled Abdullah Ocalan, former leader of the separatist Kurdish Workers Party (PKK). Syria concluded an anti-terror agreement with its neighbor and regularly extradited PKK activists to Turkey until the fall-out between the countries in 2011.

The Syrian-Turkish honeymoon began with Asad's ground-breaking visit to Turkey in January 2004. At the end of the same year both countries signed a free-trade agreement. Turkish President Ahmet Necdet Sezer returned Asad's visit and travelled to Syria in 2005. From this moment on nothing seemed to be able to stop the breathtaking momentum of bilateral affairs. The sides started to hold regular government consultations with each other. Citizens of both countries were allowed to cross the common border without a visa. In particular for Syria, which has been a closed country for decades, this meant a lot. In Syria, only Iranian travelers enjoyed the same privileges.

The mines at the border were cleared and Syria reduced its area of maritime sovereignty. The neighbors intended to use the new free spaces for joint marine and agricultural projects. The former enemies even cooperated on a military level. Against this background, it almost seemed forgotten that Syrian maps still portrayed today's Turkish province of Alexandretta with the cities of Antakya/Hatay and Iskanderun as Syrian territory. However, a sensational exception occurred in the state-run newspaper *Tishreen* in September 2005 that, for the first time, printed a map without the disputed areas. The new realities no longer left room for nationalist revisionism. Syria's advantages from a friendship with Turkey were greater than the potential rewards from national revisionism. The countries did not sign anything official on their borders but agreed on keeping quiet on the Antakya issue.

Animosities from Ottoman times seemed forgotten. While Syria and Turkey once faced each other with a high degree of suspicion, each now acknowledged a feeling and duty of "family bonds"—if one believed the words of leading politicians from both sides—until the beginning of 2011. This family affair made certain details appear politically inopportune. One of them was the oddity, as a Syrian analyst mentioned, that some of Turkish Prime Minister Tayyip Erdoğan's writings that alluded to Turkish "imperialism" were forbidden in Syria.[11] Another issue was that Turkish goods flooded the Syrian market and damaged weak Syrian industry and craftsmanship. Even more, they aggravated the economic impact of other free trade agreements such as GAFTA, not to mention Chinese imports. But political gains for Syria outweighed any of those difficulties and contradictions.

Syria had changed but Turkey had changed even more. The moderate Islamist Justice and Development Party (AKP) government under Erdoğan began the difficult task to de-ethnicize the Turkish understanding of nation. Thus, religion has become more meaningful as a connecting link within the Turkish population and between them and their Arab neighbors, without the intention of renouncing Western duties and ambitions. The Turkish-Syrian cooperation suddenly appeared in the light of a fertile common past.

The Turkish foreign policy of "zero problems" with all its neighbors made Turkey a growing influential factor in the interface between Europe and the Middle East. At the same time, Turkish political discourse—both in the street and on the level of decision-makers—has been fast approaching Arab political discourse. This is true even on the emotional level when it comes to the occupation of the Palestinian territories. Although the relations with Israel cooled considerably, Turkey for a long time still enjoyed enough confidence on both sides to play the broker between Syria and Israel.

The shuttle diplomacy that started in May 2008 was just about to enter direct talks when the Israeli delegation packed its suitcases with little explanation in December 2008. Shortly afterward, Israel started to bomb the Gaza strip with the aim to stop the launching of rockets against Israel from Hamas positions. Turkey interpreted the Israeli behavior as a profound breach of confidence. What followed were verbal attacks by Prime Minister Erdoğan against Israel's President Shimon Peres at the World Economic Forum in Davos in January 2009. Swiftly, the Turkish head of government turned into the hero of Arab public opinion since he condemned the Israeli line of action in the Gaza Strip like no Arab head of state (except Syria's).

The good relations with Turkey certainly represented the greatest success for Syria in the past years. Thus, Damascus aptly managed to diversify its foreign policy. In this respect, Syria's escape from isolation had a regional component too.

The popular uprising in Syria put Turkey's pro-democracy stance to a test. It also put an end to Ankara's ambitions to uphold a "zero problem" neighborhood in the light of fast-paced events following the Arab Spring. Ankara geared up its criticism of the Asad regime with the escalation of violence in Syria. Civilian refugees as well as army defectors found a safe haven beyond Syria's northern border, and, starting in June 2011, Turkey helped by facilitating the first major conferences of Syrian opposition figures. In the end Erdoğan followed through his role as an advocate of change in the Arab world after having opted for determined criticism of Tunisia's and Egypt's autocrats. The rhetoric of "family bonds" between Turkey and Syria vanished into thin air as quickly as it had been born. The blunt rejection of Turkey's attempts of mediation during the Syrian uprising represented one of the many lost chances of the Asad regime.

Iran

The short-sighted war in Iraq led to results that, in many ways, were neither in the interest of the United States onr Israel but instead endangered their security interests. One of the points in question is the Kurdish issue. A very practical community of interest emerged between Syria, Turkey, and, so far, Iran because of the fragmentation of Iraq and Kurd ambitions for autonomy in northern Iraq. All these states feel threatened by Kurdish nationalism.

Turkey has chosen diplomatic tones instead of a policy of confrontation with Iraq, following its "zero problem" policy. The relations between Syria and Iran, in contrast, were shaped more by political opportunism than by a far-reaching congruency of interests or by shared ideology. A high-ranking Syrian diplomat framed it this way: "We don't share the same ideologies but we agree on strategies."[12]

Trade with Iran developed more sluggishly than with Turkey despite all rhetoric. However, with increasing isolation and domestic threats, Syria intensified the links with Iran. Both states ratified free trade agreements in 2011 and broadened their cooperation in the areas of oil and gas, the banking system, traffic, tourism, and of the construction and health sectors. Iraq served as a zone of influence and a trade hub for both countries alike. Despite all this representatives of the old school of Syrian diplomacy rejected the term "alliance" with regard to Iran. A more than one-dimensional adjustment of Syrian foreign policy toward Iran could damage Syrian interests in the long run. Iran did not serve as an ideal partner either when it came to keeping Syria's military up to date. But above all, it was in Iraq where dangers for the bilateral relationship between Syria and Iran lurked. [13]

It was an illusionary endeavor of the West to push Syria to give up its cooperation with Iran. The country was Syria's staunchest ally in time of urgent need as the world (including most Arab governments) had turned away from Damascus and the voices of regime change had become stronger and stronger in Washington. The more Syrian politicians felt dictated to from Western capitals, the more defensive of their independence they became especially when incentives to break with Iran were missing. Under certain circumstances it looked as if it was even in the interest of the West that Syria held a working connection with Iran—as long as Syria was perceived as a constructive element in the regional setting.

Having said this, of Syria's three critical points mentioned above—cooperation with Hezbollah, Hamas and Iran—the relation with Iran was about to temporarily lose some of its importance. Syria had diversified its foreign policy and put the relationship with Iran in a broader context through its friendship with Turkey. Breaking with Iran would still have entailed more disadvantages than advantages for Syria in the late 2000s. Meanwhile Iran increased its presence in Syria with three offices of the Iranian *mukhabarat* in Damascus and independent military bases in the country. Iran had a much stronger presence in Syria than Turkey. According to opposition figures, Asad pursued a division of labor: Security and military from Iran; diplomacy and economy from Turkey. People who called for loosening ties with Iran were quickly denounced as pro-American and had to suffer consequences.[14]

As analysts in Damascus conceded, there was a breaking-point in the Iranian-Syrian relationship that could have become more visible in the coming years under normal conditions. Syria—as well as Turkey—was interested in keeping the Iraqi state intact whereas Tehran was gradually widening its influence in Iraq's Shiite south. If one day the Shiites were to demand autonomy or at least strive for an ideological union with Iran, the Kurds would certainly use the opportunity to leave the state structure. Such a scenario would have put a heavy strain on Syrian-Iranian relations. In addition, Iran's growing ambitions in Lebanon after decades of clear Syrian predominance there made the Syrian leadership uncomfortable. Iran's influence could have even jeopardized Syria's national interests if it had provoked tensions in the region; indicative of this is that it took all Asad's art of persuasion to keep Ahmedinejad from visiting the border fence with Israel during his visit to southern Lebanon, where he wanted to throw stones at the Zionist enemy.

However, for a foreseeable future Hezbollah—apart from an anti-American stance—was to remain the strongest common interest between the Syrian and the Iranian regimes. The Israeli-Palestinian arena upheld the bonds. However, if Syria and Iran parted ways, Hezbollah would certainly stick to Iran, Kilo was convinced: "Hezbollah is an Iranian organization and is led by Iranian officers."[15]

Iraq

Syria's view of Iraq changed in the late 2000s. Initially, the regime in Damascus was interested in encouraging unrest in the neighboring country as survival insurance by keeping the Americans tied down and diverted from Damascus. It was opportune for Damascus to let militant Islamists travel to Iraq and be killed by the Americans. Asad made it clear that Syria could do more to secure the border with Iraq but would not do it for free. In the secret cables unveiled by Wikileaks he was quoted, demanding an end to sanctions that banned the sale of commercial airplanes and their parts to Syria.[16]

In his effort to stand up against the United States' Iraq policy, Asad had called the violence of Iraqi rebels "legitimate resistance."[17] This was open provocation for the stumbling US forces and poured fuel on the flames. However, Syria did not remain obstinate or resentful in spite of all its bitterness and criticism of US policy in Iraq. After the United States withdrew its administration from the Tigris in the summer of 2004, the ice began to thaw between Damascus and Baghdad. It was by no means a matter of course that Syria would recognize the new Iraqi government so soon, but the pragmatists prevailed. When the temporary Iraqi Prime Minister Iyad Allawi visited Damascus in July 2004 for the first time, the two sides agreed on a resumption of diplomatic relations, which had been broken off in 1982. Asad and Allawi set up a joint committee to improve the controls of their shared state borders. A railway connection was planned to be opened again between Aleppo and Mosul. At the end of September 2004, an Iraqi aircraft landed at Damascus airport for the first time in twenty-two years. In January 2005, the Syrian government permitted exiled Iraqis to vote in the first democratic Iraqi elections—while residing within the Syrian dictatorship. Some twenty thousand Iraqis made use of this opportunity.

Interestingly, the government in Damascus at that time adopted a less ideological stance than some of the opposition, who wrote a letter of protest over Allawi's first visit to Syria, saying that Iraq was the tool of an occupying power, controlled by the Americans, the Israelis, and foreign secret services. Michel Kilo and Haitham Maleh were among the signatories.

In a final turn of policies, Syria's interest in preventing the fragmentation of Iraq started to prevail in its policy as a matter of self-protection. After 24 years of interruption, the states took up diplomatic relations in 2006. They started to cooperate in the fields of trade and security, although not without friction. Depending on the situation, Syria was able to exert constructive or destabilizing influence on Iraq's security. Therefore, the changed interest in favor of a stable Iraq as part of Syria's raison d'état was a positive sign. In any case, the relations between the countries were better than in history when the presidents Saddam Hussein and Hafez al-Asad competed for the ideological leadership of pan-Arab Baathism in the Arab world.

This held true even in the year of existential threat for the Syrian regime. In 2011 the Iraqi government supported the Syrian regime in its struggle against sanctions from the Arab League and the United Nations. Baghdad abstained from the decision to suspend Syria's membership in the Arab League in November. Below the official level of support, Shiite fighters from the al-Mahdi and Sadr's militias flocked into Syria in buses in support of the Syrian security forces, according to opposition sources. As a counter reaction, Iraqi Sunnis formed the so-called Anbar Force at the Anbar border crossing between the countries and attacked buses heading West. And radicalized Syrian Sunni fighters started to head back from Iraq toward their home country to direct their weapons away from the Americans and toward the Syrian regime.[18] Syria's civil war scenario started to blend with the Iraqi one and vice versa.

Saudi Arabia

The geopolitical strengthening of Iran after the Iraq war brought the issue of Arab solidarity back to the table. The Saudi-Syrian animosity (with Egypt under ousted President Mubarak in the anti-Syrian camp) had long been a determining factor after the assassination of Lebanese Prime Minister Rafiq Hariri, who had strong economic links to Saudi Arabia and carried a Saudi passport. At times this led to paralysis. Pan-Arab cooperation was fragile, as demonstrated during the wide boycott of the Arab League summit in Damascus in March 2008.

Later in 2008, relations gradually started to improve. President Bashar al-Asad and King Abdullah bin Abd al-Aziz exchanged a series of letters, political delegations and even personal visits. The détente in Lebanon between the pro-Syrian and pro-Saudi-Western camps was a consequence of more pragmatic relations between the countries. Riyadh and Damascus were still ideological and socio-political antipodes. But to Riyadh, in case of a war against Iran, being on better terms with Damascus was of strategic significance. Although developments in Lebanon (in particular the Hariri Tribunal) still endangered Syrian-Saudi reconciliation, the wave of pro-democracy protests in the Arab world created a common ground between the Syrian and Saudi autocrats. Not surprisingly, Syria declared the Saudi military intervention in Bahrain to suppress the protests there to be justified (separating itself in this regard from Iran).

As in many other things, the achievement of a Syrian-Saudi détente collapsed with the escalation of violence in Syria. The old cleavages broke open again. Saudi Arabia together with Qatar pushed forward sanctions against the Baath regime within the Arab League. Obviously, Saudi Arabia would not have sounded very credible, surfing on the wave of a pro-democracy discourse, and had to maneuver carefully. Syria, for its part, smelled a US-driven conspiracy.

With Syria weakened and its regime entangled in a web of home-made difficulties, time had come to pay open bills.

The United States

Although Syria and Israel entered negotiations with the mediation of Turkey, all participants knew that an agreement between the archenemies could not be reached or upheld without guarantees from the United States. Syria, in particular, was interested in walking the last mile with the US because no one else could press Israel for compromises. Asad underlined that, with regard to the global balance of power, a strong US is better for the world than a weak one.[19] But the US was far from playing a dynamic role in the Middle East. Despite its changed tone toward the Muslim world, many Arabs were disappointed in the US administration. The expectations had been high, though it appeared that President Obama gave his Cairo speech too early, long before he could start to put into practice his new intentions.

This was due less to a lack of consciousness with regard to the problems, as Obama knew that his two predecessors had entangled themselves in the strings of Middle East diplomacy in their last months in office instead of presenting themselves as effective peacemakers. Domestic hurdles within the US made impossible a Middle East policy according to Obama's ideas. The crisis of the economy and other domestic issues preoccupied him and became his priorities. As soon as Obama would have tried to raise stakes in the Middle East conflict, the political constellations at home would have changed even more to his disadvantage. Obama needed to resolve the most important domestic projects first before trying to find allies in political Washington to put pressure on Israel's leadership to stop the building of settlements or to enter into concrete negotiations with the Palestinians or Syria. Otherwise, he would have endangered his entire political legacy. Building alliances in Congress became even more difficult after the sweeping victory of conservative Republicans in the November 2010 mid-term elections.

Despite these obstacles, important progress was visible in US-Syria relations. Syria declared itself ready again to take up an exchange of information with the CIA and the British MI6. At the same time, Asad made clear that the cooperation could not be a one-way-street as it used to be under George W. Bush. Otherwise, Syria would once again stop its cooperation.[20]

After a vacuum of six years, a US ambassador returned to Syria in January 2011. The US President was so convinced that Ambassador Robert Ford had to go to Damascus that he sidelined Syria-skeptical Congress. This was the last major foreign policy victory for the Syrian regime before the popular protests broke out barely two months later. Without any doubt, a US ambassador in place was an important investment in bilateral relations because the reestablishment of a political eye level was a factor for Syrians that could not be underestimated. Obama's decision came just in time. Since then the relations soured due to the brutal suppression of the protests. Nevertheless, the United States turned against Asad only hesitantly while hoping for a political solution in Syria. With the death toll rising in Syrian streets, international condemnations and sanctions became the rhetoric of the day.

International Factors & Three Waves of Suppression

When Syria's domestic and international policy contexts are juxtaposed in a timeline, certain patterns emerge between both realms. The following table shows the phases of ten years of Asad's rule. Three waves of domestic suppression took place before the big bang in 2011.

The first wave of repression took place in 2001 as a clampdown on the mushrooming debating clubs of the Civil Society Movement. The leading figure imprisoned at that time was ex-Member of Parliament Riad Seif, who dared to announce the foundation of a new social democratic party (see Chapter VII "Opposition, Islam, and the Regime"). The regime feared a kind of Russian Perestroika that would destabilize it, a fear especially shared by members of the traditional power structure such as hard-liner Vice President Abdul Halim Khaddam. When it came to foreign policy, in the first years the new leadership was still in a phase of orientation. No major changes were taking place either in discourse or in major foreign policy initiatives. Nevertheless, there were lively debates within the leadership on the course of Syria's foreign policy, basically between westward looking protagonists and eastward oriented figures who favored contacts with Russia, Iran, and China.

Not long after the Damascus Spring was suppressed in 2001, it became clear that economic reform remained as a minimum common denominator after political and administrative reforms were discarded. But things may have turned out better if international events had not put considerable strain on Syria's development. Among these were the 9/11 attacks that changed the whole board game in the Middle East and beyond, the military approach of the US administration under George W. Bush, the subsequent war in Iraq in 2003 and its violent repercussions, the wave of Iraqi refugees that hit Syria in particular, the French-US-Saudi-Sunni connection to expel Syria from Lebanon in 2004/05, the war between Hezbollah and Israel in 2006, and the economic sanctions that lasted more or less since the preparations for the Iraq war. Under these conditions no democratic experiments could be expected.

Nevertheless, hope for change persisted even through the years of 2003 and 2004 while the Syrian Baath regime was entrenched in harsh ideological opposition to the Iraq war. With increasing pressure on Syria, especially by Saudi Arabia, France, and the United States, to leave Lebanon, and the Hariri assassination in February 2005, the strangling of Syria's opposition reached a new climax.

Phases of Bashar's Rule
June 2000 till 2011

Foreign Policy		Domestic Policy	
2000 thru 2002	**Orientation** No significant steps, continuation of known problems and discourse.	2000 thru mid 2001	**Cautious Opening** Damascus Spring, debating clubs, Civil Society Movement.
2003 thru 2005	**Ideologization** Stiff ideological positioning against the Iraq war, isolation, strengthening ties with Iran but mending relations with Turkey from 2004 onward.	mid 2001 thru 2002	**First clampdown** Suppression of the Damascus Spring, first losses of the Civil Society Movement, arrest of Riad Seif.
		2003 thru 2004	**Stagnation** Civil Society Movement simmers.
2005 thru 2007	**Contraction** Hariri assassination and consequences, withdrawal from Lebanon, further isolation also by Europeans (France) and Arabs (Saudi Arabia).	2005 thru 2006	**Confrontation** Opposition gains courage, Damascus Declaration (Oct '05), collision course between regime and Civil Society Movement; Rising influence of Islamists.
		2006	**Second clampdown** End of open confrontation, silencing of the Civil Society Movement, arrest of Michel Kilo, Anwar al-Bunni.
2008 thru 2010	**Re-emergence** Start of liberation from foreign policy dead-ends and pariah status, back on the international stage, well-thought alliances and decisions (Turkey, Lebanon, Saudi Arabia), consolidation of the regime.	2007 thru 2009	**Silence** The comeback of fear to the streets, rest-opposition is in the underground; continued rise of Islamist influence.
		2009 thru 2010	**Third Clampdown** Arrest of further senior opposition members and HR activists like Haitham Maleh, rising suppression of secularists and secular ideas; increased influence of Islamists up to the legislative level.
2011	**Fall-back into Isolation**	2011	**Crisis** Existential regime crisis and military crackdown on mass protests.

In the face of the obvious weakness of Asad's regime, the secular opposition caught momentum. At that time a historical step toward a more unified opposition had been achieved through the Damascus Declaration of 16 October 2005 (see Chapter VII "Opposition, Islam, and the Regime"). Opposition figures said that they were additionally encouraged by European diplomats and politicians to become more aggressive. But later Michel Kilo became convinced that the Europeans had secretly decided to keep the Asad regime in Damascus. "Why did the Europeans not tell us that they had an interest in maintaining the Asad regime? Why didn't they tell us that this was supposed the frame of our actions? They should have warned us!" he said in disappointment.[21]

The second wave of suppression followed in the first half of 2006 when those who had been spared in 2001, like Michel Kilo and Anwar al-Bunni, were arrested. The hunt for signatories of the Damascus Declaration was justified with the accusation against the activists of pursuing the agenda of Western interests. The Syrian regime suffered from the "Lebanon trauma" of increased isolation and stigmatization.

The first and the second wave of suppression followed some kind of logic where foreign and domestic events dovetailed. When the regime felt threatened, no experiments could be expected. However, the third wave of suppression against secular opposition and human rights activists started at the end of 2009 when Syria had already celebrated its re-emergence onto the international stage. In other words: The setback in human rights contradicted a quite stable and successful, even liberating, phase of foreign policy from a Syrian perspective.

Attempts at explanation of the regime's behavior have proven difficult. Intellectuals referred to the "trauma of Lebanon," when more or less the whole world—Western and Arab countries—were standing against Syria after the assassination of Lebanon's Prime Minister Hariri in February 2005. This underlined the perception of persisting nervousness of the regime as the reason for the overall tightening of red lines.

The hope that Syria would adopt domestic reforms if it did not continue to feel threatened from abroad did not materialize. In previous years, the thesis was plausible that with Syria's isolation and existential threat against the regime, the political leadership was less ready for experiments and cracked down all the more on opposition movements. The reversal of this thesis did not come true. Despite a relaxation in international affairs and Syria's re-emergence on the Arab and international stage, the suppression of political dissenters and human rights defenders even increased since 2008. Correlations between domestic and foreign policies that were visible in the past were replaced by contradictions between these realms. In other words: Syria was by no means on a path toward political reforms when the Arab Spring hit the country.

9
Che Not Usama:
Syrian Society & Western Ideals

THE BEARDED WARRIOR IS LEADING THE FIGHT AGAINST a superior colonial occupying power on behalf of those deprived of their rights. He is hiding in the mountains—conducting guerilla warfare. His followers are motivated by his charisma and unshakeable ideological convictions to such an extent that they are ready to die for him. Almost everywhere in the world he is revered as a saint. This figure, symbolizing resistance to oppression and Western capitalism, also used to look down from posters in Damascus during the Baathist reign. Young demonstrators used to carry his picture as a protest against the American occupation of Iraq, against the oppression of the Palestinians, against the perceived threat of globalization, and against a "new Western imperialism."

The man who stood for all these goals was not Usama bin Laden—not in Syria, at least. No one found bin Laden's likeness here. The hero who frequently appeared at public demonstrations was Che Guevara! T-shirts, banners, and stickers with the socialist revolutionary's portrait were just as common in Damascus, Aleppo, and Homs as in Havana, Berlin, or Boston. Red flags, some still bearing the Soviet hammer and sickle, fluttered in the streets of the Syrian capital when people demonstrated against the war in Iraq in 2003. Time seemed to stand still. Of course, Islamic demonstrators also walked next to communists with their own slogans, but without foaming at the mouth and calling for a worldwide jihad. After all, the protest marches were controlled by members of the civilian branch of the *Mukhabarat* and staged for the TV cameras. These were the old days.

Che Guevara was also seen on posters hanging in student hostels, not only during political demonstrations. Syrian society is a colorful cocktail of lifestyles and convictions. It is a melting pot of Islamists, humanists, atheists, pan-Islamists, pan-Arabists, nationalists, liberals, communists, and traditionalists. Not all of them were able to act openly, let alone engage in politics. But because of its isolation, Syria remained a bizarre biotope. Some things appeared dusty, dreamy, and old-fashioned. But Syria has certainly not been a hotbed of Islamic fanaticism whose members wanted to carry the Prophet's ensign to the West and proclaim international terrorism as a legitimate means to this end. US neoconservative propaganda was out of place here. US rhetoric for a long time disregarded the social reality in Syria. If it was a matter of social values instead of oil, the Syrian people believed, the United States would align itself with secular Syria instead of with the totalitarian Saudi regime from the "Islamic Stone Age." The negative image that Syria had in the West could be explained in many ways, reasons which had to do with Damascus itself and with the political system. Syria would have been assessed differently, however, with regard to social aspects if the criteria of Western ideals were truly applied.

Until about 2008, some people in the Syrian government used this argument as well, presenting themselves as a partner of the West in view of growing international pressure on Syria after the Iraq war. "If the United States seriously wanted the Middle East to be peaceful, safe, and prosperous, Syria would be the most obvious partner in the region," said Buthayna Shaaban, then Minister of Expatriates in 2004. "It's the only secular regime in the region. We have a multi-ethnic, multi-religious society like in the United States. For forty years, we have had the best policy in the Arab world for promoting women's rights. I can't see why the United States would have any problem with us. If you take Israel out of the equation, I can't see any collisions of interests."[1]

Particularly in comparison with its neighbors in the region, Syria retained a qualified but remarkable social secularism. This was an important realization at a time when Western decision-makers were concerned about the rise of a radical political Islam in the Arab world. After all, this kind of Islam was regarded as a hotbed of international terrorism, such as the world experienced, especially since 11 September 2001. Societies in the Arab world have become more Islamic in recent years. A central reason for this is that the unending conflict between Israel and the Palestinians has been distorting the realities. Another reason is the authoritarianism of secular regimes such as Tunisia, Egypt, or Syria that created a defiant, defensive, and oppositional Islam. In Tunisia and Egypt strength became visible after the first democratic elections there. The influence of conservative Islamic scholars and the numbers of women in head scarves have visibly increased also in Syria. Nevertheless, a relative variety of lifestyles and customs endured in the country that were not based on religion.

For example, in Jordan, eating in public places during the day is forbidden during Ramadan. In Syria, on the other hand, many restaurants stayed open, and not only in the Christian quarters. Although an old Syrian law from 1971 did forbid eating and smoking in the street during the Muslim fasting period, it was hardly ever enforced.[2] The cones of golden, grilled chicken and juicy kebab meat sizzled openly on spits along the boulevards in downtown Damascus with hardly anybody taking offence.

Many restaurants and bars sold alcohol, again not only in the Christian areas. There has been Syrian wine, Syrian beer, and of course the national drink araq, a high-proof aniseed schnapps. A topless pin-up girl hung on the wall of a tiny den near the East Gate (Bab Sharqi) in the Old City of Damascus, where mostly old men sat in the evenings at three small tables with their heads close together. This was another part of the Syrian mosaic.

Nightclubs and cabaret shows, usually with Russian or Iraqi girls, were part of the street scene in Damascus and were mainly patronized by Saudi men during the summer months. Here they were able to gratify their sexual desires, for which there was no outlet in the radically puritanical society of Saudi Arabia. If they were married, their wives, who may number up to four, remained in the hotel suite. Syrian TV shows developed a tradition in caricaturing the Saudis' behavior during their summer holidays in Syria. For many Arabs in the Middle East, Syria was a place of social liberty compared to their home countries, which increasingly displeased conservative circles. Only in Lebanon, a special case because of its large Christian population, did everyday life appear more liberal.

It was not uncommon to see long manes of hair, skintight T-shirts and leggings, audaciously low necklines, and provocative make-up on university campuses in Damascus, Homs, Aleppo, or Latakia—as well as in the streets and shopping quarters. The university also played a part in the marriage market. Girls with and without *hijab* (headscarves) mingled with one another in groups. Guys wore jeans, T-shirts, sunglasses, baseball caps, and had gel in their hair.

In spite of certain restrictions, everyday life for women was better in Syria than in many other Muslim Arab countries. The Civil Code of 1949, which to a large extent has kept its validity, was modeled on the secular French code. Women were allowed to file for divorce, which was far from the convention, as debates in Egypt have shown. They enjoyed equality with men in the eyes of the law and received equal pay for equal work, which is not always the case even in some Western countries. These achievements were to be challenged by the increasing influence of Islamic conservatives. The heated debates about a planned new, reactionary, Personal Status Law showed that the status of women was still being challenged (see Chapter VII "Opposition, Islam and the Regime"). Nevertheless, there was a large number of Syrian women in middle-management positions, and women accounted for more than half of the students in the universities. Since 1980, the military was no longer an exclusively male domain, and since 1983, boys and girls had been taught in common classrooms.[3]

Despite all of this, religion, and traditions influenced by religion, played a significant role in the everyday life of all Syrians—Sunnis, Christians of all stripes, Alawites, Druze, Shiites, and Jews. Some communists, for example, regularly went to the mosque or church. Religion and tradition were most noticeable in the case of marriage. The Sharia, the Islamic law, governed matters relating to the family and inheritances. In 1970, Hafez al-Asad, startled by widespread protests, yielded to the demands of the Muslim Brothers and had the Sharia anchored in the constitution as "the main source" of legislation, rather than "a main source," as the constitution of 1950 had stated. It remained impossible to marry at a registry office. People who wanted to marry had to profess to a religious faith. In case they were registered without any faith, they were automatically considered Muslims. Islamic marriage law states that Muslim men may marry Christian women, but the latter will not be allowed to inherit wealth or property. Christian men who marry Muslim women have to convert to Islam. In these respects, Syria has hardly been different from any other Muslim country.

The Islamic command for tolerance was, in fact, superior to the intolerant Christian practice until the early twentieth century. However, in comparison with today's legislation in the Western world influenced by the Enlightenment of the eighteenth century, the Islamic command looks more like toleration than real tolerance. Although it technically accepts members of other scriptural religions, it does not meet them eye-to-eye, but looks down on them morally. Why else—as the final argument in a chain of reasons—must a man who marries a Muslim woman convert to her religion, or only a Muslim is allowed to be head of state in most Muslim countries? Even in secular Syria there was no social or legal room for atheists or members of other than the traditional scriptural religions.

The free spaces in private and social life untouched by Islam had been decreasing in the past years. Islam became a stronger base of orientation for many Syrians, not in spite of but because of the new openness, the erosion of traditions, and Western influences through the media and the Internet. This was less a "return to Islam" than an entirely new development, as headscarves testified.

The black veils of the radical Wahhabis from Saudi Arabia, who for a long time had been unable to get a foothold in Syrian society, gradually became part of the street scene, even if they only played a marginal role. The origin of the new Wahhabi influence in Syria dates back to horse-trading between Hafez al-Asad and Saudi Arabia in 1980. Asad managed to dissuade the Saudis from supporting the militant Muslim Brothers in Syria, an important step that assured his political survival. In return, the secular Asad allowed Saudi Arabia to set up Quranic schools, welfare organizations, and mosques in Syria. According to estimates from Islamic sources of the year 2004, within the preceding fifteen years $1.5 billion had poured into Syria, Jordan, and Lebanon to promote Wahhabism. "The petro-dollars have destroyed the remarkably tolerant Islam over time," said analyst Samir Altaqi. Sufism and tolerant, popular Islam in Syria were the greatest victims of this trend. Altaqi recalled his childhood, when even Jews sometimes had gone to sheikhs because they had been more open-minded and tolerant than their own rabbis. What seems incredible today was quite common sixty years ago. "If an unmarried girl got pregnant, she went to the sheikh in her predicament. He then protected her in order to prevent a scandal."[4]

Traditions shared by Muslims, Christians, and others were increasingly losing their bonding power. But the West, whose values were often only perceived in a distorted manner through cheap Hollywood movies, did not offer a convincing alternative. The West's Middle East policies also led people to discount Western values at times.

A Syrian photographer, aged around fifty and an experienced world traveler, described the paradoxical change of values in Syria. "When I was small, it was almost impossible to speak to strange girls. I had a crush on a girl and we always made a date for four o'clock every afternoon to wave to each other at the windows of our apartments. After many months we even dared to start writing to each other. Those were the traditions. Today you can approach any girl in the street and give her your mobile phone number or she will even give you hers. When you go to a university campus, you see naked belly buttons and you don't know where to look. This is why so many people are escaping to Islam and headscarves, because they have lost their orientation."

The contrasts had become more extreme. "Either you cover yourself up or you run around half-naked," a student of economics pointedly remarked. "Either you say, 'Long live Islam!' or you demonstrate that you are against Islam. There is hardly a middle way," said twenty-five-year-old Shuruq in 2003, who attended lectures in ordinary blue jeans and without make-up.

Looking at old family photos, you can often see mothers in mini-skirts, which would be quite daring today. An Alawite friend told me that her family used to have a holiday house at the beach north of Latakia, but they sold it because they did not feel comfortable living there any longer. "In the end, we were almost the only women still bathing in bikinis," she reported. "More and more women were coming from the countryside, bathing with all their clothes and veils on, and the large number of Saudi tourists reinforced this trend. Today when you're the only person who wants to swim in a bikini, people stare at you and consider you a slut."

The wife of Sadiq Jalal al-Azm, Iyman Shaker, a vivid lady with short, uncovered hair, recounted how she had been asked by an Islamic zealot to wear a veil at the market in the Old City of Damascus. She had never seen such a behavior in old times. He pressed a sheet of paper into her hand that described in detail how "the sister" should put on a *hijab*. It had to be gray, without any lively colors, and without perfume. Mosques in Mohajereen, the district where she lives, she continued, used spies in the neighborhood to check up on the lifestyle of the faithful. Taxis had at times passed her by only to stop a few yards farther on to pick up a veiled woman. A secular, Muslim intellectual from Aleppo recounted that a taxi driver had thrown him out of his taxi merely because he had a bottle of araq with him. "This wouldn't have happened twenty-five years ago. They learn all that from the hate-preachers in the mosques," he said in frustration.

Another well-known intellectual from Aleppo, Abdul Razaq Eid, added: "There are conservative sheikhs who preach all kinds of things. For example against the woman—we have to kill her if she does this and that. But the *mukhabarat* doesn't have a problem with that. Radical positions in questions of belief and society are ok. The main thing is that they don't talk against the regime. Syria is fighting Islamism on a security level but not ideologically and culturally."[5]

Attempts by the secret service to put an end to radical tirades by Islamists increasingly led to open conflict. Sometimes it seemed that there was a risk that the balance of power between radical preachers of hate and the government would be tipped. The murder of a member of the political secret service in Homs at the end of 2004 brought things to a head. The dead man's assignment was to observe the Ghufari Mosque in Homs. In this capacity, he had forbidden radical religious instruction to children under the age of eighteen. The mosque supervisor was implicated in the murder. This incident was of course not reported in the Syrian press because the case was explosive for another reason—the murderers were radical Sunnis and the victim was an Alawite.

The increasing frequency of these incidents demonstrated a growing trend in Syria. Social pressure on secular Syrians was increasing. Conservative Muslim forces dared to act in the open after the death of the elder Asad. *Mukhabarat* members could no longer be seen as often in some Islamic districts such as Bab Srija in Damascus. Passers-by were able to witness what had once been impossible: the name and symbols of the president scratched away from walls and plaques. What a contrast to the time when the female elite troops of Hafez's brother Rifaat had torn veils off women's' heads in the streets in the 1980s with an excessive zeal similar to what took place at the beginning of Kemalism in Turkey.

10
Excursus:
Secularism in Syria

THE TERM "SECULARISM" MUST BE EXPLAINED IN MORE DETAIL, especially in the context of the Middle East, as Europeans and Muslim Arabs often have different experiences and ideas about their understanding of the term.[1]

Secularism in Europe is embedded in a long process of philosophical, social, and political developments. It largely stems from the ideas of the Enlightenment, when people questioned religious dogmas and interpretations and courageously defied the powerful Christian clergy. Among the things that developed from these acts of liberation was the possibility to publicly confess to being an atheist or a deist, someone who believes in a private God without adopting the interpretations and rituals of the church. Faith increasingly became an individual decision, even though it was not until recent decades that this freedom became a social reality. Only after the social revolutions in Western societies in 1968 did individual and free self-determination win its decisive victory over tradition.

Secularism in the West is thus less a political ideology than part of social development and personal experience, with the separation of church and state only one possible result. Secularism in the European sense can also include the privatization of religion and the disappearance of personal faith and religious practices among the population.[2] These three aspects of Western secularization, however, do not have to occur everywhere at the same time.

Eastern Germany, for example, has become one of the most irreligious regions in Europe with sixty-nine percent of the population (as of 2000) professing no faith.[3] Religious practice is disappearing to a great extent in Western Germany as well. Nevertheless, church and state are not entirely separated, as the German government collects a special tax on behalf of the church. In Scandinavia a Protestant state church exists, although only a small number of people declare themselves religious. In France, on the other hand, the separation of church and state is strict and consistent, while large parts of the population are profoundly Catholic.

In the United States in recent years, one can observe an increasing role for religion and the public display of personal faith in everyday life. This is particularly true with the increasingly active Christian Right and to some elements of the Tea Party Movement. Tea Party participants often display social concerns, political ambitions, and a missionary zeal that are similar to those of Islamic fundamentalists in other countries. However, rhetorical reference to "God" has always been present in political and public life in the US and is a normal ingredient of public culture. No speech of the president ends without the religious-nationalist phrase "God bless America!" But at the same time, prayer in public schools, for example, is forbidden by law and religious organizations exist independently of the government. There is no general church tax like in Germany, although the religious organizations may get financial support for clearly defined purposes. The relationship between religion and state in the United States is a very complex one that is partly in flux and also controversial within the US with some legal rulings contested in various States. Although religious forces gained influence under the administration of George W. Bush, US society and politics are known for their ability to self-correct and this seems to have occurred under the Obama administration.

In a nutshell, the principle difference between the United States and Europe stems, above all, from the history of the seventeenth and eighteenth centuries. For the early settlers and founders of the United States, the free practice of religion played the role of liberation ideology during the new nation-building. Religion was thus conceived as a progressive force. In contrast, the "old" Europeans increasingly saw religion as part of the oppressive political establishment, from which they freed themselves not by emigration (with religion) but by emancipation (from religion).

These examples show how the practical impact of secularism in the Western world has varied greatly. It is difficult to say which country is more and which less secular. Secularism in the Western world is a flexible concept that also leaves room for religion. However, a common denominator exists in spite of these differences. Secularism is a cultural experience, an intellectual and social movement with simultaneous and intertwined developments of liberal democracy, constitutionalism, individual liberties, and human rights, independent of personal faith or religious conviction.

Secularism is something quite different in the Arab world. The idea of a state education system, modern forms of administration, and the separation of religion and state came to the Arab region from Europe. It was Egypt that first came into contact with the ideas of the French Revolution when Napoleon landed there for an expedition in 1798. Radical reforms were initiated in 1801 by Muhammad Ali, an Albanian officer, who initially went to Egypt on behalf of the Ottoman Empire to get rid of the Mamlukes. Afterward he proclaimed himself regent of the Nile. The country soon became the first modern, secular nation-state in the region.[4]

With the rise of pan-Arab nationalism, shortly before the collapse of the Ottoman Empire in World War I, secular elements increasingly entered the rhetoric and finally the politics of the Arab Middle East (see Chapter XI "The Bankcrupty of Baathism"). The concept, however, suffered a major defect: it came along with European colonization. In the Middle East, the Western powers in charge of colonized territories scarcely applied the values that they praised and implemented at home, which explains the defiant attitude of many Muslims who reject ideas simply because they come from the West. (This attitude also exists the other way round, of course.)

Secularism as many Arabs have experienced it up to the Arab Spring meant the replacement of one tyranny by another. It was an imported ideology grafted in a distorted form onto societies that had entirely different backgrounds of experience. Secularism was associated with imperialism and later with Western-backed authoritarian regimes, with etatism (state socialism), cultural disorientation, and often with the violation of human rights and personal liberties. Secularism became a platform for Western-educated elites to legitimatize their rule without themselves adhering to the intellectual and social pillars of Western secularism.[5]

Secularism was thus degraded to a political instrument and an ideological facade. This explains why secularism was so easily exchangeable with Islamic populism in Iraq. Saddam Hussein, for example, felt that he needed more support from Sunni religious scholars and believers after the disaster of the Gulf War in 1991. So he switched in a flash from Baathist secularism to Islam. He had "*allahu akbar*" (God is Great) written on the Iraqi flag in green lettering. He banned alcohol and nightclubs and restricted women's rights. It is scarcely conceivable that such a U-turn could have taken place in a secular Western environment. The danger in Iraq lies in the fact that the former was not real secularism or the latter real Islam.

To summarize, in the West an embedded secularism has grown in harmony with philosophical, social and moral aspirations. In contrast, we can speak of an imposed secularism in the Arab world.

In Syria, there was no secularism in the European sense either. The spiritual fathers of secular pan-Arabism and later of the Baath ideology considered Arab nationalism and Islam (at least as a cultural factor) as inseparable components.[6] Syrian secularism was part of the state ideology, yet tolerance and religious pluralism have a long tradition in the country that went far beyond the seizure of power by members of the socialist Baath Party and the liberal Shiite sect of the Alawites. Secular views were widespread in society and politics after Syria gained its independence from France in 1946. A Christian, Faris al-Khoury, even ruled Syria as prime minister in the mid-1940s and 1950s.[7] "To a large extent Islam had lost its political and partly also its social function a long time before 8 March 1963 when the Baath Party came to power," concluded Hans Günter Lobmeyer.[8]

True, socialist ideas prevailed that impacted economic policy, especially between 1966 and 1970 when the left wing of the party (the Neo-Baathists) was in power. But sweeping secular social reforms—an inevitable consequence of atheist Marxist-Leninist ideology—did not take place. The traditional forces were too strong. Instead, socialism had become more of a signpost of foreign policy pointing toward Moscow.

The Baath Party had thus been in command for eight years when Hafez al-Asad became president in 1971. Along with him, many Alawites strengthened their positions of power. Most of them were poor peasants in the mountains around Latakia who experienced social advancement due to the French colonial policy. (Quite in contrast to their understanding of the state as a citizens' democracy in their own country, the French took advantage of the existence of different sects in their colonies and played religious groups against one another in a divide-and-rule strategy.[9]) It was no "Alawite Revolution," but rather a coincidence that an Alawite proved to be hard and unscrupulous enough to play the intrigues and power struggles of the time in his favor. Nevertheless, the fact that Asad had a personal secular background played a role. So it was not primarily a (Western) ideology—socialism—but a very traditional player—a religious group—that favored social liberalism on account of their religious teachings, implemented it, and maintained it in spite of opposition.

It was not the socialist Baath Party itself but Asad the Alawite who began to introduce secular reforms and grant more rights to women. In 1973, he even wanted to delete the requirement from the constitution that the president be a Muslim, in an attempt to gain more support from minority groups.[10] Thus he provoked intense opposition from the Islamists.

Startled, Asad backed down, shelved his proposal, and made a number of far-reaching concessions. To appease conservative Muslims he started demonstratively going to mosques and set up Quranic schools in the name of the regime, bearing the contradictory and grotesque name: "Asad Institute for Quranic Studies" (m'ahad al-Asad li tahfith al-quran). Secular critics in Damascus maintain that the Mamlukes, who ruled in the thirteenth and fourteenth centuries, and the Alawites under Asad had more mosques built than any other rulers in Syrian history. Both had the same goal: as former political and religious outsiders, they wanted to prove their faith to the Sunni majority and thus avoid public unrest. Islamic trust properties (auqaf), that arrange for the construction of mosques funded by private and public money, were nationalized under the Baathists and put under the control of a government ministry. This is a clear example of how institutional formal laicism—the separation of church and state—does not necessarily entail social secularism. As of the year 2009 there were 8,500 mosques in Syria of which 4,500 were in Damascus.[11]

Paradoxes can be found at all levels. Shortly after becoming president in 1971, Asad re-introduced the religious oath of office that the Baathists had abolished two years earlier. He established a ban on eating in public during the fasting period of Ramadan and was not averse to including religious expressions in his speeches.

Deep inside, however, the pragmatist Asad detested religious conservatism and the politicizing of religion. He demanded that Islam be free of "the ugly face of fanaticism" and maintained that moral values, not religion, should be the crucial component for the development of a society.[12] In his polemics against the Muslim Brothers, Asad stressed that "No party has the right to monopolize Islam or any other religion." He also said, "The Arab Ba'th Socialist Party is a nationalist socialist party that does not differentiate between religions . . . . If Syria had not always been above sectarianism, it would not now exist."[13]

The Muslim Brotherhood of the 1970s and 1980s, however, no longer used religious arguments but anti-Alawite ones, thereby trying to take advantage of the fact that Alawites were the backbone of the regime. During that time many Alawites were assassinated. The Muslim Brothers presented them as a sect of non-believers who abused the country and oppressed the faithful Sunnis. The Islamists discredited Baath secularism as an Alawite heresy.[14]

The Alawite card had always been played in the Syrian system of loyalty. Membership in a particular religion had increasingly become part of the political poker game. However, as previously mentioned, it was not justified to speak about an "Alawite rule." There was no exclusive clientelism by and for Alawites in Syria. The Baath Party was not an Alawite party and its base was formed out of various social, not religious, groups. Alawites did not dominate society, let alone business. Neither were they supported by special infrastructure measures. Most Alawites did not fare any better than the other groups in Syria.[15] Some of Asad's most faithful supporters were Sunnis, including Mustafa Tlass who retired in May 2004 after a record thirty-two years as minister of defense. Bashar al-Asad, in a politically astute move, married a Sunni woman and was anxious to achieve a balance in the machinery of power. There was also enmity and distrust between the Alawite tribes and a large number of Alawites were in prison for opposing the government. They often got harsher sentences from the regime than members of other religions.

The Muslim Brothers pursued concrete political interests, namely the fall of Hafez al-Asad and the Alawite clique. Islam served as a mobilizing ideology to this end. Nevertheless, both sides used Islamic rhetoric, claiming that the other side was not truly religious and accusing them of misusing Islam for political purposes. The conflict escalated and Hafez al-Asad was no longer able to pacify the Islamists with cosmetic and symbolic religious action. The mistrust between the two sides was too profound.

The public trial of strength between the regime and the Sunni Islamists continued over several turbulent years. It was not a religious conflict. Asad was supported by large segments of the Syrian population—the peasantry, a liberal-minded class of Sunni traders especially in Damascus, Kurds, Sunni Bedouin tribes, and religious minorities were largely on his side. "These combined forces were just able to prevent the country from Islamization," said the historian Abdullah Hanna. "The odds were fifty to fifty."[16] The tactician Hafez al-Asad made large concessions to Sunni businessmen in Aleppo, after which they handed over more and more Muslim Brothers from their street quarters to the authorities. In addition, Asad managed to pull off the previously mentioned deal with Saudi Arabia that stopped Saudi support for the militant wing of the Muslim Brothers.

The decisive turn of events though was finally brought about by the military. As mentioned above, in 1982 Hafez al-Asad together with his brother Rifaat put a bloody end to the civil war by the notorious Hama massacre. It is likely that tens of thousands of people died during the bombardment and storming of the Old City, where the Muslim Brothers had barricaded themselves among the population. Since then, radical Islamists have no longer been able to gain a foothold in public life in Syria until they emerged again in the garb of an exiled opposition group.

A high price was to be paid for maintaining the status quo. Yet even critics of the Syrian regime did not dare risk the regime's hard-won stability in view of the social and political Islamization that was encircling Syria.

11
The Bankruptcy of Baathism

Oₙₑ ᴏꜰ ᴛʜᴇ Bᴀᴀᴛʜɪsᴛs' ᴘᴏʟɪᴛɪᴄᴀʟ sʏᴍʙᴏʟs ᴡᴀs a map uniting all the Arab countries around the Mediterranean in a dark green semicircle. A pennant in the pan-Arab colors of black, white, red, and green was stuck in the heart of Syria. Usually a portrait of Hafez or Bashar Asad was pictured next to it—the leader of the Syrian Baath Party as the guarantor of and fighter for pan-Arab unity. The map was also part of a gigantic mural in the Baghdad National Museum until it was looted after the American invasion in 2003. In the mural Iraqis were carrying the map as an ensign, only this time the masses were following Saddam Hussein who was riding toward Jerusalem on a proud, white horse with a sword in his hand.

For outsiders it was hard to grasp why two countries that had committed themselves to the same ideology had been bitter enemies for decades. Branches of the Baath Party were ruling in both Syria and Iraq, but they seemed to hate each other more than their archenemy Israel or the United States. What were the reasons for this brotherly feud? And what are the roots of pan-Arabism anyway as a political force?

The development of Arab nationalism coincided with numerous social and economic upheavals in the Middle East that were strongly marked by European influence. A better infrastructure came into being and with it arose greater social mobility. More and more people moved to the fast-growing cities. As a result, traditional ties and identities dissolved. A middle class started to develop, as did new possibilities for mass communication with the use of printing presses. A modern educational system resulted in more uniform curricula, and along with it came higher literacy rates. These are factors that have fostered a homogenization of cultural units (or what were then perceived as such), as well as nationalist movements in other parts of the world.[1]

The history of ideas also plays a role. Nationalist ideologies that spread to the rest of the world from Europe in the nineteenth century exerted a great influence on the Orient. The ethno-national ideas of the German Romanticists occupy an important position in the Arab case. Pan-Arab nationalism sharpened its political profile on this spiritual foundation at the end of World War I in order to demarcate itself from the ethno-national ideology of the Young Turks, whose revolution had shattered the traditional foundations of the Ottoman Empire. European imperialism and colonialism were other sources of friction for the young Arab ideology. In addition, political pan-Arabism was fed by its resistance to Zionism, the growing Jewish nationalism in Palestine.

The phenomenon had many facets, political causes, and social circumstances. The framework after the collapse of the Ottoman Empire was a fragmented political landscape—newly formed states whose frontiers were artificially drawn by the European colonial powers. The nation-state identity created a counterforce to pan-Arabism and developed surprisingly rapidly into a significant and distinctive social and political framework for action. "One of the most extraordinary features of the modern Middle East is indeed this strength of the states and their ability to resist pressures either to disintegrate into their local components or to coalesce into some larger union," Bernard Lewis writes.[2]

More recent historiography focuses on the socio-economic factors of nationalism in the Arab region. It tries to embed Arab nationalism in its political, institutional, and social context—with less emphasis on the aspects of the history of ideas. Recent approaches do not consider Arab nationalism to be a purely mechanical reaction to the weakness of the Ottoman Empire, the Young Turks, or European colonialism. They nevertheless recognize that there is a close connection between the phenomena. Here the focus is on the players, the functions that nationalism has in various contexts, and its different forms in the various regions.[3]

Thus Philip S. Khoury, for example, states that during the inter-war period, Arab nationalism was strongest where large religious and ethnic minorities existed and where nation-building and gaining independence from colonial powers was a particularly difficult process. This applies to Syria and Iraq.[4] Syria had to struggle with comparatively greater problems during its state-building. While the monarchy had an integrating effect in Iraq until 1958 and oil revenues helped to assure a certain degree of stability, the political landscape in Syria was hopelessly fragmented.[5]

By the 1970s, Arab nationalism had passed its zenith as a political force. Recent historiography deals with Arab nationalism more as a tool of the rulers than a deep-rooted ideology. As Malik Mufti has pointed out, seventeen attempts to permanently merge the individual Arab states into various combinations have so far failed. He sees scarcely a more profound purpose to Arab nationalism than as a political diversionary tactic on the part of the Arab heads of state. "Lacking the dynastic claims to leadership of their royal predecessors and too preoccupied with the struggle for survival to worry about economic and social issues, most rulers who managed to claw their way to the top sought support and legitimacy through pan-Arab unity schemes."[6] Under these circumstances, nationalism was an important instrument to stabilize the young state structure. On the one hand, the new states were too narrowly focused for pan-Arab ideas to take off and, on the other hand, too large for clear, traditional, primordial ties to hold people together.[7] "State building in

Syria, unable to fall back on distinctively Syrian historic loyalties or myths, could, paradoxically, only succeed by the exploitation of both pre-existing sub-state loyalties, such as sect, and the dominant pan-Arabic ideology," writes Raymond Hinnebusch.[8] Both become even more important as pillars of legitimacy and stability when authoritarian regimes fail to create strong institutions.

Even during its early years, during World Wars I and II, Arab nationalism had been a mosaic of different persuasions and intentions that partly worked against each another. Behind the ideological façade, bizarre alliances emerged. As an example, in spite of juxtaposed, ethno-national ideologies, the Young Turks were able to win over high-ranking Arabs as their supporters. They came from the local administrative dynasties of the Ottoman Empire, such as Rafiq al-Azm from Damascus or the Arab general Mahmoud Shawkat. Both were members of the Young Turkish Committee of Union and Progress (CUP) based in Saloniki. One of their common denominators was secularism.[9] In contrast to this, in 1913-14 some Arab nationalists were ready to conclude an anti-Ottoman agreement with the Zionists.[10] Others, in turn, allied with France against the British and the Zionists, hoping to obtain self-determination and to maintain their own positions of power.[11] On the other side, there were Egyptian nationalists who thought in terms of nation-states and rejected any form of pan-Arabism as reactionary and a form of foreign control. Finally, after the dream of Greater Syria had collapsed in 1918, Palestinian nationals sometimes fought quite solitarily—abandoned by all the Arab states—against both the British and the Zionists for a political identity of their own.[12]

Despite the many contradictions in everyday politics, a glance at the ideological origins should not be omitted. This is necessary for a better understanding of the ideology of the later Baath parties in Syria and Iraq.

Since nationalism in Europe arose as a mass movement with the French Revolution in 1789, two ideological variants have been competing with each other. One is the so-called French concept of nation and the other is the German variant.[13] The French concept of a citizens' democracy leaves the choice to the individual if he wants to belong to the nation or not (subjectivity). The nation is an open society, a community of choice. First the state is created and then the nation grows within its borders. Its members share common values and legal opinions (Immanuel Kant). What counts is what people think and profess, not where they come from. The protagonists of the Enlightenment advocated this variant.

On the other side, the German or ethno-national concept divides people into various categories from the beginning. They have no choice (objectivity). What counts is origin and lineage, not convictions—origin is more important than rational thought and belief. People "of the same blood" are automatically members of the nation. According to this idea, a nation comes into being before the state, which then ideally embraces the whole nation within its borders. The nation is an organic structure, a cultural nation *(Kulturnation)*, a closed community with a common origin, language, history, etcetera. This variant gained popularity in the nineteenth century, particularly on account of the German Romanticists Johann Gottfried von Herder (1744-1803) and Johann Gottlieb Fichte (1762-1814).

Today the ethno-national concept has undoubtedly prevailed over the democratic citizens' concept of nation. Wherever in the world someone speaks of a nation, he mostly means the German variant with all its negative consequences. When the two concepts overlap, a particularly explosive blend results, as happened in the Balkans in the 1990s.

Herder and Fichte's ideas were also received in the colonies. The later ideologues of ethno-nationalism largely went to schools in Europe or enjoyed a Western education in their homelands. Thus, Hindu nationalism in India is based on the German thinkers. The pan-Arab ideologues of the Baath Party likewise drew their ideas from this body of thought.[14] As with the German Romanticists, language played an eminent role in the idea of the nation. In this case, all who speak Arabic are members of a nation whether they like it or not—and the political borders must be adapted to this situation if possible. Arabic, as the original "sacred language" of the Quran and rich in tradition, was particularly suited to postulating a sublime "soul of the people" (Volksseele) in Herder's sense. With reference to the Quran, it was also possible to skillfully emphasize the Islamic heritage that many Islamic scholars correctly saw was threatened by nationalism.

As with all forms of ethno-nationalism, the Arab version is strongly fed by imagination that, depending on the situation, can flourish or dry up. Benedict Anderson has elegantly described nations as "imagined communities."[15] Modern ethnologists such as Wolfgang Kaschuba call the ethnic group, the skeleton of the ethno-nation, a "fictive reality."[16] Despite all of this, the affective power of the unreal can become real on the social level—so real that it triggers political consequences. Unfortunately, there is no room here to delve into the long debate of scholarship on nationalism as to how real or constructed an ethnic group actually is and how it should therefore be treated.

A brief hint of this paradox should suffice in the Arab case. The Arabic language, the main component of the "Arab nation," has developed in so many different directions in everyday life that Arabs from different regions can barely understand each other. For example, Moroccans who visit friends in Syria often resort to French for their conversations. There is a standard Arabic language (fusha) that dominates in the print media and news broadcasts, but the colloquial spoken language is characterized by a large number of dialects (amiyya). Although many Arabs do not speak classical Arabic, this does not represent a major problem. If one compares this with what is today called the Serbian, Croatian, and Bosnian languages, one becomes aware of the irony. These languages have been scrupulously distinguished and deliberately developed apart by ethno-nationalists after the collapse of Yugoslavia. The idioms belong to three different nations although they are so similar to each other that one has to use grammatical sophistry to locate the differences. Serbs, Croats, and Bosnians have no problems understanding each other— at least linguistically. The South Slav movement, a counterforce to ethno-nationalists, used to stress the commonness among the Balkan population (the common language was known as Serbo-Croatian). Pan-Arabists play a similar role in Arab countries. It simply depends on where the emphasis is placed. The motives are of a purely political nature. Nowadays the differences have prevailed in the Balkans. In the Arab world, contradictory developments are taking place. One could point to the new mass media, particularly the Arab TV news broadcasters, which create a stronger world of common experience with their content and the use of standard Arabic.

Another provocative question for Arab nationalists is whether some religious groups in the Arab region could instead be defined as ethnic groups. Here we come back to the basic difficulty of defining the term "ethnicity." Academic literature so far has not been able to deliver a clear answer. But if it has to do with a common origin and lineage, as ethno-nationalists advocate, one could claim that the Druze now constitute an ethnic group of their own. They are a relatively small group whose members for centuries have married only among themselves according to strict rules. It would be far easier to ascertain their lineage than the larger group of the Arabs, for example. But such discussions resemble shadow boxing, since from Ibn Khaldun to Max Weber and up to today, all serious scholars have stressed that actual lineage has no importance in the end, for people think themselves apart or together.[17] It is all about a feeling of community (assabiyya).

In spite of all the paradoxes, this feeling of community, as well as the Arabic language itself, became the pillars of pan-Arab ideology. The French concept of the nation, in which language had a less ideological importance in the formative stage, did not appear to come into question at all for the Arab region, since initially there were no Arab states in the modern sense and only later were their borders drawn by the Europeans. Nevertheless, the concept of a democratic nation of citizens can be found in individual cases among Arab thinkers. It is no coincidence that they lived and wrote only a few decades after Napoleon's expedition to Egypt in 1798. In his concept of the nation the Egyptian Rifaat Rafi' Tahtawi, who had studied in France, linked values such as patriotism, equality, and justice in a liberal, democratic sense. It was the first time that an Arab had spoken of the nation in a secular sense.[18]

When Muhammed Ali went from Egypt to Syria in 1831 and took over rule there, the region further opened up to European influences. His son Ibrahim Pasha continued his father's policy of reform and the first generation of nationalists grew up in the Levant. The protagonists were mostly men of letters and Christian Arabs. They were influenced by American Protestant and Russian Orthodox missionaries who promoted translations into Arabic and the printing of books. The philologist Boutrus Boustani (1819-1883) for the first time linked the renaissance of Arab literature and culture to the idea of a national union of Arabs. He worked at the Syrian Protestant College, an institute that was founded by American missionaries and later became the American University of Beirut (AUB). Today, AUB is still the intellectual window to the West for students in the region.

The Arabic language, with the help of Western missionaries, became the source of modern pan-Arab thinking. Bassam Tibi writes, "The revival of the national language signified a revitalization of the national culture and with that the creation of a new, national identity that pushed the previous religious identity—the substance of the Arabs' loyalty to the Ottoman Empire—into the background."[19] The rather apolitical literary revival turned into a more and more distinct ethno-national current among intellectuals. Their views were, at the same time, in contrast to traditional Islamic thinking and also connected to it. Thus, the Islamic scholar Abdul Rahman al-Kawakibi (1849-1903) stressed that only Arabs were legitimate representatives of Islam. He called for the caliphate to be moved from Istanbul to Mecca and entrusted it to members of the Arab Quraish tribe. People like Kawakibi or Jamaleddin Afghani strove for the modernization and strengthening of Islam, partly with reference to Western ideas and experience. They were less concerned with a political movement against the Ottomans. A Turkish-Arab dichotomy did begin to take shape, and some people called for more cultural autonomy. Nevertheless, until shortly before the collapse of the Ottoman Empire there was no pan-Arab national "awakening" or political mass movement for independence. The champions of nationalism were intellectuals as well as the administrative and military elites, with people in the countryside scarcely taking part in its development. Broader forces were not mobilized until the Great Arab Revolt started in Mecca in 1916, although its primary aim was to preserve Islam.[20]

There had been no ideological differences worth mentioning between the Arabs and the Ottoman administration for four centuries. The reason for change and the fact that Islam increasingly lost its bonding power lay mainly in developments at the Bosporus itself. For a long time the Ottoman Empire had been the model anti-nation, where minorities lived relatively undisturbed and enjoyed the right of self-administration (millet system). Neither did the colorful mixture of languages present any obstacle to the neutral state administration. Kurds and Arabs felt integrated into the empire as Sunnis, just as Christians or Jews found their places as Muslim protégés (dhimmi) with plenty of freedom in place of being second-class citizens.

However, the huge empire stretching from Bosnia to Baghdad and Mecca increasingly lost power and internal stability from the nineteenth century onward. Ethno-national uprisings and secessions shook the Balkan provinces. European nations interfered more and more ambitiously in the internal affairs of the empire as "protective powers" for the minorities. Reforms (tanzimat) aimed at modernizing and centralizing the administration and education system showed only initial success. However, a new generation who grew up during this period of reforms became the champions of either Turkish or Arab ethno-nationalism.

The Young Turks under Kemal Ataturk (1881-1938) gained increasing influence in the Ottoman Empire beginning in the early twentieth century. They had also read the German Romanticists and promoted an extreme ethno-nationalism called Turanism. It culminated in the thesis that Turks were of Aryan descent and thus came from the pre-Islamic, central Asian cradle of civilization (which incidentally the Hindu nationalists as well claim for themselves).[21]

Such an ideology in the Ottoman Empire conceptually excluded a lot of ethnic groups and religious minorities, including Arabs. Most Young Turks looked down on them with contempt and in their own circles described them as "the dogs of the Turkish nation."[22] At the same time, this nationalism was, as in other parts of Europe, a vehicle for democratic ambitions against the ancien régime, as last embodied by Abdul Hamid II in the Ottoman Empire.[23] In 1909, when the Young Turks overthrew the sultan, they could still count on the help of Arab officers. Even an "Alliance of Arab-Ottoman Brotherhood" was established but was dissolved again only eight months later as tensions between the two sides rapidly increased. From Istanbul, the revolutionaries began to "Turkify" the Arab provinces in an authoritarian manner by means of language and education policies. This increased the displeasure of many Arabs toward the Ottomans. More and more people began to see the Turks as an occupying power.[24]

The secular Young Turks also undermined the pan-Islamic embrace as they regarded language and culture rather than religion as the national binding factor. On top of this, Ataturk abolished the pan-Islamic caliphate in 1924, offending many Muslim believers. Until then the caliph had been regarded by most Sunnis as the highest religious authority.[25] The focus thus increasingly shifted from the distinctively religious idea of a pan-Islamic community of believers (umma) or an Islamic nationalism (umma as nation) to political units of nation-states (watan) or pan-Arabism ('uruba). After the collapse of the Ottoman Empire, the short-lived Syrian King Faisal Ibn al-Hussein said in 1919, "We are Arabs before being Muslims, and Muhammad is an Arab before being a prophet."[26] Pan-Arab nationalism was in direct opposition to Islamic forces because of its increasingly secular and later socialist coloring. Many Islamists rejected any form of nationalism—not only the pan-Arab one but also that of nation states—as incompatible with Islam.

Islam was also of secondary importance for Sati al-Husri (1882-1968), the most influential pan-Arab ideologue. Husri, who was born into a Syrian family, spent his youth in the Ottoman Balkans. Ironically, he mastered Turkish and French before he learned Arabic, thus speaking the core language of his ideology with a Turkish accent.[27] His thinking was also strongly marked by the German philosophers and Romanticists. He admired Fichte, Hegel, and Herder, and his key ideological role in the Arab world earned him the nickname of "the Arab Fichte."[28] Accordingly, Husri put forward an organic understanding of the nation with common language as its backbone. In his thought, there was no place for the individual, as individuals were completely absorbed into the pan-Arab nation that, in his view, stretched all the way to the Maghreb. This was a new idea, for since the Napoleonic invasion, Egyptian nationalists defined themselves in terms of a nation-state (watan). Husri strongly influenced the new educational curricula in Egypt, Syria, and Iraq in its various functions.

Ethno-national ideas of this kind were not so far from the racist Nazi ideology. Because Germany was not a colonial power in the region, but an enemy of England and France in both world wars, many pan-Arabists sympathized with Germany (as did Hindu nationalists for the same reasons). The strongest influence of pan-Arabists was first witnessed in Iraq in the 1920s and 1930s when Hitler rose to power in Germany. In 1941, Husri supported a fascist coup in Baghdad, though in this case everyday politics likely played a more important role than ethno-nationalist ideology. In an alliance with the axis powers Germany and Italy, the Iraqi pan-Arabists aimed to expel the British colonial power.[29]

Pan-Arabism especially offered new opportunities for non-Muslim minorities in the Middle East. "Arab Christians, when they thought in a nationalist way, could free themselves from the status of a tolerated minority—as Arabs they could regard themselves as equal to Muslims," Gerhard Schweizer wrote.[30]

The main ideologue of the subsequent Baath Party in Syria was himself a Christian (however, he reportedly converted to Islam shortly before his death, although this has never been confirmed). Michel Aflaq was born in 1910 in Damascus and went to Paris to study philosophy at the Sorbonne University. There he found the idea of Arabness in Western literature, as had many others before him. He viewed Islam as an essential part of the Arab socio-cultural heritage, but thought that it had become obsolete as a political means for Islamic nationalism. It had now been superseded by pan-Arabism with Islam as a humanistic foundation.[31] However, neither Aflaq nor other proponents of the ideology were able to eliminate the basic contradiction between Islam, which is a stranger to nationalism and does not differentiate between ethnic groups, and ethno-national pan-Arabism, which refers to Islam rather as a national heritage.

This lack of logic was compensated for by the political agitation of the pan-Arab ideologues. For Aflaq and his supporters the idea of Arabness was mixed with anger from the humiliation of colonialism. When Aflaq was a boy of six, England and France planned to split up Greater Syria (bilad ash-sham) between them in the secret Sykes-Picot Agreement. It became evident that the Arabs were being led up the garden path, particularly by the British. During World War I and following the struggle against the Ottoman Empire, the British government had promised a uniform and independent Arab kingdom under the rule of the Hashemite King Faisal (1883-1933). The betrayal soon came to light, and in 1920 and 1921 the colonial powers realized their plan against the will of the Arab population. Palestine and Jordan (Transjordan at that time) were placed under English occupation and today's Syria and Lebanon under French occupation. Faisal was fobbed off with a semi-sovereign Iraq (formerly Mesopotamia) under English mandate after the French had expelled him from Syria after a regency of only five months. That was not all. One year after the Sykes-Picot Agreement, the British guaranteed the Zionists the establishment of a Jewish "homeland" in Palestine in the Balfour Declaration of 1917. These decisions were a severe blow to the Arabs and sowed the seeds for the persistent conflict in the Middle East that are still far from resolved today.

The persecution and extermination of European Jews by the Nazis and subsequently an increasingly aggressive Zionist immigration to Palestine with the approval of Great Britain gave an additional boost to pan-Arabism. Eberhard Kienle holds that "had it not been for the massive Zionist immigration to Palestine which increasingly exacerbated Arab sensitivities, and the uprising of 1936-1939 which definitely became the key issue of Arab politics, Arab nationalism might not have survived as a unifying ideology aimed at the creation of a political entity encompassing the entire Arab world."[32]

Tibi sums up the ideological development as follows: "While the Arab nationalism of pre-colonial times, as formulated by the Syro-Lebanese Western-educated intellectuals, strove for the introduction of liberal freedoms and a citizens' democracy after the Western model in a secular Arab nation-state, it has become an apologetic, reactive, *völkisch,* and sometimes aggressive ideology under colonial rule." Husri and Aflaq, in particular, paved the way for this change. "Arab nationalism, once Francophile and partly Anglophile, has changed with English and French colonization and became anti-English, anti-French, and Germanophile."[33] Adeed Dawisha considers this nationalism to be inherently authoritarian—an ideology that does not know any civil liberties but only freedom from colonialism, indifferent toward domestic conditions and social progress. According to him, this "illiberal character" of nationalism à la Husri and Aflaq is partly to blame for the failure of the pan-Arab movement because they did not set up any institutions that could have supported them in times of crisis.[34] The neo-Baathists tried to correct this defect and managed to implement some social changes, but in the end they remained authoritarian.

Aflaq did not conceal his sympathy for Hitler.[35] He became a history teacher in Damascus, and in the 1940s he led a movement called the Arab Revival *(harakat al-ihyā' al-'arabi)* together with his Sunni colleague Salahadin al-Bitar. In 1945, the movement merged with a party that had borne the name Baath ("Rebirth") five years earlier. It had been founded by the Alawite Zaki al-Arsuzi from Antakya who had subsequently withdrawn from politics in frustration. The role of the philosopher and linguist Arsuzi is disputed among Baathists. Arsuzi was not rehabilitated as the spiritual father of Baathism until 1966, by Hafez al-Asad among others.[36] Incidentally, all three teachers— Aflaq, Bitar, and Arsuzi—had studied in France and after their return fought the French occupation in various places in Syria.

The first party conference of the new Baath Party was held in Damascus after independence on 7 April 1947. In November 1952, the organization merged with the Arab Socialist Party (ASP) of Akram al-Howrani to become the Socialist Party of Arab Rebirth *(hizb al-Ba'th al-'arabi al-ishtiraki)* with the slogan "Unity, Freedom, Socialism." The ASP was the first peasant movement in Syria. Thus the Baathists considerably extended their social base and political program. Rural players, especially from the middle class and influential families, began their march through the Baath institutions.[37]

Thanks to the staunch republican Howrani socialist ideas and peasants' interests had entered mainstream politics in Syria. This was a challenge for the conservative and feudal city of Hama where he came from and for whom he later served as a deputy in parliament. Howrani also defended the pan-Arab cause in demarcation from English or American influence in the Arab world. From his early days as a college student, Howrani's ideal was the achievement of Greater Syria. For that purpose he had joined the Syrian Socialist National Party (SSNP). In the 1940s Howrani advanced to a popular national figure in Syria who got involved in various political intrigues and military coups and who changed allies several times. But he always remained faithful to his socialist and pan-Arab sentiments. Thus he became one of the most powerful supporters of Egypt's President Gamal Abdul al-Nasser in the late 1950s who rewarded him with the vice presidency in the newly founded Syrian-Egyptian United Arab Republic (UAR). In this position Howrani pushed through a land redistribution program in Syria. When Howrani became too popular among Syrian peasants for Nasser to bear, he was sidelined. Howrani finally supported the coup that ended the UAR. This cost him credibility among conservative Baathists. In 1962 Howrani fell out with the Baath Party and revived his Arab Socialist Party. Subsequently, he was forced into exile in 1963 and worked against the Syrian Baathist governments from Iraq.[38]

The new start of the Arab Socialist Baath Party with Howrani still on board in the 1950s took place in turbulent times. World War II had just ended; the Cold War and the Soviet socialist period had begun in Eastern Europe; the Arab League was founded as the first practical result of pan-Arab ideas; and in 1946 the last French soldier left Syrian soil. Finally, a hopelessly overtaxed England surrendered, like a hot potato, its mandate over Palestine to the United Nations. In 1948, the UN decided to divide the piece of land and pave the way for a Jewish-Israeli state.

The Baath Party was not the only secular voice in independent Syria. There were communists, socialists, Syrian nationalists (many of whom also thought in pan-Arab categories), and naturally conservatives and Islamists in the other camp. But Aflaq's, Bitar's, and Howrani's organization became more and more powerful, especially after the 1954 elections that were regarded as the first free elections in the Arab world.[39]

In the years after independence, hopeful democratic intermezzi and military coups alternated at a rapid pace. With Faris Khoury, the country—and the Arab world as a whole—saw its first and last Christian prime minister. But above all, Syria became the synonym for instability and chaos in the region. As A.R. Kelidar joked, "It was a time when all the Syrian officers had to get up in the morning at the same time; otherwise one of them would initiate a coup."[40] On 8 March 1963, it was the Baathists that jumped out of bed a moment earlier and staged a putsch in Damascus.[41] This date became a national holiday.

Particularly young people from minorities such as the Alawites, Druze, or Ismailites were attracted to the Baath Party. Its radical pan-Arab ideology and social reform agenda gave them an opportunity to integrate into the young nation. Uprooted Alawites from the province of Alexandretta (the area around Iskanderun and Antakya), which France had ceded to Turkey in 1939, and Palestinian refugees—both victims of imperialist policies—saw their political home with the Baathists.[42] The Baathists were also able to win the support of those who were tired of the old elite and critical of the encrusted and unjust social conditions.

The main driving forces in Syria in the 1950s and 1960s were a combination of pan-Arab ideology and the struggle for an overdue land reform. The Baath Party skillfully combined the two elements, which broadened its base and mobilized the peasants according to the national agenda. The national revolution therefore became, in turn, a social one. Those who prospered were the small and medium-sized farmers who profited significantly from the redistribution of land.[43] The Baath Party today still has a significant number of rural supporters, in addition to workers, students, and members of the lower urban middle classes. Even though the economic benefit of the land reform, which dragged on for two decades, is controversial among scholars, it did in fact fulfill its social and political purpose. "Without it," writes

Raymond Hinnebusch, "Syria would probably be ruled today by the kind of military regime in alliance with the landed class against the peasant masses found in many areas of Latin America."[44]

Pan-Arab nationalism and socialism, however, have two very different grounding social principles. As previously described, pan-Arabism and Syrian nationalism are rooted in ethno-national thinking where members of the nation are classified according to primordial characteristics, i.e. according to external and a priori principles based on lineage. In contrast, socialism takes social classes that come into being through socio-economic development as a starting point. In spite of this contradiction, the Baath Party incorporated both Arab nationalism and socialism in a difficult balancing act.

Socialism was only the vehicle of Arab nationalism, as the founders of the Baath Party themselves admitted. Michel Aflaq wrote, "Our socialism is thus a means of building up our nationalism and our people, and it is the door through which our Arab nation will make its new entry into history."[45] The Christian Aflaq was irreconcilably opposed to atheistic Marxism. In this context, socialism was scarcely more than a diffuse but understandable call for social justice.

The very issue of socialism soon threatened to split the Baath Party. On one side were Aflaq, Bitar, and their supporters who advocated moderate socialism with democratic liberties, and who primarily followed their pan-Arab program. This also included a revival of Syria's union with Nasser's Egypt that became reality in 1958 only to fall apart three years later. On the other side were the more radical young intellectuals who saw Marxism and Leninism as the main pillars of the Baath Party. For them the social revolution in one country had priority over the distant goal of a pan-Arab state. Thus representatives of Greater Arabia were lined up against supporters of a social-revolutionary "Syria first" vision.[46]

In 1966, the old guard around Aflaq and Bitar were driven from their positions of power in a bloody internal coup in the Baath Party staged by the officers Salah Jadid and Hafez al-Asad. The left-wing neo-Baathists now had a free hand for their "revolution from above." Its motor was set in motion by a quasi-Leninist cadre party.[47] They went ahead with the land reform, nationalized banks and firms, and the monopoly for international trade was given to the state. These measures won the neo-Baathists support from rural and urban lower classes but antagonized businessmen and traders in the urban middle class. Also as "representatives of the Palestinian cause," they adopted a sharper tone toward Israel. But, as mentioned earlier, an accelerated secularization in the Marxist-Leninist sense did not go far beyond rhetoric.

A year later, the Arab countries experienced a traumatic defeat in the Six-Day War against Israel. Another year later, the branch of the old Baathists staged a coup in Iraq. After some hesitation, Aflaq emigrated to Baghdad in 1970 and became secretary-general of the Iraqi Baath Party, where he soon befriended Iraq's new president Saddam Hussein. The all-embracing National Command (al-qiada al-qawmiyya) of the Baath Party had degenerated into a farce. Since that time, the power in Syria has been held by the Regional Command (al-qiada al-qutriyya). The "national" level of the Baath Party still exists. As an institution it might be roughly compared to the idea of the Communist International, maintaining its pan-Arab claim only symbolically.

The schism between the old guard and the neo-Baathists increased due to the personal enmity between the two stubborn egos of Hafez al-Asad and Saddam Hussein. It was also about regional power politics and about who blazed the trail of the Baath ideology in the Arab world. This was a crucial question of internal legitimacy, especially for the Syrian regime. Paradoxically, this brotherly hatred between Syria and Iraq only ended in the last years and months before the Anglo-American attack on Iraq in 2003.

The enmity of the Baath regimes lingered on even after the so-called socialist revolution in Syria suffered another setback. In 1970, Hafez al-Asad from the nationalist wing, a pilot and head of the Syrian Air Force, finally emerged the winner of the power struggle among the leading Baath figures, consisting of, above all, the Alawite, Druze, and Ismailite military. He dismissed President and acting Prime Minister Nured-din Atasi, who held doctrinaire neo-Marxist views in what was termed the progressive wing of the Syrian Baath Party, but had adopted a less militaristic and irreconcilable stance toward Israel. At that time, nobody would have foreseen that it would be the last coup in Syria till this day. Asad did not call it a coup but merely a "corrective movement" (al-harakat at-tashihiyya).

Asad, the clever son from a mountain farming community, mainly corrected the socialist economic policy, thus forming an alliance with the bourgeoisie. In the 1970s, Syria experienced an economic boom by opening up its market to the outside world (infitah). In the following years, Asad went ahead with industrializing the country. He invested in infrastructure, urban construction, the health sector, and the education system. This contributed to create a relatively broad middle class, increased Syrians' economic mobility and drastically reduced illiteracy.[48] Asad turned the Baath Party into an organization with mass appeal. The number of members skyrocketed from 65,398 in 1971 to 374,332 in 1981, and 1,008,243 in 1991 in a country that had approximately thirteen million inhabitants in the early 1990s.[49]

After his coup, Asad initially began a limited liberalization of domestic politics and reduced the powers of the feared secret services (which, however, lasted a short time only because of the confrontation with the Muslim Brothers). Most Syrians welcomed the changes with great relief. In 1971, Asad had himself elected president by an appointed People's Council of Baathists, Nasserists, and communists with ninety-nine percent of the vote. A new era had begun.

Since then, the country had been marked by pragmatism aimed at maintaining power and stability both in domestic and foreign policy. Lobmeyer writes, "Since November 16, 1970, Syria's politics have been largely de-ideologized and Baathism has declined into a mere ideology of justification and a reservoir for propagandist phrases."[50] The initial euphoria disappeared and was soon tempered by a hard line in domestic policy. Instead of liberalization, Syrians experienced a "presidential monarchy."[51] Asad fostered a gigantic leader cult. Streets and squares were dominated by statues and posters of the "leader throughout all eternity" *(al-qa'id ila al-abad).*[52] "In the end it was his personal authority and that alone which held the country together," writes Asad's biographer Patrick Seale. "He was the only pole that held up the tent."[53]

It was therefore a real possibility that the tent might collapse on 10 June 2000, when Asad died of leukemia. But the death of the "leader" and "constructor of modern Syria" again threw open a question that had been smoldering for a long time: What actually happened to the ideology of the Baath Party? What about its two substantial components: pan-Arabism and socialism?

The answer was simple as far as state socialism is concerned. It went bankrupt after the collapse of the Soviet Union and the Warsaw Pact. It was true that Syria still offered a touch of communist nostalgia in dusty government offices, subsidized food and medicine, five-year plans, one-party rule, an inflated civil service, government propaganda, shaky Soviet military jeeps, and other anachronisms such as US vintage Chevys from the 1950s that created a Cuban-like atmosphere (due to once horrific import duties on automobiles). But this was only a distorted picture of an increasingly modern and capitalist reality. Pragmatic as always, Hafez al-Asad had already started looking West as the Berlin Wall fell in 1989.[54]

Most of the members of the communist opposition in Syria had long since changed direction and called themselves secularists or humanists. Apart from elements of a planned economy, the main thing that remained from Baath socialism was in fact Syrian secularism—or let us call it the qualified social liberalism that was so remarkable for the Middle East. However, it also ran the risk of getting worn down. Even the socialist facade was crumbling more and more. Since mid-2004, the state media no longer referred to leading members of the Baath Party as "Comrade" but simply as "Mister." The final nail in the coffin of the socialist façade was the new Syrian constitution of February 2012, in which the term socialism was erased once and for all.

The balance sheet did not look much better where pan-Arabism was concerned. In spite of its claims, the Baath Party had never grown beyond its role as the Syrian national party. Pan-Arab ambitions failed. The union of only two Arab states—Egypt and Syria—ended in a debacle. Other union plans did not come into being in the first place. The Baath brothers, Iraq and Syria, ground each other down in jealous competition and symbolic trench fighting. Finally, with the Iraq war in 2003, pan-Arabism—the second historic pillar of the Baath Party—ceased to exist altogether. Arab states always formed temporary political alliances, even against each other with the help of non-Arab states, as was shown particularly in the second Gulf War and, of course, in the Iraq war. The principles of behavior among Arab states were based on the sovereignty of nation-states and on independence from pan-Arab stipulations. Petro-dollars counted more than revolutionary pipe dreams. In its history before the Arab Spring in 2011, the Arab League had more often been the stage for inter-Arab disputes than for pan-Arab cooperation. Neither had there been talk of Arab unity on the Palestinian issue or on a comprehensive policy toward Israel.[55]

One positive effect of Baath ideology was less its pan-Arabism than its nationalism, which served as a common umbrella for religious minorities who could feel integrated into the state concept. The majority of Sunnis who rejected a sectarian policy also equally identified with it. However, the idea of "common Arabness" ignored the problem of ethnic minorities such as the Kurds. Here lay a predetermined breaking point in the ethno-nationally connoted "Arab Republic of Syria" that had begun to creak, especially since the war in Iraq. Kurdish-Arab disputes boiled to the surface again in the period when the opposition was trying to demonstrate unity toward the international community in 2011.

Bashar al-Asad was aware of the ideological crisis of the Baath Party. He lacked his father's charisma and therefore needed all the more institutional and ideological foundations. Party committees were set up at various levels to discuss the role of the Baath Party in modern Syria. Observers reported fierce debates between the president and other Baath functionaries, where Asad was said to have often appeared openly frustrated. Surprisingly, even opposition members from the Civil Society Movement were at times invited to these debates. The big question in Damascus was whether a reform of the Baath ideology was possible despite its many inherent contradictions.

Apart from the intellectual debates about direction and ideology, critical voices also questioned the party base. Baath member and former friend from Asad's youth, Ayman Abdul Nour, pointed to increasing contradictions within the Baath Party as well as a lack of leadership. "In the Baath party are Muslim Brothers, intellectuals, businessmen, trade unionists, soldiers and what have you. It's not a party but a collective movement. There is no ideology anymore."[56] Yet, the party was not to be underestimated as a power factor, warned analyst Samir Altaqi. "The ideological role of the party is weakened, but the party is still the main kitchen for cooking up loyalty."[57]

During the Iraq war, pan-Arab ideology gained support from an unexpected corner. In search of a direction for his foreign policy, Asad used the Anglo-American attack on Syria's neighbor to revive pan-Arab rhetoric. It was a matter of debate whether this had helped or hindered him.

On the one hand, Syria's rejection of a military intervention in Iraq was definitely understandable. Raymond Hinnebusch justified Syria's stance with ideological raison d'état: "Opposition to the US was a collective decision that would have been taken by any nationalist leadership in Damascus. Not only did the invasion threaten vital Syrian interests in Iraq, but it was also an egregious affront to the Arab nationalist values so ingrained in Syrian thinking." After all, the invasion of Iraq was in Israel's best interest.[58]

Against this background of domestic and regional popularity the debate is certainly controversial if Asad's actions were to be politically useful in the long run. Discussions with Syrian intellectuals at that time indicated that Asad could have reacted to the Iraq war with more political foresightedness and less ideological fervor. In search of a direction for his foreign policy, Asad used the Anglo-American attack on Syria's neighbor to revive pan-Arab rhetoric. People in the tea houses wondered how Hafez al-Asad would have acted in this situation. Some considered the young Asad's policy to be even more ideological than his father's in this respect. In the end most Syrians were glad that Saddam was overthrown, the Syrian Baathist establishment included.[59] Why should Syria have suddenly lent support to the Iraqi dictator, its Baathist archrival? Michel Kilo is convinced that "Hafez al-Asad would have avoided the conflict with the United States."[60]

It is hard to say if Asad really became more ideological than his father. He might have been less intellectually flexible and less politically shrewd to have changed sides at opportune moments. The young Asad's ideological hard-line position on the Iraq issue was part of a search for political orientation, a learning process concerning foreign policy rather than an entrenched ideology. It is scarcely surprising that it was the Baath cadres in particular that were said to have advised Bashar to adopt such a strict pro-Iraq and anti-American position. For them it was a welcome opportunity to begin to replenish the empty reservoir of the Baath ideology in a time when they were otherwise running out of answers.

Syria's critical position in the Iraq war was also embedded in a wider context. The terrorist attacks of 9/11 had fatal repercussions in the Arab world. "The September 11 attacks hit us Muslims as much as it did the United States," said Minister Buthayna Shaaban. "It was the most terrible thing that has happened to our region."[61]

First of all, 9/11 was a severe blow to Americans that caused great pain, physical and psychological. But the US overreacted to the attacks in rhetoric and action, and this was perceived by the Islamic world as collective punishment. Thus the Bush administration provided terrorists with the platform they needed to gain broader support for their Islamist hate campaigns. In addition, US policy caused many moderate Muslims to lose their orientation, as they wavered between revulsion toward the September 11 attacks and indignation at what they perceived to be Washington's insensitive, "neo-colonial" policy.

The neo-conservatives in the White House and the Pentagon, whom George Packer described as "fevered minds" in the prelude to the Iraq war,[62] advocated an explosive blend of policies: A glorification of violence and military action; an unwillingness to engage in deeper policy analysis (or a blindness toward the need for this analysis); a tendency toward groupthink—a dangerous auto-dynamic where decisions were taken without critical minds having the opportunity or encouragement to question basic assumptions;[63] a simplistic, dualistic, and state-focused division of mankind into "good guys" and "bad guys" reminiscent of the Cold War; and the conviction that the United States had a historical and religious mission as a chosen people under the banner of American Exceptionalism. In addition, the US was estranged from many Arabs, most of whom were far from being Islamic radicals, because of its uncritical stance toward Israeli and its settlement policy. The neo-conservatives did not season their policies with a knowledge of Islamic culture or take into account the deeply entrenched social and political grievances in the Middle East. The result was an approach devoid of sensitivity and lacking serious political diplomacy, at least during George W. Bush's first term in office.

These factors fueled anti-Americanism which in turn fed a new pan-Arabism of a much stronger Islamic or even Islamist hue. With Washington's help, an ideology believed to be almost dead returned to the political agenda. Arab politicians exploited it in order to distract their people from their own contradictions, weaknesses, and unresolved problems.

Syria found itself in this interplay of forces, in which the Baathists had to perform another ideological bridging feat. If they wanted to swim with the tide of Islamic neo-pan-Arabism, they would have to play down their secular concept of pan-Arabism that restricted Islam to a cultural role. This showed how watered down—or flexible—the Baath ideology had become. This also caused erosion from within the Party. Since socialism and secularism had been marginalized as pillars of Baathism, it went without note that members of the Baath Regional Command began to attend the haj in Mekka, accompanied by wives and daughters wearing veils. Prayer rooms were created in the offices of the Baath Party. "The Baath Party is being undercut by Islamists. This is dangerous." Michel Kilo observed in 2010. "We are heading toward a post-Baath phase."[64] Louay Hussein was convinced that "Baathist leaders could be easily converted into sheikhs," since Baathism had been increasingly soaked with Islamic ideology. Louay said that Baathism added nothing to the secularism of the country because secularism existed long before, even in Syria's constitution.[65]

Since Baathist secularism was nearly drained of its appeal, the question in Syria during Bashar's rule hinged on this neo-pan-Arabism cum anti-Americanism. Would it be sufficient to give Bashar al-Asad the backing he needed to negotiate the many crags of domestic and foreign policy? Or would Bashar be forced to give up an overarching ideology and to craft a solution to each challenge pragmatically?

The war between Israel and Hezbollah in summer 2006 offered another opportunity to intensify pan-Arab rhetoric. Similar to the period after the Iraq war, Asad was again perceived in the region as the only Arab leader—together with Hezbollah leader Hassan Nasrallah—who successfully upheld the flag of resistance on behalf of Palestinians facing the Israeli enemy. For the second time Asad became the hero of the Arab street, and pan-Arabism was his vehicle. Consequently, Asad stressed the significance of the ideology in his second inauguration speech on 18 July 2007. The president spoke "of the people's will to continue to pursue our national and pan-Arab doctrine, an embodiment of this giant national unity which is impossible to break and which has been our real support in everything we have done or achieved."[66]

Asad, however, did not make use of this pan-Arab popularity in the long run. Paradigms had started to shift. With a more moderate administration in place under President Barak Obama the anti-American side of modern pan-Arabism was losing its edge. Rapprochement and détente became the principles of the day.

But in the end it was the unexpected Arab Spring that turned the discourse upside down. The Arab people did not take to the streets in anti-American, anti-capitalist, anti-imperialist or anti-Western protests but against their own Arab governments. Pan-Arab Baathism cum anti-Americanism had lost its effectiveness to serve as a forge for Syria's nationalism. Asad remained convinced for too long that Syria's ideological discourse, fed by anti-Western Baathism, would remain a reliable insurance against the mainly socio-economic grievances of the people. From one month to the other in the spring of 2011 Asad turned from being the hero of the Arab street to one of the most detested autocrats in the Arab world in the perception of Arabs themselves, not only from a Western perspective.

Pan-Arabism had become a farce due to the fact that some Arab countries were on the way toward democracy while others remained authoritarian monarchies. In addition, the Saudi-Syrian fault line and other dormant rivalries revived. In practical terms, Syria lost an important pan-Arab institution when the Arab League decided to transfer the permanent headquarters of the Arab Parliament from Damascus to Cairo in December 2011 in response to Syrian atrocities and political obstinacy. Baathism as such became increasingly associated with totalitarian rule. It was perceived as the ideological *überbau* of one of the cruelest police states in the region and possibly the world. Baathism had degraded into a concept bereft of content, whether it be socialism or pan-Arabism.

In another symbolic move, the opposition in Syria's streets in 2011 chose to carry the old Syrian flag—green, white, and black horizontal stripes with three red stars in the middle—that was valid from 1932 to 1958 and from 1961 to 1963. Thus it detached itself from the Syrian flag that echoed pan-Arab and Baathist motives from the coup 1963 onward—red, white, and black horizontal stripes with two red stars in the middle. This was another indication that Syria's days as a champion of the pan-Arab cause were over. From a Syrian perspective, the closure of the Hamas premises in Damascus in December 2011 and the organization's transfer to Cairo and Qatar was yet another nail in the pan-Arab coffin. This development, however, was in line with new ideologies and cleavages that had more to do with religious antagonisms—Alawite / Shiite versus Sunni—than pan-Arab aspirations.

Criticism of the Baathists' rhetoric of resistance had increased in the prelude to the Arab Spring. At the end of 2010 Michel Kilo asked: "What does the resistance consist of? Where is the Golan issue in Syrian politics?" Many Syrians who bore pan-Arab convictions had lost faith in the regime as defender of Syrian national or even Arab interests. "The policy of resistance has ruined the whole of the Arab world," Kilo summarized. The strategy to stigmatize anyone as an "agent of the Zionists" had replaced real national policies. "Even I have already been denounced as a Zionist henchman when it was politically opportune." In a biting reflection, he added: "For 40 years we have been fighting against Zionist henchmen while the Zionists are having a quiet time sitting on the Golan. Where is the resistance? Where is the nationalist policy?"[67] Accordingly, during the upheaval in Dara'a in March 2011 one of the first slogans of the protesters was directed against Maher al-Asad, who was head of the Fourth Brigade and responsible of the Golan dossier. The people asked why he was shooting his own people instead of liberating the Golan.

Criticism also grew outside the usual opposition circles. Syrian scholars like historian Sami Moubayed, who previously supported the regime, drifted away when they realized that promised reforms would never be implemented. Moubayed wrote at the end of 2011:

> Arab nationalism has been tested, and milked, for nearly 50 years. It failed drastically at answering people's political, economic, and social worries. So has Baathism, which has already started its long march into history. In fact, it is precisely because Baathism failed that people began searching elsewhere for answers—at mosques, for example, in online Islamic forums, and at the theology lessons of people like Said Ramadan al-Bouti and al-Qubaisi. And it is precisely because moderate Islamic parties were denied a platform for decades that Al Qaida-inspired fundamentalists hijacked Islam throughout the Arab World.[68]

In November 2011, the newspaper *Baladna (Our Motherland)*—owned by the son of a senior Alawite officer close to Asad—carried a bold opinion piece that caused the newspaper edition's confiscation. The actor Bassam Jneid wrote:

> Today, the last slogan of the Baath Party has collapsed, after the fall of the "freedom" slogan more than 40 years ago, and the "socialism" slogan 11 years ago. Today, according to all the loyalists, members and leaders of the party, the "unity" slogan has collapsed and the supporters went out to declare that this is not a unified nation and that its message is not immortal. For God's sake, what is left of this party other than a group of thieves who have stolen all they could under the cover of nationalism?[69]

Even the official discourse in Damascus began to radically break with the ideology of the past decades. The Syrian Baathists in ire and under attack from all sides said good-bye to pan-Arabism. Their set of arguments was, of course, entirely different. The state media painted Syria as a victim of Arab treason and thus attacked the "conspiracy" of the Arab League against Syria. Titled "A Letter to the Heart of Pan-Arabism," the private regime mouth-piece *al-Watan* published a leading editorial in November 2011 that reflected the Syrian regime's spite and pride:

> The time may have come—at the level of both the words and the action—for Syria to distance itself from that name [i.e. the Heart of Pan-Arabism] and from the chronic problems, calamities and catastrophes of the Arabs and all the obligations they induce. In the past, it was inappropriate to say, "Syria first" while Palestine, Lebanon, and Iraq were bleeding and while crows and hyenas were multiplying in their skies and on their soil. Now, Syria is the one bleeding and the crows of the Arabs are once again adopting their favorite position, i.e. that of the stab in the back, while awaiting to stand proud over the victim with the traditional Arab dagger. This time, it is our blood that is being spilled, and not that of our brothers and neighbors. . . . Maybe the time has come to close the doors, even the windows, tend to the domestic affairs and relinquish Pan-Arabism, which only brought Syria one catastrophe after the other, one refugee after the other and one embarrassment after the other . . . .[70]

It was supporters and critics alike that put a final end to Baathism and pan-Arabism as an ideology for Syria.

12
Syria: A Rogue State?

W HEN TERRORISM WAS THE PARADIGM THAT dominated international debates in the decade following 9/11, the term "rogue state" was in vogue, too. Roughly speaking, a rogue state was considered to be a country that—especially in the eyes of the Bush administration—behaved badly with regard to US or Western interests or against international norms in general and supported terrorists abroad. In a certain sense, these countries intended to "export" terrorism into Western societies or were developing arsenals of chemical or nuclear weapons to directly threaten Israel or Western states. Or those states acted in a way that destabilized a region. The term rogue state was a handy label that played well with the media and fit into the Bush world-view that tidily divided the world into an "axis of evil" versus the "empire of good." In contrast to his predecessor, US President Obama has mostly refrained from using such polarizing expressions as "war on terror" (since a war is usually known to have a beginning and an end), "rogue state," or "axis of evil." He also applied the term "terrorists" more cautiously and did not lump all kinds of violent phenomena into this category.

What really emerged with the term "rogue state" was the classic clash between values and strategic interests. When it came to values, obviously the American and European policy makers have applied the term rogue state very inconsistently. Saudi Arabia, for example, has a long record of exporting militant and dogmatically radical Islamists into various areas of the world, sometimes without and sometimes with the blessing of the United States (as in Afghanistan). Despite dissent even within the USA on this matter, criticism of the important Western ally of Saudi Arabia has remained modest at best. The domestic violation of human rights was not part of the definition of a rogue state. When Libyan Revolutionary Leader Muammar al-Qaddafi embarked on a political U-turn in 2002/03, he turned from the camp of rogue states to the camp of friendly faces by giving up his nuclear arms program and by paying compensation to the victims of Libyan terrorist attacks of the 1980s. But nothing at all changed with regard to the human rights situation inside Libya, not to mention political freedom or even political pluralism.

In the context of the Arab Spring, the autocrats that were threatened by the street protests turned their propaganda and state machinery against their own people. Stability as it had been known for years did not hold any longer, even more, it did not make sense any longer. Western-friendly autocrats turned into rogue states with regard to their relations with their own people, polity and political culture. Also, of course, anti-Western states such as Syria turned into the worst imaginable rogue states when it came to suppressing their domestic opposition.

This chapter sheds a light on debates about Syria's role in the classical concept of a rogue state whose behavior was supposed to have regional or international repercussions. As mentioned above, the type of political system and government, and the way things looked domestically did not play a major role in this definition. A-priori, dictatorship was not a rogue state by definition. Additional elements were needed to make it qualify as one. In the Syrian case the discourse mainly revolved around Syria's ideological defense of the Palestinian cause, its role in Iraq and Lebanon. The picture is manifold and complex. Depending on the context, Syria was at times regarded as a source of stability and a bastion against radical Islamism in the region even by its enemy Israel and Western countries, and on other occasions the Asad regime was perceived as a source of instability and danger. Indeed, it was Hafez al-Asad who often managed to play both roles at the same time, as did his son, for a while.

The Palestinian Issue

As dawn breaks, a rumble drifts over the desert, quickly approaching. The hands of the clock show 4:30 AM on 5 October 2003. Two F-16 jet fighters fly over the border of the Golan Heights and reach the Syrian capital in less than half a minute. People are fast asleep, including in the town of Ain Saheb. Israeli pilots fire three missiles into the small town, only fifteen kilometers north of Damascus, then turn back and disappear as fast as they had come. One person is injured. It is the first time in thirty years that Israel had attacked Syrian core territory.

At 2:14 PM the day before, Hanadi Jaradat, a pretty Palestinian lawyer, had buckled on a belt loaded with explosives and had gone to the Maxim beach café in the northern Israeli city of Haifa. There the twenty-nine-year-old in jeans and head scarf pulled the ignition, killing herself and twenty-one other people, including two families spanning three generations, three children, and a baby. Five months earlier, Hanadi had lost her brother in the West Bank city of Jenin. Her lover had also been killed by Israeli soldiers for coordinating an attack on Jewish settlers.[1]

What did the incidents in Ain Saheb and Haifa have in common? Israel took the suicide attack as an occasion to establish a direct link to Damascus. As Israel and the United States read it, Palestinian attacks were planned in Syria and assassins trained there. In the Israeli government's view, this must also have been the case with Hanadi. The spiral of violence had assumed interstate dimensions. For a moment in October 2003, observers feared that a new war between Syria and Israel could no longer be ruled out. Press releases from the Israeli government ticked away on fax machines in the offices of correspondents. The statements claimed that the missiles had hit a training camp of the Islamic Jihad. Israel had the right to take measures in "preventive defense." The Syrian authorities hushed everything up. The terrain, now with a gaping crater in the ground, was cordoned off. Not until a week later did the Syrian government hold a press conference. By that time, hardly anyone was interested in the subject anymore—a typical example of the lost media war.

In reality, the rockets fell on a long-abandoned camp where members of the General Commando of the left-wing Popular Front for the Liberation of Palestine (PFLP-GC) used to train. It had since been turned into a sports ground, where children took swimming lessons, residents of Ain Saheb reported.[2] The camp had not been used to train Palestinians for several years. Israel wanted to teach the Syrians a lesson and demonstrate their vulnerability. At the same time, then Israeli Prime Minister Sharon presented a map of Damascus and announced that more attacks would follow on targets in the Syrian capital. As he put it, he intended to destroy the offices of Palestinian organizations in Damascus in the same way it had been done in the West Bank or in Gaza. A few weeks before the attack on Ain Saheb, Israeli jets had attacked Syrian positions in Lebanon and had flown low over Bashar's summer residence in the Syrian coastal town of Latakia. The incidents of humiliation did not stop there. US troops destroyed the Syrian trading center in Baghdad during the war and even encroached on Syrian territory in June 2003, taking Syrian soldiers to Iraq as prisoners.

It is true that the Syrian regime saw itself as an advocate for the Palestinian cause and used aggressive rhetoric. In addition, as previously mentioned, Syria granted hospitality and freedom of movement to members of Palestinian organizations such as Hamas, Islamic Jihad, and the PFLP. These groups established a network of hospitals, schools, and welfare institutions for Palestinian refugees in Syria. However, this did not necessarily mean that Damascus had become the center of command for suicide attacks in Israel. In fact, there was always some uncertainty as Syria treated military matters with the utmost secrecy. But if Israel had a better target, it certainly would not have fired on Ain Saheb. This happened later on when Israeli warplanes buzzed closely over Asad's summer residence in Latakia once more at the end of June 2006 and bombed, according to Western intelligence, a nearly-complete nuclear reactor in a desolate desert canyon east of the Euphrates River in September 2007. An intrusion of Israeli war planes into Syrian territory became almost a yearly exercise, mostly without Syrian military intelligence taking notice.

With regard to the Palestinian file, the Syrian regime took every opportunity possible during past decades to create a fog of anti-Israeli propaganda. Thus, in parallel to the hardliners in Israel, the Syrian regime built an atmosphere that created considerable obstacles to peace between the peoples of the region.

An example was Syria's school textbooks, which described Zionism across the board as racism without going into the various historical currents in Jewish nationalism such as early socialism or Marxist Zionism. Anti-Semitic clichés and conspiracy theories about Judaism could be found in the books, as well as the statement that Zionism was the real reason for Arab backwardness and the prevention of pan-Arab unity. The books also contained a glorification of the martyr's death in the "holy war" against Israel. This was a grotesque manipulation since these Islamist ideas conflict with the secular Baath ideology.[3]

It was equally contradictory that, on the one hand, the textbooks spoke about the relentless struggle against Israel until all land that was unlawfully taken was returned to the Arabs, while on the other hand they described peace with Israel—as long as it is "comprehensive and fair"—as Syria's "strategic choice." This could be interpreted in such a way as to pave the way to new circumstances, such as peace negotiations with the supposed archenemy, in the minds of the next generation. Incidentally, in 2004 the eight block parties in the National Front under the leadership of the Baath Party proposed deleting the section in the Front's National Charter that prohibits negotiations with Israel or recognition of the Israeli state. Instead, reference was made to UN resolutions, the Madrid peace process, and even the wish for peace with Israel. Furthermore, the proposal suggested that the term "war economy" should be replaced by "economic growth" in the charter and the "unitary" political structure of the country replaced by a "pluralistic" one.[4]

It must be pointed out as well that the so-called regional peace process, starting with the Madrid conference in 1991, found a place in more recent school textbooks in Syria. But the books also contained the criticism that the United States was using this opportunity to give Israel preferential treatment. Only since 1991 the Syrian textbook authors used the name "Israel" rather than "Zionist entity." In contrast, the elder Asad since the 1970s had insisted on calling Israel by its name and had never questioned its sovereignty, even in interviews with the Syrian military magazine Jaish as-Sh'ab (People's Army). This was a remarkable contrast to the official former Baath wording.[5]

In a nutshell, the newer school textbooks used a more conciliatory language than their predecessors. Even when the authors complained that the United States misused the term "terrorism" and that the Zionist occupation violated international law, they did not represent a particularly aggressive or exclusive Syrian position.[6] A German study found out in 2006 that Syrian textbooks—together with Palestinians—depicted the Christian community better than in any other Arab country. In contrast, Egyptian books showed a particular bias against Christians.[7]

What propaganda sticks in peoples' heads always depends on a variety of factors. Young Syrians, whose modern world consisted mainly of satellite television, spoke with a touch of humor about their education at school and university. "I'm good at lying," one student told me. "That's why I always got top grades in 'nationalism.'" After numerous interviews, it became clear to me that many people saw through the Baathist propaganda or even rejected it. Stirring up hatred in school textbooks was one of the greatest dangers for long-term peace. But propaganda did not necessarily translate, out-and-out, into public opinion and certainly not when the state had lost its monopoly over the media through satellites and the Internet. Even Israeli television could be received without problem in Damascus, and Jews watched the news in Hebrew every day. Many Syrians had been exposed to a traditional Islamic education and therefore did not know religious hatred for Jews, but rather integrated them into their world view as an ancient scriptural religion. They separated this fact surprisingly clearly from Zionism as a worldly, modern, and political phenomenon in spite of the often cruel pictures that emanated from the Occupied Territories.

Since 1979, Syria had continually been on the United States' black list of countries. Syria was a "supporter of terrorism" in the eyes of many other Western states as well. But, paradoxically, Syria was the only rogue state with which Washington had normal diplomatic relations and from time to time even exchanged political opinion at a high level. This happened despite the fact that President Bush counted Syria as part of his extended "axis of evil."

The problem of assessing Syria as a "rogue state" was twofold. Part of the issue had to do with distinguishing the 1970s and 80s with the later decades. The Baath regime did have a record of proxy wars and international terrorism, but the last incident took place in 1986. Some actions subsumed under terrorism were supported by secular-nationalist Palestinian groups who conducted attacks against Arafat's PLO in the late 1970s and early 1980s. Moreover, Syria linked up with both radical Palestinian and Lebanese groups in Lebanon who carried out attacks against Lebanese, Israeli, and Western targets following Israel's invasion of Lebanon in 1982. This was to prevent the Lebanese government from signing a peace treaty with Israel. After Israel provoked Syria by intercepting an airliner carrying Syrian officers and shooting down two Syrian fighters in Syrian airspace in 1985, Asad attempted to blow up Israeli jetliners at airports in London and Madrid in 1986. Both operations failed and caused severe international reactions. After that, Asad followed a more indirect approach.[8]

The second problem in assessing Syria was the fact of widely varying definitions of the term "terrorism." The definition was far from clarified, several political and scholarly attempts worldwide notwithstanding.[9] Israel's move after 9/11 was to extend the term to include anything connected with Palestinian resistance—even when such a resistance was directed at an occupation that violated international law and did not exclusively consist of suicide attacks against Israeli civilians. With this use of rhetoric, the Israeli side managed to drive their archenemy Syria into a corner on the international level.

The ideology of the regime in Damascus was diametrically opposed to that of Sunni Islamist movements such as Hamas. Hamas developed out of the Palestinian Muslim Brotherhood, who at that time was supported by Israel as a counter force to Arafat's PLO in an attempt to drive a wedge between the Palestinians. Hamas was not even allowed to open an "agency" in Damascus until in the late 1990s. As mentioned above, Syria had for many years made great efforts to combat the activities of Islamic extremists. Instead of making use of these fundamental differences, the United States and Israel in the years under Bashar al-Asad brought Islamist forces and the Syrian regime closer together—even Hamas, the secular PLO, and other Palestinian groups in Damascus—by condemning all of them across the board as terrorists and, at the same time, narrowing political options for Syria. After Arafat's death, the joining of forces between different Palestinian groups with diverging ideological outlooks took a step forward with the Cairo Declaration in March 2005. The groups agreed to develop the PLO to include all factions and as the sole legitimate representative of the Palestinian people. This aim, of course, was torpedoed by the sweeping victory of Hamas in the Palestinian parliamentary elections in January 2006 and Hamas's subsequent violent takeover of the Gaza strip.

However, the bonding between Damascus and Palestinian groups continued despite the fracturing of their representative movements and bodies. Hamas leader Khalid Mashaal could feel relatively safe in Syria after the murder of his predecessor. "Syria has adopted a courageous attitude," he said frankly in an interview at the end of April 2004. "It isn't putting any pressure on us."[10] This changed, however, after Syria felt more pressure regarding Lebanon, and after a Palestinian suicide attack took place in the Negev desert on 1 September 2004, for which Israel again threatened Syria with retaliation. Three days later, Mashaal was reported to have left Syria, although the government denied any official order expelling the Hamas leader.[11] Mashaal never left or, if he did leave, he returned soon and again made public appearances in Damascus.

Multiple rumors that Mashaal left the country or was expelled existed throughout the years. This sheds light on the delicate relationship between the Baathist regime—closely linked with Shiite Hezbollah—and Sunni Hamas. Again in September 2008 rumors spread that Syria planned to expel Hamas chief Mashaal from Damascus. But in the end, nothing came of the story. Syria was probably testing waters with regard to its improving relationship with the United States.[12] It became clear once again that Hamas was no natural partner for Syria when secret cables were documented by Wikileaks in November 2010. Asad was quoted as calling Hamas an "uninvited guest" in his country and indicated that Syria's support for Hamas was negotiable.[13]

Syrian-Palestinian relations became increasingly tense during the popular uprising in 2011. Initially, it seemed that the Syrian regime would quickly start to regionalize the conflict by making use of its Palestinian refugees. Unarmed Palestinians from Syria and Lebanon illegally trespassed the sealed Golan Heights' borders on Naqba Memorial Day on 14 May 2011. Twelve people were killed under Israeli army fire and hundreds wounded. This showed a new quality of agitation and it was the first trouble on the Israeli-Syrian border since ex-US Secretary of State Henry Kissinger had negotiated the line of separation on the Golan Heights in 1974. However, shortly afterward, Palestinian mothers in Damascus protested against the abuse of their sons for these political purposes. Since most Palestinians are Sunnis it became tense in the Palestinian refugee quarters in Damascus and elsewhere. Violence and threats against Palestinians were also reported. The ideological alliance between the pro-Palestinian Baath regime and the Palestinians inside Syria broke under the strains of regime violence.

Another political consequence of the estrangement between the Syrian regime and the Palestinians was the final closure of Hamas' premises in Damascus. The organization had started to distance itself from Iran and Syria. Despite an Iranian threat to stop its funding, Hamas left Damascus in December 2011 and made Cairo and Qatar their new exile headquarters.[14] According to Arab media, the rift between Asad and Mashaal occurred when Mashaal had urged Asad to be more sensitive to the people's demands and initiate sweeping reforms without further delay. Hezbollah-leader Nasrallah was not able to mediate the clash. Asad refused to meet Mashaal to discuss his demands.[15] Hamas' giving up on Syria represented yet another crack in the regime's previous pillars of ideological legitimacy and, above all, another relapse of pan-Arab ambitions.

These developments show the complexity of the relationship between Syria and the Palestinians. The previous rhetoric from Washington that put the Syrian regime, the Palestinians, and al-Qaida into one boat of "global terrorism" was far off the mark. This was a kind of propaganda that had previously proved to have little substance in Iraq—although it became a self-fulfilling prophecy in the post-war chaos.[16] On the contrary, Syria had long been cooperating with the US secret service, especially after the 9/11 attacks. It was no coincidence that George Tenet, who resigned from his position as head of the CIA, was, with his organization, one of the few moderating voices with regard to the Syrian regime within the US administration. Many long-wanted terrorists and Iraqi Baath members were caught with the help of Syria. On at least three occasions, Damascus had furnished information that prevented terrorist attacks against US interests, including planned strikes against Navy bases in the Middle East. Al-Qaida had issued a warning to its members not to travel through Syria since the risk of arrest or having large sums of money confiscated was too high.[17]

Just a year after the attacks in New York and Washington, the US State Department praised Syria for having saved "American lives." After that, the relationship again cooled down. Washington complained that the source of information in Damascus was drying up. It was not surprising that Syria was not too enthusiastic about cooperating in the "war on terrorism" with a country that reviled it as being "terrorist" itself. Snubbed, Syria finally broke off any intelligence collaboration with the United States in May 2005 (the Syrian embassy in Washington said that it was the US government that was no longer interested). Only two months before, Damascus had handed over Saddam Hussein's feared half-brother, Sabawi Ibrahim al-Hassan, in an effort to appease the United States after the Hariri killing. At the end of April, Syria formally acceded to a UN treaty designed to cut off funding for "terrorist activities." And at the beginning of 2005, the government was reported to have closed two al-Qaida facilities in Aleppo and Homs run by sheikhs.[18]

Washington under the Bush administration did not understand how to separate the fight against fundamentalist al-Qaida terrorism from the Palestinian Intifada. The United States was roped in by Israel in this matter and, at the same time, had fallen right into Usama bin Laden's trap. During most of his life, the al-Qaida leader who was killed by a US military operation in May 2011 near the Pakistani capital Islamabad had not shown any great interest in Palestine. However, he used the widely perceived injustice by Arabs of US foreign policy in the Middle East, among other things, to justify the 9/11 attacks. In the critical phase of the fight against al-Qaida terrorism, Washington had estranged valuable allies, among them Syria. This also rebuffed the westward-looking part of the Syrian elite. Syria's disillusion with the West went deep. A high-ranking Syrian diplomat said in 2009: "We can look West as an orientation, import cars and machines but we can't import respect."[19]

The Golan and Lebanon

Syria's link to the Shiite organization Hezbollah in Lebanon has been another reason to link Syria with terrorism. According to Damascus, Syria only granted "moral support" to the organization. But in reality Baathist Syria was the hub for arms supplies from Iran to Shiite fighters. Syria and Iran paid millions of US dollars to the organization in support on a yearly basis. Hezbollah was founded as a response to the Israeli invasion of Lebanon in 1982.

One very formal argument from Damascus to justify its support of Hezbollah was the continuing Israeli occupation of a tongue of land, the Shebaa farms in southeast Lebanon. The twenty-six square kilometers of land is Syrian territory that was occupied by Israel when it took the Golan Heights. That is why Israeli troops kept the farms when they withdrew from southern Lebanon in 2000. But the Shebaa farms are only a pretext that Israel could easily invalidate by withdrawing its troops from this tiny piece of land, especially because Syria has toyed with the idea of handing it over to Lebanon as part of a new border agreement.[20]

It was a successful strategy on the part of the elder Asad to stand up to Israel in a proxy war in southern Lebanon with the aid of the Hezbollah militia, without entering into direct conflict with its neighbor, who was clearly superior in military terms. At the same time, Syria was the only regional power that was able to control Hezbollah. Bashar al-Asad continued this policy.

Hafez al-Asad was highly indebted to the Shiites. After the coup that brought him to power in 1971, he received a religious legal statement (fatwa) from the Shiite High Council, led by Musa Sadr, confirming that Alawites were Muslims. This was significant because many Sunnis consider Alawites to be heretics, and the Syrian constitution insisted that the president be Muslim.[21]

Throughout the years Hezbollah concentrated on Lebanon and branched out far into society by providing welfare organizations and social services that the weak and fragmented state has not been able to deliver. In 1992, the Party of God (*hizb 'allah*) entered parliament for the first time and took part in elections recognized by the West as democratic. Hezbollah's participation in politics has presented a dilemma for the West. Arabs asked how democratic states such as the United States or Israel could ignore other peoples' democratic wills and dismiss their choices as "terrorism." The victory of Hamas in the Gaza Strip further aggravated this dilemma. This question must be tackled despite the fact that observers report that some votes for Hezbollah are not freely cast votes, but are made under social constraints.[22] This is a serious problem. But how can this social pressure be measured and included in the assessment of democracy worldwide? This aspect is alien to the classic theories of democracy, for the societies of ancient Greece and later England and other Western countries assumed that individuals acted with self-determination and free will to make their own choices.

Hezbollah's reorientation as a Lebanese political party was not undisputed within the movement itself. The leadership, as a rule, adopted a more moderate tone when speaking to international listeners. The spiritual leader of the organization, Hassan Nasrallah, said that "the Islamic state is not the end but a means of achieving justice. If there is another realistic means available and this way is the only possible one, it will be supported by Islam. This is not a contradiction to Islam." According to Nasrallah, this was the case in Lebanon, where a number of strong religious minorities have to live in one state.[23]

Hezbollah lived up to this philosophy of shaping cross-sectarian coalitions after the Hariri killing when it struck electoral alliances with Jumblatt's Socialist Progressive Party and the Future Movement *(tayar al-mustaqbal)* led by Hariri's son Saad. Later on the alliances broke apart and new constellations emerged. The Christian general Michel Aoun returned from his exile in 2005 and to the surprise of many his newly founded Free Patriotic Movement (CPL) forged a pro-Syrian alliance with Hezbollah that has been holding since then. Aoun was, by reputation, unpredictable and could become a burden for Hezbollah and vice versa when tensions spill over from Syria.

After the heyday of its popularity in the Arab world in 2006 following the summer war against Israel, the nimbus of Hezbollah began to fade, nationally and regionally. Not much of its cross-sectarian discourse was left when Hezbollah fighters seized control of much of Christian dominated Western Beirut in May 2008. This was the first time that Hezbollah had publicly turned its arms inward. A taboo was broken. The organization opted for violent means in an escalating political confrontation with the American-backed government of Saad Hariri. Working to roll back Hezbollah's octopus-like power in the Lebanese state, Hariri had indirectly touched on the delicate issue of disarmament of the group.

Hezbollah' was attempting to extend its telecommunications network from core Shiite areas to other neighborhoods—an effort that provoked resistance among Lebanese Christians and Sunnis. Suspicion has also been rising as Hezbollah has purchased vacant land and apartments throughout Beirut to create a strategic network of bases in case of civil war. In addition, Hezbollah has been exposed: drug dealing in Latin America and money laundering through the Lebanese Canadian Bank. The strongest reason for the decline of Hezbollah's popularity, however, has been the Arab Spring. This Shiite resistance movement had claimed for years to fight for freedom and statehood for the Palestinians and yet it was now supporting the killing machine of a Arab dictator. And this at a time that resistance and freedom became the slogans of the Arab street. Nasrallah lost the Arab street in 2011. Would Hezbollah seek to recover Arab popularity in a confrontation with Israel? This risk was significant, but secondary. The real risk was local: The trenches were opening up inside Lebanon again in the wake of a falling regime and looming civil war in Syria.[24]

For many years Hezbollah had attempted to reassure the Lebanese that resistance against Israel remained a national endeavor and not a sectarian one. Hezbollah leaders knew that the organization would face harder times with the Syrians gone from Lebanon and that the pressure to disarm according to UN Resolution 1559 would increase. The head of the Hezbollah foreign relations unit, Nawaf al-Musawi, made it clear in June 2005. "I believe that by striking these [electoral] alliances we have managed to close the door to disputes of a sectarian nature. . . . I believe we have made significant success in showing how the resistance is part of the national defense mechanism."[25]

Nevertheless, the religious groups were split on this issue. Most of the Christian Maronites favored the disarmament of Hezbollah, whereas thirty-one percent of the Sunnis and seventy-nine percent of the Shiites opposed it.[26] Considering Hezbollah's fading popularity it is likely that voices will be rising again in favor of Hezbollah's disarmament. This does not make the demand more viable in practice.

Returning to the debates on terrorism, it was the nascent Hezbollah movement that introduced the practice of suicide attacks in the 1980s.[27] More than twenty years later in a conversation with Western scholars in February 2004, Nasrallah clearly condemned violence against civilians as a means to achieving goals in domestic policy.

Dressed, as always, entirely in black with turban, cloak, and trimmed beard, the spiritual figure sat reflectively in a deep armchair and spoke calmly in a gentle, low voice. Small glasses of sweet black tea are on the table. The shutters were down in the small lounge situated in the guarded enclave in a suburb of Beirut that was destroyed two years later by Israeli bombs. "Defining terrorism is currently one of the most difficult problems worldwide," Nasrallah admitted. "But it's clear that resistance must be excluded from the definition of terrorism. . . . Israeli soldiers are aggressors when they go into Lebanese territory. Do you expect us to offer them coffee? . . . Therefore this war is legitimate resistance and certainly not terrorism. By contrast, it is terrorism when someone, for instance in Lebanon, pursues a domestic policy goal by killing people—men, women, and children. If someone parks a car loaded with explosives in the middle of a market or in front of a cinema and blows it up, this is an instance of terrorism, even though the political objective may be perfectly legitimate and just." Thus Hezbollah adopted a different strategy than Islamists in Egypt or Algeria, who had worn themselves down in direct confrontation with authoritarian regimes.

The propaganda posters that were common in the streets, especially in southern Lebanon, showed the forty-four year old with bulky plastic glasses and a kalashnikov in his raised hand, the Dome of the Rock in Jerusalem shining golden in the background. This is the message that frightens Israel and the West. Nasrallah did not distance himself clearly from suicide attacks in Israel. "It's up to the Palestinians themselves to define the limits of their resistance," is how he cautiously formulated it, "be it in the land occupied in 1967 or in the territories of 1948 [in today's "Israel proper"]. Our responsibility is merely to help them."[28]

However, Hezbollah's occupation of West Beirut in 2008 raised suspicions about the organization's real intentions in Lebanon. With Syria possibly sliding into a civil war, rearming intensified in the fractured country of Lebanon. At the end of 2011, some Arab media reported that—if the Syrian regime fell—Hezbollah together with the forces of ex-general Aoun planned to occupy Beirut.

Throughout the years Syria was double-dealing. On the one hand, it stressed its willingness to hold peace talks with Israel and tried to rekindle its relationship with the United States. On the other hand, Damascus naturally intended to keep as many options open as possible. "We don't need any nuclear bombs," someone told me in Damascus. "Our atomic bombs are Hamas and Hezbollah." From a Syrian point-of-view, it was clear that the regime was not prepared to give up Hezbollah as its right hand in Lebanon, because of its own military weakness. This was even more obvious after the withdrawal of Syrian troops from Lebanon. After all, the Israeli-Palestinian conflict was far from resolved. Encouraged by the war in Iraq, Israel adopted an increasingly aggressive strategy that included the spontaneous bombardment of targets in Syria as well as the outspoken intention of integrating large West Bank settlements into Israel and doubling the number of settlers on the occupied Golan Heights.

From an Arab point-of-view, peace negotiations with Israel were always a vague affair because of the "democratic uncertainty factor." Israeli political opportunism based on election strategies had again and again led to the revision of previously agreed upon negotiation results. It would be oversimplifying matters to attribute an obstructive attitude exclusively to the "evil dictatorship" that was threatening a "good democracy." The progressive Israeli historian Avi Shlaim joined the criticism that "the Middle East peace process is being held hostage to the vagaries of Israel's internal politics."[29] Deep rifts could not be overcome by merely changing short-lived majorities.

This became clear in the negotiations between Syria and Israel in January 2000. According to American participants, Hafez al-Asad had made exceptionally far-reaching concessions in security issues and in matters of normalizing relations (diplomatic exchange, open borders, trade, etcetera). But his counterpart, Ehud Barak, sensed among the Israeli population a growing opposition to the return of the Golan Heights to Syria. Barak backed down on this crucial issue and no longer wanted to commit himself to a complete withdrawal to the borders of 4 June 1967.[30] Syria saw this as a betrayal. The negotiations in Shepherdstown, USA were a missed opportunity. In Geneva in March 2000, US President Bill Clinton once again attempted on Barak's behalf to persuade the terminally ill Asad to surrender land east of Lake Genezaret that belonged to Syria before 1967, and according to the international borders of 1923. Hafez al-Asad had splashed around in that lake as a child. He remained unbending in the final big decision of his life. He refused to participate in any further discussions and in a rage flew back to Damascus where he died three months later.[31]

The issue of the Golan Heights has given Syria a reason to maintain its relationship with Hezbollah, which, in turn, lent the country the image of a supporter of terrorism. Bashar al-Asad, likewise, referred to national security to justify Syrian troops stationed in Lebanon. In 1982 Israel had invaded Lebanon, reaching the Syrian border in just forty-eight hours. Their troops had stood some twenty kilometers away from Damascus. Even after its withdrawal from Lebanon in May 2000, Israel repeatedly encroached on Lebanese air space to spy or bombard Hezbollah or Palestinian targets. This had served Asad as an argument for making the pullout of his troops from Lebanon dependent on the Middle East peace process. Syria's fear had not been allayed that Israel might again try—as it had done in the 1980s—to win over the Lebanese Christians and turn Lebanon into a satellite state. A vicious circle of mistrust and a balance of deterrence were in place until the assassination of Hariri turned the tide irrevocably against Syria.

The Syrian bargaining position had not improved since the breakdown of the negotiations in Shepherdstown. Powerless, Syria accused Israel of using the Golan as a nuclear waste dump and building extensive settlements there.[32] Israel was able to feel secure with its unqualified American backing. For the first time, the neo-conservatives in Washington were able to set up conditions on Syria's even participation in the peace process. Among these conditions were demands to expel the Palestinian militant factions from Damascus, to cut off support for Hezbollah, and—until 2005—to withdraw from Lebanon (two of these demands were fulfilled by the end of 2011, be it voluntarily or not). The isolation of Syria was at its peak shortly after the Iraq war. Damascus was not invited to negotiations on the Road Map in the Egyptian beach resort of Sharm al-Sheikh in June 2003. Washington's intention was to knock Syria's diplomatic cards out of its hand and subject the country to conditions dictated by Israel, criticized Raymond Hinnebusch. The Syria expert quoted Shlomo Gazit, former head of the Israeli secret service, that the Syrians would not be able to accept such a situation. If they accepted such preliminary conditions, it would be a "public surrender to Israeli-American dictates."[33]

Apart from tightening the screws on this front, the United States under George W. Bush also used Lebanon as a tool for eroding the regime in Damascus. For a long time, the Syrian regime underestimated the seriousness of the situation, failing to recognize the U-turn in US policy. The demand to withdraw from Lebanon could have been made years ago. But a Syrian military presence in this fragile state was in American and even Israeli interests. "Better a politically administered Lebanon than an unhindered point of crystallization for terrorists," as the opposition figure Kilo put the argument (although he and other Civil Society activists were in favor of a withdrawal and reiterated this stand in a press communiqué about one week after Hariri's assassination).[34]

Because of this rigid stance and sudden change in the paradigm, many Syrians experienced a sense of injustice, which the Syrian ambassador to the United States, Imad Mustafa, expressed, alluding to Israel's practices in the Palestinian territories. "I just want to remind you that Syria went to Lebanon to end a bloody civil war that cost almost one hundred thousand lives. We did not annex a single square kilometer of the Lebanese territories. We did not impose our social, political, or economic system on Lebanon. We did not build any settlements in Lebanon, we did not demolish houses there, and we did not, of course, build a wall deep into the Lebanese territories."[35]

It was a fruitless lament because priorities had changed, and Lebanon once again served as a game board for greater interests. Here, the US and French interests diverged. Both supported UN Resolution 1559, but France was interested in Lebanese sovereignty and democratization, which would also increase its historical influence on the country. The United States aimed at weakening Damascus and had no further stakes in Lebanon itself.

But if Syria was supposed to be the guarantor of stability in Lebanon, it failed in its role when Rafiq Hariri was assassinated on 14 February 2005. This was the mildest reproach that the regime in Damascus had to accept. Of course, public opinion in Lebanon and abroad did not stop here, but blamed Syria much more directly. The professionalism of the assassination and the strength of the explosion hinted at a well organized and well backed enterprise in a country that was suffused with Syrian military and intelligence. Asad's personal fallout with Hariri a few months earlier fueled the speculation.

The head of the UN fact-finding team that was investigating Hariri's death, Detlev Mehlis, made it clear from the beginning that he was convinced that Syria was involved in Hariri's murder. He was heavily attacked because it was not up to the UN team to make political statements, much less at this stage. But Mehlis did not go so far as to blame Bashar al-Asad directly. In an interview with the newspaper *al-Sharq al-Awsat,* Mehlis was asked, "Do you feel you are on the right track? Do you feel Syria is definitely behind this [Hariri's] killing?" Mehlis answered, "Yes."—"The Syrian government?"—"Well, let us say Syrian authorities."—"How high up [in the government] do you go?"—"Well, that is speculation so I cannot comment on this."[36]

Since then the UN investigations—that were accompanied by a series of technical flaws and scandals[37]—and the opening of the Special Tribunal for Lebanon in 2009 put heavy strains on Syria precisely at the time it was striving to find its way back onto the international stage. The first indictments of the Tribunal in January 2011 solidified traces that led to an implication of Hezbollah in the Hariri murder case (although the Tribunal as such never published names, they leaked through Lebanese officials and the media). In June 2011, the Special Tribunal issued four arrest warrants against senior Hezbollah members. Hezbollah leader Hassan Nasrallah rejected the indictment and vowed that the accused individuals would not be arrested under any circumstances by any government. He also denounced the Tribunal as a foreign plot against his party.[38] Since the establishment of the UN investigations they had always threatened Lebanon's delicate political fabric. Yet in parallel to the challenge of popular protests in Syria, the Tribunal was a pain in the neck for Hezbollah. Hezbollah and Syria were even more put on the defensive. But the flaws the Tribunal had exposed in its investigation again played into the hands of Hezbollah and the charge that this was no exercise of international law but an American conspiracy against the organization, politically motivated justice at best.

Whatever turns out to be true, if the truth ever comes to light, the Hariri investigation left early scars on the face of the Syrian regime. In October 2005, the spectacular death of Interior Minister Ghazi Kanaan added to the tension. It boosted speculation that not only the Syrian *mukhabarat* was involved, but Syrian government representatives, too. Consequently, it would be less likely that Asad had known nothing about the developments.

Kanaan's death was also linked to the subsequent defection of former Vice President Abdul Halim Khaddam at the end of 2005. Both men, together with former Chief of Staff Hikmat Shihabi, were rumored to be plotting against Bashar because they considered him incompetent, and because they wanted to secure their own economic interests in Syria and Lebanon against the Asad family. At the least, Kanaan and Khaddam were the only men powerful and politically resourceful enough to represent a realistic threat to Asad. The president was well aware of this.

The sixty-three-year-old Kanaan had been a key player in Lebanon for nineteen years as Damascus' military intelligence chief there until Asad removed him in 2003. From this time on, Kanaan's authority had started to crumble. He finally felt cornered by the UN fact finding team and by rising accusations of bribery. Kanaan had been interrogated by Mehlis and denied any involvement in Hariri's murder. In the summer of 2005, Washington froze Kanaan's American bank accounts. (His children studied in the US. He even used to have good ties with US intelligence officials and had interceded with kidnappers to release Western hostages in Lebanon.)

Shortly before noon on 12 October 2005 Kanaan, who was one of the last living Alawite strongmen from the time of Hafez al-Asad, once again denied on Lebanese radio that he had accepted bribes from Hariri, or ordered the man's death. He concluded ominously: "This is the last statement I can make." An hour later, the Syrian news agency SANA announced his suicide. According to reports, he shot himself in his office. Rumors started to circulate that he was murdered as a scapegoat for the Hariri assassination or because he simply knew too much. Of course, Kanaan had many enemies within the regime's growing internal power struggle. In particular, relations had soured between Kanaan and Syria's military intelligence chief, Asef Shawkat (Bashar's brother-in-law), whom Mehlis also listed as a suspect. Various other factors might have played a role but, given the timing, a link to the developments in Lebanon seemed unavoidable.

The question, "Who killed Hariri?" was, of course, a component in assessing whether modern Syria under Bashar al-Asad showed the traits of a "rogue state." It was a complex mix of factors. On the one hand, it soon became clear that Syria was the main loser in these events. It lost Lebanon as its military backyard (although Syrian influence over Lebanon continued unabatedly by other means) and, therefore, had to reassess its security policy in the region. Political options narrowed and Syria's image had been shattered. The words from the mouth of a US official made things clear. "It doesn't matter [who killed Hariri]. Why are you worrying about the fact there's no empirical evidence for who killed him?…It doesn't matter what reality it is. It's—Syria did it. That's all we say and that's all the world wants to believe and that's it."[39]

Before following the trail of blood to Damascus, several counter-arguments stood in the way. The brutal and spectacular assassination of a personal enemy had been far from Asad's style, at least in the overall perception of that time, judging from his prior political and personal behavior as well as from his educational background. In addition, Hariri was a moderate and cooperative politician who had supported Syria in critical times. Other figures had been much more outspoken and radical anti-Syrian mouthpieces, especially the old protagonists from the civil war such as Druze leader Walid Jumblatt or the exiled Christian General Michel Aoun (who later switched sides and became a pro-Syrian Hezbollah ally, as mentioned above). The Maronite Patriarch Mar Nasrallah Sfreir had also joined the ranks of those who called for the implementation of Resolution 1559. If there had been a plan to assassinate adversaries, these figures would have made a good, if not better, target according to this logic. The counter-argument to this was that Hariri had been the only Lebanese politician who could have really challenged the Syrian regime, and with his money and charisma he could have gathered broad support to rule Lebanon on its own for the first time after more than thirty years. If someone in Syria wanted to prevent this from happening, it was Hariri who had to be erased from the scene. In addition, he was an ally of Asad's rival, Vice President Khaddam, who represented a threat to Asad from within the regime.

The core issue in this context pointed to domestic Syrian politics and the pluralization of power centers. If Hariri was killed by Syrian hands—be it in cooperation with Hezbollah, Lebanese intelligence, Hariri's business rivals, or others— the question fell back on Asad. If Syrians were involved and he had not been consulted or even informed, it would have been the final proof that he had lost control. The same logic would have applied if he had gotten wind of it but had not been able to prevent it. If Asad ordered the murder or even condoned, the situation was even worse. This put him in a lose-lose situation, for he was blamed either way and culpable either way because he carried the responsibility. A similar situation occurred again during the popular protests against Asad in 2011 as we have seen above (see Chapter II "Regime's Reflexes and Reactions").

Several facts indicated direct or indirect Syrian involvement in Hariri's assassination. According to a well-informed and leading Syrian opposition figure, the reshuffle of positions in the Syrian and Lebanese *mukhabarat* six months before the assassination could be interpreted as having prepared the ground for this big event. Moreover, a media smear campaign had been launched to chip away at Hariri and other anti-Syrian voices. Hariri had been exposed to repeated personal threats from Syrian officials in Lebanon, according to the source. This had escalated to the point that, in a sense of anticipation, Hariri told Jumblatt that "it's either you or me."[40] Only two weeks later Hariri was dead.

Certainly, creating an atmosphere of hatred was as much or as little evidence that Asad killed Hariri as concluding that Benjamin Netanyahu was guilty of the 1995 assassination of his opponent, Prime Minister Yitzhak Rabin. However, this remains a question of political responsibility. And it rested on Asad's shoulders. Khaddam's allegations from his exile in Paris that Asad was not only involved in intimidating but also in killing Hariri were the most serious attacks the president faced. But Khaddam, a staunch hardliner and corrupt politician, had several personal accounts to settle with Asad and had always had ambitions to play the leading role in Syria himself. This dented his credibility.

Nevertheless, with or without Khaddam's accounts, more details raised concern: according to the same Syrian opposition source cited above, Asef Shawkat, at that time widely regarded as the second most powerful man in Syria, traveled to Paris a few days after the assassination. There the French confronted him with Russian evidence that the ammunition powder used in the attack had been delivered by Russia only two months earlier. According to this information, Syria was the only country in the region that used the powder.

Most people, even in Syria, believed that a complex combination of interests and actors from the political and possibly from the business arenas led to Hariri's death. Hardly anyone wanted to bet on the fact that no Syrian hand was involved. At least, public wisdom held, the feared Syrian intelligence chief in Lebanon, General Rustom Ghazaleh (Kanaan's successor in this post), must have been in the picture. Others also pointed to the 2 June 2005 assassination of the liberal Lebanese journalist Samir Qassir, who was a staunch critic of Syrian influence in Lebanon. He was killed shortly after the pro-Syrian director general of internal security in Lebanon, Jamil al-Sayed, was forced to resign. Sayyed happened to be Qassir's political and personal enemy. The time for settling accounts had begun and drew a trail of blood through Lebanon with more murders such as of the politician and leading critic of Syria, Gebran Tueni, in December 2005 and others.

Another theory in the puzzle was the view that Bashar's uncle Rifaat al-Asad masterminded the disaster in order to further weaken the president.

According to this thesis, Rifaat was preparing for the role of "savior" and was waiting to be invited to end his exile and take over the family business in Damascus. Rifaat had backing from parts of the military. Why? Because in military circles doubt was rising as to whether Bashar could save the country from more disasters. A real déjà-vu as a prelude to 2011.

Another version was that Israel could be behind it all. It would not have been the first time that Israel was involved in liquidations in Lebanon and Syria. Both Israel and the United States have a long record of finalized or planned assassinations of political opponents, be it in the Middle East, Latin America, or elsewhere. If this were the case, the Mossad or the CIA would not have used ammunition powder from Israel, of course, but from Syria. Not surprisingly, this version had most of its adherents in Syria itself, although US intellectual rebel Noam Chomsky also uttered this view. Interestingly, also Khaddam blamed Israel when he was still Syrian vice president. The logic of this theory went that the Hariri killing and the following military withdrawal weakened Syria. Thus it reduced Syria's cards in possible peace negotiations with Israel, dimming the prospects of recuperating the Golan Heights. The findings of the UN investigation, however, made this version appear as rather one of many conspiracy theories in the Middle East.

The Hariri case sent Syria into yet another pressure cooker of international dimensions. UN Resolution 1559 had been pressuring Syria, but it was replaced by Resolutions 1595 and 1636 that called for Syria to cooperate with the UN fact finding team. Otherwise, Syria would face tighter sanctions or even worse. The regime was accused of failing to cooperate, of having destroyed evidence and intimidated witnesses, and of trying to discredit the work of the UN team. However, in a gesture of good will, the Syrian government later issued travel bans for figures listed as suspects. It also agreed to conduct its own investigation, just as the members of the UN Security Council had asked Syria to do.

Mehlis' original list of interviewees, apart from high-ranking Lebanese *mukhabarat* officials, read like a who's who of the Syrian powerful. Reportedly, the list also included the name Asef Shawkat, but he was spared an interview after negotiations between the Syrian government and the UN. Some of the men on Mehlis' list were interviewed in Damascus, like then Vice Foreign Minister Walid al-Mu'allim, a former friend of Hariri. Mu'allim, who later became foreign minister, had tried to convince Hariri to change his political course and not work against Syria a few days before his assassination. Others had to face Mehlis in Vienna, chosen as neutral ground because the Syrians refused to come to Mehlis' office in Lebanon. Among those were General Bahjat Suleiman, former chief of Syria's internal intelligence, General Rustom Ghazaleh, who was Syrian intelligence chief in Lebanon when Hariri was killed, General Jam'a Jam'a, Ghazaleh's assistant in Beirut, General Abdul Karim Abbas, head of Syrian intelligence's Palestinian section, and General

Zafer Youssef, head of the intelligence's communications and Internet section. The list did not include Asad's younger brother Maher, head of the Presidential Guard, who was originally named along with Shawkat in a copy of Mehlis' interim report to the UN Security Council. Asad's close family circle had been spared—at that time.

However difficult and flawed the investigation was, at first glance it seemed a remarkable victory of international law: a prosecutors sent by the UN to investigate a political murder had the power and international backing to force a reluctant regime to cooperate. This, however, only works if a state is already softened up. Experts on international law criticized that the investigation confused the solving of a crime with the political interest of powerful countries to isolate a state and its regime. These voices worried about the nexus created between a judicial interest to solve a murder or several murders and UN resolutions that threatened a whole country and its population with sanctions or worse. This, they said, ran counter to international law.

Even before the Lebanon disaster, the transfer of power from the elder Asad to his son had resulted in a weakening for Syria in matters of foreign policy. Nevertheless, the regime still benefitted from the heritage of the deceased president, who had transformed Syria from a pinball in the political game to an independent force in regional politics. Its influence on Lebanon, too, has always remained high, not least because of economic ties, the infiltration of Syrian intelligence, and even Syrian influence on the Lebanese administration.

Syria's motto in its relationship with the United States could be summed up as, "cooperation as much as necessary with as much restraint as possible. Go into hiding and wait until the storm has passed." An analyst in Damascus said that "the Syrian regime's biggest trick is to live from the crisis and on the edge of the crisis, to play the role of a stabilizing factor but to let the crisis simmer." This was a dangerous gamble, especially with George W. Bush on the other side.

In principle, the whole question as to whether Syria was a "rogue state" or not revolved around the Palestinian-Israeli conflict, the root of political chain reactions. On this issue Syria was on the "wrong" side of the conflict, on the weaker side of realpolitik. If Syria had been on the "right" side, for example, the United States would not have cared if Syria had a foothold in Lebanon. Those who were on the "right" side received a blind eye with regard to human rights violations and other rogue matters. Just take Mubarak's Egypt. When it came to the realities of the political system, Egypt hardly resembled a democracy and was closer to the Syrian model in many respects. A never-ending martial law was only one example. This held true in spite of Mubarak's hypocritical "multi-candidate" election in the fall of 2005. Pointedly, one could say that Egypt was granted the title of a "democracy" by the Western media mainly because it showed the boldness and vision to sign a peace treaty with Israel. This classification changed, of course, when the

Arab Spring caught Egypt. This rapidly turned Mubarak's image into one of a "dictator" in the West. Nearly forgotten was Egypt's long record of arbitrary and collective arrests, high numbers of political prisoners, torture, extreme levels of corruption, an impoverished society controlled by the strong secret service, and press censorship. In 2004 there were 20,000 political dissidents behind bars in Egypt.[41] This was more than thirteen times the estimated number in Syria at that time. Even if Egypt's population of eighty million was taken into account, the number of political detainees was still proportionally almost four times higher than in Syria. Comparing the numbers with other Arab states and Turkey, the US expert of Syria, Joshua Landis, came to the conclusion that Syria was doing quite well, even with regard to Turkey.[42]

The picture turned upside down with the second and third waves of suppression against the Syrian opposition in May 2006 and at the end of 2008, not to mention the humanitarian disaster from 2011 onward. The regime was struggling for survival. Apart from applying unrestricted domestic violence, it once again became prepared to lash out with into the region and beyond.

The Nuclear File

Simply speaking, part of the definition of a rogue state has been that it possessed or was developing nuclear weapons even though it was not supposed to in the eyes of those powers that already had nukes.

During the long reign of Hafez al-Asad Syria remained out of the loop while other countries went ahead with their nuclear ambitions such as India, Pakistan, Libya (until 2003) and Iran. Syria chose to turn the nuclear issue around and pursued a moral discourse that branded Israel as the one that threatened the Middle East with such arms. In 1969 Syria signed the Nuclear Non-Proliferation Treaty. The Syrian regime used to point out that Israel, by contrast, refused to place its nuclear plants under the supervision of the International Atomic Energy Authority (IAEA), in violation of UN Resolution 487. The head of the organization, Muhammad al-Baradei, still confirmed in July 2004 that there was no evidence that Syria had atomic weapons.[43] Syria, however, has not signed the Chemical Weapons Convention. It was said to possess chemical weapons, most of them were allegedly stockpiled near Homs.

More than once Syria decided to use the United Nations in order to condemn nuclear weapons. The last time was in December 2003 when Syria drafted a UN resolution for the Middle East as a region free of weapons of mass destruction. Before this date, Iran had made unsuccessful attempts in this direction in 1974, Egypt in 1985, and Syria once more in 1989. But in 2003 the United States showed no interest in such a resolution for Israel's sake, and so Syria voted the resolution postponed until "a better time."

After the Iraq war Syria radically changed its strategy. With the Palestinian problem and the Arab-Israeli antagonism unresolved, with rising pressure on the Syrian regime and suffocating isolation, the Asad government apparently went ahead with plans for nuclear enrichment. First suspicions came up in the media around 2004. These aspirations were short lived. For the above mentioned bombardment of a site by Israeli airplanes close to al-Kibar in Syria's north-east in 2007 apparently meant the end of the program, at least according to public knowledge. US intelligence said that bombs hit an almost full-fledged nuclear reactor of North Korean origin of the type used in Yongbyon. The Syrian government was anxious to hide the traces and had the damaged building erased by bulldozers in record speed so that satellite images were unable to identify any details of a possible nuclear production site.

By 2011, clear evidence appeared that Syria had been tinkering with a nuclear program. There were implications of involvement by both North Korea and Pakistan. The Syrian regime followed two separate tracks in its attempt to develop a nuclear program: plutonium based technology from North Korea and uranium based technology from Pakistan. In that year UN investigators identified another complex in the Kurdish city of Hasaka in the far north-east of Syria that bore resemblance to a uranium enrichment plant that the Pakistani scientist Abdul Qadeer Khan had planned to build in Libya. According to reports, IAEA officials had obtained correspondence that proposed cooperation between Syria and Khan, who held the nickname of Pakistan's "father of the atomic bomb" but was secretly active in nuclear proliferation to Iran, North Korea, Libya, Algeria, and Saudi Arabia. He was the world's leading expert in providing nuclear technology via the black market.[44]

The facility in al-Hasaka, however, showed no signs of ever having been used for nuclear production as the investigators believed. According to media reports, the building appeared to house a cotton spinning plant. However, the discovery of this second facility raised new suspicions about the extent of Syria's nuclear weapons program. Syrian opposition figures (with reference to high-ranking pensioned army officers) spoke of up to seven nuclear facilities in Syria of which two had been active. They also held that North Koreans were killed in the 2007 bombing. Moreover, they passed on information that Iran had forced Syria to accept outsourcing of part of its nuclear research program on Syrian soil.[45] This constituted another strong link of conspiracy between both states, something like a community of fate against the rising external threat that the Asad-Ahmedinejad tandem was exposed to. In June 2011 the IAEA reported Syria to the UN Security Council over its failure to cooperate with inspectors who intended to examine the facility bombed by Israel.

In addition, Syria had acquired hard steel technology from North Korea to upgrade its long-range missiles. The production sites lay in the hotspots of the 2011 revolts around Homs and Hama. According to Western media, part of the plan was to equip Hezbollah with pinpoint strategic weapons. Thus the whole territory of Israel would have been in the range of Syrian rockets.[46]

With the regime fighting an existential struggle, it was highly unlikely to cooperate with international institutions on the nuclear issue. Some may see a parallel to the Iraqi case here. However, Syria never used weapons of mass destruction such as Saddam Hussein did in 1988. In that year the Iraqi dictator bombarded his Kurdish population with chemical weapons that left an estimated 7,000 people dead and 20,000 wounded. The parallel, however, is that Bashar al-Asad chose to fight his ugliest fight not against an external enemy but against his population at home. In the end, he was about to reach the same number of casualties without the help of any weapons of mass destruction.

13
After Arab Spring:
Shifting Discourses & Alliances

THE ARAB SPRING PLUNGED SOME OF THE MOST notorious police states into turmoil. The secret services of Tunisia's Ben Ali, Egypt's Mubarak, and Libya's Qaddafi had long been regarded as invincible and even as stabilizing factors by Western strategists. Furthermore, these were the more secularist states in the Arab world. They were all presidential republics, whereas the monarchies proved more stable. The same held obviously true for Syria where one of the toughest regimes with a secularist ideology was struggling for survival. Whereas the autocrats in the other Arab countries had looted their people for 30 to 40 years until they rebelled, Syria faced the abyss of civil war after only a decade of rule by Bashar al-Asad, although after more than four decades of Asad dynasty.

The fate of the Arab Spring states was far from decided when this book was being edited. Tunisia had gone through successful elections and toward a working coalition government of moderate Islamists and secular forces, while Egypt remained deeply divided. The most populated country in the Arab world had witnessed elections amidst increasing violence exerted by the military against civilian protesters. The Egyptian revolutionaries were deeply disillusioned of the military rulers whom they had once greeted with joy on Tahrir Square. People soon started to ask if the generals had deliberately sacrificed Mubarak, who had become senile and of no use, in order to maintain its grip on power in a different garb. At the same time, the radical Salafists in Egypt gained the second largest number of votes after the Muslim Brotherhood and frightened many secular and Christian Egyptians. The new government in post-Qaddafi Libya had to overcome existential challenges before embarking on a democratic experiment, such as rebuilding the country's administrative structure and the state's monopoly of power. Yemen in turn remained unruly and in political uncertainty after the reluctant renunciation of President Ali Abdullah Saleh who had claimed immunity for all his deeds in office.

Despite the uncertainty of the different outcomes of the wave of popular protests in the Arab world, they have altered the regions' social and political discourse, public policies, and regional alliances beyond return. Politics found its way back to the Arab street after decades of stagnation, intimidation, and submission. People started discussing, voicing their opinion, writing what they really thought and, of course, hoped for a better future. This was the most difficult part. Social and economic grievances and the feeling of injustice had triggered the uprisings. What people needed most was, expressed in Western terms, good governance and a more just distribution of resources. When looking at the demography and at the run down economies of the predatory regimes, the task to achieve fast alleviation looked unmanageable. But the protests had a magnetic effect as well. They even affected countries that had been spared for the time being. Their governments suddenly realized that they had to be more sensitive about corruption, and they started to distribute more subsidies, raised salaries, allowed more incremental freedoms—or else. Although handing out goodies was not part of elaborate long-term strategies of economic development, a preemptive reallocation of resources had started to set in as a reflex to the uprisings next door. In some cases, it helped to alleviate the immediate pressure. In Syria it did not.

With events running in a fast pace the chronology of events is easily overlooked. In the beginning the protests were civil in nature and almost carnival in spirit, unheard of in modern Arab political history. It was, as Sadiq Jalal al-Azm put it, "an epistemological break with the past."[1] Part of the Arab Spring in 2011 had similar features of the social uprisings that had swept Western countries in 1968. Without anticipating or judging the subsequent developments in post-revolution countries, the Arab Spring movements proved four postulates. First, the aspirations of peoples were indeed universal. As people in other parts of the world had done before, Arabs revolted against poverty, social injustice, corruption, censorship, police intimidation, disrespect for the rule of law, and lack of individual opportunity. The calls for accountability, freedom, and political pluralism in the Arab world—at the time of their eruption—had no cultural or religious coloring and were very much compatible with demands elsewhere. Second, the protesters articulated these grievances without any foreign impetus, save the urge to emulate the achievements of fellow Arabs. The revolts were homegrown.

Third, the civility, creativity, peacefulness, communitarian spirit, and social, religious and ethnic solidarity during the protests showed in a remarkable way that, whatever their rulers said, Arabs were mature enough for democracy. The militarization, primordialization, and fragmentation of the uprisings materialized mostly as a matter of regime reaction, survival strategy or at best because of regime failure. The autocratic regimes and their authorities were not morally, conceptually, or technically equipped to cope with social unrest. These outcomes have to be considered separately from the origin of the protests.

Fourth, the carriers of revolution came from many strata of society, including an educated but politically muzzled middle class that was exposed to economic shock and feared of socioeconomic decline. People with various religious, educational, and political backgrounds joined in the streets in order to protest against the situation in their provinces or in their countries. Most of the protesters in the Tahrir Squares of the Arab world were not inspired, and apparently not very impressed, by the slogan "Islam is the solution."

The Arab peoples, as Rashid Khalidi pointed out, reasserted their dignity by refuting the patronizing attitudes of kings and presidents-for-life.[2] These revolutions, he continued, were not the first democratic ones in the Arab world but the first directed against Arab, rather than colonial, rulers.

In another break with Arab traditions, the revolutions did not produce charismatic leaders nor were they fixed on a particular ideology. In comparison to anti-colonial revolutions and wars of independence this was unusual indeed. The leaders in the street did not often participate in shaping political parties and programs. Some of the bloggers who were instrumental in the Egyptian revolution, for example, publicly declared that they intended to go back to their previous jobs. They saw their place at Google, not in Government. Thus the revolutions remained leaderless to a large extent but not necessarily less effective. The downside was, however, that some of their aspirations remained short-lived. Some staggered after the first wave that broke up the old structures at the surface at least. If adequate structures had followed, technocrats could have followed up what the protesters had in mind. But this depended a lot on transitional arrangements and leaders. In Egypt, it appeared that the military council had second thoughts about the country's future.

Another novel feature of the Arab Spring was a new form of national Arab nationalism—civil in nature—that began to crystallize around the demonstrations. In Egypt the Facebook organizers of the Tahrir-Revolution at one point called the people to leave their religious symbols at home and only to carry the Egyptian flag. Throughout history Arab nationalism used to be directed against something. It was defensive in nature. Once it was anti-colonialist, then anti-imperialist, at times anti-capitalist, subsequently anti-American or anti-Western in general. During the Arab Spring, a new civil-secular form of national Arab nationalism *(wataniyye)* was not directed against any external concept or actor. It was a new platform that served to galvanize anger against Arab rulers and systems themselves. Egypt's kifaya-movement, a motley platform that was formed in 2005, might be considered one of the first precursors of this kind of national opposition. The movement had criticized President Mubarak's fake elections. The common message was "Enough!" *(kifaya!)* The movement embraced Muslim Brothers and secularists alike. Kifaya lacked any religious or ideological predisposition and was not directed against an external scapegoat. It displayed this very nationalism of civil nature that emerged during the Arab Spring.

After the first successful revolution in 2011 Egyptians expressed their nationalism in very practical terms. They placed photos on Facebook showing themselves holding up ink-colored fingers as proof of their participation in the March 19 referendum on constitutional amendments in advance of the free elections in the fall. Others uploaded a new status message: "Proud to be an Egyptian." Still other Facebook pages displayed the crescent and the cross—the twin religious symbols of the protests in Cairo and then Damascus. Similar observations were made for the protesters in Syria. Most of the slogans during the protests emphasized the unity of the Syrian people and Syrian patriotic feelings.

In another important shift of paradigms, the Arab Spring bore the potential of reconciling Arab and Western connotations of democracy. The Iraq war had alienated the discourse almost beyond recognition. Now it was the Arab street that demanded regime change, not a president of the United States. Furious protesters went out with their voices, banners, and fists. Nobody promised democracy on the back of a foreign tank. The polarization between Arab and Western narratives was shrinking, thanks to the Arab Spring on the one hand, and thanks to the absence of neo-conservative missionary militarism on the other hand. This was a great opportunity and a step toward universal acceptance of freedom, pluralism, and a basic understanding of human rights—at least with reference to the demands of ordinary Arab citizens and at least at the point of time when the ideals of the Arab Spring were (still) flying high.

To make clear the sharp contrast to past discourse, it makes sense to look back into the years of confrontation between the United States and the Arab world, in which Syria was positioned in a crucial spot. In the years after 9/11, the United States had ruined its moral and political credibility in the Arab-Muslim environment to such an extent that foreign policy and public diplomacy implied high costs and had an extremely hard time combating the tide of anti-Americanism. The low attitudes toward the US in the Arab world were closely linked with the US government's perceived bias toward Israel, the Iraq war, but also, more generally and more problematically, with the perceived "American treatment of Arabs and Muslims," according to a poll conducted in 2005.[3]

When it came to public diplomacy the war in Iraq played the ball easily into the court of anti-American protagonists like Bashar al-Asad. "For the first time," he said in May 2004, "the United States has turned into a source of instability instead of stability. The war in Iraq has unleashed a hatred that is finding an echo in terrorism." Asad added that sectarian groups had gained momentum, weapons were being smuggled through Syria, extremists were getting a boost, and the streets were filled with an unprecedented amount of anti-Americanism. Most Europeans and even many Americans would have hardly disagreed.[4] The irony was, as Samir Altaqi put it, that "the conservative bureaucratic hardliners in Damascus say that making concessions to the United States is much easier than to the European Union, because the Europeans demand real domestic reforms, the guarantee of human rights, and so forth. For the United States a superficial adaptation would suffice."[5]

By systematically ignoring international law during the "war on terrorism," by legalizing some forms of torture through internal memos (written by

President Bush's counsel Alberto Gonzales, thus making torture an approved tool with the blessing of the Pentagon, the Justice Department, and the White House), the United States, in the perception of many Arabs and Westerners alike, had allied with the crude methods of authoritarian regimes in the Middle East. Incidents against captives in the Abu Ghraib prison in Iraq or the prison camp in Guantánamo Bay on Cuba added to the gruesome picture. The United States had outsourced torture, as suspects had been sent to countries where mistreatment was notoriously used as an interrogation practice. For this purpose, the CIA used a Boeing 737 in clandestine missions that carried detainees to distant interrogation facilities, including Afghanistan, Egypt, and Jordan. Until 2002, US officials sent al-Qaida suspects even to Syrian dungeons.[6]

Also in the past under previous governments, the United States had nourished some of the very forces that caused danger later on: Islamist fighters in Afghanistan, among them Usama bin Laden, to counter Soviet influence, some of whom merged with the nascent Taliban movement; initially, until 1997, the Taliban themselves as a force of "stability" and a bastion against Iran's influence;[7] and Saudi Arabia, the country from which great amounts of funding have flown to the most radical Islamists in the world outside and inside the US. Also, Washington condoned the civil war in Syria which was unleashed by the Syrian Muslim Brotherhood in the 1970s and 1980s and militarily supported by Israel and Jordan at that time.[8]

Subsequently, after 9/11, instead of a victim of terrorism, the US became widely seen as arrogant and anti-Muslim, as a report of the Washington based Brookings Institution conceded. "What the United States calls a 'war on terrorism' is broadly interpreted as a 'war on Islam' by the world's Muslims," Hady Amr wrote in this report. "This credibility gap is worrisome not just in itself, but also because it presents real complications for the success of our foreign policies, ranging from seeking cooperation in the pursuit of terrorists to supporting the expansion of democracy." This problem turned into a security issue, as Amr emphasized. "The paradigm through which America chooses to answer this question of 'why do they hate us?' and how it responds will be crucial to national security in the decades ahead."[9]

Francis Fukuyama pointed out the contradiction that, according to results of another poll in the UN Arab Human Development Report, many Arabs still admired the US and would emigrate there if they could. Not to mention the fact that Arab autocrats possessed uncountable assets that lay in Western bank accounts and were frozen in the wake of the Arab Spring. Also, many of the leading political functionaries sent their offspring to Western universities, preferably to the US. Fukuyama concluded: "We are disliked or hated not for what we are, but rather for what we do."[10] When US foreign policy changed, there was a chance that Arab public opinion would change as well.

President Barak Obama's widely acclaimed speech, in Cairo's al-Azhar

University in June 2009, represented a step to embark on changing mutual (mis-)perceptions. With his carefully chosen words that differed so significantly from his predecessor's saber-rattling Obama caused enthusiasm among the Egyptian student audience as well as in many countries worldwide, including those in Europe. Obama did not spare touching the wounds of the past decades: ". . . tension has been fed by colonialism that denied rights and opportunities to many Muslims, and a Cold War in which Muslim-majority countries were too often treated as proxies without regard to their own aspirations. Moreover, the sweeping change brought by modernity and globalization led many Muslims to view the West as hostile to the traditions of Islam." He emphasized that "Islam has demonstrated through words and deeds the possibilities of religious tolerance and racial equality. . . . And I consider it part of my responsibility as President of the United States to fight against negative stereotypes of Islam wherever they appear. . . . America is not—and never will be—at war with Islam."

At the same time Obama shed a self-critical light on his country's policies after 9/11: "Unlike Afghanistan, Iraq was a war of choice that provoked strong differences in my country and around the world. . . . 9/11 was an enormous trauma to our country. The fear and anger that it provoked was understandable, but in some cases, it led us to act contrary to our traditions and our ideals." He also promised to abolish torture by US authorities.

Part of the disillusion of Obama's Cairo speech was that many of its promises were never kept. The president did not manage to shut down the Guantánamo camp; he did not hold Israeli settlements as he promised in Cairo, and he did not even succeed in getting another peace process going between Israelis and Palestinians, let alone a Palestinian state. The US and Western politicians in general have always been viewed by Arabs through the prism of the Israeli-Palestinian conflict. Will this change in the wake of the Arab Spring? This is an open question. Instead of tackling this issue of issues, the United States found itself entangled in deep domestic trench warfare on universal health care, the financial crises, and the ideological role of the state facing a growing gap between rich and poor. In addition, it faced a hard-line Israeli government. The US superpower withdrew from the scene and had hardly any resources left to return with full force in whatever sense. When the last US soldiers left from Iraq—at the end of 2011, unexpectedly and symbolically in parallel to the Arab Spring—the US appetite for political or military experiments in the troubled region was satisfied for the time being. This gave room to rearrange distorted perceptions on both sides. At the same time, it became clear to everyone that the problem in the Middle East was by far not American presence alone but an abundance of unresolved Arab issues from social injustice, to lack of development, to religious and denominational cleavages.

Despite growing disillusion about President Obama's realpolitik in the

Arab region, he had uttered important thoughts in Cairo in order to correct the image of a supposed clash of civilizations between the West and Islam. And he said something that appeared even more interesting in the light of the Arab Spring: "I know there has been controversy about the promotion of democracy in recent years, and much of this controversy is connected to the war in Iraq. So let me be clear: No system of government can or should be imposed by one nation by any other," Obama emphasized.[11]

In 2011 it was the Arab people themselves who chose to call for democracy and human rights. If the United States had continued to push an aggressive anti-terrorism and regime-change agenda in the Middle East, the Arab Spring would have been much less plausible. Previous US policy had dragged down democratic activists in Arab countries. The leaders of authoritarian regimes imputed to the activists an American agenda. This made democratic reformers weak and vulnerable. In many cases, they became victims of Islamist hotheads and also of the cheap populism of authoritarian regimes surfing on the Islamist tide. In countries such as Syria, where anti-Western pan-Arabism was also widespread among opposition figures, the fear of any kind of US-Israeli dominance would have overshadowed aspirations for domestic regime change that was likely to create a dangerous power vacuum yet to be filled.

US policy under George W. Bush had remained noticeably cool toward social players who tried to defy both religious fundamentalism and authoritarian regimes. According to the US anthropologist Augustus Norton, the prospects of strengthening civil society had dimmed in these countries as a result. Violations of human rights had increased under the authoritarian regimes during the years, without much protest from the United States. These regimes were only too happy to jump on the bandwagon of the "war on terrorism" and, in its name, batter the tender shoots of civil society that were growing in their countries. Critics and human rights activists were silenced and liberal reforms shelved. According to Norton, this had been the result of the Western states having exchanged their human rights agenda for an anti-terror agenda.[12] Interestingly, throughout his lengthy speech in Cairo President Obama avoided the use of the word terrorism. Instead, he spoke of the challenge of (religious) extremism.

Syria's Civil Society Movement had always been split over the question of whether American pressure was a help or a hindrance to their cause. Alluding to the US record of supporting benevolent dictators from the Middle East to South America, human rights activist Haitham Maleh did not count on American involvement of any kind. "Take your nose out of our affairs and out of this region. Don't support any dictatorship. This would automatically help us," he said in 2003.[13] This showed that the loss of trust in its intentions had become a big burden for the United States in the region. The Syrian professor of political science, Imad Fawzi Shu'aibi, summed up the defiant mood: "We can agree with the slogan that democracy is the best system and that freedom is a basic right for human beings, but we can't accept it from someone who is violating this freedom and this democracy."[14]

On the other hand, some of the activists adopted a more pragmatic wait-and-see approach. "The Americans won't come because of democracy. They have supported so many dictators in the past," Anwar al-Bunni held. "But their pressure is helping to get things to change in Syria." Without the US turning up the heat on Syria, more people would have been sitting in prison, he was convinced in 2003.[15] In the market places, one was able to hear Syrians utter the minority view that "our corrupt Arab regimes are much worse than the United States." This is how it was summed up by a young carpet merchant in the Old City of Damascus who went to the mosque five times a day for prayer.

The relationship between Syria and the United States had always been a mixture of threats, revilements, face-saving, and flattering. It was a love-hate relationship between dialogue and speechlessness, between rapprochement and repulsion. Flynt Leverett, a former member of the US National Security Council, pointed out that President Bush's policy toward Syria lacked profound analysis and was far from coherent.[16]

The big picture started to change, however, as early as at the end of 2005 when the Syrian regime was weakened by the Lebanon disaster. The US and other Western states started to take into account that the Syrian political system could actually collapse in a heap of noise and dust and cause considerable instability in Syria and the region. This also entailed Israel's more cautious approach toward regime change in Damascus. Israel realized that a violent regime change in Damascus might turn out to be against its national security interest: Hezbollah was deeply entrenched in Lebanese politics; Islamists of all kinds and colors were on the advance in Iraq; Iran was ruled by a religious fanatic; the Muslim Brothers were gaining hold in the political process in Egypt; Hamas was temporarily on the rise in the Palestinian territories; and Lebanon was deeply divided over the Hariri Tribunal. This U-turn added a new dimension to Syria's situation and to the premises of Middle East politics. It was also at the end of 2005 when representatives of Syria's Civil Society Movement started to feel abandoned by the West, according to their accounts (see Chapter VII "Opposition, Islam and the Regime").

The view started to prevail that the Baath regime had always been a guarantor of stability in Syria. Before the Baathists came to power Syria had been the country with the highest number of military coups in the Arab world between 1949 and 1970. The United States was hardly interested in a second Iraq, neither were the Syrians. In this respect, the Iraq war in one of its numerous collateral effects became a stabilizing factor for the Syrian regime, far into the months of the Arab Spring.

The reasoning that Syria needed to remain stable in a shaky region became stronger through the years while Lebanon became more unstable and Iraq hardly better. In addition, as described in Chapter VIII, Syria's foreign policy became more creative and constructive again. Western politicians, negotiators, and development agencies became frequent visitors in Damascus. In January 2011, Syria achieved its last major foreign policy victory when US President Obama dispatched the first US ambassador to Syria after a gap of five years. Hence the Syrian tragedy: At the moment when the Arab Spring hit Syria, nobody—including Israel—was actually interested in a fall of the Asad regime.

Simultaneously, though, the picture inside Syria began to look quite different. Frustration with the regime was growing at the end of the decade, and surprising statements could be heard even from people who had pursued a strong pro-regime discourse during their political careers, which included an equally pronounced anti-Americanism.

The remarkable development about the Arab Spring is that anti-Americanism had been so deeply entrenched in the Arab countries' discourse after 9/11 and the war in Iraq that it seemed that it would take generations for attitudes to change. This may still be true in the long run, especially if an Islamist discourse was to prevail in the Arab countries of transition. Yet who would have thought that, one day soon, a US representative would be more welcome and more secure in a Syrian city than any functionary of the Syrian regime? In an unusual move, US Ambassador Robert Ford supported the Hama demonstrations with his physical presence in July 2011 together with his French colleague Eric Chevallier. This was a first sign that the US administration no longer put much value on long-term working relations with the Syrian regime. The opposition Local Coordination Committee in Hama helped to guarantee Ford's and Chevallier's security. People in the street chanted "The people want the fall of the regime!" while greeting Ford's embassy SUV with roses and olive branches—something the US troops in Iraq had waited for in vain.[17]

Later, with escalating violence, the narratives started to shift even more. Some Syrian protesters in their desperate fight for survival, in anger about the dragging of sanctions by the Arab League, and in disappointment at Western restraint recalled the time of US President Bush. Opposition sources reported in December 2011 that in the Sunni stronghold of Idlib in northern Syria demonstrators had put up a banner that said "Obama's procrastination kills us, we miss Bush's audacity. The world is better with America's Republicans."[18] Not even George W. Bush himself would have predicted such a slogan in Syria eight years after the war in Iraq. Nevertheless, it must be added that something similar had occurred before. Prior to the designation of Burhan Ghalioun as the head of the Syrian National Council, for example, banners with his name were seen in the streets of Syria, according to a member of the opposition outside the SNC.

The desperation of Syrian civilians grew while the situation went more and more out of control. Armed gangs contributed to mistrust and intimidations on both sides. The longer the conflict lasted, the less likely it was to prevent the emergence of engineered religious hatred and the nascence of a civil war that would tear the country apart even after the formal establishment of a new regime. At the same time that Syrians struggled for their lives and the remnants of their mosaic nation, two other developments went hand-in-hand. Post-revolution violence broke out in Egypt and Yemen, and it became increasingly clear that democratically elected institutions and the nascent constitutions would be strongly influenced by an Islamist majority. It became clear that the shifting of political parameters in the Arab world was not over with the Arab Spring of 2011 but was just about to begin.

Skeptics in the West concentrated on the phenomena of Islamism and tended to cast aside the initial spirit of hope for change and personal freedom that spread through the stagnating region from the moment that the Tunisian vegetable seller Mohammed Bouazizi immolated himself in his village of Sidi Bouzid on 17 December 2010. Nobody claimed that transforming the Arab autocracies would be an easy ride. But Islamism was about to become the dominant issue again, from the perspective of Western audiences, threatening to tie in with previous discourse. Hard-line US Republicans even drew parallels between the Arab Spring and the Iranian revolution of 1979—which had originally not been an Islamist upheaval either but was carried by secular people and even communists, too, before the movement was hijacked by Khomeini's followers. Most Islamist figures who emerged as political leaders after the Arab Spring referred to Turkey as their model rather than Iran. Rachid al-Ghannouchi, Tunisian's long-standing Islamist opposition leader and founder of the moderate Islamic party al-Nahda, explicitly rejected a Khomeini-like state.

The stakes for the Arab Spring states and their neighbors were high, and so has been the risk of failure. The danger became particularly obvious when radical Islamist parties like the Salafis in Egypt gathered strong support at the early stage of the democratization process. Thus they were likely to be involved in shaping the new constitutions. In such cases, the difference to Turkey would become salient where an Islamic party was elected but within a solid secular framework. Unfortunately, a ban of ethnically or religiously connoted parties as in Yugoslavia up to the moment of its collapse was not envisaged in most Arab transformation states. In contrast, the Syrian Baathists had always implied such a ban in the planned party law. The problem was that, by the time the law could have taken effect, the country had already been run down, and the Baathists had drowned their remnants of credibility in blood.

In any case, "Islamism" as such is a much too rough term to cover what has been developing in the Arab societies before and after the Arab Spring. Each Arab country has its social, political, and ideological particularities. In each

Arab country Islamists crystallized as political forces that had their specific discourse—from Tunisia's moderate and consensus-oriented al-Nahda Party to Egypt's Salafists and their al-Nour Party. Over the previous decades, suppressed Islamist groups shifted their discourse away from the slogan "Islam is the solution" *(islam hua al-hall)* to demanding democracy and human rights—precisely the items that the authoritarian secularist regimes most painfully denied. At the same time, Islamic charities strived to fill the vacuum left by the corrupt state apparatus in the field of social inequalities. Religious charities dealt with the losers of economic liberalization and fast-paced population growth.

In contrast, secularism, as an ideology at the political surface, had been strongly tied to authoritarianism in the Arab world of the past decades. Similarly, socialists and even social democrats did not manage to gain majorities after the collapse of Yugoslavia, even if they had elaborated reformist party programs, but the ethno-nationslists did, with simple messages. Against this background in the Arab world, liberalism and secularism as values were unlikely winners of popular support in the first rounds of elections. Even in Syria, where the Civil Society Movement for years had tried to fill secularism with a discourse on civil society, the discrediting of secularism went so far that the new opposition protagonists avoided the term altogether. SNC President Burhan Ghalioun, for example, said in an interview in December 2011:

"All parties are calling for a civil, democratic pluralistic state [that] treats its citizens as equal in front of the law. Civil is a version of secular—secular in the way that it assures it is neutral toward religions and sects, and assures the separation of state and society. The exact term 'secularism' has a negative connotation in the Arab world, so we prefer use the term 'civil'."[19]

This is interesting because the original Arab Spring movements were actually secular in the sense that there was not much of a religious momentum as a tool of motivation. Islamists jumped on the bandwagon when the revolutionary tide was about to tip the balance of power. In a clever move, they did not burn themselves too early in the fight against the common enemy and kept a low profile when change was about to take place, also without much ado. In Syria, for example, Islam gained importance after other groups had stayed away from the protests because of the escalation of state violence or because of (founded or unfounded) fear of post-revolutionary chaos that was feared to be filled by Islamists later on, similar to Iraq. *"Allahu akbar"* also became a slogan of desperation while expressing grief about fallen victims or was used as a call to mobilize courage to continue despite an overpowering state machine. In any case, the first protesters—urban educated professionals or desperate people from the provinces from Sidi Bouzid to Dara'a—who took to the streets had no religious agenda. This was true even if they had to hide in mosques when the state security attacked them as in Syria. Islamism as a political movement was no issue. Al-Qaida was out.

The killing of Usama bin-Laden in early May 2011 by US Special Forces in the vicinity of Islamabad, Pakistan, did not cause shock waves in the Islamic world at all. The Arab Spring with its secularist and material demands had become the prime preoccupation of the people. It was no zealous war against the West any longer but against the octopus-like *mukhabarat* and military at home. The death of Usama bin-Laden coincided with the Arab Spring and occurred at a point when al-Qaida's ideology had long been in decline. As the French Middle East experts Gilles Kepel and Jean-Pierre Filiu pointed out, bin-Laden's physical death followed his political death. "The democratic revolutions in the Arab world, whose slogans formed an anti-thesis to bin-Laden's radical Islamist ideology, swept him away," Kepel wrote. "If he had been killed under George W. Bush in the war against terror, he could have easily become a martyr of the Jihadists, even an icon of the various anti-Western movements in the Muslim world. His death ended a dark chapter in the relations between Orient and Occident that reached from the 9/11 attacks to the Tunisian Jasmine Revolution. Cairo's Tahrir Square and the striving of the Arab peoples for democracy and human rights put an end to this era."[20]

Would such optimism be supported by long term developments? This was an open question. The first wave of enthusiasm had exhausted itself quickly, and Tahrir Square and other places showed scars of post-revolutionary violence. After they have broken open the cage of authoritarian rule, Arab people have faced the painstaking process of reforming entrenched economic and social arrangements. The challenges lie in developing a more just social system and an economy that grows significantly faster than demography, constructing a new social contract and a democratic political culture, respecting minority rights and dissenters of all kinds. Islamist parties, slogans, and protagonists overshadowed much of the post-revolutionary events, partly because Islamists possessed the best organization and infrastructure. But "opposition" Islam had to convert itself into "governing Islam," and on the way much of its religious zeal might give way to pragmatic approaches and every-day restraints.

Even some secular intellectuals like Sadiq Jalal al-Azm warned not to overreact to the new Islamist ghosts that haunted the young democracies or that emerged in bleak scenarios of fragmentation and violence as in Syria. Others held that it was precisely these pre-modern elements that would leave their footprint in the post-revolutionary societies. The appeal of the Islamists lay ". . . in large part in their promise to rebuild Arab societies while remaining faithful to traditions that al-Azm—like many secularists today—believed had outworn their use. Perhaps they have; but they cannot simply be wished away, or purged by revolutionary fiats, as al-Azm might have wished," Adam Shatz wrote in a review of Azm's 1968 book *Self-Criticism After Defeat* in the light of the new contexts. "The Arab revolutions have been an exhilarating leap into the future. The post-revolutions will be a slow and difficult effort to reconcile revolutionary change and respect for tradition, with all the uncertainties—and potential reversals—that popular sovereignty and democracy entail."[21]

Others spoke of post-Islamism in order to get near to a description of the phenomenon that had been taking hold. Although a religious momentum was missing during the revolutions themselves, subsequently a dominant movement—or perhaps even a societal mood—crystallized that aspired to combine a pious society with democracy. According to Asef Bayat, it was far from decided if post-Islamism was to prevail or a renewed fundamentalism similar to the one that ravaged through the Arab world in the 1980s and 1990s.[22]

In order to get a grip on the term "Islam" and to avoid a catch-all use for whatever purpose, al-Azm offered a differentiation of three groups that were contending in a fierce struggle to define Islam in the present Arab world and beyond. The first one is the official state Islam nourished by autocratic governments, their clerical elites or monarchs. Often, it was financed by petrodollars like in the Gulf States. Official state Islam, which has even existed in Turkey, sidelined dissenting and autonomous Islamic currents. This explained the vigorous protest movement in Iran in which many clerics had participated who felt marginalized.

The second current, according to Azm, is insurrectional Islam. This was the marginalized opposition Islam that radicalized itself during the years of authoritarian repression. In their extreme form, these groups produced terrorist attacks like those on the Grand Mosque in Mecca in 1979 or against the targets in New York and Washington in 2001. These dissident Islamic groups had popular support and bore similarities of 20th century liberation movements, according to Azm.

The third current is the good-for-business Islam or commercial Islam, as Azm coined it. Bearers are the chambers of commerce, investment houses, and small entrepreneurs from the backbone of the spouts of civil societies in the Middle East. This form of Islam abhors projections from the radical left as much as from Islamist frenzy. In order to pursue good business, people need a minimum guarantee of rule of law, good governance, and democratic rule. Turkey's Justice and Development Party (AKP) represented such a current, said Azm, and most Arabs used the Turkish experience as a guide. It is no coincidence that the Muslim Brotherhood in Turkey named their party according to the Turkish model in the first post-revolutionary elections. Turkey, however, had a staunch secularist fundament before an Islamist party started to walk on it. This is not the case in Arab states.

Especially Syria has, as mentioned above, an important Sunni merchant class that has traditionally championed commercial Islam. This is why they found shelter in an arrangement under the Baathist umbrella. Religious frenzy and extremism has been alien to the Syrian religious and societal landscape. The violence that started in 2011 has represented a serious challenge to this heritage. With caution Azm concluded in October 2011: "If and when Arab societies stabilize, this form of business Islam will prevail for quite some time."[23]

Undoubtedly the tides will move back and forth until some form of equilibrium is reached between the worldly demands of a dynamic and young population, which requires a functioning economy and a welfare arrangement, and the religious traditions on which the new social contracts and polities will most likely be built. It will take time until a suppressed, distorted, and radicalized Islam can transform itself into a force that serves politicians to carry political responsibility for the whole of the population.

A lot depends also on how the Israeli-Palestinian conflict will evolve. This point of ideological and religious crystallization in the Middle East had been pushed into the background during the turbulent months of the Arab Spring and its aftermath. But it may gain importance again when elected governments have to respond to their Islamic constituencies and take sides more vigorously in favor of the Palestinians.

Meanwhile, Israel finds itself in a predicament. The country is deeply divided between an increasingly aggressive Jewish orthodoxy and secular Israelis. Moreover, Israeli society faces a hardening antagonism between rich and poor, which produced massive protests in Tel Aviv's boulevards parallel to the Arab Spring. If the transformation of the Arab Spring states turns out to produce pronounced Islamist tendencies in government or even instability with radical armed groups holding sway, Israel's security concerns will obviously mount. The unabated construction of Israeli settlements in East Jerusalem and the West Bank will remain a catalyst of conflict with the Palestinians, with an Arab world that is gaining new self-confidence, and with Western governments. For years Israeli politics have been facing an increasing public diplomacy problem. Turkey did not help to promote sympathy for Israeli concerns. Apart from the settlement issue, Israel's former strategic partner was repelled by the massive retaliation against Hezbollah in south Lebanon in summer 2006, the Gaza war in 2008 - 2009 and the violent storming of the Turkish vessel Mavi Marmara. The latter involved a flotilla of activist NGOs who intended to confront the Israeli maritime blockade of the Gaza Strip at the end of May 2010.

Confrontations may turn more asymmetric in nature as demonstrated when Syrian Palestinians crossed the border into the Golan in May 2011. Israel's security concept has been challenged. "Israel's is facing the biggest erosion of its strategic environment since its founding," as US author Thomas Friedman put it. At the same time he criticized Prime Minister Benjamin Netanyahu for a lack of appreciation of the democratic movements in the Arab world. "Israel's fear of Islamists taking power all around it cannot be dismissed," Friedman wrote. "But it is such a live possibility *precisely* because of the last 50 years of Arab dictatorship, in which only Islamists were allowed to organize in mosques while no independent, secular, democratic parties were allowed to develop in the political arena."

The other side of Israel's predicament is that if the Arab Spring goes well and produces outcomes of rule of law, respect for human rights, and democracy in Israel's Arab neighborhood, Israel will lose its singularity in the region, and its own human rights record will shift more into the focus again. The title of being "the only democracy in the Middle East"—a kind of Israeli moral self-definition—would not be sustainable any longer. Unconditional support from an economically ailing and increasingly disinterested United States may not be a matter of self-evidence any longer either. Preventing the Palestinians from obtaining acceptable living conditions, working institutions, and dignity was prone to provoke a similar Arab Spring movement among the Palestinians. Therefore, Friedman warned Israel against digging in as the only response to the drastic changes in the region. "That could be the greatest danger of all for Israel: to wake up one day and discover that, in response to the messy and turbulent Arab democratic awakening, the Jewish state sacrificed its own democratic character."[24]

Israel and Syria have one thing in common: If the external enemy breaks away for whatever reason, domestic rifts will all the more surge to the surface. The situation of a cold but stable non-peace does have winners on each side. Israel has not felt under time pressure to tackle the Palestinian issue either. Time was working for the Israeli side while international pressure remained unlikely. The moment of the Arab Spring may have been one of the last opportunities to work for a peaceful two-state-solution before demography and the expansion of settlements were to create irreversible realities on the ground.

At a second glance, for Israel not only dangers lingered in the Arab Spring. The decline of popularity of religiously radical, morally hypocritical, and politically opportunistic groups such as Hamas and Hezbollah was an extraordinary development. It was the Arab street itself that cast them from their pedestal, at least temporarily. Hamas' bad governance and moral intolerance faced rising domestic criticism in the wake of the Arab Spring. Hezbollah's role of anti-Israeli resistance became overshadowed by the group's support of a Syrian dictatorship that slaughtered civilian Arab protesters calling for a better life. It was a surprise that the Israeli side failed to develop an adequate discourse that plugged into these new sentiments.

The question of questions was how to find a way to democracy without jeopardizing stability. The previous notion of stability for the region meant basically stagnation. Western states had accommodated themselves with this trade-off. How hard it was to change the established paradigms became obvious when former French Foreign Minister Michèle Alliot-Marie as a first reflex had offered help to Tunisia's President Ben Ali when the first protests broke out. When events unfolded, she was obliged to resign, and after some hesitation France's President Nicolas Sarkozy put himself to the forefront of democratic change in Libya and beyond. Also Turkey was hesitant in the beginning before it chose to side with the forces of change. Similarly, other Western states had to readjust their compass for the Arab region. The delicate trade-off still remains between a new dynamic and stagnation-stability. The latter is still applied in the Gulf States, for example, where strong economic interests and the distribution of oil are at stake.

Nevertheless, the old definition of stability as social, economic, and even moral stagnation became untenable after the Arab Spring. It needed courage and foresight to redefine a new notion of stability in the Arab region. This necessarily implied some kind of a free play of political forces. Majorities uncomfortable to the West have become possible outcomes of this process. In 2003, Raymond Hinnebusch pointed out the risk: "If these regimes are really to become democratic, they will have to combat social inequality and Islamist movements." Therefore, he concluded, the United States—and one could add other Western countries as well—preferred pluralization to democratization and their goal was to establish "liberal oligarchies." "If democracy were to be promoted [in the Middle East], Washington would evoke the very forces that are against US interests."[25] But it is worth repeating that the Arab Spring protesters did not have any anti-American agenda. Nevertheless, the Arab populations are manifold and nobody had ever asked their political preference before, much less in the impoverished and less educated countryside. Surprises were part of the transition. Despite this mixed outlook Western states should have the courage to hold on to this new notion of stability because in the long run it will prove more viable than the encrusted structures that imploded with noise and dust. A free play of forces—within constitutional limits—is able to better absorb shocks without falling apart.

Hardly anyone seemed to remember that, until the Arab Spring broke out, Lebanon looked like a highly volatile country waiting with angst for the indictment of the Hariri Tribunal. Two polarized political camps opposed each other. But what happened was that the National Unity government collapsed, and a new government was formed peacefully in January 2011. The political system allowed an abrupt change from a rather anti-Syrian and anti-Hezbollah cabinet to a strongly Hezbollah-influenced and Syria-friendly cabinet without rocking the boat. Nobody had guessed that Lebanon might look more stable than neighboring Syria at one point soon. If Lebanon drowns in civil war again it is not because of its fragile democratic arrangement but because of proxy forces that drag the Lebanese game board toward the abyss.

Another example in favor of an open society and polity can be taken from Egypt. Censorship was part of everyday life in Mubarak's country. Only one thing was not barred from free speech and from the media: Criticism of Israel and, much more importantly, anti-Semitism, which almost became part of Egyptian popular culture. This was a safety-valve to compensate the fact that Egypt had signed a peace treaty with Israel in 1979, that Mubarak kept the border sealed with the Gaza strip, and that gas pipelines led through the Sinai Peninsula to Israel. The airing of anti-Jewish conspiracies theories flourished in a closed system, whereas an open society with alternative access to information leads to more differentiated views. A pluralization of accessible ideas and options automatically brings about a gradual diversification of discourse.

A new notion of stability would equally imply a strong social and economic component. Without fast-growing economies the hopes of the street protesters will be dashed and their patience will run out soon. At the same time, ingredients of a fair distribution of resources, welfare, good-government and rule of law are indispensable in this new notion of stability. People who fought for their freedom with high sacrifices have also become more sensitive to personal liberties. All these are Hercules-like tasks in countries that have been run down, if not during then after colonization, up to the day of transition. It remained to be seen how countries like Jordan, Morocco, or the Gulf monarchies would manage to combine incremental change with an old notion of stability that granted them at least a more stable dynastic legitimacy.

In his 2009 speech in Cairo, US President Obama had offered a dose of the new notion of stability when he said:

"Governments that protect these rights are ultimately more stable, successful and secure. Suppressing ideas never succeeds in making them go away. America respects the right of all peaceful and law-abiding voices to be heard around the world, even if we disagree with them. And we will welcome all elected, peaceful governments—provided they govern with respect for all their people."

This was an innovative promise after Western countries had sanctioned Hamas after its democratic victory in the Palestinian territories in 2006. In this regard, Obama even met those on the other side of the political spectrum that precisely, therefore, had criticized the double standards of the Bush government. One of them, right-wing hawk Robert Kagan, held that "if the Bush Administration isn't willing to let Islamists, even radical Islamists, win votes in a fair election, then Bush officials should stop talking so much about democracy and go back to supporting the old dictatorships."[26] This daring statement gained unimaginable importance after the Arab Spring. Once again, the West had to let itself be measured by its own standards; its credibility was at stake. This represented also a great chance to open a new chapter between the West and the Arab world after the antagonisms, misconceptions and conspiracy theories that had accompanied the relationship after 9/11 and the reactions to it. It was also a chance that democracy and human rights be considered as really universal values indeed, and not Western ones, even less Western-imposed ones.

In his speech Obama added another thought that carried weight and unfolded its real meaning after the Arab Spring. The educated urban demonstrators of Tahrir Square and elsewhere will probably come back to the following caveats of the promise to recognize any democratic outcome. Alluding to the Islamists' discourse of democratic change, Obama said:

"This last point is important because there are some who advocate for democracy only when they're out of power; once in power, they are ruthless in suppressing the rights of others. So no matter where it takes hold, government of the people and by the people sets a single standard for all who would hold power: You must maintain your power through consent, not coercion; you must respect the rights of minorities, and participate with a spirit of tolerance and compromise; you must place the interests of your people and the legitimate workings of the political process above your party. Without these ingredients, elections alone do not make true democracy."[27]

A thin notion of democracy that consisted of not much more than formal elections needed to give way to a thicker notion of democracy that implied its administrative, social, economic, and political preconditions. The problem of the Arab Spring states was that elections were an organizational challenge but relatively quickly done whereas the other improvements were to take much more time. The same was true in Eastern Europe. This generation who fought for democracy and freedom, risking their lives, will cherish and defend democracy with more vigor than following generations who are born into it but may not see any benefit in their everyday lives. Democracy needs a welfare component or at least economic perspectives that are worth defending the system. Otherwise, religious rabble-rousers will have easy game in the region again, as in the old days when they played the suppressed alternative to the authoritarian secularist regimes.

Despite persisting dangers, the Western reflex should not be staring at "Islam" like a deer in the headlights. For decades, the West failed to become a constructive agent of change in the Middle East—even though it made several attempts ranging from military action to building institutions such as the Mediterranean Union. Western politicians should be far-sighted. Faced with post-revolutionary election results and the sometimes messy process of forming governments, they should forbear. Above all, these new governments reflect a breaking up of old structures. The Arab people will have to demonstrate patience with their new governments despite the high costs of the revolutions and the extremely high expectations they entailed. Equally, the West should be able to apply patience on its side to judge the new governments according to their deeds.

Western actors should not fall into the trap of measuring each twitch in the Arab world with reference to Islam, lest their fear of political Islam does not become a self-fulfilling prophecy. Westerners and Arabs alike should always remember that there was a reason why Islam did not play a role in the early days of the revolutions. Islam as a catch-all term that crystallizes the hope for a golden future, surges in popular usage in times of crisis when worldly life appears to be less worth living.

Moreover, it would be unfair to reduce the ample achievements and repercussions of the Arab Spring movements to the emergence of a degraded form of Islamism. As elaborated above, Islamists did not bring up the power to topple any of the regimes they had opposed for years and decades. They just jumped on the bandwagon when other segments of society had tipped the balance in favor of change. Of course, Muslims were involved in the upheavals, simply because the Arab states are Muslim majority countries. So it was revolutions of Muslims not of Islamists—together with Christians and others, even atheists. Keeping in mind the chronology is the only way to pay tribute to the real character of the Arab Spring. Everything that followed from here has been a development of political competition in a new and unfamiliar framework for all. It is now up to the Arabs—what they make out of the new possibilities and how they shape the heritage of the Arab Spring.

The violence in Egypt since the first free elections showed a first rift between those who originally tipped off the revolution and the Muslim Brotherhood. The Brotherhood, which obtained the majority of votes, did not participate in the street protests against the post-Mubarak military council because it was interested in obtaining seats in parliament and less inclined to waste more of their human resources in the street. This enraged the urban secular protesters who did not represent a majority of Egypt's population but the majority of those who let themselves be beaten up and killed in Tahrir Square—this time by soldiers and not by Mubarak's policemen. When politics returned to the Arab street, new scenarios opened up and unleashed new dynamics that were previously kept under the lid, positive and negative ones. In some cases, the revolution will be considered incomplete, like possibly in Egypt or in Yemen. In Libya and Syria, the protests unleashed violence and varying degrees of counter violence in a last resort of self-defense. This occurred not only in one central square but across each country. The physical destruction and moral wounds will obviously have an impact on the future construction of institutions, and on each country's polity, political culture, national identity, and social cohesion. Transitional justice will become an important challenge in those countries that suffered high violence. Much will also depend on improving access to and quality of education. This will automatically reduce the fertile ground that cheap religious propaganda can exploit.

European contributions, instead of trying to impose values or ready-for-use concepts, can be more credible and constructive if they accompany the developments in their southern neighborhood with at least three major policies. First, Western borders should become more permeable for young Arabs who seek to qualify themselves in Western universities or professional education centers. Secondly, European markets must become more open for imports of their southern neighbors, especially in the field of agriculture. Thirdly, and not less importantly, Western countries in their political relationships with the Arab states must live and cherish the very ideals and liberal values for which the Arab youth took to the streets. The so-called war against terror and the US engagement in Iraq were definitely no such model. A solution to the Israeli-Palestinian problem represents another difficult objective that would help overcome religious stereotypes and political antagonisms in the region and beyond. Even the Arab Spring was not able to end the political stagnation between Israel and the Palestinians.

But it was encouraging to see that a radical shift of discourse during the Arab Spring set aside previous ideological constellations in other areas. Especially those demonstrators who suffered for months under state brutality did not care any longer who was to protect them but cried for help to whomever would listen. When the Arab League hesitated to impose sanctions on Syria and shifted their ultimatum to Syria again and again, they lost credibility with the result that people in the streets looked increasingly to the West. However, the sudden expectations that Syrians and other Arabs connected with Western stands were also a burden. The European Union that had hardly spoken with one voice when it came to the Middle East, much less during the Iraq war, had very limited influence and found itself in the worst financial and monetary crisis of its history. When the Arab Spring broke out, the EU was in a painstaking process of self-discovery (similar to the time of the Bosnian war in the 1990s when the EU first had to come to grips with shaping a common foreign policy during the double processes of integration and extension).

The United States for its part was caught in profound domestic struggles. Signals pointed toward withdrawal rather than additional engagement after the Iraq war—a war that had cost the superpower a tremendously high price in finance, personnel, and public diplomacy. Obama had acted with restraint in the Libyan case and preferred to keep US engagement under the radar while France and Great Britain played the leading role in the UN-backed NATO mission against the Qaddafi regime.

On the other hand, it was precisely the Libyan case that curbed efforts to stop human rights violations in Syria later on. Russia and China vetoed a condemnation and further measures against the Syrian regime. The UN Security Council blocked itself because Russia and China argued that UN Resolution 1973 of March 2011 had been overstretched by the NATO forces. This Resolution had empowered UN members to establish a no-fly-zone over Libya to protect the civilian population, since Qaddafi's forces had also used war planes to clamp down on protesters. The Resolution also empowered UN member states to take "all necessary measures" to protect civilians. In the end, the Libyan rebel forces would probably not have gained an upper hand against the Qaddafi troops without the far-reaching help of NATO.

But the real reasons for China's and particularly Russia's resistance against further pressure on Syria lay deeper. Syria had billions of dollars in arms deals with Russia. Hardly anybody, except Russia, was ready to sell arms to Damascus under long-standing international sanctions. Thus old Cold War alliances re-emerged in the wake of Syria's antagonism with the United States and gradual estrangement from the Europeans. The Russians lost $4 billion of contracts when the UN Security Council had issued the arms embargo against Libya[28] and wanted to prevent a similar outcome in Syria. And one more thing: For Russia, Syria offered strategic value by offering a military base in Tartous that would be the only Russian staging facility on the Mediterranean Sea. Syria (apart from Algeria) remained the only Russian ally in the Arab world. Russia kept its word and delivered tanks and other shipments to the port of Latakia during ongoing violence. For China the Syrian market was peanuts. The blocking of sanctions against Syria stemmed rather from an anti-Western impulse in addition to well developed ties between both countries.

When it became increasingly clear that Asad did not have his country under control and would likely not be capable of solving the crisis, Russia and China began to act more cautiously. Delegations from the Syrian National Council visited Moscow. Russia also knew that it could lose by supporting the Syrian regime for too long. What would happen to its business contacts and dreams of a maritime military presence in the Mediterranean under a new, and probably anti-Russian government? Russian flags had been frequently burned by Syrian protesters. In addition, Russia came under domestic pressure itself when the largest demonstrations since the foundation of the new Russian state in 1991 filled the streets in Moscow and elsewhere to question the legitimacy of the parliamentary elections of December 2011. So Russian President Dmitry Medvedev, as well as his antecessor and successor Vladimir Putin, suddenly depended on Western goodwill in order to keep business as usual. After year-long negotiations Russia was finally accepted into the World Trade Organization (WTO), also in December of that year. All these were factors that played a role with Russian strategists. Russia was not interested in an escalation of events. Under Russian influence, the Asad regime held a (very ambiguous) referendum for a new constitution in February 2012. However, Moscow remained obstinate in the UN Security Council and hoped that the Asad regime would weather the storm.

Historically remarkable was the fact that Arabs, after decades of infighting, struggled to build a consensus. Western intervention, as in Libya, bore high political costs in Syria and was not a welcomed option by either side. For the first time in its history, the Arab League showed determination and announced suspension of the membership of one of its members and founding states, Syria. However, tensions among the Arab states remained and Syria managed to outmaneuver the League by posing conditions of an observation mission. Thus it bought several months' time until a reduced and not very effective mission was finally on the ground. The Arab League's declaratory determination may never be equal to its opportunities for political and military action. And, it soon became clear that the Arabs did not speak with one voice on the Syrian. The Gulf monarchies took a tougher stand. They condemned the regime in Damascus even though other Arab states kept silence in an attempt to avoid an internationalization of the conflict.

However, looking at the general picture, after the revolutions in Tunisia and Egypt human rights violations became an issue in the League that had awakened. New democratic voices now formed part of the once mildewed club of autocrats. This new impetus blended with old animosities among the remaining autocrats themselves. This led to a more and more anti-Syrian stance, however temporary. It was a tightrope walk for anti-Syrian Saudi Arabia, Qatar, and other autocratic monarchies to condemn human rights violations in Syria. Obviously, a pro-democracy discourse from their side did not look very credible. A few months earlier, Saudi Arabia had sent tanks into Bahrain to help the Sunni Kingdom clamp down on a mainly Shiite driven democracy movement. Accordingly, fear of an increasing Shiite influence in the Levant through Iran was one of the driving forces to get tough on the Syrian regime. There was also rising concern about long-lasting instability in Syria and a rising influence of al-Qaida or other radical groups once the country had been ripped apart by civil war. Reconstructing stability and a monopoly of state power is a painstaking process, as the experience in Iraq have shown.

A realignment of power structures in the new Arab World was in full progress. The Gulf Cooperation Council—a club of Gulf monarchies—suddenly invited Morocco and Jordan to join them. The only similarity between these groups of states was that they were monarchies that started to design an axis of their own. Cooperation among the countries in transition or in internal conflict was limited by contrast. The reformers had plenty of national tasks ahead of them instead. Apart from pan-Arab TV stations that created a common audience and a similar narrative of events, official declarations of solidarity remained rare. National Arab nationalism proved again stronger than pan-Arab bonds. Exceptions were the Tunisian engagement of taking over thousands of Libyan refugees in their common border zone or the participation of some Libyan rebels in the Syrian scenario. After the Libyan government, the authorities in Tunis followed suit by recognizing the SNC as the legitimate Syrian representative while, at the end of 2011, it closed down the Syrian embassy and expelled the Syrian ambassador. In a bitter irony, the only formal pre-Arab-Spring democracies—Lebanon and Iraq—stood by the side of the Syrian regime and did not participate in the Arab League's sanctions. This was due to significant Syrian influence on their Shiite-dominated governments. Harmony within the Arab League has always been a rare and short-lived experience.

14
Syrian Scenarios

Every Syrian considers himself a politician, one in two regards himself as a national leader, one in four thinks he is a prophet, and one in ten thinks he is God. How is it possible to rule such a country?

Former Syrian President Shoukri al-Quwatli issued the above warning to his Egyptian counterpart Gamal Abdul Nasser in 1958 on the eve of Syria's union with Egypt. These words have since become a proverbial saying throughout Syria. When Quwatli coined this bon mot, Syria had just gone through a brief and turbulent phase of democratic experiments. It was also a heyday of ideological politics and a struggle for self-orientation following colonial oppression. Throughout Syria's modern history, debates have always been heavily loaded with ideas and ideology, less with religious or ethnic discourse, despite its societal mosaic. This became obvious again at the time of the uprising when it proved a headache for Syrian opposition currents to find a common platform. Domesticating the tribal patchwork of Libya during the battles against Qaddafi's forces almost looked like a cakewalk, by comparison.

A lead blanket of silence had been lying over the Syrian population for five decades of Baath rule, crippling civil society and many political ideals. Under the cover, however, Syrian society had not become entirely silent. Be it in spite of, or because of, the domestic rigidity during the Asad years, Syrian society possessed a large variety of moderate forces, an intelligent opposition, and the capacity for religious tolerance—something that appears almost naïve and unreal to mention following rising sectarianism in the wake of the violence against the popular protests of 2011. But it was indeed a remarkable achievement that could not be taken for granted in the Middle East. Below the surface, mistrust between religious groups had always existed. Yet it had not become the primary element of discourse until the regime finally unmasked itself and chose sectarianism as a tool for its survival.

With the outbreak of the Arab Spring in Syria, the waves of popular protests were edging ever further toward the Middle East conflict. With Syria in turmoil, repercussions for the Middle East conflict were more significant than the impact of other revolutions, such as in Tunisia, and even in Egypt. Unlike Egypt, Syria had not signed a peace treaty with Israel. Any new political leadership would not be bound to formal agreements in this respect. And an old leadership struggling for survival was likely to cross formerly respected lines. For a stumbling old regime, regional confrontation was one option of last resort, a desperate gambit before the downfall. For a new political elite of whatever kind, the Golan question would become an issue of equal importance, regarding domestic legitimacy. In their manifestos the opposition platforms that came up in 2011, most notably the SNC, all referred, in some way or the other, to the Golan problem. Although they stressed that they intended to pursue this issue with all possible diplomatic and political means. The Syrian-Palestinian intrusion into Israeli occupied Druze villages in the Golan in May 2011 was a foretaste of what kind of alternative forms of protest existed beyond negotiation tables. In any case, the unresolved territorial dispute with Israel—more than the unresolved Israeli-Palestinian issue—was likely to remain a tool to divert the Syrian people from domestic problems.

Moreover, in the years following the Iraq war from which Iran emerged as a net winner, Syria and Lebanon developed more notably into the interface of the Saudi-Sunni and Persian-Shiite spheres of interest. The fault lines of this growing power struggle extend right through the Levant. In a long-term perspective, Syria had to worry about its influence in Lebanon. Syria's rising domestic challenges put a question mark on the degree of influence that Damascus still had over Hezbollah, and to what extent Hezbollah would overcome its weakness and reestablish sufficient power to dictate terms of its own. Moreover, Iran's direct influence in Lebanon was rising. A Syrian nightmare was that one day Syria would be reduced to a logistical interface between Iran and Hezbollah, or even a junior partner. The overwhelmingly warm welcome of Iran's President Ahmedinejad in Lebanon in mid October 2010 was the most visible aspect of this development. During Ahmedinejad's visit, the British *Daily Telegraph* presciently titled: "A landlord visiting his domain."[1]

As for radical Sunnis: Syria, because of its proximity to Israel, could turn into a strategic playground for al-Qaida. The call from al-Qaida leader Ayman al-Zawahiri in February 2012 to support the protests in Syria did not help the opposition's cause at all. It rather reflected an ancient and deep animosity between the Asad regime and the Islamic fanatics. No one in the Syrian opposition picked up this statement of support. It was embarrassing because it played into the tactics of the regime that had always presented itself as the defender of secularism and rule of law against Islamic fundamentalism and civil war. But as part of the self-fulfilling prophecy, al-Qaida inspired jihadists were reported to be on their way from Iraq to Syria to help topple the Asad regime—some of whom were Syrians who had radicalized in Iraq when they had supported the Iraqi resistance against the United States.

Syria, a country that for many years had been fighting Islamic extremism and terrorism—although often left alone in its efforts by the West because of US and Israeli pressures—might lose the capacity of fighting on this domestic front. Sadiq Jalal al-Azm had predicted weeks before the Syrian uprising: "If the revolts reach Syria, it will become far bloodier than in Tunisia or Egypt because of the sectarian nature of Syrian politics."[2]

Instability in Syria was also a worst-case scenario for Israeli security strategists. Syria had always been a stable and reliable enemy. If it was politically opportune, Syria used to be capable and willing to restrain Hezbollah's shelling of northern Israel. It was Asad who dissuaded Ahmedinejad, during his visit to southern Lebanon, from throwing stones toward the Israeli border. The occupied Golan Heights served both Syria and Israel as a welcome status quo, too. During the upheavals, Syrian opposition figures commented with skepticism on the lifting of Syria's Emergency Laws from 1963. They reminded everyone that the regime had always justified the state of emergency as a response to the state of war with Israel. Suddenly, without a peace treaty the state of emergency was lifted—at least rhetorically—due to street pressure. Adding fuel to the fire, the fourth branch of the presidential guard that was commanded by Bashar al-Asad's brother Maher was militarily responsible for the Golan dossier—and it was Maher who commanded the bloody clampdown on the people's protest in Dara'a and thereafter. Some of the protesters shouted: "Maher you coward. Send your troops to liberate the Golan."[3]

And thus in May 2012 as this book goes to press, the outcome of the Syrian struggle was unclear. On the other hand, it *was* clear that regardless of the way events unfolded, in the end the region would face an altogether changed neighbor. The events of 2011 and beyond represented a point of no return for Bashar al-Asad, personally and politically. At this moment, the following five scenarios still look possible.

One: Regime Survival with Bashar al-Asad

After a months-long war of attrition, the regime may be able to suppress and suffocate the upheavals through brutal force, targeted arrests, sophisticated intelligence work, and clever stonewalling tactics vis-à-vis the Arab League and Western governments. Asad would, ever more, grow into the traditional role defined by his father Hafez who had successfully ruled with blood on his hands after the massacre in Hama in 1982. At that time however, his father faced a stark choice vis a vis militant Islamists: kill or be killed. At the outset, his son did not face a violent threat. Instead, *he* was the one who chose to kill.

In this scenario of regime survival, the younger Asad would be able to continue his career in Syrian politics, at least for some time, by playing the sectarian card. At the very least he would face a more sectarian society fueled by extremists on all sides. Asad himself might still be able to rely on most Christians and Alawites (although they, like the opposition, might be personally appalled by the regime's violence). The alternatives presented by the United States in Iraq did not look convincing to Syrians. The primordialization of politics next door provided the Syrian regime—and large parts of the Syrian population—with arguments for preserving the status quo. It did not matter if Syria was different from Iraq. This was the narrative.

Asad might also manage to forge new alliances, in an alternating manner, as his father did. With promises of restoring stability, he might also be able to maintain the bond with the pragmatic Sunni merchant class, although it would be a crumbling pillar of acquiescence and support. For this to succeed, an economic upswing was required in order to distribute wealth and privileges, as in the past. At this point, this looked almost impossible to manage after the damage the crisis had inflicted on Syria's economy, and after the imposition of strangling sanctions. No easing of Syria's isolation was to be expected if the regime stayed in place. However, Syria still enjoyed loyal neighbors and trading partners such as Lebanon, Iraq, and Iran. In addition, Russian and Chinese relations remained commercially important.

Domestically, power relations have started to be fundamentally renegotiated. Key posts were reshuffled amidst rumors of open discord between Asad and the security services, between Asad and the army, between Bashar and other members of the Asad clan and, possibly, between Alawites, Sunnis, and others in the upper echelons who belonged to other sects. In this scenario, Asad would hardly have any legitimacy left based on soft power and would depend almost exclusively on his security apparatus and on ruthless members of his family clan like Maher al-Asad, Asef Shawkat, or (in the economic realm) Rami Makhlouf. After deciding in favor of the "security solution," Asad owes the clan a great deal. He is especially indebted to Maher, who was responsible for starting the violence. The country would be run by a new triumvirate of power—Bashar, Maher, Asef—with Bashar trying to play the good cop (or the less evil cop) to the bad cops played by his partners. Despite the thorough reshuffling of power elites after the death of his father, Bashar did not have a power base that could have supported him through the violence. It was Maher who controlled the army units on which the clan could still rely, and Asef Shawkat had his hand on the secret services. Somewhere floating in between were the *shabbiha* gangs that ravaged the country by command of local Alawite thugs. Whatever the precise lines of authority at a given moment, this crew would continue to be close. They were a team. And they were playing a game with extremely high stakes.

As long as Bashar al-Asad was of use to the clan, it did not make sense to dispose of him. He could reach certain constituencies inside Syria, perhaps, or he could connect with internationals. Bashar at times seemed to be a political lightweight, muddleheaded, crazy, aloof from reality, aloof from reality (or from everything a bit). The crisis also steeled his cynicism and ruthlessness, and he turned out to be a ruler with an iron but shaking fist.

In this scenario, Asad would continue to play the tunes of false alternatives such as "Islamism and chaos, or Baath rule and law and order." And he may see a need to get tougher with the external enemy, Israel, to compensate for his loss of credibility among Syrians. Those who had still hoped that the president would embark on reforms would finally turn away from him. Asad would survive for some time in a wounded and crippled country. Syria's ruined economic and narrowed foreign policy options would be a heavy burden for him. The foreign policy successes of the past two years, before the revolution, are lying in tatters.

Even if Asad survived the protests, it was improbable that he would ever recover politically, and be able to rebuild the foreign policy environment that he had so arduously worked to achieve. He would have to rely, ever more, on his staunchest ally Iran, and on Hezbollah, whereas during his father Hafez's times, it was rather Hezbollah that relied on Damascus. The Asads had their backs against the wall. A radical perestroika would have destroyed their regime as they understood it. After clamping down on the Damascus Spring, Asad would become known as the grave digger of the Arab Spring in Syria.

Two: Regime survival without Asad

Since 2005, Asad has had to live with rumors or real threats of coup d'états. People in his entourage doubted if he would be able to defend the interests of the country or, more importantly, of the ruling elites. After the catastrophe of 2011, a putsch would likely be led by Asad's brother Maher who would have had much to lose in case of a transition or regime collapse. For many years, the circle around Asad's sister Bushra and Asef Shawkat had its share of friction with the president and his wife In addition, a few key intelligence and military figures could also participate in a coup. It is possible, however, that removing Bashar would lead to a collapse of the regime. Anyone else from within the power circle would possess even less recognition and allegiance from the remaining loyalists among the Syrian people, mostly minorities, who still adhere to the status quo.

If Asad survived such a scenario, he could paint himself as the weak but willing reformer who was unable to finish his task because of insurmountable vested interests. In particular, Syrians who had profited from the selective economic opening Bashar brought to Syria might be inclined to accept this version of events.

Three: National Reconciliation & Gradual Transition with Asad

This possibility was especially supported by Michel Kilo, and the CCDC, for a considerable period of time, as mentioned in detail above. But the minimal precondition—stopping the violence and releasing all political prisoners—was never met by the regime. At the time when this book was written, it remained questionable if these initiatives would survive the dynamic of events. One year after the uprising started, even moderates like Kilo had to admit that one cannot prevent people from taking up arms in self-defense, given the indiscriminate slaughter of civilians.

Four: Chaos and Civil War

This scenario has been the most deterring one for many Syrians. The fear of the unknown was stronger than in Tunisia or Egypt. A mere thirty years ago, the last civil war in Syria ended with the massacre in Hama. Since then Syrians enjoyed a period of exceptional security and stability whereas examples of civil strife, sectarian clashes, crime, and terrorism ravaged around Syrian borders. The Baath regime tapped these fears—a well-known discourse also to other Arab Spring states. It was the autocrats who inferred chaos and intended to criminalize the opposition shortly before they finally stumbled. Also in Syria, thousands of protesters who dared to go out into the streets were labelled criminals, terrorists, Islamists, or sectarian bandits. Having said this, radicals and thugs mingled with the protests because of the scale, length, and brutal escalation of events.

The narratives started to drift apart amidst violence, fear, and propaganda. Alawites complained about Sunni gangs who raided their villages and vice versa. Slogans such as "Christians to Lebanon and Alawites into coffins" intimidated the minorities. Since the 1960s, mostly Alawite peasants had risen in the Baathist and military circles and migrated to the urban centers. Hafez al-Asad himself was Syria's first ruler of peasant extraction.[4] Historically, Syrian had few ghettos. Mixed or at least open cities and also mixed neighborhoods had been the norm.

At the end of 2011 observers on the ground said that Alawite families started to sell their apartments in Homs, one of the areas most affected by the protests and increasingly divided in animosity between Alawite and Sunni neighborhoods. They withdrew into the Alawite mountains between Homs and Latakia. Many still had family houses or holiday houses in the pleasant climates and green landscape. Some Alawites moved back to the mountains for good. Other observers reported that weaponry and money were transported to the mountains from Damascus. Some even spoke of an Alawite rump state that was to be defended in the worst case. This made reference to the short-lived Alawite State of Latakia *(Dawlat Jabal al-'Alawiyin)* in time of the French Mandate in 1922. In a strategy of divide-and-rule the French had granted the Alawites a state of their own as a reward for their political support.

But this tendency to return to the roots went counter to the more recent historical record of Alawites who had been fighting side by side in nationalist struggles in modern Syria starting from the upheaval against the

French mandate to Alawite participation in nationalist, leftist and pan-Arab movements and parties. During the violence of the 21st century, however, Syrian society began to segregate.

On the military level, Syria was drifting more toward a Libyan scenario than an Egyptian or Tunisian one. Elite troops such as the Presidential Guard were under tight control of the Asad clan. Mostly composed out of hand-picked Alawites, they faced a win-all or lose-all scenario. During the protests the regime mainly fell back on these troops for good reason. For the ordinary army of conscripts, mostly Sunni in nature, was in a dismal state of frustration, corruption, poverty and poor equipment. Cases of intra-army strife bloodily increased, including the killing of soldiers by soldiers who had refused to shoot civilians. The Syrian government at some point stopped using Sunni pilots because there were reports that defectors had planned to bomb the presidential palace in Damascus. Segregation took its course in Syria's institutions, too.

The Local Organization Committees—the grass roots bodies of the street demonstrators—tried to prevent a violent escalation and insisted on peaceful protests despite of the mortal danger involved. This did not always succeed. The army was in danger of splitting into frustrated and appalled soldiers who joined the rebels of the Free Syrian Army on the one side and Asad loyal elite troopers on the other side. Other than in Libya, the Syrian rebels did not hold a coherent territory and the regime's troops made great efforts to prevent precisely this scenario.

This led to a prolonged conflict of attrition. Since any form of regional or international intervention would affect the complex power fabric in the region, any action in Syria implied much higher costs than in Libya. Thus the Syrian actors on the ground were likely to continue their struggle without a major foreign intervention in sight. Support trickled in on sub-state levels, instead, and increasingly by arms deliveries from Gulf countries. According to the opposition, the Asad regime brought in Shiite militias from Iraq and Iranian revolutionary guards to support the dismembering Syrian armed forces. Hezbollah tried to keep a low profile because of its shrinking popularity among Arabs in the street. But the group obviously feared the collapse of the regime in Damascus and contributed with fighters and arms, too. In addition, the pro-Hezbollah government in Lebanon did not prevent Syrian forces from entering its territory to track down fleeing opposition figures. Syria's continued presence in Lebanon on the level of *mukhabarat* activities aggravated the fact that Syrian refugees could not feel safe in Lebanon. In turn, according to the Syrian government, arms smuggling increased in favor of the Free Syrian Army and possibly other groups. Avenues were available via Turkey, Jordan, and Lebanon.

With centrifugal forces in full sway, with the segregation of society and institutions under way, the stockpiling of arms meant very dim prospects. The longer the conflict ravaged the country, the more difficult it would become to restore Syria's peaceful societal mosaic. The notoriously strong monopoly of power of the Syrian state was crumbling in one of the most contested regions of the world. Part of this scenario was the possibility that pockets of the country would remain "liberated territory" for a while to come. Dozens of mostly Sunni villages in the Idlib province in Syria's north-West were referred to as liberated zones by the opposition in 2011. The power vacuum was an additional invitation to drug dealing and gang crimes. In the worst case, some main urban centers such as Aleppo, Damascus, or the Druze capital of Sweida in the south might remain under full government control while wide areas in between became no-go zones for the regime's forces.

Syria, once the self-confident, pragmatic middle power under Hafez al-Asad and the incarnation of authoritarian stability in the region, could turn into a chessboard of conflicting interests, a hub for arms trade and instability. The terrain for proxy wars would extend from Lebanon on the one side and Iraq on the other. It would turn Syria into a new crescent of instability. No matter how the events in Syria unfolded and to which scenario they would follow, Syria was shaken beyond return. Domestic power structures were shifting. The regime had destroyed its legacy. Only a less evil scenario than the one described here would avoid the decomposition of Syria's social fabric and stop the decline of Syria's weight in the region.

Five: Regime Change & Democratization

In spite of these dim projections a glance at Syria's history brings about encouraging aspects, too. First, Syrian society for centuries had been known for its moderate and tolerant approach in religious matters throughout the rule of foreign dynasties and empires. Most of Syria's Sunnis (roughly two-thirds of the population) have traditionally been more interested in good trade relations than in religious dogmatism or fanaticism. The politics of the Baath regime continued this tradition of a peaceful co-existence of religious groups and of granting privileges for religious minorities. The predominantly Alawite regime had always relied on minority support, especially from Druze and Christian constituencies. Finally, the Asad dynasty promoted moderate religious leaders (although sometimes opportunists) and had a record of fighting Islamist currents.

The entrepreneur, Ihsan Sanqer, calculated in 2004 that Asad would have gained a popular election for president because of minority and moderate Sunni support. After all, in the good times he had the support of the minorities who accounted for nearly a third of the population. "These people [the minorities] may be the most unsecular of all in their way of thinking," said Sanqer when he resided still in Damascus, "but they have to pretend to be secular because it is necessary for their financial and political survival." If we add ten percent of progressive Sunnis to the minorities, we come to a secular base of forty percent of the population. "Syria is perhaps the only country in the region that can regard itself as secular. Even Turkey and Israel are becoming less and less secular," the businessman added.[5]

Historian Sami Moubayed presented a similar estimate in 2011. He held the view that demographics in Syria spoke against even the surge of political Islam in general. In his words: "Ten per cent of the population is Christian, and they would never vote for the [Muslim] Brotherhood. Neither would the fifteen percent Alawite and Shiite communities, or the three per cent Druze, or two per cent "others" (Circassians, Jews, Ismailis). Then come fifteen per cent Syrian Kurds and ten per cent tribes and Bedouins, who although Sunni Muslims, would also never support an Islamic party. That adds up to fifty-five per cent, topped with no less than twenty-five per cent of Syria's seventy-five per cent Sunni majority, who are seculars or ordinary Syrians simply un-attracted to political Islam." If this calculation would also hold true after a civil war remained an open question. According to Moubayed, in any parliamentary elections the Muslim Brotherhood or its sister groups would not take more than twenty to twenty-five per cent of any incoming Chamber. "Meaning, in true internationally-monitored parliamentary elections, Islamic-driven parties like the Brotherhood would be unable to rule on their own with no coalition parties, as [is] the case with the Al Nahda Party in Tunisia," Moubayed concluded.[6]

One important thing would be the design of the political arena: parties with an exclusively ethnic or religious orientation could remain banned, as was the case in socialist Yugoslavia, for example. On the other hand, the argument that Islam and democracy do not go together was qualified by enlightened Muslim representatives in Syria and the experience in neighboring Turkey.

In contrast to other Arab states, including Arab Spring states, Syria can look back on some democratic experience. The country enjoyed intermezzi of civilian rule during its turbulent phase after independence in the 1950s. The 1954 elections were regarded as the first free ones in the Arab world. One of the most respected prime ministers of that time, Faris al-Khoury, was a Christian. Although most civilian cabinets were short-lived, Syria has a tradition of democratic thinking and articulation on which political decision-makers could build political narratives. As mentioned above in the chapter on Baathism, the anti-Asad opposition in 2011 chose the old Syrian flag—green, white, black—that was precisely valid during the time of civilian governments in Syria. So the green color that appeared on the opposition flag was no particular allusion to Islam, as some Western observers erroneously presumed, but it showed the will to tie in with Syria's short, albeit turbulent, experience of democracy.

This tradition has led to the self-confidence of parts of the Syrian intelligentsia that sees the roots and key contents of today's Arab revolutions in the Syrian Civil Society Movement and its numerous declarations from the Damascus Spring to subsequent years. The example of Syria's opposition also shows that moderate Islamists and secularists were able to take great steps and approach each other respectfully, at least on an intellectual level. Their rapprochement, or at least their mutual acceptance of each other, was more than simply presenting a common front to the Baath regime. However, this cooperation has never been exposed to the strains of practical politics in Syria, much less to the challenges of a possible moral, political, and physical reconstruction in a post-conflict scenario.

Nevertheless, judging by past experience, Islamists and secularists may be able to find common ground despite their different origins and world views. The Islamic camp in particular continues to face an internal struggle among a wide range of conservative and radical forces. Neither should all Islamic welfare institutions as well as other activities based on religious identity and traditional ties be confused with civil society. The idea of a civil society is that all individuals can engage themselves in projects by their own motivations and out of their own free will. The playing fields should remain open to all. Everybody should be able to freely enter activities or exit them at any time. This was part of the development from a parallel existence of closed communities to an open society. In turn, this is the best foundation for a democracy that does not divide populations into ascribed groups, but leads them to policy-oriented competition. At least, this has been the aim of Syria's Civil Society Movement.

Unfortunately, despite the potential for a rapprochement between religious and secular intellectuals, the reality of everyday life in Syria even before the violence gave reason for skepticism. During the past years, Syrian society has become visibly more conservative. Above all, social pressure on women to obey ever stricter religiously interpreted norms increased; others found new niches of freedom through mobile phones and the Internet; and again others combined conservative Islam with modern technology and status symbols. The rift in the population between supporters of secularism and conservative Islamic forces has grown.

With the escalation of violence and its longer term repercussions, former prerequisites for democracy that existed in Syria might lose importance— or they might help to prevent the country from sliding into a worse state. Among them was the general level of education that, despite its deficiencies and rising influence of both Saudi financed *madrasas* and the distortions of Baath textbooks, looked good compared to other Arab countries. Important contents of education, including a high proficiency of classical Arabic, were part of the informal and oral family tradition of urban merchants. Women have enjoyed considerable rights and might be able to exercise a perceptible political influence under democratic conditions.

In addition to those observations, the economic divide was not as great as in other countries, thus the danger of social tension was smaller. But the gap had been growing, also very notably between urban progress and rural stagnation. The economy has been additionally strangled by the violence. Before 2011 the low non-state violence had also been a positive indicator for chances of a transition toward pluralism or even democracy. Syria possessed a state machinery that functioned down to the lowest levels: parking tickets were issued and generally paid, to list just one example that was far from a given in some other Arab countries. In other words, internal stability—that was thoughtlessly destroyed in Iraq—gave the country the potential basis for a relatively fair and orderly transition to some form of political participation. All this had been put at stake for the survival of one family clan.

There was another helpful factor: Syria does not have much oil. As Herbert Kitschelt and others concluded after evaluating data on several Muslim nations, the chances for democracy are greatest in countries with low oil reserves. Conversely, the staying power of authoritarian and predatory regimes is highest when those in power can fall back on rich oil resources, and/or when a large amount of oil wealth is accumulated in the hands of a few people. When lacking oil resources, the rulers have to look for a more differentiated constituency, including peasants, traders, and craftsmen. Neither are they able to pacify the population with endless acts of generosity.[7]

On the level of international and regional politics, a new Syria led by members of the Syrian National Council, for example, would experience an abrupt shift of power alignments, too. Taking declarations of the SNC as an indicator, in which the Sunni Muslim Brotherhood was strongly represented, Syria would orient itself more toward the Arab states again, toward Turkey and cautiously toward the West and, most importantly, away from Iran. This was an obvious reason why Iran beefed up its efforts to prevent this from happening.

Iran was interested in a stable Syria—under its influence. When it came to stability, Asad might not have been the man anymore. But there was little choice from the Iranian point of view, until things cooled down, to open the way for an intra-regime replacement of the president. By contrast, what SNC-President Burhan Ghalioun had in mind was a horror scenario for Teheran: "The current relationship between Syria and Iran is abnormal. It is unprecedented in Syria's foreign policy history," he said in an interview in December 2011. "A new Syria will be an indispensable part of the Arab League and it will work on improving the role of the Arab League and the role of Arab states regionally, specifically because they took a historic and unprecedented decision to back the Syrian people. . . . Breaking the exceptional relationship [with Iran] means breaking the strategic military alliance. We do not mind economic relations." Breaking with Iran would also have repercussions for Lebanon. "As our relations with Iran change, so too will our relationship with Hezbollah," Ghalioun said. "Hezbollah after the fall of the Syrian regime will not be the same. Lebanon should not be used as it was used in the Assad era as an arena to settle political scores."[8] From a tactical perspective, with these declarations Ghalioun hardened the Iranian regime's support for Asad and closed doors for possible two-track diplomacy between the SNC and Teheran. Obviously, the breaking away of Syria from the Iranian orbit could only be achieved by regime change. It was something that Western states had tried in vain for years with Asad in power.

In the case of regime change and the absence of civil war, the necessity of shaping a new social contract in Syria would come to the fore. National unity needs to be redefined as an equality of religions and ethnic groups alike. Arab nationalism proved a flawed vehicle, although when looking at Syria's opposition, there is a possibility that future decision-makers will chose it, once again, as an umbrella for national unity. This time it may be embedded in a new form of inter-Arab cooperation within a revitalized Arab League. This is a positive development without any doubt. It creates political ownership and capacities of intra-Arab conflict solution after colonialist and neo-imperialist discourse in the past. It is also a logical consequence of the Arab Spring, since it was Arabs, without any foreign help, who managed to shake the region and topple at least some of their dictators. Arabism, however, should be used with caution and not as an antipode to ethnic minorities as it happened with the Kurds in the past. Otherwise, also Asad's successors will face a Kurdish problem and perhaps a self-inflicted Iraqi scenario of some sort. Veritably, civil societies and polities would be a modern outcome of a revolution with modern features and impulses.

In any case, particular sensitivity must be given to the minorities that had supported the Asad regime for presumed reasons of safety and collective survival. The challenge for possible new rulers of Syria will be to refute the false alternatives of either chaos or the Asad regime, either radical Islamism or authoritarian secularism. The various grey shades in between will determine possible paths of the future. New leaders will need time and a lot of effort to convince the minorities that an Iraqi fate can be avoided.

The problem lies in the fact that powerful external players tend to intrude into Syrian affairs, including Saudi Arabia. Since the 1980s, the Wahhabi Kingdom has been able to establish a plethora of Quran schools and cultural institutions in Syria. This patchwork of islands of influence can be widened by additional petrodollars as has happened elsewhere. Not many Syrians are interested in falling from an Iranian embracement into a Saudi one. It will be up to the moderate Sunni believers, sheikhs, and merchants to resist this pressure and to make sure that they will not fall into traps either in the direction of intolerance and radicalism nor in that of opportunistic alliances with totalitarian ideologies in the name of stability.

Despite incredible violence and the engineering of sectarian provocations, Syrian society has not let itself be infected yet by this virus on a large scale. Only in some hot spot areas like in Homs and surrounding villages violent sectarianism has been on the rise and will probably continue to simmer in a post Asad scenario until the wounds are healed. Syrian history of religious accommodation speaks a different language. Even in 2011 and beyond, it was a hopeful indicator that the civil protests and the organized opposition, inside or outside Syria, at no point targeted Alawites as a group or made minorities responsible for the existence or stability of the Asad regime (although they could have done more to placate minorities' fears).

Contrary to the negative incidents described above that fueled communal mistrust or even violence, there existed positive examples where residents counteracted sectarian provocations with inter-communal communication and demonstrated solidarity. In other Arab Spring contexts, minorities were equally hesitant to support the protests in the beginning. In Egypt the Coptic minority supported the Mubarak regime until fall. Then, it sided with the revolutionaries. In Syria, too, nothing indicated that Christians or Druze would take up arms in order to defend an increasingly dysfunctional Asad regime.[9] Still, with the tactics of regime survival, civil strife and sectarianism had become an imminent danger for Syria as hardly ever before in its recent history.

Very probably, on the political level one of the uniting platforms in post-Asad Syria will be a new impetus to recover the Golan Heights—in a negotiated agreement. This issue has already been included in the first declarations of Syria's new opposition. A post-Asad Syria would be too weak and too unwilling to embark on military adventures. It would be even less apt to match Israel in asymmetric warfare than the Asad regime. From an Israeli perspective, instability would be the worst enemy because, in the complex Levantine scenario, it would entail a high degree of asymmetric threat. Syrian politicians should avoid, however, using the Golan file once again as a distraction from domestic insufficiencies. Nothing is wrong with getting back the Golan from a Syrian perspective but it would be wrong to neglect problems that affect the Syrian population more directly. No Arab leader after the Arab Spring should forget why the rebellions broke out. The future will be measured by economic growth and acceptable public policies on the technocratic side as well as accountability—or dignity as the protesters called it—and freedom on the normative side.

Also in Syria it is time to thrust aside overloaded ideological debates that stem from times of heteronomy (colonial times) and to tackle the practical problems of the country. Dwindling oil resources, an underdeveloped countryside where large parts suffer from drought and bad public policy management, a growing gap between rich and poor, weak economic performance, insufficient education for world market competition, wealth threatening demographic growth, and the necessity to break up long-standing predatory arrangements are some of the challenges that lie ahead. Of course, on the ideological side the role of Islam will remain a major issue of intra-societal contest. The hope of the majority of the Syrian population lies in the predictions given by many Syrians themselves—including opposition figures—that moderate Islam would prevail in a new Syria.

Another challenge will be a successful management of transitional justice after the scale of cruelties that occurred. The balance between justice on the one hand and peace on the other hand is a tightrope walk. As in other countries of transition—be it in South Africa or Latin America or in this very Arab neighborhood after the Arab Spring—peace and justice remain in a state of tension. Both will not be entirely fulfilled at the same time. The degree to which citizens are ready for reconciliation depends a lot on the establishment of trust in the new institutions and on credible moral leaders who have a moderating influence and who stand for the fulfillment of promises. In the Syrian context it will also be crucial how much sectarianism will prevail in a new political setting, not only with regard to violence but also in legislation, and how much of the state's monopoly of power can be re-established. If people feel the threat of revenge, they will hesitate to give up arms, and reconciliation will remain a distant goal.

In every transition it proves a challenge to convince people not to dash everything that had existed before simply because it belonged to the old order. As described in the chapters above, Syria has developed valuable assets—some because of and some in spite of Baathism—that are worth keeping. A rich heritage has also developed from Syria's intellectual history, most recently by the year-long struggle of the Civil Society Movement. Although its protagonists were overtaken by the developments and protesters in the street, they had developed moderate, conciliatory, and secular ideas to build on. Whatever the long-term results of the Arab Spring will be in Syria, one thing is certain: Against the background of the tremendous tasks that lie ahead, the Syrian people cannot afford and do not deserve another decade of lost chances. If the most grim scenarios unfold, however, the next decade may be much worse for many Syrians than it was, prior to Arab Spring, under the rule of Asad.

- Resources -

Endnotes

1 Hariqa: The Fire Spreads

1 Al-Makhadhi, in: *Global Post*, 18 February 2011. The Hariqa scene on *youtube*: www.youtube. com/watch?v=qDHLsU-ik_Y (retrieved on 26 Nov 2011).

2 "Syrian MP calls for review of harsh emergency laws," in: *The National*, 11 March 2011.3 "Middle East unrest: Syria arrests Damascus protesters," in: BBC *online*, 16 March 2011 (www. bbc.co.uk/news/world-middle-east-12757394).

4 Abbas, in: *Arab Reform Brief* (2011).

5 Fischer, in: *Internationale Politik* (2011).

6 "Syrian Businessman Becomes Magnet for Anger and Dissent," in: *New York Times*, 30 April 2011.

7 Abouzeid, in: *Time online*, 19 March 2011.

8 Abouzeid, in: *Time online*, 19 March 2011.

9 "Tortured and killed: Hamza al-Khateeb, age 13," in: *al-Jazeera online*, 31 May 2011.

10 Ismail, in: *Index on Censorship* (2011).

11 www.youtube.com/watch?v=hciFvV-7wOw&feature=player_embedded&skipcontrinter=1.

12 Abbas, in: *Arab Reform Brief* (2011), mentions 450,000 to 500,000 soldiers while Hermann, in: *Frankfurter Allgemeine Zeitung*, 8 February 2012, writes about 220,000 ground troops and 100,000 air force soldiers. He puts the number of tanks at 5,000 and the number of combat planes at 550.

13 The earliest incident of mass casualties on the government side was reported from Jisr al-shughour close to the Turkish border where 120 security men were killed in an ambush in early June. The official version is that rebels were responsible. The opposition says that they were shot by their own comrades because they refused to obey the orders to shoot at civilians. Subsequently, the army entered the town and caused many more deaths as well as the first considerable flow of refugees toward Turkey.

14 Hermann, in: *Frankfurter Allgemeine Zeitung*, 9 November 2011.

15 See also Abbas in: *Arab Reform Brief* (2011).

2 Regime Reflexes & Reactions

1 Abdulhamid, in: *The Guardian*, 7 February 2011; Luca, in: *Now Lebanon*, 10 February 2011; Haddad, in: *Jadaliyya*, 9 March 2011.

2 Interview with Syrian President Bashar al-Asad, in: *The Wall Street Journal*, 31 January 2011.

3 Dahi/Munif, in: *inamo* (2011).

4 For more on the fragile alliance between the regime and the Sunni merchant class, see: Ismail, in: Lawson (2009).

5 Interview with Thomas Pierret, in: *Le Nouvel Observateur*, 30 November 2011.

6 Quoted from : Al-Jazeera English service on 8 April 2011 (http://english.aljazeera.net/news/middleeast/2011/04/20114711251531744.html9).

7 "President al-Assad's Speech to the New Government," *SANA* (original English translation), 17 April 2011.

8 In an interview with the author in Italy on 29 October 2011.

9 Interview with the author in Damascus on 6 June 2007.

10 More on the Asad cult see: Wedeen (1999).

11 Interview with the author in Damascus on 23 October 2010.

12 " Neuer Ärger für Assad—Hochrangiger Regierungsbeamter rechnet ab," *dpa*, 4 January 2012, see also the SRCC bulletin "Syrian Revolution News Round-up" of the same day.

13 " Neuer Ärger für Assad—Hochrangiger Regierungsbeamter rechnet ab," *dpa*, 4 January 2012, see also the SRCC bulletin "Syrian Revolution News Round-up" of the same day.

14 "Transcript: ABC's Barbara Walters' Interview With Syrian President Bashar al-Assad," in: ABC *News*, 7 December 2011.

15 Quoted in: ICG Report II, p.12.

16 "Assad's Detachment Reveals Life in Cocoon," *Bloomberg*, 14 December 2011.

17 "President al-Assad to The Sunday Times: Strike Syria and the world will shake," *Sunday Times*, 20 November 2011 (http://www.dp-news.com/en/detail.aspx?articleid=103707).

18 Interview with the author in Italy on 29 October 2011.

19 "Die Vorgabe lag bei 15 bis 20 Demonstranten: Assads Abschussquoten für Scharfschützen," in: *Die Welt*, 16 December 2011.

20 *Al-Sharq al-Awsat*, 9 December 2011; statement published in German on *www.inamo.de* on 15 December 2011.

21 "Makhlouf Says Syria Will Fight Protests Till 'the End'," in: *New York Times*, 10 May 2011.

22 "Re "Syrian Elite to Fight Protests to 'the End'," in: *New York Times*, 11 May 2011.

23 *Al-Akhbar*, 19 June 2011.

24 "Transcript: ABC's Barbara Walters' Interview With Syrian President Bashar al-Assad," *ABC News* 7 December 2011.

25 In this context the primordialization of the conflict means to reduce it to sectarian thinking and incitement.

26 *Al-Jazeera* and *Facebook* sources, 19 June 2011.

27 Ismail, in: *Studies in Ethnicity and Nationalism* (2011).

28 Khaled Yacoub Oweis, *Reuters*, 6 May 2011.

29 "Still bubbling: In Syria's third-biggest city people fear for the future," in: *The Economist*, 16 June 2011.

30 Details and analyses on the new constitution can be found in: El Husseini, in: *spiegel-online* (24 February 2012), Moubayed, in: *Mideast Views* (14 February 2012), Sydow, in: *Zenith* (21 February 2012), interview with Naseef Naem, in: *Zenith* (22 February 2012).

3 A Decade of Lost Chances

1 Inauguration speech of Bashar al-Asad, 17 July 2000, according to the English translation of the state news agency SANA.

2 Inauguration speech of Bashar al-Asad, 18 July 2007, according to the English translation of the state news agency SANA.

3 *Al-Safir*, 15 March 2003.

4 Interview with the author in Berlin on 15 July 2011.

5 Abdul-Ahad, in: *The Guardian*, 11 December 2011.

6 This debate stirred emotions and hit taboos in the United States. In July 2002, Laurent Murawiec, a French neo-conservative who worked in the RAND think tank in Washington, heavily attacked the Saudi connection to international terrorism. In a presentation before the US Defence Policy Board Advisory Committee he called for an "ultimatum to the House of Saud" and described Saudi Arabia the "kernel of evil." When the briefing was leaked, Pentagon and State Department officials distanced themselves from his comments to avert a major diplomatic crisis between the United States and its longtime ally less than a year after the terrorist attacks of 2001. Murawiec was subsequently expelled from RAND (see: "Laurent Murawiec, 58; Strategist Said Saudis Backed Terror," in: *Washington Post*, 14 October 2009).

7 Interview With Syrian President Bashar al-Assad, *The Wall Street Journal*, 31 January 2011

8 According to reports from the opposition Strategic Research and Communication Center (SRCC) in a briefing from 12 November 2011, "the family members of Assad regime officials have been fleeing the country as over a hundred security, army, and government cars are seen daily at the Aleppo International Airport, with mostly women and children accompanying massive loads of luggage. According to airport employees, most of the passports are Latakia issued [i.e. with Alawi background], and most of the flights are fully booked departing to Malaysia, Iran, UAE, China, Ghana, and Nigeria."

9 *SANA*, 20 October 2011.

10 "Syria, Russia, India and China are east," Asad said. "There are many countries that have good relations with Syria whether in the east, in Latin America or in Asia. . . . I don't recall any period in which there weren't [*sic*] under some sort of Western blockade on Syria, but this blockade intensifies during crises, which is why we decided six years ago—in 2005—to head towards the east." President Asad to Rossiya 1 TV on 31 October 2011, quoted according to SANA.

11 Interview with the author in Damascus on 23 October 2010.

12 "Syria Justifies Saudi Military Intervention in Bahrain," in: *al-Sharq al-Awsat*, 20 March 2011.

13 Interview with the author in Damascus on 23 October 2010.

14 Interview with the author in Damascus on 24 October 2010.

15 "Asad Admits Mistakes," in: *The Daily Star,* 11 August 2011. Statement quoted from a release of India's UN mission after a meeting with a delegation from UN Security Council members Brazil, India and South Africa.

16 "Unruhen in Syrien 'Wenn Sie Krieg wollen, können Sie ihn haben'," in: *Süddeutsche Zeitung*, 09 August 2011, translated from German by the author.

17 Hillary Clinton on CBS program "Face the Nation," 26 March 2011.

18 "Assad Has 'Lost Legitimacy,' Clinton Says," in: *Bloomberg*, 11 July 2011 (www.bloomberg.com/news/2011-07-11/clinton-says-assad-lost-legitimacy-after-mob-attacks-embassy.html).

19 "Syria: No Message Was Conveyed between Assad, Davutoğlu," in: *Naharnet Newsdesk*, 6 October 2011 (http://www.naharnet.com/stories/en/16787-syria-no-message-was-conveyed-between-assad-Davutoğlu).

20 Moubayed in: *Mideast Views*, 21 September 2011.

4 Bashar & Breaches in the Leadership

1 "Which Asad?" in: *Associated Press*, 18 March 2005, quoting statements of Makhlouf from July 2000.

2 Landis, in: *The Syria Review* (2004), p.2-3.

3 On Hafez al-Asad's leader cult see: Wedeen (1999).

4 Ayman Abdul Nour in an interview with the author in Damascus on 16 May 2004.

5 Ayman Abdul Nour in an interview with the author in Damascus on 16 May 2004.

6 Interview with the author in Damascus on 5 May 2005.

7 *Akhbar al-Sharq*, 12 April and 16 May 2005.

8 Hinnebusch (2001), p.165.

9 Interview with the author in Damascus on 30 September 2003.

10 Interview with the author in Khaliye Qudsiye on 7 June 2007.

11 Interviews by the author in Damascus; see also ICG Report I, p.4.

12 Interview with the author in Damascus on 23 October 2010.

13 Lesch (2005).

14 "Assad's Detachment Reveals Life in Cocoon," *Bloomberg*, 14 December 2011.

15 Interview with the author in Damascus on 2 November 2003.

16 A concise overview of such key figures can be found in: Leverett (2005), p.71ff.

17 As quoted by *Reuters* on 6 January 2006 ("Syria's Assad slams ex-deputy Khaddam-paper," taken from the Egyptian *Al-Usbua* newspaper), Bashar said: "I wish to say here that no one joined us in the last meeting between me and Hariri, so where did these allegations come from?"

18 Interview with the author in Damascus on 5 May 2005.

19 Interview with the author in Damascus on 28 April 2005.

20 *Reuters*, 7 June 2005.

21 Interview with the author in Damascus on 28 April 2005.

22 The opposition member Haitham al-Manna, quoted from ICG Report II, p.10.

23 Interview with the author in Damascus on 28 October 2010.

24 A good analysis of the Asad regime's handling of resistance is the short piece by Ismail, in: *Index on Censorship*, 8 July 2011.

25 An excellent account of the political and sectarian discourse during the rise of the Baath Party can be found in: van Dam (2011).

26 According to conversations of the author with members of the Syrian opposition during the months of upheaval.

27 *Aljazeera* and *spiegel online*, 23 April 2011.

28 *Al-Arabiya, Now Lebanon, Facebook* sources, 16 January 2011, Bauer, in: *Der Tagesspiegel*, 1 February 2012.

29 "Syrian Minister Appears to Defect and Join Opposition," *New York Times*, 8 March 2012; "Erster syrischer Top-Politiker läuft zu Aufständischen über," *spiegel-online*, 8 March 2012.

30 A good overview with different primary sources is delivered by: "The Mysterious Downfall of Assef Shawkat," in: *Mideast Monitor*, Vol. 3 No. 2, August 2008.

31 "Sicherheitskreise: Putschversuch in Syrien gescheitert," in: *Die Welt*, 7 June 2008 (http://www.welt.de/politik/article2075124/Putschversuch_gegen_Assad_in_Syrien_gescheitert.html).

32 Interview with the author in Damascus on 6 July 2009.

33 "Syrian leader's uncle calls for him to step down," in: *Reuters*, 17 November 2011 (http://af.reuters.com/article/libyaNews/idAFL5E7MH4AU20111117).

5 The Pillars of the Ancient Regime

1 The most widely reported case was that of 15-year-old school boy Mohammed Mulla Eissa who was beaten with truncheons by militiamen in front of his classmates in the streets of Deir al-Zour because he refused to take part in a pro-Asad demonstration. When he lay on the dusty ground, blood streaming out of his mouth, the officer ordered a militiaman: "Shoot him again to make sure he dies!" Some 20,000 people were reported to have taken part in Mohammed's funeral. See: "'Shoot him again to make sure he dies': Boy, 15, gunned down in front of his classmates after refusing to join march in support of Syria's President Assad," in: *Daily Mail online*, 20 November 2011 (http://www.dailymail.co.uk/news/article-2063874/Mohammed-Mulla-Eissa-murder-Boy-15-refused-join-march-Syrias-President-Assad.html#ixzz1fMl9d5Lrhttp://www.dailymail.co.uk/news/article-2063874/Mohammed-Mulla-Eissa-murder-Boy-15-refused-join-march-Syrias-President-Assad.html#ixzz1eLohsL5y).

2 ICG Report II, p.9.

3 UNWRA statistics as of 1 January 2011 (http://www.unrwa.org/etemplate.php?id=253).

4 Perthes (2002), p.212; Leverett (2005), p.124.

5 Quoted from Leverett (2005), p.125.

6 "Politik, Gewalt und Religion in Palestine," Interview with Mashaal, in: *Neue Züricher Zeitung*, 8 May 2004.

7 "Hamas leader Meshal 'leaves Syria for Sudan'," in: *Haaretz*, 2 September 2008 (http://www.haaretz.com/news/hamas-leader-meshal-leaves-syria-for-sudan-1.253064).

8 "Syria's Assad seems to suggest backing for Hamas negotiable, leaked cables say," in: *The Chicago Tribune* and *Los Angeles Times*, 2 December 2010 (www.chicagotribune.com/news/nation-

world/la-fg-wikileaks-syria-20101202,0,2255930.story).

9 *Al-Hayat*, 6 December 2011.

10 "Syria's Assad seems to suggest backing for Hamas negotiable, leaked cables say," in: *The Chicago Tribune* and *Los Angeles Times*, 2 December 2010 (www.chicagotribune.com/news/nationworld/la-fg-wikileaks-syria-20101202,0,2255930.story).

11 Interview with the author in Damascus on 2 November 2003.

12 Perthes, in: *Adelphi Paper* (2004), p.63.

13 Interview with the author in Damascus on 29 March 2004.

14 *Al-Hayat* 28 July 2003.

15 Interview with the author in Damascus on 28 April 2003.

16 Interview with the author in Damascus on 4 April 2003.

17 Interview with a representative of the Jewish community in Damascus on 17 September 2003.

18 Hinnebusch (2001), p.19-20 from Quilliam (1999).

19 Interview with the author in Damascus on 23 October 2010.

20 *New York Times*, 5 August 2004; *Counter Punch*, 10 August 2004; *Washington Times*, 23 February 2005.

21 "Iraqi refugees in Syria reluctant to return to home permanently: survey," UNHCR, 8 October 2010 (http://www.unhcr.org/4caf376c6.html).

22 Interview with the author in Damascus on28 April 2005.

23 Interview with the author in Damascus on September 2003.

24 A detailed reconstruction of the events and a discussion on the local power structures during the massacre can be found in: Fawaz (1994); Schatkowski Schilcher (1985), p.87-106.

25 *Al-thawra*, 19 June 2011.

26 Jallouf, in: *Im Land des Herrn* (2011), translation by the author.

27 *Al-Arabiya TV*, 16 September 2011.

28 *Al-Sharq al-Awsat*, 19 September 2011.

29 *Facebook* sources and *SANA*, 18 December 2011.

30 Interview with the author in Damascus on 9 October 2003.

31 Perthes (1990), p. 230.

32 Ismail, in: *Studies in Ethnicity and Nationalism* (2011).

33 Interview with the author in Damascus on 15 September 2003.

34 Interview with the author in Damascus on 25 March 2004.

35 *EFE*, 8 February 2005.

36 George (2003), p.2, the data refers to the year 2001.

37 George (2003), p.1.

38 This rank of order of public universities follows the Ministry of Higher Education's classification according to the number of enrolled students and the universities' performance.

39 The constitution of the Baath Party stipulates that "freedom of expression, assembly, religion, and artistic expression" must be protected, preserved and defended, and that "no authority has the right to restrict or repress them." Quoted according to: Kawakibi (2010), p.7-8.

40 المركز السوري للإعلام و حرية التعبير (www.openarab.net/ar/node/1398).

41 Haidar, in: *Syria Today*, April 2009.

42 Kawakibi (2010), p.16.

43 Owned by the son of one of Syria's high-ranking officers and respectively soft on political issues.

44 Kawakibi (2010), p.6.

45 Interview with the author in Damascus on 25 October 2010.

46 A more detailed glance behind the scenes of the private media can be found in: Kawakibi (2010).

47 "Ex-Syrian news anchor slams state 'propaganda'," in: *France 24*, 21 February 2012 (http://www.france24.com/en/20120220-former-syrian-news-anchor-hani-malathi-bashar-

assad-regime-resign-dubai).
48 Wedeen (1999).
49 *SANA*, quoted from the official English translation.
50 "Assad könnte zurücktreten," in: *Der Spiegel*, 45/2011, 7 November 2011.
51 "President al-Assad to The Sunday Times: Strike Syria and the world will shake," *Sunday Times*, 20 November 2011 (http://www.dp-news.com/en/detail.aspx?articleid=103707).
52 "Transcript: ABC's Barbara Walters' Interview With Syrian President Bashar al-Assad," *ABC News*, 7 December 2011.
53 Denselow, in: *The Guardian online*, 11 May 2011.
54 Interview with the author in Damascus on 31 October 2010.
55 Interview with the author in Damascus on 4 April 2003.

6 The Negative Balance

1 Quoted from the English translation of *SANA*; see also: George (2003), p. 32.
2 Interview in *Syrian Times*, 25 May 2003.
3 Interview with the author in Damascus on 28 October 2010.
4 Interview broadcast on 29 March 2006, translation per a transcript published by *SANA*.
5 George (2003), p.170.
6 Interview with the author in Damascus on 12 November 2009.
7 Interviews with the author in Damascus on 4 April 2003 and 30 September 2003.
8 Interview with the author on 23 October 2010.
9 Interview with the author in Damascus on 16 May 2004.
10 Interview with the author in Damascus on 29 March 2004.
11 Interview of the author with Riad Seif in Khaliye Qudsiye on 7 June 2007.
12 More about the suppression of the Damascus Spring in: George (2003), p.47ff. Kilo and Seif are reported to have had different approaches for political change and had personal differences. However, opinions differ as to the extent of their disagreement, p.42.
13 Perthes (2002), p.210.
14 Interview with the author in Beirut on 17 February 2004.
15 *Al-Safir*, 15 March 2003, quoted from ICG Report II, p.10; Sadiq Jalal al-Azm in an interview with the author in Damascus on 22 May 2003.
16 Perthes, in: *Adelphi Paper* (2004), p. 27.
17 *Akhbar al-Sharq*, 12 August 2004 and 22 September 2004.
18 *Al-Hayat*, 21 November 2004.
19 Interview with the author in Damascus on 5 May 2005.
20 Perthes, in: *Adelphi Paper* (2004), p.13.
21 Interview with the author in Damascus on 5 May 2005.
22 Report of the Syrian Committee for Human Rights (London), in: *Khaleej Times*, 28 June 2004.
23 "Deputy Head of Syrian Journalists Union wonders at the term 'Syrian Kurdistan' launched by Masaud Barazani," in: *al-Sharq al-Awsat*, 21 March 2004.
24 Interview with a Kurdish communist on 28 March 2004 in Damascus and others who were involved in the developments.
25 Interview with Abdul Yusef, chairman of the Kurdish Yakiti Party (which split off from the Democratic Kurdish Party, the largest Kurdish party in Syria) in Damascus on 26 October 2003.
26 Interview with the author in Damascus on 17 March 2004.
27 *Al-Hayat*, 10 May 2005.
28 Buthayna Shaaban in an interview with the author in Damascus on 29 March 2004.
29 "Some Reactions to the Presidential Referendum," in: *The Syria Monitor*, 30 May 2007 (http://syriamonitor.typepad.com/news/2007/05/some_reactions_.html).
30 Interview with the author in Damascus on 23 October 2010.

31 Interview with the author in Damascus on 27 October 2010.

32 Interview with the author in Damascus on 12 November 2009.

33 Quilliam (1999), p.45-46, 81-84.

34 Interview with the author in Damascus on 28 April 2003.

35 Habermas, in: Balakrishnan (1996), p.290.

36 Hinnebusch (2001), p.2ff.

37 Dahi / Munif, in: *inamo* (2011).

38 First figure from: "بالوثائق 111 مليار ليرة سورية ثروة رامي مخلوف الظاهرة" (http://www.arflon.net/2011/04/11.html#ixzz1JyA2LH4R); second figure from: Leverett (2005), p.84.

39 *Cham Press*, quoting *The New York Times*, 1 November 2005.

40 Dahi/Munif, in: *inamo* (2011).

41 Perthes uses this term in spite of misgivings and integrates it into debates on theories of development, Perthes (1990), p.33, 209ff.

42 Samir Altaqi in an interview with the author on 7 May 2004, see also ICG Report II, p.13; Perthes (1990), p.205ff makes a somewhat different classification.

43 Interview with the author in Damascus on 28 April 2003.

44 Ismail, in: Lawson (2009), p.14.

45 Dahi/Munif, in: *inamo* (2011).

46 Ismail, in: Lawson (2009).

47 Syria Opposition Leader Interview Transcript, *Wall Street Journal*, 2 December 2011.

48 "Transcript: ABC's Barbara Walters' Interview With Syrian President Bashar al-Assad," *ABCnews*, 7 December 2011.

49 Interview in *Syria Times*, 25 May 2003.

50 Hinnebusch, in: *DOI-Fokus* (2004), p.10; figures of the Delegation of the European Commission to the Syrian Arab Republic.

51 Government of Austria factsheet on Syria 2011 (http://www.dfat.gov.au/geo/fs/syri.pdf) and figures mentioned by SNC-President Burhan Ghalioun in: Syria Opposition Leader Interview Transcript, Wall Street Journal, 2 December 2011.

52 CIA World Factbook (https://www.cia.gov/library/publications/the-world-factbook/geos/sy.html).

53 Perthes, in: *Survival* (2001), p.144; ICG Report II, p.13.

54 Interviews by the author; ICG Report II, p.13 states 20 percent. Figure of 2010 from the *CIA World Factbook*.

55 Approximately one out of ten children has to work for money in Syria to support their family financially. Perthes, in: *Adelphi Paper* (2004), p.35.

56 According to official estimates, quoted from: *Al-Hayat*, 17 July 2005. The most recent data available in the CIA World Factbook of 2006 put the number at 11.9 percent.

57 Interview in: *Der Standard*, 1 April 2003, quotation from the interviewer's original text.

58 Interview with the author in Damascus on 6 July 2009.

59 Seifan (2010), p.17.

60 Seifan (2010), p.7ff.

61 European Commission figures of 2005 and interview with a European diplomat in Damascus on 1 May 2005, also: www.indexmundi.com/g/g.aspx?c=sy&v=71.

62 First figure: George (2003), p.10. Second figure: Samir Altaqi in an interview with the author in Damascus on 7 May 2004.

63 CIA World Factbook 2011.

64 *New York Times*, 13 May 2004 (from interviews in *El País* and *La Repubblica*).

65 Landis, in: *The Daily Star*, 28 July 2004, he cites IMF figures.

66 Perthes/Schwitzke, Paper (May 2003), p.7; Perthes, *Adelphi Paper* (2004), p.43; MacFarquhar, in: *New York Times*, 30 March 2003, even states the amount of $4 billion worth of Syrian exports to Iraq. According to Perthes/Schwitzke the Syrian state budget amounted to some

420 billion Lira (approx. $8.2 billion).

67 Ali Saleh in an interview with the author in Damascus on 4 November 2003.

68 "EU set to target Syrian oil industry," in: *Financial Times*, 19 August 2011.

69 Among them were 3.590.273 million Arab tourists, 1.436.679 million foreign tourists and 1.064.937 million Syrian expatriates according to the Syrian ministry of Tourism (www.syriatourism.org/index.php?module=subjects&func=viewpage&pageid=2848).

70 Tallal Kudsi, in: *All4SYRIA*, 2 May 2005.

71 The pressure came from neo-conservative, fundamental Christian members of the US Congress and supporters of the Maronite ex-general Michel Aoun, whom the Syrians neutralized in the Lebanese civil war. At the hearing in Congress at the end of 2003, nobody who rejected the Accountability Act was allowed to speak. The majority leader in the House of Representatives at the time, Tom DeLay, claimed that Syria was waging a war against the entire civilized world and was a threat to all free nations. Hinnebusch, in: *DOI-Fokus* (2004), p.9.

72 The United States exported goods worth $214 million to Syria in 2003. Syrian exports amounted to $259 million, mostly in the form of oil and similar products, which in any case are exempted from the embargo. *Associated Press*, 12 May 2004. For the amount of Syrian exports to the USA: Economist Risk Service 2003, p.7.

73 *Al-Hayat*, 29 June 2004.

74 "Putin Confirms Sale of Short-Range Missiles to Syria," in: *afp*, 22 April 2005.

75 *Al-Hayat*, 21 December 2005.

76 Interview with the author in Damascus on 23 May 2004.

77 *The Daily Telegraph*, 1 June 2004; "Syriens geheimes Atomprogramm: Die Spur führt nach Hanau," in: *Spiegel online*, 28 February 2004.

78 Interview with the author in Damascus on 6 July 2009.

79 Seifan (2010), p.12-13, and foreign experts that were interviewed by the author.

80 Müller-Armack (1976).

81 Inauguration speech of Bashar al-Asad, 18 July 2007, according to the English translation of *SANA*.

82 Interview with the author in Damascus 24 October 2010.

83 Interview with the author in Damascus on 23 October 2010.

84 Interview with the author in Khaliye Qudsiye on 23 October 2010. There was a minor strike effort during the diesel price hikes in May 2008. But when two bus drivers had their service taxis confiscated by the secret service, the strike broke down quickly.

85 Interview with the author in Damascus on 31 October 2010.

86 Article from Ehsani in *SyriaComment*, 2 January 2012. Ehsani referred to an unnamed economic expert at Damascus University and to the original version in Arabic on *Syria Steps* (http://www.syriasteps.com/?d=126&id=80294&in_main_page=1).

87 "Government to Cut Overhead Expenses by 25 Percent," by Jihad Yaziji, in: *Syria Report*, 26 December 2011, also published by *SyriaComment*.

88 Ehrhardt, in: *Frankfurter Allgemeine Zeitung*, 21 February 2012.

89 Figures by the Syrian economic expert Nabil Sukkar, quoted in: Frefel, in: *Frankfurter Rundschau*, 13 February 2012.

90 Interview with the author in Damascus on 28 April 2005.

91 Perthes (2002), p.192.

92 Interview with the author in Damascus on 15 October 2003.

93 *Cham Press*, 12 August 2004.

94 Helberg, in: *Deutschlandfunk*, 6 March 2004.

95 Interview with the author in Damascus on 28 February 2004.

96 Interview with the author in Damascus on 15 October 2003.

97 Amnesty International and Syrian Committee for Human Rights (London). See: *The Region*, 19 June 2004, *Khaleej Times*, 28 June 2004, *Scoop*, 30 June 2004.

98 Statement by Amnesty International on 24 April 2004.

99 From a conversation with Wadia Kilo and Raghida al-Bunni in Damascus on 7 June 2007.

100 Interview with the author in Damascus on 2 July 2009.

101 Interview with the author in Khaliye Qudsiye on 23 October 2010.

102 Report of the independent international commission of inquiry on the Syrian Arab Republic, UN Human Rights Council, 23 November 2011 (http://www2.ohchr.org/english/bodies/hrcouncil/specialsession/17/docs/A-HRC-S-17-2-Add1.pdf).

103 Quoted according to: "UN rights council condemns Syrian abuses," in: *CNN*, 2 Dec 2011

7 Opposition, Islam & the Regime

1 Perthes (1995), p.70.

2 Lobmeyer (1995), p.399, 402.

3 For more information see: Wild, in: *Der Islam* 48 (1972) 2, p.206ff; Schweizer (1998), p.336ff; Moubayed (2006), p.428-430.

4 These forces are united under the National Democratic Assembly, which is illegal but tolerated. It includes: the Arab Socialist Union (Nasserists) under Hassan Ismail Abdul Azim, who left the National Front a year after it was founded in 1973; the Syrian Communist Party Politbureau under Riad al-Turk (not to be confused with the legal Syrian Communist Party which belongs to the National Front); the Revolutionary Workers' Party; the Movement of Arab Socialists; and the Democratic Socialist Arab Baath Party.

5 Petition of 17 May 2003, published in the newspaper *Akhbar al-Sharq*, quoted from MEMRI Newsletter of 15 June 2003.

6 Interviews with the author in Damascus on 11 February 2004, and 11 May 2004.

7 Signatories to the new alliance: National Democratic Assembly; Committee for Reviving Civil Society; Al-Atasi Forum; Human Rights Association in Syria; Committee for the Defense of Liberties and Human Rights; Arab Association for Human Rights—Syrian branch; Communist Workers' Party; Democratic Kurdish Alliance; Kurdish Democratic Front; Kurdish Yekiti Party; Kurdish People's Union; Committees for the Defense of Denationalized Syrians. (From *al-Sharq al-Awsat*, 21 January 2005).

8 *Gulf News*, 31 May 2005.

9 Interview with the author in Damascus on 11 February 2004.

10 Interview with the author in Damascus on 1 May 2005.

11 English translation taken from *Cham Press*, 17 October 2005.

12 Interview with the author in Damascus on 23 October 2010.

13 Interview with the author in Berlin on 21 October 2010.

14 Interview with the author in Khaliye Qudsiye on 7 June 2007.

15 *Al-Nahar*, 24 January 2006.

16 In a bold article that was first published in the Lebanese paper *The Daily Star*, Seif described his experiences of corruption and suppression that pushed him into bankruptcy: "Former MP Riad Seif's Experience in Parliament," in: *The Syria Monitor*, 21 April 2007 (http://syriamonitor.typepad.com/news/2007/04/former_mp_riad_.html).

17 Interview with the author in Khaliye Qudsiye on 7 June 2007.

18 Interview with the author in Damascus on 23 October 2010.

19 Interview with the author in Berlin on 21 October 2010.

20 In a conversation with the author in Damascus on 24 October 2010.

21 Starr, in: *Forward Magazine*, 3 March 2010.

22 Haidar, in: *Syria Today*, March 2010.

23 Husrieh, in: *Syria Today*, March 2010.

24 In a conversation with the author in Damascus on 24 October 2010.

25 Interview with the author in Damascus on 28 October 2010.

26 Interview with the author in Damascus on 12 November 2009.

27 Interview with the author in Berlin on 21 October 2010.

28 This passage must remain vague because of the danger of the people involved.

29 Interview with the author in Khaliye Qudsiye on 23 October 2010.

30 Ayman Abdul Nour in an interview with the author in Damascus on April 28, 2005; George (2003), p.93.

31 In April in Damascus, Bashar met, among others, Sheikh Yusef al-Qaradawi, who is active in Qatar and heads the European Council for Fatwa and Research; Fathi Yakan, one of the founders of the Islamist Organization al-Jamaa al-Islamiyya; the Lebanese representative of the Muslim Brotherhood; and Hamza Mansour, secretary general of the Islamic Action Front, the political arm of the Jordanian Muslim Brotherhood. The spiritual leaders and activists came together for a conference over the interpretation of Islamic law in Damascus. See: "Damascus, Brotherhood set to reconcile?" in: *The Daily Star*, 26 May 2004, also: "Would civilians succeed where security men failed?" in: *Al-Nahar*, 1 June 2004.

32 Interview with the author in Damascus on 6 June 2004.

33 George (2003), p.92.

34 *Al-Madjalla*, 6 May 2001, *al-Hayat*, 6 May 2001.

35 George (2003), p.92-93.

36 *Al-Hayat*, 27 November 2005.

37 Lobmeyer (1995), p.347ff.

38 Interview with the author in Damascus on 28 April 2003.

39 *Al-Nahar*, 24 January 2006.

40 Interview with the author in Damascus on 28 April 2005.

41 Interview with the author in Damascus on 4 April 2003.

42 Interview with the author in Beirut on 17 February 2004.

43 "Mixed signals from Washington leave Damascus confused," in: *The Daily Star*, 26 April 2004.

44 Moubayed, in: *Mideast Views*, 11 December 2011 and Alhaj (2011).

45 Lobmeyer (1995), p.364.

46 Interview with the author in Damascus on 15 November 2003.

47 Interview with the author in Damascus on 30 June 2004.

48 Interview with the author in Damascus on 9 February 2004.

49 Interview with the author in Beirut on 17 February 2004.

50 *SyriaComment*, 30 November 2011.

51 Interview with the author in Damascus on 12 November 2003.

52 Heck (manuscript 2004), p.6, 19, 26, 30-31.

53 Singh (1996), p.69; Athar (1996), in: *Social Scientist*, p.83ff; Ruthven (2000), p.272ff.

54 More on contemporary moderate Islamic figures worldwide in: Esposito/Voll, in: Petito/Hatzopoulos (2003), p.255ff.

55 Concerning early Islamic pantheism and the rational approach of the Mutazilites, see: Tizini (1972), p.27.

56 Interview with the author in Damascus on May 4, 2005.

57 Hinnebusch, in: *DOI-Fokus* (2004), p.14, quoted from: Stalinsky/Carmeli, "The Syrian government," Oxford Business Group, "Online Briefing," March 31, 2005.

58 Habash (2003), p.16, 35.

59 Interview with the author in Damascus on 11 May 2004.

60 Interview with the author in Damascus on 16 March 2004.

61 Batatu (1999), p.261.

62 www.youtube.com/watch?v=LDHDBSXWRnQ/.

63 *Akhbar al-Sharq*, 15 January 2004; ICG report II, p.16.

64 Moubayed, in: *Mideast Views*, 11 December 2011.

65 Heck (2004 manuscript), p.23.

66 Interview with the author in Damascus on 4 May 2005.

67 According to Habash, this Centre was reopened again under the camouflage license of a trade company. Thus it has to pay taxes but it is allowed to sell books and make conferences, however, not on the scale it used to.
68 Interview with the author in Damascus on 24 October 2010.
69 "Syrian MP calls for review of harsh emergency laws," in: *The National*, 11 March 2011.
70 *Al-Arabiya*, 4 October 2011 (http://www.youtube.com/watch?v=bjiUVxY_Qp8).
71 "McCain talks about military options in Syria," in: *AP/Washington Post*, 23 October 2011 (http://www.washingtonpost.com/politics/mccain-talks-about-military-options-in-syria/2011/10/23/gIQAl0Gf9L_story.html).
72 "Syria reaches agreement with Arab League on solution to months-long crisis," in: *Xinhuanet English*, 2 November 2011 (http://news.xinhuanet.com/english2010/world/2011-11/02/c_131224607.htm).
73 Interview with the author in Damascus on 31 October 2010.
74 Interview with the author in Kassab on 14 July 2009.
75 Interview with Sausan Zaqzaq, member of the Central Committee of the Communist Party in Damascus on 26 October 2010.
76 The SWO is the English name of the website *Nisa' Suriyya* (Syrian Women) (www.nesasy.com) launched in 2005 by Bassam al-Kadi. See: Maktabi (forthcoming).
77 Interview with the author in Damascus on 6 July 2009.
78 Maktabi (forthcoming), *"ash-shakhsiyya al-haqiqiyya limashru' qanun al-ahwal ash-shkhsiyya,"* in: *www.swo.org*, 8 June 2009.
79 The ten signatories included seven civil society groups (*al-jam'iyya al-wataniyya litatwir dawr al-mar'a; rahibat al-ra'i as-salih; rabitat an-nisa' as-suriyyat; al-mubadara an-nisa'iyya; al-muntada al-fikri; lajnat da'm qadaya al-mar'a; muntada suriyyat al-islami*), and three electronic sites (*thara; Ishtar;* and SWO).
80 "Syria moving away from equality: report," in: *The National*, 26 November 2009.
81 Maktabi (forthcoming), see: *dirasat midaniyya hawlal-unf al-waqi' alal-mar'a* [fieldwork study on violence against women], a joint report by the Syrian Central Bureau of Statistics (CBS), UNIFEM, The Syrian Commission for Family Affairs (SCFA), and The Syrian Women General Union (SWGU) issued in 2005.
82 Interview with the author in Damascus on 10 November 2009.
83 Interview with the author in Damascus on 27 October 2010.
84 Interview with the author in Damascus on 31 October 2010.
85 Interview with Louay Hussein, in: *Junge Welt*, 11 February 2012.
86 Haidar/Fares, in: *Syria Today*, June 2011.
87 Haidar/Fares, in: *Syria Today*, June 2011.
88 Kilo, in: *al-Safir*, 16 April 2011, quoted according to *Mideast Wire*.
89 Ibid:
90 Syria Opposition Leader Interview Transcript, *Wall Street Journal*, 2 December 2011.
91 Interview with the author in Berlin on 8 July 2011.
92 Interview with the author in Berlin on 8 July 2011.
93 Azm, in: *Reason Papers* (2011).
94 Inauguration speech of Bashar al-Asad, 18 July 2007, according to the English translation of *SANA*.
95 Saliba, in: *The Middle East Magazine* (2011).
96 Interview with Sadiq Jalal al-Azm, in: *Zenith*, 6 December 2011.
97 Interview with the author in Berlin on 8 July 2011.
98 Interview with the author in Vienna on 6 October 2011.
99 "The Launch of the Syrian National Council," SRCC Briefing, 15 September 2011.
100 "The Launch of the Syrian National Council," SRCC Briefing, 15 September 2011.
101 *Aksalser*, 11 October 2011.

102 "Syrer treffen Arabische Liga," in: *Frankfurter Allgemeine Zeitung*, 10 November 2011.
103 SNC Statement on the Formation of Military Bureau, 1 March 2012 (http://us4.campaign-archive1.com/?u=857bd82c962e619f33d2a9b1e&id=59fb0fa919&e=7d60dd67d3).
104 Zalewski, in: *Foreign Policy*, August 2011.
105 Syria Opposition Leader Interview Transcript, *Wall Street Journal*, 2 December 2011.
106 Syria Opposition Leader Interview Transcript, *Wall Street Journal*, 2 December 2011.

8 Syria's Policy Paradox

1 A critical summary on the interaction of US foreign policy and Syria's development in the past decade can be found in Hinnebusch, in: Hinnebusch/Kabalan/Kodmani/Lesch (2010).
2 Hariri in a press conference on his visit to Italy, see: "Hariri: Scuds story similar to US claims of Iraq WMDs," in: *The Daily Star*, 21 April 2010.
3 "Hariri to his media staff: Those who want to criticize Syria must resign," in: *Al-Akhbar*, 24 March 2010.
4 "Hariri says was wrong to accuse Syria over killing," *Reuters*, 6 September 2010 (www.reuters.com/article/2010/09/06/us-lebanon-hariri-idUSTRE68510420100906).
5 McElroy, in: *The Telegraph*, 14 October 2010.
6 "Israel warns Syria it would lose future war," *AP*, 4 February 2010; "Why did Al-Muallem warn Israel against attacking Syria or South Lebanon?", in: *Al-Akhbar*, 5 February 2010; "Israel's Aussenminister droht Asad mit Sturz," in: *NZZ-Online*, 4 February 2010.
7 Hersh, in: *The New Yorker*, 3 February 2010.
8 "Syrian sources: here's what will happen if war is imposed on us," in: *Al-Rai al-Aam*, 26 April 2010.
9 Hersh, in: *The New Yorker*, 3 February 2010.
10 Interview with the author in Damascus on 23 October 2010.
11 Interview with the author in Damascus on 23 October 2010.
12 Interview with the author in Damascus on 11 November 2009.
13 ICG, *Middle East Report*, No. 92 (2009), p.8.
14 Interviews with Michel Kilo in Damascus on 12 November 2009 and on 28 October 2010 .
15 Interview with the author in Damascus on 12 November 2009.
16 Lutz, in: *Chicago Tribune*, 2 December 2010.
17 *Reuters*, 29 April 2004, taken from an interview with Asad by *Aljazeera*.
18 Syrian Research and Communication Center (SRCC) Newsletter, 27 November 2011
19 Hersh, in: *The New Yorker*, 3 February 2010
20 M. Hersh, in: *The New Yorker*, 3 February 2010.
21 Interview with the author in Damascus on 12 November 2011.

9 Che not Usama: Syrian Society and Western Ideals

1 Interview with the author in Damascus on 29 March 2004.
2 Lobmeyer (1995), p.351.
3 Lobmeyer (1995), p.353, 355.
4 Interview with the author in Damascus on 5 July 2004.
5 Quoted from: Helberg, in: *Deutschlandfunk*, 10 December 2005.

10 Excursus: Secularism in Syria

1 The following account is based on a lecture given by the author at the Islamic Institute for Humanistic Knowledge (معهد الدراسات الاسلامي للمعارف الحكمية) in Beirut. See: Wieland (2004), in: *al-Mahajjah*.
2 Among others, Theodor Hanf made this distinction during the international conference, "God's Rule and Caesar's Rule: Exploring the Spaces between Theocracy and Secularism," in Byblos, Lebanon, 9 September 2003.

3 Statistics from the Protestant Church of Germany (EKD) and the Catholic Bishops' Congress.
4 Tibi (1971), p.64ff, p.83.
5 More on these different experiences with secularism in Europe and the Arab world, see: Esposito and Keane, in: Esposito/Tamimi (2000).
6 Hinnebusch (2001), p.1, 70ff; Dawisha (2003), p.295-296; Kedouri (1992), p.325ff; Mansfield (2003), p.323; Zeine (1966), p.150, 155-156.
7 More on Khoury's biography see: Moubayed (2006), p. 277-281.
8 Lobmeyer (1995), p.115.
9 More about Syria under French mandate, see: Khoury (1987); Mufti (1996), p.44ff.
10 Lobmeyer (1995), p.193ff, Schweizer (1998), p.278.
11 Interview with a Syrian analyst in Damascus on 6 July 2009.
12 Seale (1988), p.173.
13 van Dam (2011), p.110.
14 Lobmeyer (1995), p.199.
15 Lobmeyer (1995), p.211, 219ff; Batatu (1999), p.227-229, 327; Perthes (1990), p.16; Perthes, in: *Orient* (1990); van Dam (2011).
16 Interview with the author in Damascus on 2 February 2004.

11 The Bankruptcy of Baathism

1 Among many others, particularly see the groundbreaking works by Deutsch (1966), Gellner (1983), and Anderson (1991).
2 Lewis (1998), p.104.
3 A good comparison of old and new historical writing is to be found in Jankowski / Gershoni in: Jankowski / Gershoni (1997), p.3ff.
4 Khoury, in: Jankowski / Gershoni (1997), p.286.
5 Mufti (1996), p.187.
6 Mufti (1996), p.256.
7 The great Arab sociologist Ibn Khaldun (1332-1406) called this feeling of community or be-longing together *assabiyya*. The term may derive from ties based on religion or common origin (tribe, clan) or both. In an ethno-national sense it is now also translated as "national feeling," to coin a modern phrase.
8 Hinnebusch (2001), p.20.
9 Muslih (1988), p.55.
10 Bunzl (1983), p.17-18.
11 Khoury (1987), p.535-562; Dawisha (2003), p.79.
12 Jankowski/Gershoni in: Jankowski/Gershoni (1997), p.12; about Egypt, see Jankowski/Ger-shoni (1986); about the Palestinians, see: Muslih (1988), p.131ff.
13 For a detailed description of the concepts of the nation and the debate about the problematic term "ethnic group," see Wieland (2000), p.45ff. Specific to the Arab context, see, above all, Dawisha (2003), p.1ff, 52ff; Tibi (1971), p.80ff.
14 Tibi (1971), p.103ff; Lobmeyer (1995), p.35ff; Kedouri (1992), p.282; Kienle (1990), p.18; Aoyama/ Khansa/al-Charif (2000); Arsuzi-Elamir (2003).
15 Anderson (1991).
16 Kaschuba (1997), in: *Ethnologie française*, p.502.
17 Weber (1921), p.528; Khaldun (1377, English edition 1969), p.102-103.
18 Tibi (1971), p.73.
19 Tibi (1971), p.87.
20 Dawisha (2003), p.27ff; Muslih (1988), p.60, 67.
21 Kedouri (1992), p.288.
22 Muslih (1988), p.60.
23 For a historiographical assessment of Hamid's rule between reform and reaction, see: Muslih

(1988), p.47ff.

24 Tibi (1971), p.94ff; Muslih (1988), p.60ff; Zeine (1966), p.92; Mansfield (2003), p.128ff; Kienle (1990), p.4ff.

25 For the prehistory of the caliphate since Muhammad, see: Halm (1988), p.10ff, 17ff, 661. For political history, see Schulze (1990), p.446ff, (1994), p.88ff; Schimmel (1983), p.119ff. Schimmel points out that the caliphate is not provided for in Islam but represents an ex-post facto.

26 Mansfield (2003), p.228.

27 Dawisha (2003), p.49.

28 Tibi (1971), p.110. For Husri's ideology, see in detail Tibi from p.103ff; also Dawisha (2003), p.49ff.

29 Kedouri (1992), p.295; Thomas von der Osten-Sacken/Thomas Uwer: "Die Araber-Macher," in: Die Zeit 14/2003; Tibi (1971), p.113ff; Aoyama/Khansa/al-Charif (2000).

30 Schweizer (1998), p.261.

31 Lobmeyer (1995), p.35-36.

32 Kienle (1990), p.8.

33 Tibi (1971), p.104.

34 Dawisha (2003), p. 298-302. Avineri argued in a similar manner in: Winkler (1985), p.240ff with a view to the components of social change and compares this with Jewish nationalism. Khoury also refers to this problem in: Jankowski/Gershoni (1997), p.286.

35 Tibi (1971), p.190.

36 For more about the life and work of al-Arsuzi, see Arsuzi-Elamir (2003); Aoyama/Khansa/al-Charif (2000).

37 Concerning the details on the composition of the peasantry and their role in Syrian politics, see Batatu (1999).

38 More on Howrani's biography see: Moubayed (2006), p. 245-250.

39 Perthes (1990), p.49; Petran (1972), p.107.

40 Kelidar (1974), in: Asian Affairs, p.16-22; quoted from Lobmeyer (1995), p.64.

41 Initially, they were still supported by Nasserists and independent Unionists, whom they, however, discarded after the Nasserists' unsuccessful coup on July 18, 1963.

42 Hinnebusch (2001), p.31.

43 Hinnebusch (2001), p.3, 120.

44 Hinnebusch (1989), p.99.

45 Lobmeyer (1995), p.35, quoted from Abu Jaber (1966).

46 Hinnebusch (2001), p.47ff; Lobmeyer (1995), p.101ff; Kienle (1990), p.10ff.

47 Hinnebusch (2001), p.52ff.

48 Literacy doubled between 1960 and 1989. In 1960 only 37 percent of the Syrians lived in towns; but in 1990 it increased to 50.5 percent. Hinnebusch (2001), p.104.

49 Batatu (1999), p.177.

50 Lobmeyer (1995), p.184.

51 Hinnebusch (1990), p.145.

52 More about the leader cult and its sometimes grotesque excesses, see Wedeen (1999).

53 Seale (1998), p.440.

54 Concerning the opening of Syria after 1991, see Kienle (1994).

55 Concerning the failure of pan-Arab practice, see Mufti (1996) and Dawisha (2003).

56 Interview with the author in Damascus on 28 April 2005.

57 Interview with the author in Damascus on May 7, 2004.

58 Hinnebusch, in: DOI-Focus (2004), p.12.

59 ICG Middle East Report No. 23/24 Vol. II (2004), p.i.

60 Interview with the author in Damascus on 5 May 2005.

61 Interview with the author in Damascus on 29 March 2004.

62 Packer (2005).

63 Janis (1982) gives an array of examples that ended in fiascoes because of groupthink. Packer (2005) mentions this dynamic in connection with the Iraq war, too.

64 Interview with the author in Damascus on 23 October 2010.

65 Interview with the author in Damascus on 31 October 2010.

66 Inauguration speech of Bashar al-Asad, 18 July 2007, according to the English translation of *SANA.*

67 Interview with the author in Damascus on 28 October 2010.

68 Moubayed, in: *Mideast Views*, 11 December 2011.

69 "Let us now tend to a country called Syria," *Baladna*, 22 November 2011, translation from *Mideast Wire.*

70 "A letter to the heart of Pan-Arabism: Syria First," in: *al-Watan*, 28 November 2011

12 Syria: A Rogue State?

1 "Warum Hanadi zur lebenden Bombe wurde," in: *Die Welt*, 15 January 2004.

2 According to information from international journalists who visited the spot directly after the incident.

3 Examples in: Wurmser (2000) and Elhadj, in: *All4SYRIA*, (2011).

4 *All4SYRIA*, 13 June 2004, *al-Hayat* June 11, 2004.

5 Frisch (2004), in: *Political Studies*, p. 401-403.

6 National (pan-Arab) socialist education for the 12th grade (*tarbiyya al-qawmiyya al-ishtiraqiyya*), 2002/2003, p.103-104, 242-243.

7 Hoffgaard, *epd*, 4 September 2006. The article refers to a study done by scientists from the universities Rostock and Erlangen-Nürnberg.

8 See also: Leverett (2005), p.10-12.

9 A good manual on this is: Hoffmann (2001). The international law expert Shukri (1991) provides an early view that also includes state terrorism.

10 Interview in the Egyptian newspaper *al-Ahram*, 24 April 2004.

11 *Al-Sharq al-Awsat*, 4 September 2005; *Elaph*, 9 March 2005.

12 Putz, in: *spiegel-online*, 3 September 2008.

13 Lutz, in: *Chicago Tribune*, 2 December 2010.

14 *Ria Novosti*, 14 December 2011.

15 *Al-Hayat*, 22 December 2011.

16 Final Report of the Commission on Terrorist Attacks upon the United States (2004), p.66. The Commission conceded that there was "no evidence" of a "collaborative operational relationship" between al-Qaida and Iraq. "Nor have we seen evidence," it continued, "that Iraq cooperated with al-Qaida in developing or carrying out any attacks against the United States."

17 *Al-Hayat*, 21 December 2003; "A Tale of Extraordinary Renditions and Double-Standards," in: *spiegel online* 21 November 2005.

18 *Al-Hayat*, 30 March 2005.

19 Interview with the author in Damascus on 11 November 2009.

20 If Syria decides to go ahead with the plan to hand over the Shebaa Farms to Lebanon, the pressure on Israel to withdraw from the land will rise. If it does not, as Bashar indicated at the end of 2005, Hezbollah would have justification to continue its operations in southern Lebanon against the "Israeli occupation," although legally it is not Lebanese territory. Shebaa is recognized by the UN as part of the Israeli-occupied region of the Syrian Golan Heights since 1974, and not as Lebanese territory. Therefore, the UN announced in 2000 that the Israeli withdrawal from Lebanon was complete.

21 Seale (1988), p.173.

22 Danawi (2002), p.92.

23 Interview with the author and other journalists and scientists in Beirut on 19 February 2004.

24 See also: Berti (2011).

25 Interview in *al-Ahram Weekly*, 9-15 June 2005.

26 *The Daily Star*, 21 April 2005, and *Le Monde Diplomatique* (German edition), June 2005.

27 Nasrallah stresses, however, that these were Shiite fighters before the Hezbollah organization was founded.

28 Interview with the author and other journalists and scientists in Beirut on 19 February 2004.

29 Shlaim (2000), p.xiv.

30 Miller (2008), p.286.

31 ICG Report I, p.1-2, Enderlin (2002).

32 This accusation is made in a twenty-four-page report by the Syrian Foreign Ministry to a UN fact-finding committee, a*l-Hayat*, 8 June 2004.

33 Hinnebusch, in: *DOI-Fokus* (2004), p.17.

34 Interview with the author in Damascus on 28 April 2003; the communiqué was published in the Lebanese newspaper *al-Nahar* on 23 February 2005.

35 *New York Times*, 29 March 2005.

36 *Al-Sharq al-Awsat*, 18 December 2005.

37 Among the rich literature on the problems of the Tribunal, a good and summarizing insight is delivered by Wimmen, in: *MERIP* (2010).

38 The names are Mustafa Badreddin, Salim al-Ayyash, Assad Sabra and Hassan Unaisi. "Hezbollah leader Nasrallah rejects Hariri indictments," in: BBC *online*, 3 July 2011 (www.bbc.co.uk/news/world-middle-east-14004096).

39 Seymour Hersh in a panel discussion at the Saban Center for Middle East Policy of the Brookings Institute on 25 April 2005. Quoted from: "Doomed but at What Cost?," by Azmi Bishara, in: *al-Ahram Weekly*, 19-25 May 2005.

40 Fakih, in: *al-Ahram Weekly*, 17-23 February 2005.

41 Kassem (2004), p.156; *al-Ahram Weekly*, 3-9 March 2005.

42 Landis, in *SyriaComment*, 11 August 2004.

43 Baradei in: *Al-Jazeera*, 22 July 2004; Leverett (2005), p.13.

44 "Syria enlisted help of 'father' of Pakistan's atom bomb," in: *The Telegraph*, 2 November 2011.

45 Interview with the author in an undisclosed location in Syria in summer 2009.

46 "Das heimliche Rüstungsprogramm Syriens," in: *Die Welt*, 25 November 2011.

13 After Arab Spring: Shifting Discourse and Alliances

1 Azm, in: *Reason Papers* (2011), p.227 and in an interview with the author in Berlin on 15 July 2011.

2 Khalidi, in: *Jadaliyya* (2011).

3 Zogby (2005), p.12.

4 *New York Times*, 13 May 2004 (from interviews in *El Pais* and *La Repubblica*).

5 Interview with the author in Damascus on 26 April 2005.

6 "Aboard Air CIA," in: *Newsweek*, 28 February 2005. The Syrian cases involve the Canadian of Syrian descent, Maher Arar, who was intercepted by US authorities on a flight in New York and shipped to Syria where he was tortured. The same is true for Mohammed Haydar Zammar, a German citizen, who was brought to Syria at the end of 2001 and was interrogated there by German officials in summer 2002, which is against German law ("A Tale of Extraordinary Renditions and Double-Standards," in: *spiegel online*, 21 November 2005).

7 One of the best accounts in this field is Ahmed Rashid's book about the Taliban (2001).

8 Dreyfuss (2005).

9 Amr (2004), p.iii, 1.

10 Fukuyama, in: *The National Interest*, 2004.

11 Official transcript of President Obama's Speech in Cairo, 4 June 2009.

12 Augustus R. Norton (Boston University) in a lecture at the conference: "The Middle East after

the Invasion of Iraq" at the Danish Institute in Damascus on 22-24 October 2003. See also: Mansfield (2003), p.398-399.

13 Interview with the author in Damascus on 15 October 2003.

14 *New York Times*, 8 November 2003.

15 Interview with the author in Damascus on 11 March 2003.

16 Leverett (2005), p.147ff.

17 "US ambassador to Syria, Robert Ford, greeted in Hama with flowers and olive branches," in: *Washington Post*, 8 July 2011, see also the following *youtube* sequence: www.youtube.com/watch?v=BEjLLqHoVbM.

18 News Bulletin of the Strategic Research and Communication Center (SRCC), 16 December 2011.

19 Syria Opposition Leader Interview Transcript, *Wall Street Journal*, 2 December 2011.

20 Kepel, in: *Le Monde*, 2 May 2011 (translation by the author). See also Filiu (2011).

21 Shatz, in: *Jadaliyya* (2011).

22 Bayat, in: *Foreign Affairs Snapshot* (2011).

23 Sadiq Jalal al-Azm in a lecture at the Berlin Forum for Progressive Muslims, Friedrich Ebert Foundation, Berlin, 21 October 2011.

24 Friedman, in: *New York Times*, 29 November 2011.

25 Raymond Hinnebusch (University of St. Andrews) in a lecture at the conference: "The Middle East after the Invasion of Iraq" at the Danish Institute in Damascus on 25 October 2003.

26 "Scowcroft zweifelt an Bushs Nahost-Plänen," in: *Die Welt*, 18 November 2003, interview originally from the *Financial Times Germany*. Scowcroft and Kagan quotes from: Goldberg, in: *The New Yorker*, 31 October 2005.

27 Official transcript of President Obama's Speech in Cairo, 4 June 2009.

28 "Russia to sell arms to Syria, sales overall to rise," *Reuters*, 17 August 2011.

14 Syrian Scenarios

1 McElroy, in: *The Telegraph*, 14 October 2010.

2 Interview with the author in Berlin on 4 February 2011.

3 "Bashar al-Assad's inner circle," in: BBC *online*, 27 April 2011 (www.bbc.co.uk/news/world-middle-east-13216195).

4 Batatu (1999).

5 Interview with the author in Damascus on 16 March 2004.

6 Moubayed, in: *Mideast Views*, 11 December 2011.

7 Kitschelt, in: *International Politics and Society* (2004), p.14-15.

8 Syria Opposition Leader Interview Transcript, in: *Wall Street Journal*, 2 December 2011.

9 See also: "Civil War is Unlikely—after Assad," in: *Near East Quarterly*, 31 December 2011, and Filiu (2011).

Appendix

Interviewees and partners in conversation:

Abdullah Hanna, historian
Abdul Yusef, chairman of the Kurdish Yakiti Party
Akram al-Bunni, journalist and human rights activist
Ali Saleh, economic historian
Amr al-Azm, assistant professor of history, Shawnee State University, Portsmouth (Ohio)
Anwar al-Bunni, attorney and human rights activist
Ayman Abdul Nour, engineer, founder of the online publication and forum: *All4SYRIA* (www. all4syria.info)
Bassam al-Kadi, founder of the Syrian Women's Observatory (SWO)
Buthayna Shaaban, former Minister of Expatriates
Dalia Haidar, former chief editor of *Syria Today*
Haitham Maleh, attorney and chairman of the Human Rights Association of Syria (HRAS)
Hakam al-Baba, journalist and ex-editor-in-chief of *Al-Domari*
Hanan Nejme, family lawyer
Hassan Nasrallah, leader of Hezbollah
Ihsan Sanqer, entrepreneur, former Member of Parliament
Kadri Jamil, Kurdish member of the Charter of Communist Unity
Leila Nahal, communist
Louay Hussein, publisher
Maya al-Rahabi, doctor
Michel Kilo, journalist and writer
Muhammad al-Habash, Member of Parliament, sheikh, and head of the former Islamic Studies Center in Damascus
Najib Ghadbian, member of the Syrian National Council (SNC), associate professor in political science, University of Arkansas
Nihad Nahas, communist
Jawdat Said, sheikh from Quneitra
Radwan Ziadeh, member of the Syrian National Council (SNC), director of the Syrian Center for Political & Strategic Studies (SCPSS) and visiting fellow at the Carr Center for Human Rights Policy at Harvard University
Riad Seif, businessman and ex-Member of Parliament
Sadiq Jalal al-Azm, professor of philosophy
Said al-Azm, journalist and ex-diplomat
Salam Kawakibi, political scientist, research director with the Arab Reform Initiative
Samer Ladkany, surgeon and analyst in the former Orient Centre for International Studies (OCIS)
Sami Khiyami, software engineer, consultant, economic advisor to the president in negotiations with the EU, later appointed Syrian ambassador to London
Samir Altaqi, surgeon and analyst in the former Center for Strategic Studies and Research (CSSR) later converted into the Orient Centre for International Studies (OCIS), closed in 2010
Sausan Zaqzaq, member of the Central Committee of the Communist Party and women's rights activist
Selma Karkoutli, journalist
Tayyeb Tizini, philosophy professor at the University of Damascus

. . . and many others who wish to remain anonymous.

Bibliography

Monographs, Collected Works, and Articles

Abbas, Hassan: *The Dynamics of the Uprising in Syria*, in: *Arab Reform Brief*, October 2011 (also published in *inamo*, winter 2011).

Abdoh, Samir: ألطوائف ألمسيحية في سورية: نشأتها,تطورها ,عدادها (*Christian Denominations in Syria: Their Emergence, Development, and Enumeration*), Damascus 2003.

Abu Jaber, Kamel S.: *The Arab Ba'th Socialist Party: History, Ideology, and Organization*, Syracuse (NY) 1966.

Alhaj, Abdulrahman: *State and Community: The Political Aspirations of Religious Groups in Syria 2000-2010*, Strategic Research and Communication Center (SRCC), London, January 2011.

Anderson, Benedict R.: *Imagined Communities: Reflections on the Origin and Spread of Nationalism*, London/New York 1991.

Aoyama, Hiroyuki / Khansa, Wafiq / al-Charif, Maher: "Spiritual Father of the Ba'th: The Ideological and Political Significance of Zaki al-Arsuzi in Arab Nationalist Movements," *Middle East Studies Series* No. 49, Tokyo March 2000.

Arsuzi-Elamir, Dalal: *Arabischer Nationalismus in Syrien: Zaki al-Arsuzi und die arabisch-nationale Bewegung an der Peripherie Alexandretta / Antakya 1930-1938*, Münster 2003.

Asseburg, Muriel (ed): *Moderate Islamisten als Reformakteure?* Bonn 2008.

Athar Ali, M.: "The Evolution of the Perception of India: Akbar and Abu'l Fazl," in: *Social Scientist*, 24 (1996) 1-3.

Avineri, Shlomo: "Politische und soziale Aspekte des israelischen und arabischen Nationalismus," in: Winkler, Heinrich-August (ed): *Nationalismus*, Königstein/Ts. 1985.

al-Azm, Sadiq J.: "The Arab Spring: Why exactly at this Time?" in: *Reason Papers*, Vol. 33 Fall 2011.

Ibid: *Critique of Religious Thought*, Beirut 1969, 8th edition 1997.

Batatu, Hanna: *Syria's Peasantry: The Descendants of Its Lesser Rural Notables and Their Politics*, Princeton/Oxford 1999.

Berti, Benedetta: "Can Hezbollah Cope with a Changing Middle East?" in: *Foreign Policy Research Institute E-Paper*, November 2011.

Bayat, Asef: "The Post-Islamist Revolutions: What the Revolts in the Arab World Mean," in: *Foreign Affairs Snapshot*, 26 April 2011.

Bunzl, John: *Israel und die Palästinenser: Die Entwicklung eines Gegensatzes*, Wien 1983.

Choueiri, Youssef M. (ed): *State and Society in Syria and Lebanon*, Exeter 1993.

Cleveland, William L.: *The Making of an Arab Nationalist: Ottomanism and Arabism in the Life and Thought of Sati al-Husri*, Princeton/Oxford 1971.

Council on Foreign Relations / Foreign Affairs (ed): *The New Arab Revolt: What Happened, What It Means, and What Comes Next*, New York 2011.

Daalder, Ivo/Gnesotto, Nicole/Gordon Philip (eds.): *Crescent of Crisis: US-European Strategy for the Greater Middle East*, Washington, DC/Paris 2006.

Dahi, Omar S./Munif Yasser: Schnittmengensuche—zwischen Autoritarismus und Neoliberalismus, in: *inamo*, 68, winter 2011.

Dam, Nikolaos van: *The Struggle for Power in Syria*, London 2011 (4th ed.).

Danawi, Dima: *Hezbollah's Pulse: Into the Dilemma of al-Shaihid and Jihad al-Bina Foundations*, Beirut 2002.

Davis, Scott C.: *The Road from Damascus: A Journey Through Syria*, Seattle 2003.

Dawisha, Adeed: *Arab Nationalism in the Twentieth Century: From Triumph to Despair*, Princeton/Oxford 2003.

Deutsch, Karl W.: *Nationalism and Social Communication: An Inquiry into the Foundations of Nationality*, Cambridge (Mass.)/London 1966 (2nd edition).

Dreyfuss, Robert: *Devil's Game: How the United States Helped Unleash Fundamentalist Islam,* New York 2005.

Emerson, Rupert: *From Empire to Nation: The Rise to Self-Assertion of Asian and African Peoples,* Cambridge (Mass.) 1960.

Enderlin, Charles: *Le Rêve Brisé: Histoire de l'Échec du Processus de Paix au Proche-Orient 1995-2002,* Paris 2002.

Esposito, John L./Voll, John O.: "Islam and the West: Muslim Voices of Dialogue," in: Petito, Fabio/Hatzopoulos, Pavlos: *Religion in International Relations: The Return from Exile,* New York/Houndmills 2003.

Ibid: "Islam in the Twenty First Century," in: Esposito, J./Tamimi A. (eds): *Islam and Secularism in the Middle East,* London 2000.

Faath, Sigrid (ed): *Die Zukunft arabisch-türkischer Beziehungen,* Baden Baden 2011.

Fawaz, Leila Tarazi: *Occasion for War: Civil Conflict in Lebanon and Damascus in 1860,* Berkeley/Los Angeles 1994.

Filiu, Jean-Pierre: *The Arab Revolution: Ten Lessons from the Democratic Uprising,* London 2011.

Fischer, Susanne: Das Ende der Angst: Syriens junge Generation kämpft für den Sturz des Assad-Regimes, in: *Internationale Politik,* Berlin September 2011.

Freitag, Ulrike: *Geschichtsschreibung in Syrien 1920—1990: Zwischen Wissenschaft und Ideologie,* Hamburg 1991.

Frisch, Hillel: "Perceptions of Israel in the Armies of Syria, Egypt and Jordan," in: *Political Studies,* Vol. 52, No. 3, October 2004.

Fukuyama, Francis: "The Neoconservative Moment," in: *The National Interest,* June 1, 2004

Gellner, Ernest: *Nations and Nationalism,* Ithaca/New York 1983.

Gelvin, James L.: *Divided Loyalties: Nationalism and Mass Politics in Syria at the Close of Empire,* Berkeley 1998.

George, Alan: *Neither Bread Nor Freedom,* London 2003.

Goodarzi, Jubin M.: *Syria and Iran: Diplomatic Alliance and Power Politics in the Middle East,* London 2008.

Habash, Muhammad: *A Call to the West: Lectures on the Dialogue of Civilizations,* Damascus 2003.

Habermas, Jürgen: "The European Nation-state: Its Achievements and Its Limits. On the Past and Future of Sovereignty and Citizenship," in: *Balakrishnan,* Gopal (ed): Mapping the Nation, London/New York 1996.

Halm, Heinz.: *Die Schia,* Darmstadt 1988.

Harrer, Gudrun: Kriegs-Gründe: *Versuch über den Irak-Krieg,* Wien 2003.

Heck, Paul L.: *Religious Renewal in Syria: The Case of Muhammad Al-Habash,* Damascus 2004.

Heller, Erdmute: "Die arabisch-islamische Welt im Aufbruch," in: *Weltbild Weltgeschichte: Weltprobleme zwischen den Machtblöcken,* Augsburg 1998.

Hinnebusch, Raymond A.: "Syria: From 'Authoritarian Upgrading' to Revolution?" in: *International Affairs* 88: 1 (2012).

Ibid: "Syria under Bashar: Between Economic Reform and Nationalist Realpolitik," in: Hinnebusch, Raymond/Kabalan, Marwan J./Kodmani, Bassma/Lesch, David (eds.): *Syrian Foreign Policy and the United States: From Bush to Obama,* Fife 2010.

Ibid: "Syria after the Iraq War: Between the Neo-con Offensive and Internal Reform," *DOI-Focus* No. 14, March 2004.

Ibid: *Syria: Revolution from Above,* London/New York 2001.

Ibid:/Drysdale, Alasdair: *Syria and the Middle East Peace Process,* New York 1991.

Ibid: *Authoritarian Power and State Formation in Ba'thist Syria: Army, Party, and Peasant,* Boulder 1990.

Ibid: *Peasant and Bureaucracy in Ba'thist Syria: The Political Economy of Rural Development,* London 1989.

Hinnebusch, Raymond/Kabalan, Marwan J./Kodmani, Bassma/Lesch, David (eds.): *Syrian Foreign*

Policy and the United States: From Bush to Obama, Fife 2010.

Hoffmann, Bruce: *Terrorismus—der unerklärte Krieg: Neue Gefahren politischer Gewalt,* Frankfurt / Main 2001.

Ismail, Salwa: "The Syrian Uprising: Imagining and Performing the Nation," in: *Studies in Ethnicity and Nationalism,* Volume 11, Issue 3, December 2011.

Ibid: "Silencing the Voice of Freedom in Syria," in: *Index on Censorship,* 8 July 2011 (www.indexoncensorship.org/2011/07/silencing-the-voice-of-freedom-in-syria).

Ibid: Changing Social Structure, Shifting Alliances and Authoritarianism in Syria, in: Lawson, Fred (ed): *Demystifying Syria,* London 2009.

Janis, Irving: *Groupthink: Psychological Studies of Policy Decisions and Fiascoes,* Boston 1982.

Jankowski, James/Gershoni, Israel (ed): *Rethinking Nationalism in the Arab Middle East,* New York 1997.

Ibid: Egypt, Islam, and the Arabs: *The Search for Egyptian Nationhood 1900-1930,* New York 1986.

Hinnebusch, Raymond/Kabalan, Marwan J./Kodmani, Bassma/Lesch, David: *Syrian Foreign Policy and the United States: From Bush to Obama,* St. Andrew Papers on Contemporary Syria, Fife 2010.

Kaschuba, Wolfgang: "Identité, altérité et mythe éthnique," in: *Ethnologie Française,* 27 (1997) 4, p. 502.

Kassem, Maye: *Egyptian Politics : The Dynamics of Authoritarian Rule,* London 2004.

Kawakibi, Salam: "The Private Media in Syrian, Syrian Research and Communication Center (SRCC)," 30 August 2010 (http://www.strescom.org/research/private-media-syria).

Keane, John.: "The Limits of Secularism," in: Esposito, John L. / Tamimi Azzam (eds): *Islam and Secularism in the Middle East,* London 2000.

Kedouri, Elie: *Politics in the Middle East,* Oxford / New York 1992.

Kelidar, A.R.: "Religion and State in Syria," in: *Asian Affairs,* 1/1974.

Kepel, Gilles: *Jihad,* Paris 2003.

Khaldun, Ibn: *The Muqaddimah,* Princeton 1969 [orig. 1377].

Khoury, Philip S.: "The Paradoxical in Arab Nationalism: Interwar Syria Revisited," in: Jankowski, James / Gershoni, Israel (ed): *Rethinking Nationalism in the Arab Middle East,* New York 1997.

Ibid: "The Syrian Independence Movement and the Development of Economic Nationalism in Damascus," in: *British Journal of Middle Eastern Studies,* 14/1988.

Ibid: *Syria and the French Mandate: The Politics of Arab Nationalism 1920-1945,* Princeton 1987.

Ibid: "Divided Loyalties: Syria and the Question of Palestine 1919-1939," in: *Middle Eastern Studies,* 21/1985.

Kienle, Eberhard: "Arab Unity Schemes Revisited: Interest, Identity, and Policy in Syria and Egypt," in: *International Journal of Middle East Studies,* Vol. 27, February 1995.

Ibid: (ed): *Contemporary Syria: Liberalization between Cold War and Cold Peace,* London 1994.

Ibid: *Entre jama'a et classe: Le pouvoir politique en Syrie,* Berlin 1991.

Ibid: *Ba'th v. Ba'th: The Conflict between Syria and Iraq 1968-1989,* London/New York 1990.

Ibid: *Ethnizität und Machtkonkurrenz in inter-arabischen Beziehungen: Der syrisch-irakische Konflikt unter den Ba'th-Regimen,* Berlin 1988.

Kitschelt, Herbert: "Origins of International Terrorism in the Middle East," in: *International Politics and Society,* Vol. 1/2004.

Landis, Joshua: "Is Syria Holding Fewer Political Prisoners than any other Major Middle Eastern Country?" in: *SyriaComment,* 11 August 2004.

Ibid: "Creating a Syrian dream, where none exists today," in: *The Daily Star,* 28 July 2004.

Ibid: The United States and Reform in Syria, in: *The Syria Review,* June 2004.

Ibid: "The United States and Reform in Syria," in: *The Syria Review,* June 2004.

Laqueur, Walter Z.: *Communism and Nationalism in the Middle East,* 2nd edition, London 1957.

Lawson, Fred (ed): *Demystifying Syria,* London 2009.

Lesch, David: *The New Lion of Damascus: Bashar al-Asad and Modern Syria,* New Haven 2005

Leverett, Flynt: *Inheriting Syria: Bashar's Trial by Fire,* Washington, DC 2005.

Lewis, Bernard: *The Political Language of Islam,* Chicago/London 1988.

Ibid: *The Multiple Identities of the Middle East,* London 1998.

Lobmeyer, Hans Günter: *Opposition und Widerstand in Syrien,* Hamburg 1995.

Maktabi, Rania: "State, Law and Religion—Gendered Debates on Family Law in Syria and Lebanon," in: Hinnebusch, Raymond/Zintl, Tina (eds.): *Syria under Bashar al-Asad, 2000-2010: Political-Economy and International Relations,* New York forthcoming.

Mansfield, Peter: *A History of the Middle East,* 2nd edition, London 2003.

Ibid: *The Arabs,* 3rd edition, London 1992

Miller, Aaron David: *The Much Too Promised Land: America's Elusive Search for Arab-Israeli Peace,* New York 2008.

Moubayed, Sami: *Syria and the USA: From Wilson to Eisenhower,* London 2012.

Ibid: "Syria's new Constitution: Too little, too late," in: *Mideast Views,* 14 February 2012.

Ibid: "Challenge for Political Islam in Syria," in: *Mideast Views,* 11 December 2011.

Ibid: "More Missed Chances: An offer Syria shouldn't have refused," *Mideast Views,* 21 September 2011.

Ibid: *Steel and Silk: Men and Women Who Shaped Syria 1900-2000,* Seattle 2006.

Mufti, Malik: *Sovereign Creations: Pan-Arabism and Political Order in Syria and Iraq,* Ithaca/London 1996.

Müller-Armack, Alfred: *Wirtschaftsordnung und Wirtschaftpolitik,* Bern 1976.

Murden, Simon W.: *Islam, the Middle East, and the New Global Hegemony,* Boulder 2002.

Muslih, Muhammad Y.: *The Origins of Palestinian Nationalism,* New York 1988.

Nasr, Vali: The Shia Revival: *How Conflicts within Islam Will Shape the Future,* New York/London 2007.

Norton, Augustus R. (ed): *Civil Society in the Middle East,* Vol. I, Leiden 1995.

Pace, Joe / Landis, Joshua: "The Syrian Opposition: The struggle for unity and relevance 2003–2008," in: Lawson, Fred (ed): *Demystifying Syria,* London 2009.

Packer, George: *The Assassin's Gate: America in Iraq,* New York 2005.

Perthes, Volker: *Syria under Bashar al-Asad: Modernization and the Limits of Change,* Adelphi-Paper 366, London 2004.

Ibid: (ed): *Arab Elites: Negotiating the Politics of Change,* Boulder/London 2004.

Ibid: "Der Mittlere Osten nach dem Irak-Krieg—Neue geopolitische Grundlinien und Spielregeln," in: *Neue Züricher Zeitung,* 24.04.2004.

Ibid: / Schwitzke, Anette: "After the Iraq War: Repercussions in the Levant," paper presented at the GCSP/RAND workshop in Geneva, 4-6 May 2003.

Ibid: *Geheime Gärten: Die neue arabische Welt,* Berlin 2002.

Ibid: "The Political Economy of the Syrian Succession," in: *Survival,* 43/1, Spring 2001.

Ibid: *Vom Krieg zur Konkurrenz: Regionale Politik und die Suche nach einer neuen arabisch-nahöstlichen Ordnung,* Baden-Baden 2000.

Ibid: (ed): *Scenarios for Syria: Socio-economic and Political Choices,* Baden-Baden 1998.

Ibid: *The Political Economy of Syria under Asad,* London 1995.

Ibid: *Staat und Gesellschaft in Syrien 1970-1989,* Hamburg 1990.

Ibid: "Einige kritische Bemerkungen zum Minderheitenparadigma in der Syrienforschung," in: *Orient* 4/1990.

Petran, Tabitha: *Syria,* London 1972.

Pierret, Thomas: "L'opposition syrienne: laïcs contre islamistes?," in: *Mediapart,* 28 March 2012 (http://blogs.mediapart.fr/blog/thomas-pierret/280312/lopposition-syrienne-laics-contre-islamistes).

Ibid: *Baas et islam en Syrie : La dynastie Assad face aux oulémas,* Paris 2011.

Quilliam, Neil: *Syria and the New World Order,* Reading 1999.

Rabil, Robert G.: *Syria, the United States, and the War on Terror in the Middle East*, Santa Barbara 2006.

Rabinovich, Itamar: Rabinovich, Itamar: *The View From Damascus: State, Political Community, and Foreign Relations in Twentieth-Century Syria*, Edgware 2008.

Ibid: "Arab Political Parties: Ideology and Ethnicity," in: Esman, Milton J. / Rabinovich, Itamar (publisher): *Ethnicity, Pluralism, and the State in the Middle East*, Ithaca / London 1988.

Rashid, Ahmed: *Taliban: Militant Islam, Oil and Fundamentalism in Central Asia*, London / New Haven 2001.

Ross, Dennis: *The Missing Peace*, New York 2005.

Roy, Olivier: *Globalized Islam: The Search for a New Ummah*, London 2002.

Rubin, Barry: *The Truth about Syria*, New York 2007.

Ruthven, Malise: *Islam in the World*, Oxford/New York 2000 (2nd edition).

Sakr, Naomi: *Arab Media and Political Renewal: Community, Legitimacy and Public Life*, London 2009.

Saliba, Najib E.: "The Syrian Regime: Struggle for Survival and Implications for its Fall," in: *The Middle East Magazine*, 24 September 2011 (http://www.mideastmag.com/90404/the-syrian-regime-struggle-for-survival-and-implications-for-its-fall).

Schatkowski Schilcher, Linda: *Families in Politics: Damascene Factions and Estates of the 18th and 19th Centuries*, Stuttgart 1985.

Scheck, Frank Rainer/Odenthal, Johannes: *Syria: Hochkulturen zwischen Mittelmeer und Arabischer Wüste*, Cologne 1998.

Schimmel, Annemarie: "Der Islam in unserer Zeit," in: *Italiaander, Rolf* (ed): *Die Herausforderung des Islam: Ein ökumenisches Lesebuch*, Göttingen 1987.

Ibid: *Der Islam im indischen Subkontinent*, Darmstadt 1983.

Schulze, Reinhard: *Geschichte der Islamischen Welt im 20. Jahrhundert*, Munich 2003 (2nd edition)

Ibid: *Islamischer Internationalismus im 20. Jahrhundert: Untersuchungen zur Geschichte der Islamischen Weltliga*, Leiden 1990.

Schumann, Christoph: *Radikalnationalismus in Syrien und Libanon: Politische Sozialisation und Elitebildung 1930-1958*, Hamburg 2001.

Schweizer, Gerhard: *Syrien: Religion und Politik im Nahen Osten*, Stuttgart 1998.

Seale, Patrick: *Asad: The Struggle for the Middle East*, London 1988.

Seifan, Samir: "Syria on the Path of Economic Reform," in: *St. Andrew's Papers on Contemporary Syria*, Fife 2010.

Shatz, Adam: "Prophecy and Deliverance: Reading al-Azm in an-Age of Revolution," in: *Jadaliyya*, 20 December 2011 (http://www.jadaliyya.com/pages/index/3674/prophecy-and-deliverance_reading-al-azm-in-an-age-).

Shlaim, Avi: *The Iron Wall: Israel and the Arab World*, London 2000.

Shukri, Muhammad Aziz: *International Terrorism: A Legal Critique*, Brattleboro 1991.

Singh, Yogendra: *Modernization of Indian Tradition: A Systemic Study of Social Change*, Jaipur/New Delhi 1996.

Stäheli, Martin: *Die syrische Außenpolitik unter Präsident Hafez Asad: Balanceakte im globalen Umbruch*, Stuttgart 2001.

Stalinsky / Carmeli, "The Syrian Government," Oxford Business Group, "Online Briefing," March 31, 2003.

Tabler, Andrew: *In the Lion's Den: An Eyewitness Account of Washington's Battle with Syria*, Chicago 2011.

Tatham, Steve: *Losing Arab Hearts and Minds: The Coalition, Al Jazeera and Muslim Public Opinion*, London 2006.

Telhamy, Shibley: *The Stakes: America in the Middle East*, Boulder / Oxford 2004 (2nd ed).

Tibi, Bassam: *Arab Nationalism: A Critical Enquiry*, New York 1981.

Ibid: *Nationalismus in der Dritten Welt am arabischen Beispiel*, Frankfurt/M. 1971.

Tizini, Tayyeb: *Die Materieauffassung in der islamisch-arabischen Philosophie des Mittelalters*, Berlin (Ost) 1972.

Weber, Max: *Wirtschaft und Gesellschaft*, Tübingen 1972[1921].

Wedeen, Lisa: *Ambiguities of Domination: Politics, Rhetoric, and Symbols in Contemporary Syria*, Chicago/London 1999.

Wieland, Carsten: "Between Democratic Hope and Centrifugal Fears: Syria's Unexpected Open-ended Intifada," in: *International Politics and Society*, 4-2011.

Ibid: سوريـة—الاقتراع أم ارصاص؟الديموقراطيـة و الإسلاميـة و العلمانيـة فـي المشـرق Beirut 2011.

Ibid: "Syrian Scenarios and the Levant's Insecure Future," in: *Orient*, III-2011.

Ibid: "Asad's Lost Chances," in: *Middle East Research and Information Project*, 14 April 2011.

Ibid: "The Present Context of Syria's Foreign Policy, Change in the Region and Stagnation at Home," *CMES-Report* No. 2, June 2010.

Ibid: "Turkey's Political-emotional Transition," in: *OpenDemocracy*, 6 October 2009.

Ibid: "The Gaza war and the Syria-Israel front," in: *OpenDemocracy*, 5 May 2009.

Ibid: "The Syria-Israel talks: Old Themes, New Setting," in: *OpenDemocracy*, 27 May 2008.

Ibid: "Syria's Challenges after the Election Year," in: *Papel Politico*, July 2007.

Ibid: "Syria's Quagmire, al-Assad's Tunnel," in: *OpenDemocracy*, 9 November 2006.

Ibid: "Das Erfolgsrezept der Hizbullah," in: *inamo*, 47-2006.

Ibid: *Nation-state by Accident: The Politicization of Ethnic Groups and the Ethnicization of Politics, Bosnia, India, Pakistan*, New Delhi 2006.

Ibid: "Thousands of Years of Nation-building? Ancient Arguments for Sovereignty in Bosnia and Israel/Palestine," in: Riegler, Henriette (ed): *Nation-building Between National Sovereignty and International Intervention*, (Wiener Schriften zur Internationalen Politik, No. 10), Vienna 2005.

Ibid: "The Bankruptcy of Humanism? Primordialism Dominates the Agenda of International Politics," in: *International Politics and Society*, 4/2005.

Ibid: / Bieber, Florian (ed): *Democracy and Human Rights in Multi-Ethnic Societies*, Ravenna 2005.

Ibid: "Zwischen Akbar und AKP: Moderate islamische Alternativen in Syrien," in: *inamo*, No. 40/2004.

Ibid: *Syrien nach dem Irak-Krieg: Bastion gegen Islamisten oder Staat vor dem Kollaps?* Berlin 2004

Ibid: الحـدود مـن وجهـة النظـر الغربيـة :العلمانيـة والديـن, in: *al-Mahajjah* 11/2004.

Ibid: "Syrien nach dem Irak-Krieg—Stagnation oder Umbruch?" in: *Orient* 1/2004.

Ibid: *Nationalstaat wider Willen: Die Politisierung von Ethnien und die Ethnisierung der Politik—Bosnien, Indien, Pakistan*, Frankfurt / New York 2000.

Wild, Stefan: "Gott und Mensch im Libanon: Die Affäre Sadiq Jalal al-Azm," in: *Der Islam*, vol. 48, issue 2, February 1972, p. 206-253.

Wimmen: Heiko: "The Long, Steep Fall of the Lebanon Tribunal," in: *Middle East Research and Information Project* (MERIP), 1 December 2010.

Wurmser, Meyrav: *The Schools of Baathism: A Study of Syrian Schoolbooks*, Middle East Media Research Institute (MEMRI) (ed), Washington, DC 2000.

Zalewski, Piotr: "Islamic Evolution: How Turkey taught the Syrian Muslim Brotherhood to reconcile faith and democracy," in: *Foreign Policy*, August 2011.

Zeine, Zeine N.: *The Emergence of Arab Nationalism*, 2nd edition, Beirut 1966.

Ziadeh, Radwan: *Power and Policy in Syria: Intelligence Services, Foreign Relations and Democracy in the Modern Middle East*, London 2011.

Zisser, Eyal: *Asad's Legacy: Syria in Transition*, London 2001.

Zorob, Anja: "Aufstand in der arabischen Welt: Wirtschaftliche Hintergründe und Perspektiven," in: *Protests, Revolutions and Transformations—the Arab World in a Period of Upheaval*, Center for Middle Eastern and North African Studies (Freie Universität Berlin) (ed), Working Paper No. 1, July 2011.

Reports and Analyses

Abdul-Ahad, Ghaith: "Inside Syria: the rebel call for arms and ammunition," in: *The Guardian*, 11 December 2011.

Abdulhamid, Ammar: "Syria is not ready for an uprising," in: *The Guardian*, 7 February 2011 (http://www.guardian.co.uk/commentisfree/2011/feb/07/syria-uprising-egypt-tunisia-days-of-rage?INTCMP=SRCH).

Abouzeid, Rania: "Arab Spring: Is a Revolution Starting Up in Syria?" in: *Time online*, 19 March 2011.

Amr, Hady: "The Need to Communicate: How to Improve US Public Diplomacy with the Islamic World," Analysis Paper for the Brookings Institution, Washington January 2004.

"Bashar al-Assad's Inner Circle," in: BBC (online), retrieved on 27 April 2011 (http://www.bbc.co.uk/news/world-middle-east-13216195?print=true).

Bauer, Wolfgang: "Assad hält nicht mehr lange durch," in: *Der Tagesspiegel*, 1 February 2012

Ibid: "Civil War is Unlikely—after Assad (Editorial)," in: *Near East Quarterly*, 31 December 2011 (http://www.neareastquarterly.com/index.php/2011/12/11/civil-war-is-unlikely-after-assad).

Denselow, James: "Bashar al-Assad: the dictator who cannot dictate," in: *The Guardian online*, 11 May 2011.

Ehrhardt, Christoph: "Damaszener Zweckehen," in: *Frankfurter Allgemeine Zeitung*, 21 February 2012.

Elhadj, Elie: "Syria's Islamic Textbooks: Politics, Intolerance, and Dogma," in: *All4SYRIA*, 4 May 2011 (http://all4syria.info/web/archives/6946).

Fakih, Mohelhel: "Opposition blames Damascus," in: *al-Ahram Weekly*, 17-23 February 2005.

Final Report of the Commission on Terrorist Attacks upon the United States (authorized version), Washington, DC July 2004.

Frefel, Astrid: "Generatoren statt Fernsehgeräte," in: *Frankfurter Rundschau*, 13 February 2012.

Friedman, Thomas: "The Arab Awakening and Israel," in: *New York Times*, 29 November 2011.

Goldberg, Jeffrey: "Breaking Ranks," in: *The New Yorker*, 31 October 2005.

Haddad, Bassam: "Why Syria is Not Next . . . So Far," in: *Jadaliyya*, 9 March 2011 (http://www.jadaliyya.com/pages/index/844/why-syria-is-not-next-.-.-.-so-far_with-arabic-tra).

Haidar, Dalia: "Access to All Areas? NGOs in Syria," in: *Syria Today*, March 2010.

Ibid: "Private Sector Media in Syria," in: *Syria Today*, April 2009 (http://www.syria-today.com/index.php/april-2009/273-focus/679-creeping-ahead).

Haidar, Dalia/Atef Fares, Muhammad: "Time to Talk?" in: *Syria Today*, June 2011.

Harling, Peter: "Collectively failing Syrian society," in: *Foreign Policy Brief*, 24 January 2012.

Helberg, Kristin: "Mann der verpassten Chancen," in: *taz*, 9-10 July 2011.

Ibid: "Radikale Islamisten oder muslimische Demokraten? Chancen und Gefahren des politischen Islam in Syrien," in: *Deutschlandfunk*, 10 December 2005.

Ibid: "Wir waren lebendig begraben," in: *Deutschlandfunk "Eine Welt,"* 6 March 2004.

Hermann, Rainer: "Assads Pyramide der Macht," in: *Frankfurter Allgemeine Zeitung*, 8 February 2012.

Ibid: "Ein neues System der Selbstverteidigung," in: *Frankfurter Allgemeine Zeitung*, 9 November 2011.

Hersh, Seymour M.: "Conversation with Bashar al-Asad," in: *The New Yorker*, 3 February 2010 (http://www.newyorker.com/online/blogs/newsdesk/2010/02/direct-quotes-bashar-asad.html).

Hoffgaard, Anne-Dorle: "'Syrien war die größte Überraschung'—Wissenschaftler untersuchten das Bild des Christentums in Schulbüchern islamischer Länder," *epd*, 4 September 2006.

Husrieh, Abdul Kader: "A New Way Forward," in: *Syria Today*, March 2010.

Husseini, Abdul Mottaleb: "Syriens neue Verfassung: Assads Reformlüge," in: *spiegel-online*, 24 February 2012.

International Crisis Group (ICG): "Reshuffling the cards: Syria's evolving strategy (I)," in: *Middle East Report* No. 92, December 2009.

International Crisis Group (ICG): "Syria under Bashar," in: *Middle East Report* No. 23/24: Amman/Brussels, February 11, 2004, Vol. I: Foreign Policy Challenges, Vol. II: Domestic Policy Challenges.

Jallouf, Hanna: "Die Hilfe der Franziskaner während der gegenwärtigen Unruhen in Syrien, in: *Im Land des Herrn - Franziskanische Zeitschrift für das Heilige Land,* Vol. 3 2011.

Kepel, Gilles: "La mort de Ben Laden clôt une 'sombre décennie'," in: *Le Monde,* 2 May 2011.

Khalidi, Rachid: "Preliminary Observations on the Arab Revolutions of 2011," in: *Jadaliyya,* 11 March 2011.

Kilo, Michel: "Yes, there must be a political solution," in: *al-Safir,* 16 April 2011.

Luca, Ana Maria: "Why Syria is not next," in: *Now Lebanon,* 10 February 2011 (http://www.nowlebanon.com/NewsArchiveDetails.aspx?ID=239092).

Lutz, Meris: "Syria's Asad seems to suggest backing for Hamas negotiable, leaked cables say," in: *Chicago Tribune,* 2 December 2010.

MacFarquhar, Neil: "Syrian Party Watches Iraq with Unease and Ponders Its Own Fate," in: *New York Times,* 30 March 2003.

Al-Makhadhi, Sakhr: "Syrians turn out for unprecedented demonstration," in: *Global Post,* 18 February 2011 (www.globalpost.com/dispatch/middle-east/110218/syria-protests).

McElroy, Damien: "Mahmoud Ahmadinejad in Lebanon: 'a landlord visiting his domain'," in: *The Telegraph,* 14 October 2010.

Mufleh, Ghassan: "The Silent Bloc. . . Acquiescing to Tyranny Willingly or Out of Fear," in: *Arab Reform Brief,* No. 55, February 2012.

"The Mysterious Downfall of Assef Shawkat," in: *Mideast Monitor,* Vol. 3 No. 2, August 2008.

Putz, Ulrike: "Rauswurf des Hamas-Chefs," in: *Spiegel Online,* 3 September 2008.

Starr, Stephen: "Syrian Civil Society Empowerment 2010: New Directions for Syrian Society," in: *Forward Magazine,* Issue 37, 3 March 2010.

Sydow, Christoph: "Syrien in schlechter Verfassung," in: *Zenith,* 21 February 2012.

Tallal Kudsi, Basil: "A travel consultant based in the United Kingdom," in: *All4SYRIA,* 2 May 2005.

Zogby, James: "Attitudes of Arabs: An In-Depth Look at Social and Political Concerns of Arabs," Washington 2005.

Institutional Documents

Syrian Government: *The Permanent Constitution of the Syrian Arab Republic,* Damascus, no date given (after 1973, published by: Office Arabe de Presse et de Documentation).

Syrian Government: Statistical Abstract, Central Bureau of Statistics, Office of the Prime Minister of Syria, Damascus 2003.

Syrian National Council (SNC): SNC Political Program (www.syriancouncil.org/en/component/k2/item/136-snc-political-program.html).

UN: Report of the independent international commission of inquiry on the Syrian Arab Republic, UN Human Rights Council, 23 November 2011 (http://www2.ohchr.org/english/bodies/hrcouncil/specialsession/17/docs/A-HRC-S-17-2-Add1.pdf).

UN: *UN Development Report,* 2003.

Interviews & Presidential Speeches

The following interviews are listed by the individual being interviewed:

al-Asad, Bashar (Syrian president): (original transcript), in: *ABC News,* 7 December 2011 (http://abcnews.go.com/International/transcript-abcs-barbara-walters-interview-syrian-president-bashar/story?id=15099152).

Ibid: *The Sunday Times* ("Strike Syria and the world will shake"), 20 November 2011 (http://
www.dp-news.com/en/detail.aspx?articleid=103707).

Ibid: *The Wall Street Journal,* 31 January 2011 (http://online.wsj.com/article/SB1000142405274
87038332045761147124411222894.html).

Ibid: with Seymour M. Hersh, in: *The New Yorker,* 3 February 2010 (www.newyorker.com/on-
line/blogs/newsdesk/2010/02/direct-quotes-bashar-asad.html).

Ibid: Inauguration speech of Bashar al-Asad, in: SANA, 18 July 2007 (www.sana.org/
eng/21/2007/07/18/129596.htm).

Ibid: Inauguration speech of Bashar al-Asad, in: SANA, 17 July 2000 (www.sana.org/
eng/21/2007/07/18/129596.htm).

al-Azm, Sadiq Jalal: "Syrien ist nur Kleingeld" in: *Zenith,* 6 December 2011.

Ghalioun, Burhan (SNC President): (transcript) *Wall Street Journal,* 2 December 2011 (http://
online.wsj.com/article/SB10001424052970203833104577071960384240668.html).

Hussein, Louay: "Syrien ist zum Schlachtfeld der Großmächte geworden" in: *Junge Welt,* 11
February 2012.

Naem, Naseef: "Von einem Durchbruch kann man nicht sprechen: Referendum in Syrien," in:
Zenith, 22 February 2012.

Obama, Barack (US president): "Remarks on the President on a New Beginning," official
transcript of President Obama's Speech in Cairo, 4 June 2009 (www.whitehouse.gov/the-press-
office/remarks-president-cairo-university-6-04-09).

Pierret, Thomas: "Syrie: qui soutient encore le régime d'Assad? Quel rôle jouent les religieux?" in:
Le Nouvel Observateur, 30 November 2011.

Syria Opposition Leader: "Stop the Killing Machine" in: *Wall Street Journal online,* 2 December
2011 (http://online.wsj.com/article/SB10001424052970203833104577071960384240668.
html).

Websites

The following web publications have been listed above with the name only, in italics, similar to
print publications:

Aljazeera (online): www.aljazeera.com

BBC (online): www.bbc.co.uk (British Broadcasting Service)

Time (online): www.time.com

SyriaComment: www.syriacomment.com (Founder: Joshua Landis)

All4SYRIA: www.all4syria.com (Founder: Ayman Abdul Nour)

Spiegel Online: www.spiegel.de

Jadaliyya: www.jadaliyya.com (Sponsored by the Arab Studies Institute or ASI.)

Index

Carsten Wieland (PhD) is a diplomat with the German Foreign Office. He has worked as a political consultant, analyst, author, and journalist. He spent several years in the Middle East, including two years in Syria and speaks fluent Arabic. He has published numerous articles and books on Syira and the Levant. Wieland also has worked at the Goethe Institute in Cairo and Munich. This book is based on Wieland's decade-long research as a scholar and does not represent the assessments of any institution. For more: www.carsten-wieland.de

Comment on *Syria - A Decade of Lost Chances*

"A fascinating and highly readable book, providing one of the most detailed accounts of the dramatic events in Syria over the past decade and before. Dr Wieland gives an original and critical in-depth analysis of modern Syrian history with a refreshing approach."

> —Nikolaos van Dam
> Former Dutch diplomat to the Middle East
> Author, *The Struggle for Power in Syria:*
> *Sectarianism, Regionalism, and Tribalism in Politics, 1961-1994*

"Carsten Wieland, with his first-hand experience of the country and keen analytical mind, has established himself as one of the premier contemporary Syria watchers.

"*Syria-A Decade of Lost Chances* is a must read for those seeking to understand the current uprising. The book's meticulous command of empirical detail, analytically framed and interpreted, makes it an invaluable historical record.

"Particularly strong is Wieland's analysis of the contradictory personality of Bashar al-Asad, of the power struggles within the regime, of the causes and consequences of missed opportunities for reform that might have headed off revolution and of the counterproductive violent response to protestors that propelled it."

> —Dr Raymond Hinnebusch, Director
> Centre for Syrian Studies, University of St. Andrews

www.ingramcontent.com/pod-product-compliance
Lightning Source LLC
Chambersburg PA
CBHW072059040426
42334CB00041B/1454